WITHDRAWN

S0-ABD-180

THE ENCYCLOPEDIA OF
AMERICAN
DOGS

BALDWINSVILLE PUBLIC LIBRARY
BALDWINSVILLE, N.Y. 13027

THE ENCYCLOPEDIA OF
AMERICAN
DOGS

Piero Scanziani

Consultant Editor: Catherine G. Sutton

BONANZA BOOKS, NEW YORK

Official bodies recognizing breeds and issuing standards
GREAT BRITAIN: Kennel Club of Great Britain (KC(GB))
UNITED STATES: American Kennel Club (AKC)

AUG 1 1 1986

© 1981 by Instituto Geografico De Agostini S.p.A., Novara
First published in Great Britain by Orbis Publishing Limited, London 1985

All rights reserved. No part of this publication may be reproduced, stored in a retrieval
system, or transmitted, in any form or by any means, electronic, mechanical,
photocopying, recording or otherwise, without the prior permission of the publishers.
Such permission, if granted, is subject to a fee depending on the nature of the use.

Published 1985 by Bonanza Books, distributed by Crown Publishers, Inc.

Printed in Italy
ISBN 0-517-439409

h g f e d c b a

CONTENTS

INTRODUCTION

This book has various aims: to acquaint the reader who knows little about dogs with the variety, complexity and beauty of the world of dogs; to encourage readers with some knowledge of dogs to develop that knowledge, and to find out about lesser-known breeds of dog and their uses; to tell the dog-lover or dog-fancier how to train his dog and give him some advice about how to embark on various training programmes; to improve the reader's knowledge of animal psychology and ethology, concentrating on patterns of behaviour that may be useful in this respect; to offer a guide to dog-lovers, to people who show dogs, to people who train sporting dogs, general purpose dogs, and pet dogs; to enlarge the horizons of people who are fond of nature; and lastly to show the importance, both prehistoric and historic, of dogs to man.

An encyclopedia should be a work embracing the overall state of knowledge with regard to a particular topic — in this case, cynology or the study of dogs. Now, cynology is an immense field: as a branch of the natural sciences, it deals with dogs from the physical, mental, genetic, veterinary, selective, training, economic, sporting and other viewpoints. It is also concerned with the terms of the relationships between dogs and people in various historical periods, and in a wide variety of places. It would take more than a hundred scholars writing more than a hundred books to even approach this boundless subject.

This is an encyclopedia with just one author. It will give you, in a systematic way, information and knowledge gathered in half a century from contacts with dogs, dog-lovers and cynologists, and with their books; these, alone, make up a vast library written in every language. It is a circumnavigation of the world of dogs.

As we go to press, I must thank all those who have encouraged and helped me, starting with the publishing house of Pan in Rome and Elvetica in Chiasso, who have allowed me to use my texts from previous publications. I must also thank the numerous breeders and owners, all over the world, who have permitted me to take a close look at their most interesting dogs, in terms of their mental and physical characteristics.

I must also put in a word of praise for the dogs themselves, some of them so exceptionally gifted, and invariably so patient in the face of my inquisitiveness, wagging their tails and smiling. In exchange for their kindness and co-operation, I hope that these pages will help readers to get to know more about dogs, and to encourage them to see to it that these creatures will be assured a happy future.

P.S.

ILLUSTRATED GUIDE TO DOG BREEDS

SPORTING DOGS

German Wire-haired Pointer

German Short-haired Pointer

Clumber Spaniel

Pointer

Irish Water Spaniel

Field Spaniel

Welsh Springer Spaniel

English Cocker Spaniel

American Water Spaniel

English Springer Spaniel

Cocker Spaniel (Ascob)

Sussex Spaniel

Cocker Spaniel (Black)

Brittany

Cocker Spaniel (Parti-colored)

Chesapeake Bay Retriever

Vizsla

Golden Retriever

Labrador Retriever

Flat-coated Retriever

Curly-coated Retriever

Gordon Setter

Irish Setter

English Setter

Wire-haired Pointing Griffon

Weimaraner

HOUNDS

Beagle (15 inches)

Norwegian Elkhound

Beagle (13 inches)

English Foxhound

Basenji

Irish Wolfhound

Basset Hound

Afghan Hound

Rhodesian Ridgeback

Saluki

Borzoi

Bloodhound

Scottish Deerhound

Greyhound

Whippet

Smooth-haired Dachshund

Long-haired Dachshund

Wire-haired Dachshund

Miniature Smooth-haired Dachshund

Miniature Long-haired Dachshund

Miniature Wire-haired Dachshund

Harrier

American Foxhound

Otterhound

Black and Tan Coonhound

WORKING DOGS

Doberman Pinscher

Great Dane

Alaskan Malamute

Standard Schnauzer

Giant Schnauzer

Mastiff

Bullmastiff

St Bernard

Great Pyrenees

Siberian Husky

Kuvasz

Newfoundland

Bernese Mountain Dog

Rottweiler

Samoyed

Boxer

Komondor

HERDING DOGS

Puli

German Shepherd Dog

Australian Cattle Dog

Bearded Collie

Collie

Shetland Sheepdog

Pembroke Welsh Corgi

Cardigan Welsh Corgi

Bouvier des Flandres

Old English Sheepdog

Belgian Malinois

Belgian Tervuren

Belgian Sheepdog

Briard

TERRIERS

Soft-coated Wheaten Terrier

Airedale Terrier

Kerry Blue Terrier

Lakeland Terrier

Welsh Terrier

Irish Terrier

Manchester Terrier

Wire Fox Terrier

Smooth Fox Terrier

Scottish Terrier

West Highland White Terrier

Skye Terrier

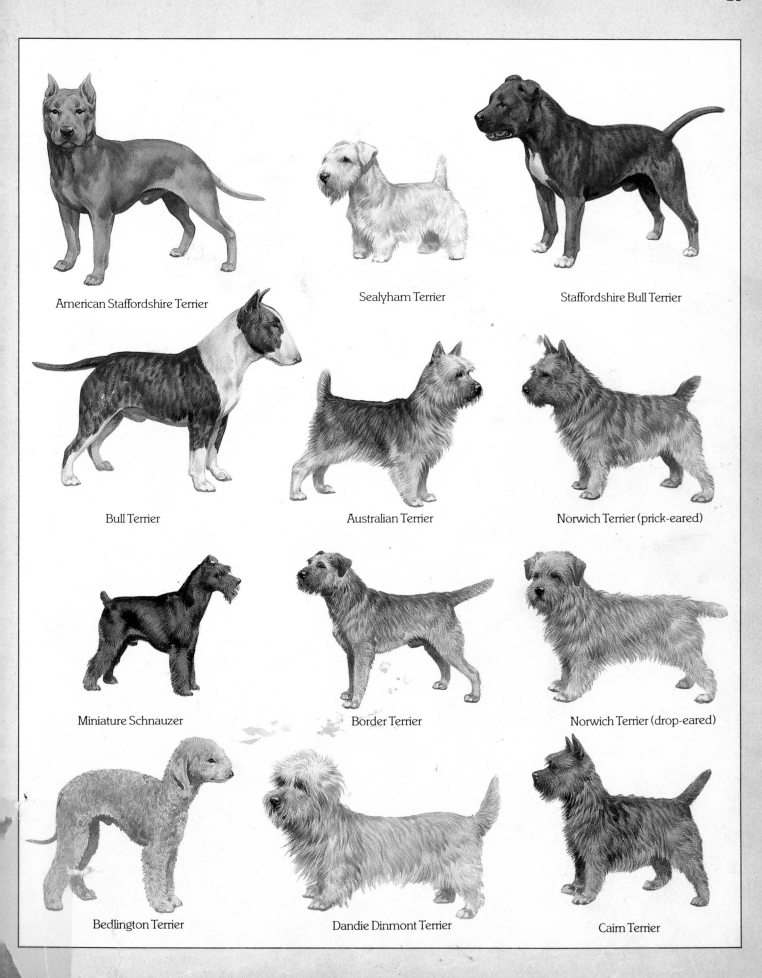

American Staffordshire Terrier

Sealyham Terrier

Staffordshire Bull Terrier

Bull Terrier

Australian Terrier

Norwich Terrier (prick-eared)

Miniature Schnauzer

Border Terrier

Norwich Terrier (drop-eared)

Bedlington Terrier

Dandie Dinmont Terrier

Cairn Terrier

TOYS

Silky Terrier

Pomeranian

English Toy Spaniel

Pug

Affenpinscher

Miniature Pinscher

Japanese Spaniel

Pekingese

Toy Manchester Terrier

Toy Poodle

Chihuahua (Smooth)

Yorkshire Terrier

Chihuahua (Long Coat)

Papillon

Italian Greyhound

Brussels Griffon

Shih Tzu

Maltese

NON-SPORTING DOGS

Bulldog

Schipperke

Lhasa Apso

French Bulldog

Keeshond

Chow Chow

Boston Terrier

Tibetan Spaniel

Tibetan Terrier

Poodle

Bichon Frise

Dalmatian

MISCELLANEOUS BREEDS

Finnish Spitz

Miniature Bull Terrier

Australian Kelpi

Cavalier King Charles Spaniel

Border Collie

Spinone Italian

CLASSIFICATION OF DOGS AND BREEDS

Fossil remains have revealed the antiquity of the Greyhound type. One of the aristocrats among recognized breeds, the Borzoi, is of the Greyhound family.

ZOOLOGY

Zoology is the science that classifies the various individual creatures belonging to the animal kingdom. It is a discipline that cannot afford to make mistakes, since its task is to categorize living creatures into groups, classes, orders and so on. Once these groupings have been decided upon, zoology announces that this is the correct classificatin and that it must be adhered to by one and all. The fact is, however, that every so often a new school of zoologists comes to the fore, and this school will revise the divisions of the classifications hitherto in force – although never from top to bottom, it must be said.

The zoological classification of the dog is as follows:

Phylum: **Chordata**
Subphylum: **Vertebrata**
Class: **Mammalia**
Subclass: **Theria**
Order: **Carnivora**

As far as the **Carnivora** are concerned, zoologists who have concerned themselves specifically with cynology have arrived at the following classification[1]:

Carnivora	Herpestoidea	Viverridae
		Hyaenidae
		Canidae
	Arctoidea	Mustelidae
		Felidae
		Procyonidae
		Ursidae

The order **Carnivora**, therefore, embraces in the separate groups, the family **Viverridae** (civets and mongoose) the family **Hyaenidae** (hyaenas), the family **Mustelidae** (martens, ermines, otters, weasels, stoats, badgers, etc.), the **Felidae** (cats, tigers, pumas, etc.), the **Procyonidae** (pandas and raccoons), the **Ursidae** (all the bears) and the family **Canidae**.

The family **Canidae** is made up of nineteen extant genera, some of which are included as members out of zoological convenience and have very little to do with the familiar domestic dog, with its 42 teeth.

These very different **Canidae** include the bat-eared fox (**Octocyon megalo-**

tis), an African insectivore with 48-50 teeth; the dhole or red dog (**Cuon alpinus**) found in Asia; the South American bush dog (**Speothos venaticus**); the raccoon-dog (**Nyctereutes procyonoides**) found in the Far East; and the African hunting dog (**Lycaon pictus**).

Of the other fourteen genera, some bear a resemblance to the fox, while others are more akin to the dog and the wolf.

The fox-like members of the **Canidae** are: the foxes themselves (genus **Vulpes**) found in the Northern hemisphere; the Arctic fox (**Alopex lagopus**) which is distributed in the Arctic regions and the Northern steppes; the American foxes belonging to the genus **Urocyon**; the fennec fox (**Vulpes zerda**) found in the Sahara and Arabia; the South American foxes belonging to the genus **Cerdocyon** (classification still provisional); and **Canis simensis**, which has the teeth of a fox although it is sometimes known as the Abyssinian wolf: its correct popular name is the Simian jackal. These animals usually have an oval-shaped pupil.

The dog- and wolf-like members of the family **Canidae** are the domestic dog (**Canis familiaris**); the wolf (**Canis lupus**); the jackals (**Canis aureus**); the side-striped jackal of Africa (**Canis adustus**); another African variety, the black-backed jackal (**Canis mesomelas**); the coyote (**Canis latrans**); the American maned wolf

The Maned Wolf (Chrysocyon brachyurus) lives in America. It is thought that it often mated with domestic dogs in the pre-Columbian period.

(**Chrysocyon brachyurus**) and the American foxes belonging to the genus **Lycalopex**. These animals usually have a round pupil.

In addition to the somatic – i.e. bodily – differences that exist between the fox-like **Canidae** and the dog-like **Canidae**, there are significant psychological or mental differences. The former group does not have any social tendencies; its members lead a solitary life, or possibly living in pairs. The dog-like species, on the other hand, lives a gregarious life, to a greater or lesser extent. Animal-lovers have often raised fox- and wolf-cubs with puppies: until the age of three or four months the young play with each other without any fuss and bother, but after this the fox-cubs tend to stay away from the wolf-cubs and puppies, and live separate lives.

The dog has thrown in its lot with man mainly because of its feelings for hierarchy. There are other animals that, while lacking any sociable quality, have also become domestic species – the obvious example being the domestic cat, Felis catus, a household pet throughout the world.

THE CANIDAE

There are few differences between the wolf-like dog and the wolf proper. The skulls differ slightly, particularly in the level of the eye-sockets or cavities; this is why the wolf's eyes appear to look out obliquely, and why the wolf-like dog has its 'honest' look. The wolf's ribcage is narrower, the knees move closer to the body, the hindquarters are more elongated, and the gait is different. In the dog the cerebral part of the head tends to extend forwards above the muzzle — a feature common to most domestic animals. The wolf howls, while the dog barks. The wolf has short, roundish ears; its eyes are gold coloured, with a black ring round them; the coat is in varying shades of tawny, but is never a uniform dense black.

There are considerable psychological (or mental) differences between wolf and dog, although these are not, in fact, divergent.

If a wolf is reared by a human being it will jealously attach itself to its master, and behave hostilely to anyone

The Black-backed Jackal of Africa (Canis mesomelas) hunts wild game but is also useful as a destroyer of rodents and as a scavenger. The Coyote (below) is found in most parts of the American continent. Its quick wits have saved it from the threat of extermination.

else. It is about 60-75 cm (24-30 in) tall and lives in Europe, Asia and America.

If a dog mates with a wolf or jackal, the offspring will be fertile, whereas the rare occasions when a dog and a fox interbreed appear to produce barren progeny. Although dogs and wolves normally have no time for one another, they will interbreed where the two species co-exist, and in the northernmost parts of the world there is plenty of evidence pointing to the fact that she-dogs or bitches have gone in search of wolves in order to mate with them. Many methodical studies have been made about the offspring of wolves and dogs. In the process of cross-breeding the differing characteristics have tended to behave like Mendelian features: in other words, in the second generation some offspring will howl, and others will bark; some have the coat of a wolf, others that of a dog; some will be timid and go about with their tails between their legs; others will be friendly, and never stop wagging their tails.

The jackal hunts mainly by night. It is an omnivorous creature, tawny in colour, with a blackish muzzle, easily domesticated, and about 45-50 cm (18-20 in) in size. It lives close to human settlements, feeding on rubbish, and is found in all parts of the world, with the exception of Oceania. There are no known methodical studies of the offspring produced by

Members of the fox genus, which belongs to the family Canidae, are much less sociable than dogs. The Arctic Fox (left), half fox and half dog, has a brownish-grey coat that turns white in winter. In the desert regions of northern Africa there is an elegant species called the Fennec (below), a name derived from the Arabic fanak. The large ears are a distinctive feature.

The Hunting Dogs (right) of eastern and southern Africa, also members of the Canidae, have an advanced social and family sense.

cross-breeding between dogs and jackals, even though this is quite common.

The coyote – also known as the prairie-wolf – is found in the great swathe of America stretching from Alaska to the Costa Rica in the south. In the United States it is found from the Pacific coast to Ohio in the east, and it is also distributed throughout Mexico and Canada. It is smaller than the wolf and larger than the jackal, weighing about 20 kg (45 lb). From earliest times it has mated with dogs, the offspring developing into the hunting dogs used by American Indian peoples. Its Latin nomenclature is **Canis latrans**. It is omnivorous, and will even eat fruit and vegetables, as well as insects; it hunts rodents and reptiles and has as its natural enemy the American red wolf (**Canis rufus** or **niger**).

The fox will not usually mate with the dog, and will not tolerate being put on a chain or lead. It can be domesticated, but the process will always leave a scar that can never be healed. Human beings find the smell of a fox unpleasant. Its coat colour ranges from bright copper-red to silver-grey; the tip of the tail, however, is invariably white. It weighs from 5-15 kg (11-35 lb), and lives in Europe, Africa and Asia.

The hunting-dog (**Lycaon pictus**) is also quite different from the domestic dog, looking at first glance rather like a hyaena. It has four toes on its front feet, instead of the five of other **Canidae**. The gestation period lasts from 70 to 75 days instead of the normal 56 to 66 days. It is the only wild member of the **Canidae** family that is distinctly three-coloured, its coat having a white background with black and red markings. The fur of each individual hunting-dog has its own pattern, but the tip of the tail is invariably white. The hunting-dog lives in packs, with a leader. It can be domesticated, and will become quite fond of man, but will always be extremely dangerous in confrontation with any other animal. It is thought that the ancient Egyptians used it in hunting. It does not mate with dogs, since there is mutual loathing between the two groups. It lives in Africa.

Wild dogs

There are many dogs living in varying degrees of wildness. The best known is the Australian dingo. It was thought that this very young continent did not have any dogs before the arrival of people from Asia and Europe, and it was claimed that the dingo was a dog that had reverted to the wild, a descendant of dogs brought to Australia by the first settlers. Recent fossil discoveries have overturned this hypothesis by showing that the dingo has been living in Australia since very earliest times; it is, in fact, the continent's only original non-marsupial mammal. This sub-

stantiates the words of Captain William Dampier, one of the first people to explore Australia, who set foot on Australian soil in 1688: 'My men spied two or three wolf-like creatures. They were starving hungry, and skeletal to the point where they looked like skin and bones.'

When the Europeans arrived with their livestock, the ravenous dingoes attacked the flocks with such zeal that for centuries they became the shepherd's main enemy.

From the very outset the dingo showed no fear towards domestic dogs, and behaved with them as if they were kith and kin.

The dingo lives in small groups of five or six individuals belonging to a

single family; in rare cases these packs may number up to a hundred animals. Australian Aborigines (according to some authorities) keep them for hunting purposes, each tribe having a couple of them. The cubs can be found in the hollows of trees (where the female dingo is happiest to give birth to her litter), and are reared with a great deal of loving care. The Aborigines let the dingoes sleep in their huts, and feed them on meat and fish. Dingoes usually act timidly towards people, which is why the Aborigines never punish them: at worst they will simply scold them while they are hunting and the dingoes act disobediently.

The dingo will mate with the dog, and the offspring are fertile. When they were crossed with the English Sheepdog or Scottish Collie, the outcome developed into the Kelpie, the highly intelligent Australian Sheepdog. Like all the wild dogs, the dingo does not bark. As soon as domesticated dogs stop living close to people they stop barking as well. The dingo is smaller and lighter than the wolf. Its coat is fairly long, and varies in colour from tawny (reddish-yellow) to straw to the red of a deer; some animals have a black coat. The feet and the tip of the tail are almost invariably white. The dingo still attacks flocks of sheep, so it is hunted by farmers, sometimes with rather cruel methods.

The wild dog found in Indonesia, the so-called red dog or dhole (**Canis alpinus**), has been taken for a dingo, but is much fiercer and virtually untameable. It lives in the jungle and hunts by night. It is a close relative of **Canis indicus**, which lives in India, resembles the Belgian Sheepdog (Groenendael or Malinois), and has shown itself to have great courage. **Canis indicus** lives in groups and will put even a Bengal tiger to flight, sending it clambering up a tree like a cat. It never attacks man, but it does not appear to be afraid of people.

In Africa, and more precisely in the high montane grasslands of Ethiopia, lives the Simian jackal or fox (**Canis**

Among the Canidae, the species closest to the dog is the wolf, which is widely distributed in Europe, Asia and North America. It lives in packs with a hierarchic structure.

a ridge of hair along its back, running in the opposite direction to the rest of its coat.

The wild-dog group also includes the pariah dog, living in bands or packs with a leader, which is common from the shores of the Black Sea to China. It lurks close to villages, and on the edge of towns and cities, feeding on all sorts of rubbish. It divides the territory into strips into which no other pariah dog may venture, and in appearance ranges from the wolf-like to a strong similarity with the Greyhound. These dogs are frequently starving, and often have mange, but seem to be unaffected by other canine diseases.

There are also wild dogs in America. **Canis cancrivorus**, a crab-eating species, as its Latin name suggests, lives near the Rio de la Plata, and the people there encourage it to mate with domestic dogs. **Canis magellanicus** is a wolf-like dog that lives between Chile and Tierra del Fuego. It can run very fast, but when it comes across people, will approach them out of curiosity.

The so-called Azara's dog or fox (**Canis Azarae**), named after the soldier and nautralist, Felix de Azara, who recorded it in 1801, is still something of a mystery. It is found in most parts of South America, lives by hunting, and is an efficient reptile-killer.

The oddest of all the American wild dogs is the bush dog (**Speothos venaticus**). It is found in the Guianas and Brazil, and, to judge from photographs of it, is remarkably ugly, looking more like a small wild boar than a dog. There are four varieties. Only one specimen has ever reached Europe, finally arriving at London Zoo. Customs officers thought it was a badger!

Things as they are now

Until the beginning of the modern period, it is not possible to talk properly in terms of breeds of dogs. Even in the early 19th century the majority of dogs were quite simply mongrels, of

simensis), which closely resembles a Greyhound. It is, in fact, thought that it made its way from Ethiopia to Egypt, where it became the forbear of all modern Greyhounds.

On the island of Phy Quoc, in the Gulf of Thailand, lives a sturdy Mastiff-like dog, in a semi-wild state. Its distinctive feature is that the coat along its

backbone and up to its shoulders is longer than elsewhere on its body, with the fur lying in the opposite direction to the rest of the coat, forming a sort of mane. The dog from Phy Quoc is the ancestor of the so-called Rhodesian Ridgeback, by now a thoroughly domestic breed, frequently bred in the English-speaking countries. It, too, has all shapes and sizes. Hunters, who were even then searching for that exceptional dog that would fill the game-bag, were spurred on in their efforts to experiment with the most extraordinary and empirical cross-breeding. This was the period when bitches on farms were mated with either Bulldogs or Greyhounds, to make their offspring either braver or swifter. The effect would be the same if a Pointer were mated now with a Boxer or a racing Greyhound, in the hope that the offspring would be superb hunting-dogs.

In the non-hunting world, dogs were sought after as guardians and watchdogs, and closer attention was paid to the steadfastness of their natures than to their distinctive features. In many litters no two puppies would be the same, either anatomically or from the point of view of character.

Dogs barked, and would sometimes bite too, and essentially this was all that was expected of them. Among people keen to have dogs as pets, the basic criterion was that the dog should be small. Ladies at every Court had small lap-dogs, and the smaller they were the more highly they were prized. As a result, each one developed into a specific breed.

There were a few exceptions. In isolated areas some breeds managed to become established and hand down their particular features. The St Bernard is a good example of this process. Another exception was provided by the isolated dog-fancier who, for his own satisfaction, might safeguard a specific breed for selection purposes. This happened in the case of the (English) Mastiff, bred for centuries by a few aristocratic English families. It was also the case with the small Italian Greyhound, taken in and protected by various Courts, and with the Abruzzi Sheepdog, which lives with shepherds and must, by tradition, be white and necessarily strong, since it may have to do battle with wolves.

Another exception is the appearance in Europe of breeds that had been selected elsewhere for centuries. Among them is the Pug, brought to Europe by Italian and Dutch seamen returning from the Far East. But for all other dogs we can only use the term 'mongrel', and in many cases the dogs seen nowadays in France, Italy, Germany, Switzerland or England are very closely related to the pariah dogs of the Near East.

As far as dogs and their history is concerned, the latter half of the 19th century was the dawn of a new era. In England, Belgium and later France, and then in rapid succession in all the countries of the West, dog-shows were held. These in turn introduced into dog-breeding the various zoo-technical principles that made it possible to classify and establish breeds on the basis of their uses. A dog is all the more valuable as a man's 'right hand' if its character is clearly defined, just as, if its capabilities are known, they can be improved. Seen in this light, every mongrel, every form of cross-breeding and every form of hybrid are steps backwards.

In the last 130 years, then, breeds of dogs have become clearly defined and established, and they have also increased in number, with man's needs and the uses to which dogs can be put. There is a powerful trend towards improving the qualities of the first domestic animal – as far back as the Neolithic Period, dogs were domesticated, before reindeer, cattle, sheep and horses – but there is also still a vast and unclassified array of unfortunate mongrels, which are not protected by their intrinsic economic value, and which thus become **res nullius** (disinherited) and consequently victims of all manner of human cruelty: from trapping to gas-chambers, and from homelessness to vivisection. This is why it is important to stop the numbers of mongrels from increasing, by preventing pregnancies and by humanely putting down new-born puppies. By replacing mongrel blood with thoroughbred blood, and by teaching people that dogs have a monetary value and that they will repay their price handsomely, it will be possible to enrich the zoo-technical stock in all countries. Furthermore, this will assist in the eradication of rabies, because the disease is spread, to some extent, by roaming dogs. Most of all, man will find that he has an even more perfect helper in any number of tasks: guard duties, protection, hunting, police duties, in sport, haulage, guiding the blind, military tasks, shows, rescue and first-aid, and so on.

All dogs, regardless of whether they belong to a breed or not, have a moral quality and value which must be respected and protected from harm by all honourable men and women. But what must be aimed at, above all else, is the thoroughbred dog.

In every country numerous associations and clubs have been set up whose purpose is to lay down guidelines for the selection of dog breeds, and to make sure that these are followed. International organizations are in charge of national activities, too. There are genealogical books published annually, in which thoroughbred dogs born that year are registered. Extracts from these books form the pedigree of each individual dog. This information enables the dog-breeder to select the innate qualities most likely to improve the breed to which he is devoting his interst and energy.

Classification

The earliest authors who concerned themselves with dogs tried, a very long time ago, to classify the different breeds on the basis of their affinities. It was immediately evident that this would be no easy task. In the 6th century BC, Aesop refers in a fable to the war between wolves and dogs, and observes that while the wolves were all equal, the dogs, on the other hand, were very diverse, '. . . black and red, white and grey', and came from very different countries. The matter of countries was mentioned later by Ovid, who speaks of dogs from Sparta, Crete, Arcadia and Macedonia, as well as dogs born of wolves, and some with long coats, either white or black or spotted.

The first lists of breeds date back to the days of Aristotle, Xenophon and Virgil, in the ancient world. In the Middle Ages Albert the Great, and in the Renaissance various authors in hunting circles, provided increasingly detailed listings. In 1576 Caius wrote a **Treatise on Breeds of Dogs**. A detailed classification was compiled in 1755 by Buffon, which lists the thirty breeds known to him on the basis of the shape and position of the ears: erect or upright, semi-erect, or drooping. These features, seem rather variable to us nowadays.

Some sixty years later, Cuvier – the founding father of comparative anatomy – established a classification based on the conformation of the skull: four classes divided into sections. In the mid-19th century Pierre Mégnin classified four types: wolf, Pointer or Hound, Mastiff and Greyhound.

In 1926 the German Schäme established two types of skull, 'decumanid' and 'veltrid', and from these made a systematic listing of all the then existing breeds. Paul and Edmond Dechambre classified the skull types into rectilinear, concavo-linear and convexo-linear. An Englishman by the name of Hugh Dalziel made a simpler, less anatomical and more practical classification: hunting- or gun-dogs, general purpose or working dogs and house-dogs and companion-dogs.

In this book the system followed was devised by Mégnin, but it has been filled out and adapted to present-day conditions. The classification is as follows (the measurements refer to the height at the withers):

(1) Mastiff type
(a) large – more than 65 cm (26 in)
(b) medium – 50-65 cm (20-26 in)
(c) small – 35-50 cm (14-20 in)
(d) miniature – less than 35 cm (14 in)
(2) Wolf type
(a) medium
(b) small
(c) miniature
(3) Greyhound type
(a) large
(b) medium
(c) small
(d) miniature
(4) Pointer/Hound type
(a) medium
(b) small
(c) miniature
(5) Pomeranian type
(a) medium
(b) small
(c) miniature
(6) Dachshund/Basset type
(a) miniature

The six basic types

Mastiff type: Head large, round or cube shaped, muzzle quite short, lips thick and long, conspicuous stop; body thickset, powerful, often very large.

Wolf type: Head resembles a horizontal pyramid, muzzle elongated and narrow, lips thin and set close together, stop moderate, ears usually erect; body well proportioned and agile.

Greyhound type: Head is in the shape of an elongated cone, skull narrow, ears small and turned back, sometimes erect, muzzle long and thin, but with powerful jaws, stop virtually non-existent, nose prominent above the mouth, lips thin and close together; the body slender and streamlined with graceful legs, a deep chest and arched loin.

Pointer/Hound type: Head rather prism-like, with the muzzle almost as broad at the base as at the tip; large, drooping ears, long, drooping lips, conspicuous stop; body sturdy.

Pomeranian type: Wolf-like head, but a broader skull and thinner muzzle, somewhat like that of a fox; ears small and erect; body short and compact; coat quite long, tail curved on to the back.

Dachshund/Basset type: Legs disproportionately small in relation to the body; either with feet turned-out (Pekingese) or straight feet (Corgi). The Dachshund type can apply to any other type, as a result of rhachitis (rickets) or malformation: there is a tendency towards it in the Mastiff group (Pekingese), in the Pomeranian group (Corgi), in the wolf group (Cairn) and in the Pointer/Hound group (Basset Hound).

Representatives of major dog types

Mastiff type
Neapolitan Mastiff

Pointer type
Italian Pointer

Wolf type
German Shepherd

Pomeranian type
Chow Chow

Grehound type
Borzoi

Dachshund/Basset type
Dachshund

Within the canine species, even when an animal is apparently clearly a member of a well-defined breed, it can possess physical characteristics that link it with all the other basic groupings. For example, there are traces of the Greyhound type in the Dobermann; there is something of the bulkiness of the Pointer in German Shepherd Dogs (in which the ears are often drooping); there are hints of the wolf in the skull of some Mastiffs, and so on. The energies of dog-breeders are directed towards eliminating as far as is possible, by selection, any specimens that have conspicuous modifying features, taking them too far from the accepted characteristics of the type.

Like all classifications, this present one has its weaknesses. The Labrador, for example, is included in the Pointer/Hound grouping, but it could just as well be regarded as a Mastiff type; because of certain of its physical characteristics (the shape of the head, for example), the wolf-like Dobermann has certain similarities with the Greyhound group. The toy group is not always wolf-like: the head of the Chihuahua is rather fox- or Pomeranian-like, and so on.

The following pages give details of the main breeds – a hundred or so – divided into the six types, and discuss the related breeds more briefly. In all, some three hundred types of dog from all the continents are included.

Measurements refer to the height at the withers.

Standards

For about 150 years people have been addressing themselves to the problem of selecting breeds of dog. In its country of origin, each breed has its own club or association, which has set up the official standard for the breed and both supports and popularizes it. The official standard is the detailed description of the dog in question, including the coat, colour and so on, and specifies the sought-after features and those that are to be avoided. The official standard sometimes refers also to the mental characteristics of the breed, and provides a scale of points intended to help show-judges, although in fact it rarely applies. Some official

standards are excellent and useful (usually the German ones); others are too superficial, and others ae overcomplicated and elaborate (some Italian and French ones). One of the world's greatest canine experts, the Belgian pharmacist, Charles Huge, after sixty years of canine studies, wrote that the best standard is a good drawing. An updated version of this criterion would be a good colour photograph.

The official standard is the basic tool of the breeder, and it also helps the ordinary dog-fancier and the judges.

Measurements

All dogs can be measured, and there are all sorts of measurements that can be made. The main one is the height at the withers. In some cases it is interesting to have the height at the chest, the circumference of the ribcage, the length of the trunk, and the length and breadth of the head. The standards for the various breeds often give a minimum and a maximum height, bearing in mind that males are

The Airedale in this photograph stands in the ideal position to show the features of the breed in terms of body structure, as laid down in the official standard, and grooming.

usually taller than the females – usually, but not always, because in the miniature breeds there is often a preference for slightly larger females (to ease the process of giving birth) and very small males (to ensure that the 'miniaturizing' genes are handed on).

The weight of the animal is an interesting detail. Unfortunately, official standards rarely deal with this. Rough weights are given below.

The coat

After the height and the weight, the feature with the greatest anatomical interest is th coat. It may be short (or close-lying) or long. The particular features may be summed up as follows:
(1) Absence of coat: bare and highly pigmented skin (hairless dogs).
(2) Short (close-lying) coat (Pointers, Boxers, Greyhounds).

(3) Long coat. This coat may differ in length and quality of hair:
   (a) Straight (Pomeranians, German Shepherd Dogs, Collies);
   (b) Curly (Spaniels, Maltese, Setters);
   (c) Hard (Spinone, Schnauzer, several types of Terrier);
   (d) Profuse (Poodles, Water dogs).

The second important feature of the coat is the colour. Some breeds have laid down colours that do not vary in their patterns (Bernese Mountain Dogs, Boston Terriers); others have a colouring in which the pattern and distribution of the colours is not important (German Shepherd Dogs).

There are, broadly, 10 main kinds of coat colour.

The colours

(1) Completley black with white markings on the chest and feet.
(2) Black with tawny markings/dappled black. In all dog breeds the tawny markings have the same pattern, but there may well be variations in their size and the intensity of the redness. The pattern is as follows: around the lips and muzzle; above the eyes; on the legs; on the chest, belly and below the tail. The dappled black pattern may include white markings on the muzzle, chest and feet.
(3) Blue, grey, mouse-grey, isabella, either all over or with white markings on the chest and feet.
(4) White all over, or with different-sized markings of various colours.
(5) Tawny – ranging from straw-coloured to russet. Often with a black mask. There may also be white markings.
(6) Various shades of red – from pale orange to the rich chestnut of the Irish Setter, with or without white markings.
(7) Roan – a fine mixture of coloured hairs, including white, blue roan, orange roan, lemon roan, etc.
(8) Light or dark brown, with or without white areas.
(9) Striped or brindle, i.e. black stripes, well defined or otherwise, on a tawny or grey background, or tawny stripes on a black background (as in the French Bulldog).
(10) Wolf grey with the hair paler at the roots and black at the tips.

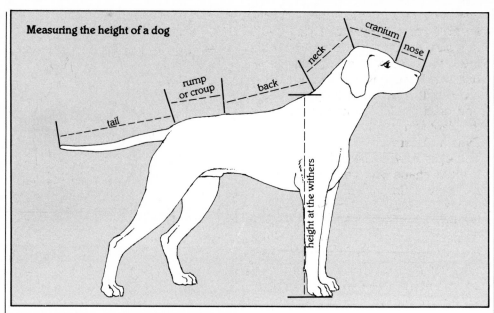

Measuring the height of a dog

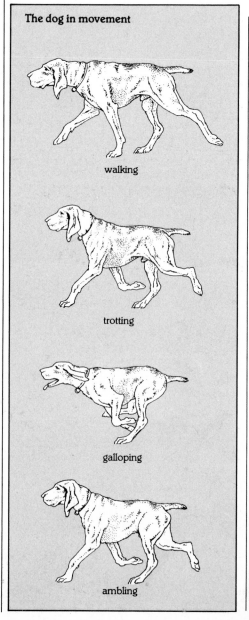

The dog in movement

walking

trotting

galloping

ambling

The body
This is the feature that constitutes the overall appearance of the breed, and gives the first impression of it. Next comes the head, the principal elements of which are the skull, the muzzle, the teeth, the eyes and the ears. Other features to be considered are the trunk, the legs, the hind-quarters and the tail.

Teeth
The arrangement of a dog's teeth is as follows:

$$\frac{3\text{-}1\text{-}4\text{-}2 \ (3)}{3\text{-}1\text{-}4\text{-}3}$$

What this indicates, as a rule, is that the jaw of an adult dog has, in the upper jaw, 6 incisors, 2 canines, 8 premolars, and 4 (or sometimes 6) molars. In the lower jaw there are 6 incisors, 2 canines, 8 premolars and 6 molars. So a dog has either 42 or 44 teeth. When a puppy is weaned it has 32; when it acquires its second set of teeth it will have 38. In some breeds, and some individuals, various teeth may be missing.

The arrangement of the teeth may vary, depending on the position of the upper incisors in relation to the lower ones. In normal dentition (i.e., closing scissor-fashion), the upper incisors slide over the lower ones, touching the front surface of the latter with their own back surface. In the pincer bite, the bottom of the upper incisors meets the tip of the lower incisors. In prognathous dentition, the lower incisors overshoot the upper ones. In the fourth form of dentition, called enognathous, the upper incisors overshoot the lower ones. Man is normally enognathous, but in any breed of dog this is a defect that involves disqualification. The official standard lays down what the dentition must be.

Eyes and ears

The eyes vary in the different breeds, in both shape and colour. There are red eyes (in albino Chihuahuas), almost black eyes (Giant Schnauzers), brown eyes of differing intensity (almost all breeds), yellow eyes (Poodle Pointer), amber-coloured eyes (Weimeraner, and some Mastiffs) and so on. Some eyes are prominent or salient (Pekingese), others sunken (St Bernard); some eyes are almond-shaped (Collies) and others round (Mastiffs). The shape of the ears also varies greatly. The broad categories of shape are: erect ears (German Shepherd Dogs), drooping ears (Spaniels), and semi-erect ears (Fox Terriers).

Trunk, legs, hind-quarters and tail

The trunk, the part of the body to

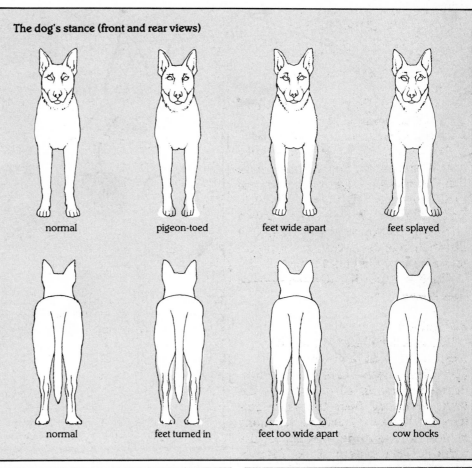

The dog's stance (front and rear views)

normal — pigeon-toed — feet wide apart — feet splayed

normal — feet turned in — feet too wide apart — cow hocks

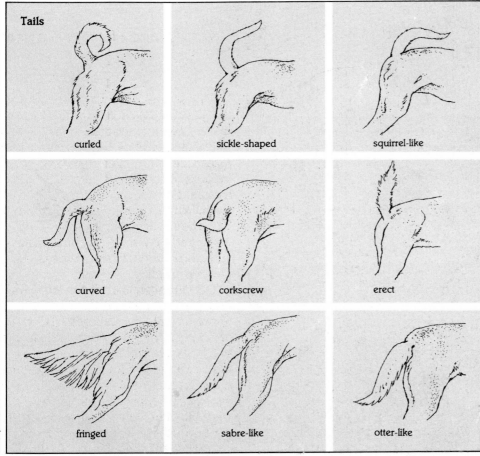

Tails

curled — sickle-shaped — squirrel-like

curved — corkscrew — erect

fringed — sabre-like — otter-like

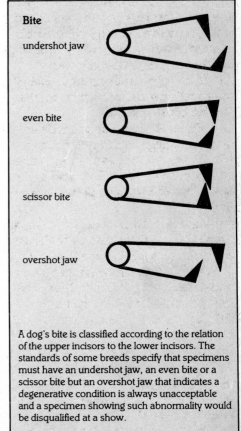

Bite

undershot jaw

even bite

scissor bite

overshot jaw

A dog's bite is classified according to the relation of the upper incisors to the lower incisors. The standards of some breeds specify that specimens must have an undershot jaw, an even bite or a scissor bite but an overshot jaw that indicates a degenerative condition is always unacceptable and a specimen showing such abnormality would be disqualified at a show.

which the neck and legs are attached, may be long (as in the Dachshund), medium (as in the Maremma Sheepdog) or short (as in the Boxer). The legs may be regular, i.e. precisely perpendicular, or irregular (as in the Bulldog). The hind-quarters may be straight (Chow Chow), bent (Greyhound) or very bent (German Shepherd Dog).

The tail may be docked to varying degrees or natural. It may have various shapes: arched over the back (as in the Pomeranian) or long, with an upward swirl (as in the Collie). Some species are more or less tail-less – the Brittany Spaniel, for example – or completely tail-less – the Schipperke or the Old English Sheepdog.

Character

After the anatomical features basic to the particular breed, all that remains to be considered are those highly important qualities called character traits (barely referred to in the official standards, and rarely mentioned in cynological volumes). They are, nevertheless, crucial, given that each breed has its own 'character' – the impressive fighting spirit of the Staffordshire Bull Terrier, the tenacity, when on the hunt, of the Jagdterrier, the good-natured friendliness of the Boxer, the alert determination of the Pointer, the calm intelligence of the Italian Greyhound, and so on and so forth.

Uses, country of origin and history

Every dog and every breed may be used for hunting, watchdog duties and companionship, but between the various breeds there are phsyical and mental differences that make each one particularly suitable for a specific use, which is precisely why it has been so selected. The Setter, for example, takes preference over the Pomeranian for farm duties, the Mastiff over the Pointer for watchdog duties, the Dachshund over the Poodle for hunting underground, and the Greyhound over the Pekingese for racing. The specific use or uses of each breed will be referred to in turn.

Another point to be dealt with is 'nationality', i.e. the country of origin, or the country that has adopted a

Ears

bat

folded

dropping

erect as a result of cropping

semi-prick

rose

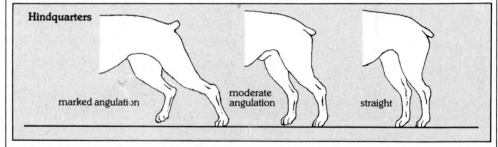

Hindquarters

marked angulation

moderate angulation

straight

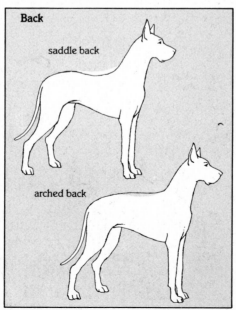

Back

saddle back

arched back

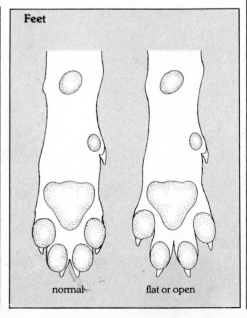

Feet

normal

flat or open

Square and rectangular build

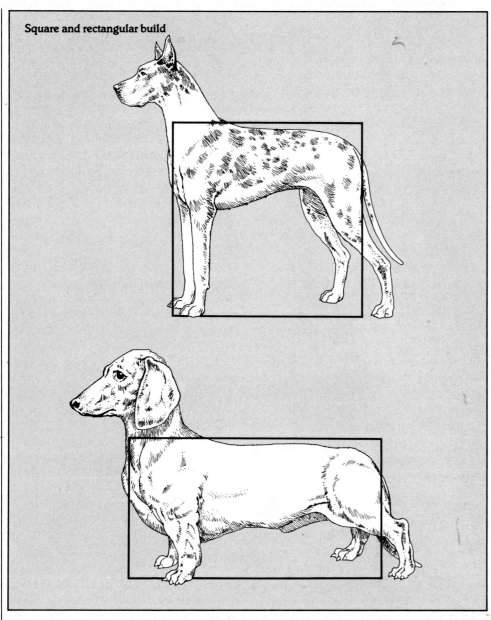

Stop

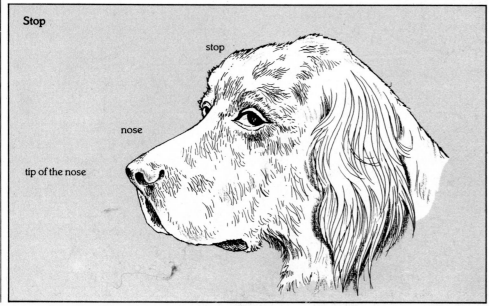

stop

nose

tip of the nose

Dewclaw

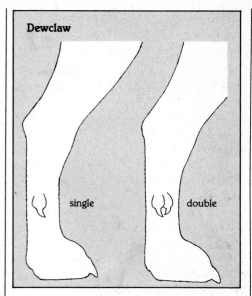

single

double

particular breed. The Pekingese, for example, comes from China, but it has been adopted by England, which is nowadays the homeland of many breeds coming from elsewhere. As a rule it is only the country of origin (or the recognized country of adoption) that is entitled to revise the official standard and, as time passes, to alter the nature of the offspring and thus of the breed as a whole.

Finally, there is the history of each breed, or the little that is known of it. Some breeds have a richer history than others, in the same way as individual human beings and nations.

A glossary of terms

Appearance, general: In dog-shows the appearance of a dog is not based on aesthetic criteria, which would be shaky ground, given that the Greyhound, the Bulldog and the Maltese all have their own particular looks. The overall beauty of a dog has to do with the physical union between the breed's features and its use: general purpose, defence, farm duties, retrieving, racing, companionship or a simple pet (the French define certain breeds as **d'agrément**, equivalent to the English notion of toy breeds).

Back: This extends from the withers to the rump and, depending on the breed, may be straight, depressed or arched.

Belly: This may be deep (Greyhounds), quite deep (Poodles) or flat (Mastiffs).

Characteristics, general: This term refers to the appearance of the breed, at first glance, and may include the physical or mental characteristics, the gait, the temperament and so on.

Classification: the dog-clubs in the various countries round the world lay down official classifications, which may be revised or modified. In Italy, for example, in 1981, the official classification was as follows: Category 1 (sheepdogs or shepherd dogs, guard-dogs, general purpose); Category 2 (hunting- or gun-dogs: Terriers, Basset Hounds, Hounds for large game, smaller Hounds, farm-dogs, British hunting- or gun-dogs); Category 3 (pet dogs); Category 4 (Greyhounds).

Cynophilia: A rather academic word describing man's affection for dogs.

Dentition: Puppies are born toothless: in about the third week the upper incisors and canines appear, and the lower counterparts in about the fourth week; during the first month the molars and premolars also appear. There are 32 first teeth, which are subsequently replaced. In the fourth to the fifth month the permanent teeth – 42-44 in number – start to develop. Dogs often lack one or more premolars – a sign of domestication – and there is no real mastication: on the contrary a dog's teeth are used for breaking and grinding. Irregularities in teeth are more common in the prognathous and miniature breeds. Greyhounds may have more than the ordinary number of teeth.

Dew-claw: A claw above the hind-feet, similar to a cockerel's spur. There may be a single one, or a pair. In some breeds (the Beauceron, for example) it is compulsory, in others admissible, and in others it must be removed. It is missing in most breeds.

Dewlap: An abundance of skin on the neck – as in cattle. In some breeds this is a requirement (Mastiffs), in others it is a flaw (Greyhounds).

Ear: The organ of hearing. The outer ear consists for the most part of a hollow cartilage, varying in shape from individual to individual: short, long, upright, drooping, small, large. The outer ear is divided from the inner ear by the membrane of the tympanum (middle ear).

Ear juncture: The place on the skull where the ears are positioned.

Foot: This may vary in shape: cat-like (compact), hare-like (oval and elongated), open (with the toes flared.)

Gait: Each breed has its own particular gait, which has to do with its skeleton, musculature and use. The gait is one of the typical or distinctive traits of a breed and may also indicate certain mental characteristics.

Height: This is measured at the withers. Minimum and maximum height of a breed are often established. Specimens that exceed or fall below the required height at the withers do not come within the minimum and maximum measurements laid down by the official standard.

Hind-quarters: The rear part of the dog's body. The hind-quarters may be straight (Chow Chow), bent (Greyhound), or very bent (German Shepherd Dog). Defects include inward-turned or outward-turned hocks, and arched hind-quarters.

Hock: In dogs, horses and other quadrupeds, this is the part of each hind leg that corresponds to the articulation of the human tibia with the tarsus.

Judge: A person with cynological qualifications who presides at dog-shows and competitions.

Lip: The lips vary from breed to breed.

Mask: Varying degrees of colouring extending over the muzzle. This may be reddish, brown or black.

Neck: The neck extends from the withers to the skull. It may be short (as in the Mastiffs), medium length (the wolf-like group) or long (as in Greyhounds).

Nose: Part of the head extending from the stop to the tip of the muzzle. In Greyhounds and the wolf-like group the nasal duct is long; in Mastiffs it is fairly short.

Pedigree: Genealogy as recorded in the Kennel Club of Britain Stud Book.

Pigmentation: An accumulation of pigment around the lips, eyes, nose, skin between the toes, nails, making these areas brown, red, dark brown or black. In some breeds poor pigmentation can be a defect.

Qualification: At shows and trials the judge's description of the quality of the dog (good, very good, excellent).

Good defines a specimen that answers to the features of the breed, but has certain flaws. Very good defines a dog that is truly representative of its breed, and has no serious flaws. Excellent describes a typical specimen with outstanding qualities. This dog may win the Champion Certificate or the International Championship Certificate, or prizes for appearance or trial performances. The Supreme Champion has to take both these prizes.

Ribcage: This may be high (not reaching the elbow), deep (reaching the knee), or very deep (going beyond the knee).

Rump: The part of the back extending from the pelvis to the tail juncture (see diagram page 38).

Skull (cranium): This extends from the neck to the angle formed by the stop. It may be broad (as in the Mastiffs), medium (the wolf-like group) or narrow (as in Greyhounds).

Splayed feet: The front feet turned outwards: the feet only, not the legs. On the whole splayed feet are a flaw, but in some breeds (such as the Bulldog, for example) they are a requirement.

Square and rectangle: The body structure, from the withers to the rump, may be fitted into a square or a rectangle, whose upper horizontal is the back, and lower horizontal the ground beneath the feet. The other two sides are vertical lines from the withers and the rump respectively. Structure differs in each breed.

Stance, true or natural: The positioning (straight or otherwise) of the front and hind legs.

Standard: The description of the features of a breed, as laid down by a club recognized in the country of origin of the breed, or in its adopted country. Breeders select their specimens, and judges hand down their verdicts on the basis of these standards. There are also working standards laying down the working potential of the breed.

Stop: The angle between the end of the forehead and the start of the nose. The presence or absence of this angle – which may be conspicuous or otherwise – is important for identifying the typical features of the breed.

Tail: The appendage at the rear of the

dog's body, varying considerably in shape from breed to breed. Its function is to protect the genitals and the anus. In differing ways the tail can express the state of mind of its owner.
Tail juncture: This is the particular area of the rump to which the tail is attached; it may be set high, low or somewhere between the two.
Weight: In some breeds the weight rather than the height is indicated in the standard specifications. Weight is vital in the assessment of certain miniature breeds.
Withers: The point at which the shoulders and neck meet, and the point at which height is measured.
Work: In order to win a championship title many breeds must undergo working trials. They include various guard- and watch-dogs, general purpose breeds, various Terriers and Basset Hounds, certain Hounds, some farm-dogs, retrievers and so on.

A Wire-haired Fox Terrier in the characteristic stance of the breed.

[1] R. Matthey, **Le chien domestique et son origine**, Lausanne, 1945

CLASSIFICATION OF DOGS AND BREEDS

A bitch and pup of a popular herding breed, the Old English Sheepdog.

AFGHAN HOUND

This breed was used for centuries in Afghanistan on gazelle and leopard hunts, often in combination with falcons, and for many years it was not allowed to be exported. In 1888 Colonel McKenzie managed to export a pair by smuggling them out of the country. It would appear that this pair was acquired from some shepherds, who used the Afghan Hound for herding.

In 1897 its fame was already spreading in Europe, to such an extent, in fact, that an English artist, A. Wardle, painted an ideal version of the breed for the magazine **The Field**, and the French painter P. Mahler did the same thing for the magazine **Le Chenil**, in France. At the same time the German book **Der Rassen des Hundes** included a picture of a specimen named Kandahar, owned by G. Radischaro, in Kabul.

In 1907 the Afghan Hound made its appearance at the London dog-show; it became the favourite dog of Queen Alexandra, wife of King Edward VII. In 1926 it was officially recognized by the Kennel Club in Britain.

TODAY'S BREED

Official classification KC (GB): Hound Group; AKC: Hounds
Country of origin Afghanistan
Height Males: 69-74 cm (27½-29½ in); females 6-8 cm (2½-3¼ in) smaller
Coat Hair long, dense, close and silky on the flanks, ribs, and front and hind feet. From the shoulders, along the back, and from the flanks and ribs upwards the coat is short and dense in adult dogs. There are plentiful fringes on the ears, legs (it is sometimes known as the 'cowboy' dog) and tail. The head has a typical top-knot of long, silky hair; there is a short hair on the muzzle; colours: all colours are permitted

General appearance An aristocratic Hound, with a conspicuous, well-coloured and shiny coat
Head Carried high on the long, powerful neck; the skull is long, muzzle elongated, tip of nose matches colour of coat; pincer-type bite
Ears Not docked, hanging, long and broad, set low and well back
Eyes Almond-shaped, sometimes even triangular. Preferably dark, but often golden in colour
Body Chest deep, belly tucked up
Legs Front legs straight, strong and sturdy-hind legs muscular; feet with large pads; toes covered with long hair
Tail Not docked, long and fringed, ending with a ring at the end, set low
Gait Loose and easy, very elegant, perfect at the gallop

Qualities First and foremost the coat, which must be plentiful, long, with silky fringes, bright, glossy colours, and just the right distribution of long and short hair. All the typical features of the Greyhound group
Defects Insufficient size and stature, curly coat, poor stance
Character Dignified but not shy, reserved with strangers, affectionate but not particularly out-going, devoted only to its master. Detached expression

Uses Courageous and even foolhardy at times; can make a good watch-dog
Future prospects Has great charm for a limited number of dog-fanciers; too aristocratic to become popular

This breed, called by some the 'pyjama dog', has superseded the Borzoi in popularity. Although Afghan by name, its real homeland now is Great Britain, where it has been selected and bred since 1910.

AIREDALE TERRIER

TODAY'S BREED

This breed came into being in the middle of the last century to meet various practical needs: fishermen angling in the River Aire (a river in Yorkshire that runs through Leeds) wanted to rid themselves of invading hordes of otters; the city's stable-boys wanted to do away with the rats; and hunters living in the nearby countryside wanted to have a capable working-dog wit a good scent, plenty of courage, and good retrieving abilities. So (through often mysterious and sometimes incredible crossbreeding) a dog came gradually into being that acquitted itself well in water and was a tracker. It was useful in the hunt, and as a guard-dog too, and it became the largest of the Terrier group. The Germans have called it 'universal' and to the French it is 'bon à tout faire'.

Historians of this breed include Holland Buckley in Great Britain, and Keirich Käuffer in Germany, the breed having caught the imagination of the Germans as far back as 1890. In fact they tried to breed a German type which was stronger, sturdier and more efficient than the elegant English variety.

The Airedale was first seen at a show in 1875. In 1886 there were 24 specimens registered with the Kennel Club. It was in this same year that the official standard was adopted, and at roughly the same time the first Airedale Club was founded.

The Airedale soon spread beyond the shores of Britain and found its way to the United States, Canada and South Africa.

Official classification KC (GB): Terrier Group; AKC: Terriers
Country of origin Great Britain
Height Males: 58-61 cm (23-24½ in); females: 56-58 cm 22½-23 in)
Coat Hair hard, dense, rough and wiry, wavy in places, with undercoat; some harder coats are 'crinkled'; may be stripped and trimmed; colour: tan (yellow-brown), in varying shades, with a broad black or dark grizzled saddle running from the back towards the ribs and the tail

General appearance The largest of the Terriers, sturdy, solid and lively
Head Long, narrow between the ears, skull flat; muzzle full; tip of nose black; lips thin and tight; scissor-type bite
Ears Not docked, small and V-shaped, with a side carriage, but pricked forward when the dog is on the alert, set high on the head
Eyes Small and dark
Body Ribs deep, and narrow, back short, muscular with no droop
Legs Front legs straight, hind legs well angled; feet small, closed, round; stance very good
Tail Docked, but long, carried gaily, set high
Gait Typical of the Terrier, free and supple, at the trot and at the run

Qualities Sturdiness, length of the head and short body
Defects Hair soft, colours dull, lack of stature, neck too thickset, shyness
Character Quick and lively, enjoys working, good endurance. Keen expression

Uses General
Future prospects Its popularity appears to have been checked by the need to trim the dog, because of the nature of its coat.
Similar breeds Aïdi (general working dog), Morocco: a rare North African breed, reminiscent of the Airedale rather because of the consistency of the coat than the shape of the body.

Over the past hundred years this breed has become very refined, as can be seen by comparing the print (above) with photographs of typical modern specimens. The changes are accentuated by the way the dog is 'dressed', which considerably alters the look of the muzzle.

BASENJI

This dog has been bred for centuries in Central Africa, where the strain has remained pure. It made its first appearance in Europe in 1895, at the London dog-show. In 1897 there was a specimen with the name of Bosc in the Paris Zoo, and there was also a pair in Antwerp, called Dibue and Mowa, belonging to F. L'Hoëst.

In 1934 the Englishwoman, O. Burns, a well-known breeder, imported four breeding Basenji dogs from the Congo (as it was then called). In 1939 an official standard was drawn up, and in 1941 a Club was established in England. At the same time the breed was spreading in the United States.

It would seem that in the Congo the Basenji was used to help in hunting, including big game. One of the requirements demanded of it was that it did not bark, and this is a feature peculiar to the breed, although it can still howl or whine.

It is often compared with the antelope, because of its graceful appearance, its slender lines and its agility – in other words, the characteristics that have ensured its survival.

The Basenji is extremely clean, and will lick itself from head to toe, like a cat.

TODAY'S BREED

Official classification KC (GB): Hound Group; AKC: Hounds
Country of origin Zambia
Height and weight Approx. 40 cm (16 in). Weight approx. 10 kg (22 lbs)
Coat Hair short; colour: fawn with white markings, also black and white, or black with fawn or tan markings, and white; cream colouring is not permitted

General appearance A small, light-bodied, lively dog, with a distinctive expression that gives it an almost puzzled look
Head Skull flat, muzzle not long and quite pointed; tip of nose black; lips tight and thin; scissor-type bite. A special feature of the head are the wrinkles on the skull, which extend as far as the forehead and cheeks; these become more conspicuous when the dog is on the alert, when its expression is half-interested and half-embarrassed
Ears Not docked, erect, turned forward
Eyes Not prominent, small, sometimes bluish, also yellow, preferably hazel
Body Brisket good and deep, belly tucked up
Legs Quite long, good stance, well muscled; feet gathered
Tail Not docked, set high, quite short, carried tightly curled over the spine, to one side, with a white tip
Gait Distinctive, like that of a horse trotting, skipping: some people see it as like that of an antelope

Qualities An important feature is the wrinkled head, the well-balanced distribution of the white markings, and the curled tail
Defects Absence or surplus of wrinkles, which tend to give the Basenji the look of a Bloodhound; tail not curled
Character Alert, keen, devoted and loyal, much more courageous than its small size would suggest, suspicious of strangers, easy to train and domesticate. Thoughtful expression

Uses Companion-dog, guard-dog, hunting-dog (for small vermin)
Future prospects A breed with a small following
Similar breeds Rhodesian Ridgeback (lion-hunting, guard-dog), South Africa: similar to the Basenji, but only in so far as it is also African; its particular feature is that the hair on the ridge of the back as far as the shoulders grows the opposite way to the rest of the coat, thus forming a sort of mane

The Basenji has two remarkable characteristics: it never barks and it cleans its coat scrupulously by licking, rather as a cat does. As the early print shows, in the late nineteenth century the breed was not required to have a curled tail.

The Rhodesian Ridgeback puppy (right) shows already some of the sturdiness of this powerful African breed.

BASSET HOUND

This (now) English breed came originally from France (where it was known as the Basset Artésien-normand). It was brought to Great Britain by Sir Everett Millais and George R. Krehl. The first such dog to win an award was the tri-coloured Model, which was shown at Wolverhampton in 1875. Later Lord Onslow imported Fino and Finette, and Krehl imported the famous Fino de Paris, who was the forefather of a whole string of champions. Sir Everett Millais is the author of the book entitled **Bassets: Their Use and Breeding**; he also drew up the official standard, which was then adopted by the first British Basset Hound Club.

The breed found its way to the United States at more or less the same time. There, from 1880 onwards, it was bred with considerable success, although the basic type was heavier and more eye-catching; it managed to attract considerable interest not so much because of its skills as a hunting-dog, but more for its amusing shape, and the affection this aroused. There is a letter written by George Washington thanking General Lafayette for his gift of a pair of Basset Hounds. Since the end of the Second World War the breed has become popular in many parts of the world as a companion-dog; and in Great Britain it has become associated with a brand of shoes.

The similarities between Mistassinis Gandolf (below), a Canadian champion Basset Hound, and the dog in the print of 1895 (above) are very striking.

TODAY'S BREED

Official classification KC (GB): Hound Group; AKC: Hounds
Country of origin France
Height Not more than 35.5 cm (14¼ in)
Coat Hair smooth, close-lying; all colours permitted

General appearance A typical 'low-slung' member of the Dachshund group, with a heavy, expressive – some would say ludicrous or grotesque – head
Head Large, with loose skin forming deep wrinkles above the eyes, dome-shaped skull, long muzzle; black or liver-coloured nose; scissor-type bite
Ears Not docked, very long indeed, set low on the sides of the head, with soft folds
Eyes Preferably dark, slightly sunken; the lower eyelids form a pouch and reveal the red conjunctiva
Body Marked dewlap, ribcage deep, belly not tucked up
Legs Short, massive, with the front legs covered with wrinkles; front feet slightly splayed, but the hind feet are straight
Tail Not docked, slightly curved, carried gaily
Gait Typically Dachshund-like, but nevertheless energetic and easy, well coordinated

Qualities Heavy bone structure is an important feature: in relation to the dog's size it must be heavier than in any other breed. Flowing movements are also important, as is the ability to follow a scent closely, nose near to the ground.
Defects More than 38 cm (15 in) tall; hind-quarters with poor stance or stiff; knees loose; front feet resting limply on toes; dew-claws must be removed when the dog is still a puppy
Character Gentle by nature, neither lively nor shy, very devoted to its master. Sad expression

Uses As a Hound
Future prospects This hunting breed has become fashionable as a companion-dog; this may assure its future, or bring it to an abrupt end
Similar breeds The Basset group is a large one. In France there are several varieties, the Westphalian Basset Hound or Dachsbracke, and others with a very limited regional following, one of which, the Basset Griffon Vendéen, is recognized in Britain. Other interesting breeds include the Westphalian Dachsbracke and the Drever from Sweden

Even when young, as the puppies of this litter show, the Basset Hound has a mournful expression.

BEAGLE

This breed originated in Great Britain in about 1570, and was very much the favourite of huntsmen at the Court of Queen Elizabeth I.

After fluctuating fortunes, it has come into its own as the ideal Hound for the lone hunter, and for hunters working in small groups, after hares and rabbits. The breed found its way to France in the 1860s, where it is so sought after and popular that many English Beagle-lovers and fanciers travel across the Channel in search of dogs.

The tuneful baying of a Beagle pack has given rise to the phrase 'singing Beagle'.

In France people have also selected and bred the Beagle-Harrier variety, the major credit for this endeavour belonging to Baron Gérard.

In the early part of this century in Great Britain there was also a Rough- or Hard-coated variety, and in County Kerry, in Ireland, there is the Kerry Beagle, which is slightly larger and weighs some 20 kg (45 lb). There is also the Elizabeth Beagle, a 'Toy' version of the breed, that was Queen Elizabeth's favourite four hundred years ago.

In the United States the Beagle has become popular as a good-natured companion-dog for all members of the family.

TODAY'S BREED

Official classification KC (GB): Hound Group; AKC: Hounds
Country of origin Great Britain
Height 33-41 cm (13-16½ in) in UK; two sizes in USA: up to 33 cm (13 in) and 33-37.5 cm (13-15 in)
Coat Hair smooth, but not too short, dense (there is also a Rough-haired variety); colours: the full range

General appearance A small, compact, well-proportioned Hound, like a miniature version of the Foxhound
Head Conspicuous but not heavy, skull broad, muzzle straight; tip of nose black; scissor-type bite
Ears Not docked, long, wide, flat and rounded
Eyes Well set (not sunken, or prominent), ranging from hazel to chestnut in colour
Body Compact, ribcage deep and well-sprung, trunk sturdy, belly not tucked up
Legs Good stance, strong and uscular
Tail Not docked, carried gaily
Gait Supple and loose, brisk, good endurance at the trot, and quick at the gallop

Qualities Neck with slight, elegant curve, stocky body of a small athletic dog, cat-like feet
Defects Ears set improperly, tail curling over the back, pale-coloured eyes
Character Strong-willed, always alert, invariably swift in movement, with quick reactions. Gentle expression. Quick to learn what is required of it

Uses A swift-footed Hound for hunting rabbits and hares
Future prospects As well as being popular with a large following because of its qualities as a hunting-dog, it is acquiring a separate following as a companion-dog, especially in the English-speaking countries
Similar breeds Briquet (Hound), France: the name derives from the word 'Braquet' (small Braque, or Pointer) used for hunting hares. There are several varieties. Hounds, in their varying shapes and sizes, are well represented in all countries. Germany has two Hounds which should be mentioned: Hanoverian Schweisshund and Bavarian Gebirgsschweisshund. There are other types of Hounds in Austria, Spain, Portugal, Sweden, Holland, Finland and elsewhere

The Beagle has become a popular breed, particularly in Great Britain, where there are numerous specialized breeding kennels as well as clubs and associations safeguarding the thoroughbred qualities of the breed and organizing and supervising field trials and shows. Packs of Beagles (above) are still maintained in Britain.

BEARDED COLLIE

The Bearded Collie's ancestry is vague but it is known that similar dogs have been working on the hills of Scotland for many years. At one time the breed was known as the Scottish Bearded or Highland Collie and even earlier as the Hairy Mountain Dog. After the Second World War it was due to the dedication and great efforts of Mrs Willison that recognition for the breed was granted by the Kennel Club in 1959. It was not until 1977 that the American Kennel Club approved them for Championship Show points.

TODAY'S BREED

Official classification KC (GB): Working Group; AKC: Herding Dogs
Country of origin Great Britain
Height Males: (53-56 cm (21-22 in); Females: 51-53 cm (20-21 in)
Coat Double, with the undercoat soft, furry and close. Outer coat flat, harsh, strong and shaggy, free from woolliness and curl; a slight wave is permissible. Length and density of the hair should be sufficient to provide a protective coat and to enhance the shape of the dog but not enough to obscure the natural lines of the body. Colour: slate grey, reddish fawn, black, blue, all shades of grey, brown and sandy, with or without white markings

General appearance A lean, active dog, longer than it is high, in an approximate proportion of 5:4 measured from point of chest to pont of buttock. Females may be slightly longer. Should show plenty of daylight under the body and should not look too heavy
Head In proportion to size of the dog. Skull broad and flat and square, distance between stop and occiput being equal to width between orifices of the ears. The muzzle strong and equal in length to the distance from the stop to the occiput. Stop moderate
Ears Medium size and drooping. When the dog is alert the ears should lift at the base level with, but not above, the top of the skull
Eyes Should tone with coat in colour, be set widely apart and be large, soft and affectionate but not protruding
Body Length of back to come from length of ribcage and not the loin. Back level and ribs well sprung but not barrelled. Loins strong and chest deep, giving plenty of heart and lung room
Legs Fore-legs straight and vertical with good bone and covered with shaggy hair all round. Hind legs well muscled with good second thighs, well bent stifles and low hocks
Tail Set low, without kink or twist, and long enough for the end of the bone to reach at least the point of the hock. Carried low with an upward swirl at the tip whilst standing or walking. Never carried over the back
Gait Movement should be effortless and supple

Qualities Should be an alert and lively dog and self confident
Defects Any departure from the standard points

Character The temperament should be that of a steady intelligent working dog with no sign of nervousness or aggression. A bright enquiring expression is a distinctive feature of the breed

Uses Good for herding and an aimiable companion-dog.
Future prospects Popularity as a show dog likely to continue

The Bearded Collie is admired for its qualities as a herding dog and for its lively and friendly disposition.

BEAUCERON
Berger de Beauce

The first dog-show in France was held in Paris on the first Sunday in May 1863. It lasted a full week, and was well attended by the public. More than a thousand dogs were shown. However, about fifty were eliminated by a committee, and the others were divided into general working-dogs, Hounds, farm-dogs and pet dogs. The show included thirteen 'wolf-like Shepherd Dogs, with erect ears and black and tan coats'. These were the ancestors of the Beauceron.

At a show held in 1897 the Beauceron was already very similar to the present-day variety; there are three prints testifying to this, all showing typical specimens (all called Fido). Credit for establishing the breed went to the dog expert Emile Boulet who also bred the Boulet Griffon (more accurately known as the Griffon à Poil Laineux), and who founded the French Sheepdog Club.

The appearance of the first short-haired specimens was in 1900. It is said that the Beauceron was one of the parents of the Dobermann.

According to some French authorities, the Beauceron has played a role in the breeding of the Dobermann. The print of 1897 shows the continuity of the breed.

TODAY'S BREED

Official classification KC (GB) and AKC: not recognized
Country of origin France
Height Males: 65-70 cm (26-28 in); females: 63-68 cm (25-27 in)
Coat Strong and thick, 3-4 cm (1-1½ in) in length, with fringes on the hind-quarters and tail; colour: black and tan (fawn markings), or tri-colour (with grey)

General appearance A sturdy working-dog, with a certain coarse quality about it
Head Long, skull quite flat, muzzle strong and not pointed; tip of nose black; scissor-type bite
Ears Not docked or may be docked; set high up on the head
Eyes Never lighter than bright hazel
Body Sturdy, ribs broad and deep, belly not very tucked up
Legs Strong bone structure, muscular, good stance, feet round; the hind legs have a double dew-claw
Tail Not docked, carried low, straight, with a slight hook
Gait Open, free, a good trotter, and an excellent runner

Qualities Although resembling the Dobermann, should be less elegant and sturdier
Defects Any sign of being Greyhound-like, absence of double dew-claws, too heavy
Character A keen worker, courageous, tending to be aggressive at times, nervous (highly-strung). Piercing expression

Uses Its large size and zeal make it more suitable for herding cattle than sheep, but it is also an excellent guard-dog and a fine police-dog
Future prospects Its spread is limited by its chief competitor, the Dobermann
Similar breeds Berger Picard (Picard Shepherd Dog), France: some people claim that the Beauceron is a smooth-haired Picard, but at the present time the two breeds do not resemble one another that closely, and the Berger Picard is becoming increasingly rare

BEDLINGTON TERRIER

This breed is on the borderline between the wolf-like group and the Greyhound group. It came into being in the town of Bedlington in Northumberland, near Newcastle. Bedlington is an industrial town, and it was in fact the working men who selected and bred this dog to hunt the rats which infested the warehouses and factories. From time to time they would also use the Bedlington Terrier to help them hunt rabbits, foxes and badgers. There was considerable crossbreeding with Whippets, which has given the breed its slightly Greyhound-like appearance.

The name was given to the breed in 1825 by a mason named Joseph Ansley, whose own dog, Young Piper, is regarded as the founding father and prototype of all Bedlington Terriers. Young Piper lived to the ripe old age of 15, and the year before he died, by then blind and toothless, managed nevertheless to flush a badger out of its set – succeeding where other Terriers had failed.

The Bedlington Terrier was one of the most popular of all dogs – in terms of numbers – at the first dog-shows held in England. In 1895 one of the most famous of all champions, Humbledon Blue Boy, was owned by W.G. Alcock, a Sunderland coal-miner.

TODAY'S BREED

Official classification KC (GB): Terrier Group; AKC: Terriers
Country of origin Great Britain
Height and weight Approx. 40 cm (16 in); approx. 10 kg (22 lb)
Coat Distinctive, thick and linty, with a marked tendency to twist, particularly on the head and face; colour: blue, blue and tan, liver or sandy

General appearance Resembles a lamb
Head Skull narrow, rounded, distinctive because of a plentiful, silky top-knot; tip of nose black; lips thin, tight; scissor- or pincer-type bite
Ears Not docked, hanging flat on the cheek, set low, with a fringe at the tip
Eyes Well sunken, small, triangular, ranging from amber to hazel in colour depending on the colour of the coat
Body Back convex in profile, distinctive, belly very tucked up
Legs Hind legs longer than the front legs; long hare-like feet
Tail Not docked, broad at the base and tapering to a point, gracefully curved at the tip
Gait Distinctive, skipping, lamb-like

Qualities Continuous line from the occiput to the tip of the nose, well arched, Greyhound-like body, linty coat, like a lamb's
Defects Anything that detracts from its lamb-like appearance
Character Mild and gentle appearance belies its energy; a keen hunter. In Austria it is also trained as a guard-dog. Gentle expression

Uses Companion-dog, hunting vermin (rats) in cellars, guard-dog for poultry to protect them against foxes
Future prospects Requires careful and constant trimming, and has a physical appearance that attracts only a small following; does not seem likely to become popular

This lamb-like dog has developed from a hunter of vermin to a gentle companion-dog. The 'toy-dog' aspect is accentuated by careful dressing and by the selection over recent years of delicate colours, including smoky blue and delicate apricot.

BELGIAN SHEPHERD DOG
Belgian Sheepdog

Selection began in 1891 at the veterinary school at Cureghem, thanks to the efforts of Professor Reul. The four varieties of coat have been given the geographical names of places close to Brussels: Groenendael (with long, black hair, selected in about 1894 by N. Rose with the famous Duc de Groenendael), Tervueren or Tervuren (long tawny hair) Laekenois (coarse-haired) and Malinois (short-haired).

Dog-fanciers split into different groups (where they still remain), one group forming the Société Royale St-Hubert and the Fédération Cynologique Internationale, and the other the Kennel Club Belge and the Union Cynologique Internationale. The two international organizations, both with their headquarters in Brussels, have rival offshoots in Europe, for all the breeds in question, with separate Pedigree Records.

The Malinois is bred for training trials, tracking and watch-dog duties. The Tervueren is sought after for its elegance, nobility and liveliness. The Laekenois has always been rare and is now bred mainly in Holland. This is a breed with an impressive temperament. It is said that to train a Belgian Shepherd Dog one must not be feared by it: one must be loved by it.

The Belgian Shepherd Dogs are divided into four breeds, named after their place of origin: the Groenendael has long black hair, the Tervueren long fawn hair, the Laekenois has coarse hair and the Malinois is short haired.

Groenendael

Tervueren

Laekenois

Malinois

TODAY'S BREED

Official classification (all varieties) KC (GB): Working Group; AKC: Herding Dogs
Country of origin Belgium
Height Males: approx. 62 cm (25 in); females: approx. 58 cm (23 in)
Coat Groenendael: long, plentiful at the neck, chest, thighs and tail; black; Tervueren: long and plentiful, fawn, grey with black overlay, preferably with a black mask; Laekenois: rough, tousled, fawn, grey with black overlay; Malinois: short, grey with black overlay, black mask

General appearance A fairly light wolf-like dog, lively, well balanced and elegant
Head Well proportioned, of good length, tip of nose black; scissor-type bite, sometimes pincer-type
Ears Not docked, quite small, triangular and erect
Eyes Quite small, not protruding, dark brown in colour
Body Trunk of medium length, back and croup horizontal, belly slightly tucked up
Legs Good straight stance with straight pasterns; cat-like feet; hind-quarters angled
Tail Not docked, medium length, held low when at rest, raised and slightly curved when moving
Gait Supple, easy, skipping, distinctive, pleasant to watch

Qualities The coat is very important in the long-haired varieties. In all the varieties there must be a clear distinction between the Belgian Shepherd and the German Shepherd.
Defects Heaviness, large ears, body too rectangular
Character Easy-going, obedient, extremely sensitive; deeply attached to its owner, easy to train; the Malinois is particularly energetic and bold. Inquisitive, searching expression

Uses Guard-dog and police duties, tracking
Future prospects Constantly on the increase, even though somewhat checked by its rival, the German Shepherd
Similar breeds Dutch Sheepdog (herding), Holland: taller and less well known than the Belgian Shepherd Dog, it is bred in three varieties, differing in the length of the coat

Three of the Belgian Shepherd Dog breeds: the Groenendael (above), the Tervueren (left) and the Malinois (below).

BERGAMESE SHEPHERD
Bergamasco

Europe has, for centuries, been the home of a medium-sized dog with a long, profuse coat, and hair falling over its eyes; a sturdy country-dog, used for sheep-herding, with differing physical features, depending on the country of origin. This family has produced the French Briard, the Hungarian Komondor and Puli, the Russian Owtscharka, the Spanish Gos d'Atura, the Portuguese Serra (Mountain Dog), the Labrit Sheepdog of the Landes in south-west France, the English Sheepdog, and even the Egyptian Armant. In northern Italy the Bergamasco was the sheep-herding dog.

Throughout the 19th century sheep-farming became increasingly rare in northern Italy, and was concentrated in Sardinia, the Maremma and the Abruzzi. With the disappearance of the age-old practice of letting the year's fallow fields out to pasture, both flocks and dogs also vanished from large areas. For a certain period of time sheep were still confined to poor areas of land, impoverished either because of aridity or altitude. But subsequently, in the north of Italy, as industry attracted labour, there was also a shortage of people prepared to tend flocks of sheep – by tradition a lowly, hard way of life.

As a result, only a few farmers still need the Bergamasco as a working dog. But those that are kept are often magnificent specimens.

TODAY'S BREED

Official classification KC (GB) and AKC: not recognized
Country of origin Italy
Height and weight Males approx. 60 cm (24 in); females approx. 56 cm (22½ in). Weight: 26-38 kg (58-84 lb)
Coat All shades of grey, including black, sometimes with fawn markings or not very large white splashes; hair very long, abundant, goat-like, with a short, dense undercoat that is oily and thus water-resistant; the hair covers the eyes and is abundant at the neck

General appearance A hardy herding-dog, sturdy, size belied by the coat
Head Large with a broad skull, good muzzle; tip of nose black; lips tight and thin; scissor-type bite
Ears Not docked, set high up on the head, semi-drooping, with fringes
Eyes Large, brown in colour, the shade matching the colour of the coat
Body Ribs and chest reaching the knees, belly not very tucked up
Legs Strong, good posture, straight; hare-like feet (oval)
Tail Not docked, should not extend beyond the hocks, with a slight curve when at rest, well covered with hair
Gait Very good at the trot

Qualities Sturdiness and endurance, abundant hair, good colouring
Defects White overall not admissible, nor are white markings accounting for more than one-fifth of the coat; too tall or not tall enough; pale eyes
Character Alert, willing, good-natured. Gentle expression

Uses Suitable for sheep-herding, farm duties, good watch-dog for homes and gardens
Future prospects This breed is now quite rare, and has competition from the French Briard, which has received more attention. Little likelihood of spreading
Similar breeds Ukraine Sheepdog (herding), USSR: this breed seems to have been selected in recent years, and is also used for military duties

The Bergamese Shepherd has a coat
varying in colour from black to fawn. In
specimens that live out-of-doors, like the
one above, it offers perfect protection from
bad weather and cold. In the breed's
native region, Lombardy in Italy, changes
in farming mean that it is less and less
used as a sheepdog.

BERNESE MOUNTAIN DOG
Sennenhund

The four breeds of Swiss Mountain Dogs (Sennenhund) all have different geographical names. They are similar in colour, but differ in size and are used for different duties. In ascending order they range from the small Entlebuch, which takes its name from the River Entlen in the Canton of Lucerne, to the Appenzeller Sennenhund, to the Bernese Mountain Dog, and lastly to the large Swiss Mountain Dog. Their selection started early in the 20th century under the patronage of Professor Albert Heim (1849-1937), a famous geologist and an even more celebrated cynologist. The Bernese Mountain Dog (which Heim called the most handsome of all the varieties) came into being thanks to Franz Schertenleib, a dog-breeder from Berthoud near Burgdorf in the Canton of Berne. The Appenzeller Sennenhund is due to the efforts of Max Siber, founder of the Club in 1907. In those days his fellow-villagers looked on him as a madman for his obsession with dogs, and there was even talk of committing him to a mental home. The large Swiss Mountain Dog survived for centuries in a non-thoroughbred state, and was sometimes considered dangerous because of its sheer size. In fact, in 1489 a Zurich magistrate ordered these dogs to be done away with altogether, but the sentence was never actually carried out.

The Bernese Mountain Dog and the Appenzeller Sennenhund are very popular in the German-speaking countries – Germany and Austria – as well as in Holland.

The Alpine dogs of Switzerland have names derived from geographical locations. The largest breeds are the Swiss Mountain Dog and the Bernese Mountain Dog. The Appenzeller Sennenhund has a distinctively curled tail and the smallest of the four, the Entlebuch, is the only variety to have its tail docked.

Swiss Mountain Dog

Bernese Mountain Dog

Appenzell Mountain Dog

Entlebuch Mountain Dog

TODAY'S BREED

Official Classification (Bernese Mountain Dog only) KC (GB): Working Group; AKC: Working Dogs
Country of origin Switzerland
Height and weight Swiss Mountain Dog: males 65-70 cm (26-28 in); females 60-65 cm (24-26 in). Weight approx. 35-50 kg (80-110 lbs); Bernese Mountain Dog: males 64-70 cm (25½-28 in); females 58-66 cm (23-26½ in). Weight approx. 30-40 kg (67-90 lb); Appenzeller Sennenhund: males 52-58 cm (12-23 in); females 48-54 cm (19-21½ in). Weight approx. 25-35 kg (55-80 lbs); Entlebuch: 40-50 cm (16-20 in). Weight approx. 20-30 kg (45-66 lbs)
Coat In all varieties black with symmetrical white and tawny markings; hair hard and short in the Swiss Mountain Dog, long and dense in the Bernese Mountain Dog, hard and short with a good undercoat in the Appenzeller Sennenhund and the Entlebuch. In all four varieties there is white on the top of and around the muzzle, on the chest, the feet and at the tip of the tail, and sometimes a white patch on the nape of the neck

General appearance Powerful, muscular, well proportioned, working-dogs
Head Strong, well proportioned, skull rather flat; muzzle strong; tip of nose black; scissor-type bite, rarely pincer-type bite
Ears Average-sized, traingular, set high up on the head, turned forward when the dog is alert
Eyes Bright, hazel-brown, chestnut, or ordinary brown
Body Neck muscular and strong, chest wide, ribs deep, back straight, shoulders muscular, belly well developed
Legs Powerful, muscular and straight; feet roundish and closed
Tail Docked by one-third, but only in the Entlebuch; curved at the tip in the Swiss and Bernese Mountain Dogs; quite distinctive in the Appenzeller Sennenhund, curled up over the rump, except when the dog is uneasy, when it drops with a slight curve
Gait Brisk, free, with a long stride, a good dog at the trot, and even better when running

Qualities Good, well-delineated muscles, uniform coat, lively, observant expression
Defects Uneven stature, irregular tail, lack of spirit, although the Swiss Mountain Dog is calmer in temperament
Character Excellent temperament

Uses The large Swiss Mountain Dog is excellent for haulage duties, and is still used by dairymen and milkmen, cheese-makers, butchers and farmers in general. The same goes for the Bernese Mountain Dog. The Appenzeller Sennenhund is the all-round Mountain Dog (like the Bouvier), capable of rounding up 200 head of cattle scattered in mountain pastures; it tends to bite when working with sheep but can control a bull. The Entlebuch, on the other hand, is still used for sheep-herding

Future prospects The large Swiss Mountain Dog is hampered by its sheer size; the Bernese Mountain Dog is popular because of its handsome appearance, which means that it is often kept as a pet; the Appenzeller Sennenhund is becoming popular as a dog for personal protection; the Entlebuch remains rare

A long-haired specimen of the Bernese Mountain Dog (above) shows the typical markings of the breed. Glay von Gampelen (right) was world champion in 1980.

BICHON FRISE

The term 'bichon' is applied to a group of small generally white dogs – including in addition to the Bichon Frise the Maltese and the Bolognese – that have had a long history of popularity in the courts of Europe. Many an eighteenth-century portrait features a companion-dog that in major respects is very close to one or other of the breeds as they are now established.

Despite its small size and somewhat frivolous appearance, the Bichon Frise is a remarkably sturdy dog. In the late nineteenth and early twentieth century the breed suffered something of a decline but thanks to its enthusiasts interest in it has revived and its qualities have been increasingly appreciated since recognition of the breed in Great Britain and North America. Intelligence, an affectionate nature, jauntiness and great mobility are combined in this breed with a physical appearance of great charm. When properly groomed the silky curled coat and gaily raised tail make it a very attractive breed in the show ring.

TODAY'S BREED

Official classification KC (GB): Toy Group; AKC: Non-sporting Dogs
Country of origin Great Britain
Height 20-30 cm (8-12 in)
Coat Fine, silky with soft corkscrew curls that are pure white. Under the white coat dark pigment is preferred

General appearance A small compact animal, slightly longer than tall
Head The head should be in proportion to the body and the skull longer than the muzzle. The hair tends to make the skull look round but it is flat when touched. The nose should be round, black, soft and shiny
Ears Narrow and delicate, dropped and well covered with tightly curled long hair. The leather should reach about halfway along the muzzle
Eyes Fairly round, dark with dark rims, expressive and alert
Body Well-developed chest with good spring of ribs
Legs Forelegs straight when seen from the front, hindquarters well angulated and the feet small and round
Tail Covered with long hair and carried raised and curled gracefully over the back
Gait Lively and stylish

Qualities Abundant coat, with plenty of pure white ringlets
Defects Snipy muzzle, poor pigmentation, corkscrew tail, eyes that protrude, overshot or undershot bite
Character Happy and alert

Uses Companion-dog
Future prospects Its popularity in the show ring and as a companion-dog is likely to increase

The Bichon Frise is a delightfully active companion-dog that is far more robust than its appearance at first suggests.

BLOODHOUND

Some cynologists maintain that the Bloodhound (the largest of the Pointer group) has as its ancestor the St Hubert Hound (Chien de St Hubert), which may possibly have found its way over to England from Belgium or France at the time of the Norman Conquest. In his work entitled **De Paris au Tonkin à travers le Thibet inconnu**, Henri, Duke of Orléans (1867-1901) makes mention of a breed of Hound encountered in the Pamir region, closely resembling the Bloodhound. The ancestors of the breed may therefore have been brought to Europe by Aryan peoples coming overland from Asia. Among the British descendants of the Hounds of the past were white and tri-colour dogs called Talbots, and black and black-and-tan dogs called Bloodhounds, a term which possibly refers to their ability to follow the scent of blood left behind by prey.

The Bloodhound in Great Britain and the Chien de St Hubert in Belgium were, for a long time, considered to be separate breeds, although they bore a close resemblance to one another. The breed was eventually standardized by the Fédération Cynologique Internationale. In the United States the Bloodhound is used for tracking human beings, and its recognition of its quarry is widely accepted as authoritative evidence in courts of law.

TODAY'S BREED

Official classification KC (GB) Hound Group; AKC: Hounds
Countries of origin Belgium and Great Britain
Height and weight 60-67 cm (24-27 in). Weight: 40-48 kg (90-108 lb)
Coat Hair short and hard on the body, soft on the skull and ears; colours tan and black-and-tan

General appearance A typical member of the Pointer group with huge ears and a very wrinkled head
Head Large and rather fat, but not broad, with large folds of skin on the forehead and on the cheeks; tip of nose black; lips large and drooping; scissor-type bite
Ears Not docked, very long, set low, hanging in graceful folds
Eyes Small, dark brown; the lower eyelid reveals the conjunctiva
Body Chest powerful and deep, back strong, belly moderately tucked up
Legs Good stance, muscular with strong bone structure; cat-like feet
Tail Not docked, curved at the extremity, never raised above horizontal level
Gait Slow and ponderous

Qualities The head is of great importance, and must have a majestic quality; another important feature are the wrinkles in the skin, which are more accentuated than in any other breed. Black saddle on tan ground is sought after
Defects Only small white markings on the chest or feet are admitted
Character Affectionate, in no way quarrelsome or difficult, receptive to kindness, should not be punished. Gentle, open expression

Uses Very keen on its duties: for the most part tracking – preferably human beings
Future prospects This specialist at tracking is earmarked for hunting down criminals and wrong-doers, and for seeking missing persons
Similar breeds Black-and-tan Coonhound (Hound), United States: as the name would suggest, the speciality of this breed is hunting out raccoons. The breed was recognized in 1947

As the print above shows, the distinctive characteristics of this breed were well developed by the middle of the nineteenth century. Bloodhounds are still commonly used to search for missing people.

BORDER COLLIE

The Border Collie is renowned as one of the world's finest sheepdogs and has been used for many centuries to work the sheep. They are sometimes known as 'creepers' from their style of working, mainly due to their ability to drop to the ground instantly. They have a more tucked up appearance than their Scottish relative, the Bearded Collie. The Border Collie has only very recently been recognized in Great Britain and is not as yet recognized by the American Kennel Club. Sheepdog trials have been held since 1873.

The Border Collie has earned a reputation well beyond its area of origin as an outstanding breed for working sheep. In action it is remarkably intelligent and active; at rest it is a gentle and good-natured animal.

TODAY'S BREED

Official classification KC (GB): Working Group; AKC: not recognized
Country of origin Great Britain
Height Males 53 cm (21 in); females slightly less
Coat Two varieties, one moderately long, the other smooth. In both the topcoat should be dense and medium textured, the undercoat short, soft and dense to give good weather resistance. A variety of colours is permissible but white should never predominate

General appearance A well proportioned dog, the smooth outline showing quality, gracefulness and perfect balance
Head Skull fairly broad, occiput not pronounced. Cheeks should not be full or rounded. The muzzle tapering to nose, should be moderately short and strong. Nose black
Ears Should be of medium size and texture, set well apart, carried semi-erect
Eyes Set wide apart, oval shaped, of moderate size and dark brown in colour, except in the case of merles where one or both, or part of one or both, may be blue
Body Ribs well sprung, chest deep and rather broad. The back should be broad and strong, loins deep, muscular and slightly arched. Slightly longer than high at shoulder
Legs Fore-legs should be round in bone and strong but not heavy. Hindquarters should be broad and muscular. From hock to ground the hind legs should be well boned and parallel from the rear
Tail Moderately long, the bone reaching at least to the hock joint, set on low, well furnished and with an upward swirl towards the end. May be raised in excitement but never carried over back
Gait Free movement with a limited lift of feet

Qualities Combination of substance to give endurance and grace
Defects Any appearance of cloddiness that would restrict ability to move with stealth and speed
Character Should be neither nervous nor aggressive but keen, alert and intelligent

Uses Outstanding merits as a working sheepdog and also makes a very good companion-dog
Future prospects As a show-dog its popularity is likely to increase

BORDER TERRIER

The Border Terrier originated in the Border Counties of Scotland and England and is used for going to ground, mainly after fox. It is a very natural Terrier and must be regarded as one of the oldest kinds of Terrier in Great Britain. It is essentially a working Terrier and will be found in most homesteads in the Border Counties. Its great ability to drive a fox out of a lair is unrivalled as the Border Terrier is full of great courage. The breed was first registered at the English Kennel Club in 1920 and its popularity has now spread throughout Great Britain and to many other countries.

TODAY'S BREED

Official classification KC (GB): Terrier Group; AKC: Terriers
Country of origin Great Britain
Weight Males: 6-7 kg (13-15½ lb); females 5-6 kg (11-13 lb)
Coat Harsh and dense with close undercoat. Skin must be thick. Colour: red, wheaten, grizzle and tan or blue and tan

General appearance Essentially a working Terrier that should be able to follow a horse and must combine activity with gameness
Head Like that of an otter, moderately broad in skull, with a short strong muzzle
Ears Small, V-shaped, of moderate thickness and dropping forward close to the cheek
Eyes Dark, with keen expression
Body Deep and narrow and fairly long, ribs carried well back, but not oversprung
Legs Fore-legs straight and not too heavy in bone. Quarters, racy with strong loin
Tail Moderately short and fairly thick at the base, then tapering, set high and carried gaily but not curled over back
Gait Free running with great staying power

Qualities Very natural Terrier that combines activity with courage
Defects Snipey muzzle or untypical head. Oversize
Character Tremendous characters that make excellent companions

Uses Hunting and as companion-dogs
Future prospects Popularity as a family pet likely to continue

In pursuit of the fox that has gone to ground the Border Terrier is absolutely relentless. His game qualities do not stop him from making an attractive companion-dog.

BORZOI

As early as the 17th century there was a Russian Hound known as the Borzoi, which was bred by huntsmen. There was, in particular, a sturdy, curly-haired variety used for hunting wolves, and another lighter, wavy-haired type used for hunting hares. Towards the end of the 19th century the court of the Tsars started selecting and breeding these dogs. Some were presented to the English Court, and the breed was much admired by Queen Victoria, a monarch who awakened considerable interest in various breeds of dog. In about 1885 Grand Duke Nicholas Nikolaievich set up his Perchino kennels, with 150 breeding dogs, including the stud called Opromiote. There were famous kennels in Great Britain, owned by the Duchess of Newcastle, and in Holland, run by Baron H. van Haaren. In Paris the kennels were in the Jardin d'acclimatation. During those years the Borzoi was painted by the English artists Emms and Earl, by the Dutch painter Eerelman, and by Mahler in France. With the collapse of the Tsarist Empire, and the decline of the aristocracy in Europe, the Borzoi became rare.

The Russian word **borzoi** is a general term for Greyhound; the precise Russian name for the Borzoi is Psovoi Borzoi.

TODAY'S BREED

Official classification KC (GB): Hound Group; AKC: Hounds
Country of origin USSR
Height Males: approx. 75.5 cm (30¼ in); females: 71 cm (28½ in). Males will sometimes measure up to 82 cm (33 in)
Coat Hair long, wavy, silky, plentiful on the neck, chest, thighs and tail; colour: white, white and yellow to red, brindle, grey

General appearance A very elegant and noble-looking Greyhound, whether at rest or in motion
Head Long and narrow, muzzle longer than the skull; tip of nose black; lips fine; scissors- or pincer-type bite
Ears Not docked, small, thin; not too far apart
Eyes Large, oval, set quite close together, dark
Body Chest deep and narrow, back arched, belly very tucked up
Legs Lean and straight, good stance; feet narrow and long
Tail Not docked, very long, carried between the thighs, slightly curved at extremity
Gait Skipping and brisk, aristocratic, slightly stiff

Qualities The overall appearance is important, and must be quite distinctive; main features are the handsome coat and the specific gait of the breed

Defects Black and tan colour, with or without white markings, is a serious defect; hair woolly and short

Character The breed is claimed by some to be 'dreamy'; and it is certainly often somewhat detached and lazy; but it is also affectionate. Rather distant expression

Uses Formerly for hunting, nowadays a companion-dog

Future prospects On the decline, with a small but keen following

An English bred Borzoi (opposite, bottom) and two International and Italian champions, Sebastian di Rocca Barbara and Jesabel di Roca Barbara, of this handsome and aristocratic breed.

BOSTON TERRIER

Boston enjoyed a reputation of being the intellectual centre of the (former) English colonies in North America, and today it is still proud of its liberal-minded aristocracy. It is also proud of its own breed of dog.

The ancestor of all Boston Terriers, called Judge, was taken across the Atlantic from Liverpool in the 1870s, and was described as half-Bulldog and half-Terrier. He was mated with a bitch of an undefined breed. There was then further cross-breeding, and a taste for dogs arriving from Europe – in particular Toy Bulldogs and the Bouledogue français – encouraged the development of the breed.

In 1878 one or two Boston Terriers began to appear at shows, then under the name of American Bull-Terrier, with the following classification: 'round-headed Bull-Terrier, of any colour'. In 1891 the American cynologist and writer, James Watson, made the point that the name Bull-Terrier was incorrect, and he recommended the name Boston Terrier. This was accepted, and it stuck. The dog quickly became popular in the United States; since 1946 it has become well known in Europe, thanks to American troops.

TODAY'S BREED

Official classification KC (GB): Utility Group; AKC: Non-Sporting Dogs
Country of origin United States
Weight Light: less than 7 kg (15 lb); medium: 7-9.5 kg (15-21 lb); maximum: 9.5-11.5 kg approx. (21-26 lb) approx.
Coat Hair short, fine and shiny; colour: brindle or black with white markings on muzzle, head, neck, chest, front and hind feet

General appearance Elegant, alert, compact, well proportioned
Head Square, with no wrinkles or folds; tip of nose black; lips large but never drooping; teeth slightly prognathus
Ears Either undocked or docked, erect, small and narrow
Eyes Large, round, set well apart, dark
Body Short but not thickset, fore-quarters quite open, hind-quarters angled; belly slightly drawn in
Legs Strong and straight
Tail Not docked, naturally short, often twisted, never lively
Gait Brisk and loose

Qualities Combines strength with elegance, and is at once distinctive and distinguished
Defects Head too heavy, gait not brisk enough
Character A lovable temperament, a good playmate, good-natured, but can be fiery

Uses A typical pet, enjoys going for walks, likes women as much as men, good with young children
Future prospects It is gradually replacing the French Bulldog, and seems to be generally on the increase in popularity
Similar breeds The Terrier group, in Great Britain and elsewhere, has a number of members: the Border Terrier, which has been officially recognized since 1920; the Lakeland Terrier, recognized since 1930, a smaller version of the Airedale Terrier; the Welsh Terrier, which is smaller than the Airedale but larger than the Lakeland Terrier; the Jack Russell Terrier (named after the priest who introduced the breed in the 19th century), which is used for hunting underground, an art in which it is unrivalled; and the Norwich Terrier, recognized in 1932

The Boston Terrier Club of America was founded in 1891 and the breed has gained a keen following ever since. Its ancestors are the British Bulldog and a English Terrier.

BOULET GRIFFON
Griffon à Poil Laineux

This breed owes its existence to the efforts of a French textile-merchant by the name of Emanuel Boulet (after whom it is named). It earned an early reputation, thanks to the President of the French Republic, Sadi Carnot, who was fond of wearing a woollen waistcoat made from the hair of Boulet Griffons. The breed was treated with considerable hostility by the envious cynologist, Mègnin.

The original progenitors of the breed were Champion Marco, Champion Diavolo and Champion Myra, all selected by Boulet at Elbeuf, a small town close to Rouen famous for its textile industry, hence the commonly used term 'drap elbeuf'. Boulet produced some 2000 dogs.

Before this revival the breed had been in a somewhat doubtful, not to say spurious, position. Boulet improved it by getting rid of the large number of Griffons which then existed in France: Nivernais, Vendéen, de Bretagne, du Grip, d'Anjou, de Picardie, and so on.

In those days there were also a Russian Griffon, an Egyptian Griffon and a variety from Central Asia, which have all since disappeared.

The Boulet Griffon is also known as the Griffon à Poil Laineux, or Soft-haired Griffon.

TODAY'S BREED

Official classification KC (GB) and AKC: not recognized
Country of origin France
Height and weight 50-60 cm (20-24 in). Weight: approx. 25 kg (56 lb)
Coat Hair long and quite silky, not with a sheen; it may be smooth or wavy, but never curly; colour: brown (as in autumn leaves), uniform or patchy, but with no black included, and no large white markings

General appearance A sturdy Griffon, plentifully covered with thick hair, an athletic dog
Head Rather bushy in appearance, with large moustache and a thick beard; tip of nose brown, matching the coat; scissor-type bite
Ears Not docked, falling, rounded, and well covered with hair
Eyes Conspicuous eyebrows hanging over the eyes but not hiding them altogether; yellow iris
Body Ribs deep, well sprung, trunk short, belly not tucked up
Legs Good stance, sturdy, muscular, covered with hair; feet oval
Tail Not docked, straight, well covered with hair, not fringed
Gait Excellent at the trot, with dashes at the gallop

Qualities A rather stern appearance, slightly heavy, clearly sturdy, strong and rugged, plentiful coat all over the body
Defects Brown eyes (a sign of crossbreeding), coarse or rough hair, large white markings
Character A clever and methodical hunter, not swift, but never loses sight of its master. Gentle, but frank expression

Uses Excellent hunter in woodland and marshland
Future prospects The fashion for fast-moving Pointer and Gun-dogs has turned this breed into something of a rarity except in its birthplace

The Boulet Griffon is a slow and steady worker in the field and is considered an ideal dog for hunting partridge. However the breed has become something of a rarity.

BOUVIER DES FLANDRES

Various types of Bouvier (literally cowherd or oxherd) came into being during the 19th century in Flanders, the great plain which stretches from the heights of Artois to the mouth of the River Scheldt. Since this territory lay partly in France and partly in Belgium, there was a French Bouvier in Lille, a Belgian Bouvier in Ghent, and a Flemish Bouvier at Roulers. There was the herding Bouvier of the lush grasslands, the barge Bouvier on the long canals, the spinning-mill Bouvier and the harbour Bouvier peculiar to Dunkirk.

They were all, more or less, Bouviers; the Flanders breed came to the fore in 1910, but it took the determination of the Belgian Captain Darby and the foundation of a Club in Ghent in 1922 to lay the foundation of the breed's uniformity. Flanders was the scene of major battles in the First World War. In the Second World War it was from Dunkirk that the British army fled back across the Channel, and the whole area was occupied by German troops until 1945. These events affected the breeding chances of the Bouvier (and of another valuable domestic animal, the large Flanders rabbit). However, in 1964 there were still three standards existing side-by-side: one for the Belgian Bouvier, one for the French Bouvier, and a third for the heavier Roulers (Flemish) variety. They were all standardized in 1965, when the breed's numbers began to increase.

TODAY'S BREED

Official classification KC (GB): Working Group; AKC: Herding Dogs
Countries of origin Belgium and France
Height and weight Males: 62-68 cm (25-27 in); Females: 59-65 cm (24-26 in). Weight: 27-40 kg (60-90 lb)
Coat Hair about 6 cm (2½ in) long, dry, rough to the touch, undercoat dense, close, water-resistant; colour: fawn (tawny), grey, variegated, charcoal, sometimes even black

General appearance Powerful, hairy, unrefined, compact, strong
Head Appears larger than it is because of the whiskers and beard; muzzle broad; tip of nose black; scissor- or pincer-type bite
Ears Docked in a triangular shape, tall, upright, movable
Eyes Slightly oval, very dark-coloured
Body Compact, thickset, ribs deep and well sprung, arched, back short, belly well developed
Legs Strong bone-structure, muscular, very good stance; feet short, solid and round
Tail Docked to second or third vertebra; some pups are born tail-less
Gait Supple, rapid, good endurance, excellent at the trot, good at the run

Qualities Simplicity and strength, solid athletic build, or that of a fighter; though not overlarge, its steadfastness is impressive
Defects Woolly or curly coat, flat hair, dull colour, lack of undercoat
Character Bold, alert, courageous, devoted to one master. Open, frank, lively expression

Uses Police and military duties, herding, guard-dog
Future prospects Its versatility and appearance, plus its temperament, mean that this breed will be increasingly used as a police-dog
Similar breeds Bouvier des Ardennes (guard-dog and general duties), Belgium: although akin to the Bouvier des Flandres, this is regarded as a separate breed, and is still bred in certain parts of Belgium

The breed has remained virtually unaltered for a century or more as can be seen from these two illustrations. Today's standards list tail-docking as compulsory.

BOXER

This breed came into being in the late 19th century in Bavaria, out of the union between a local butcher's dog called the Bullenbeisser, of dubious pedigree, and an English Bulldog, as it then was. The first people to breed the Boxer were the Bavarians, Hopper, Robert and König. Perhaps the most famous selector was Philip Stockmann, followed by his wife, from 1911 onwards. The first Boxer was shown in 1894 (this was Flocki, the son of Tom and Alt); the first Club was founded in 1896 in Munich, and the first Champion was Blanka von Angerthor in 1897. She was white-coated, but already close to the modern type of Boxer, although she also had qualities from certain late-19th-century English Bulldogs, such as Princess Ida. Both Princess Ida and Blanka are illustrated in Henry de Bylandt's book **Les races de chiens** (Brussels, 1897). In those days the Boxer was not very well known — so little known, in fact, that the dog-expert de Bylandt muddled it with the Boston Terrier. In the early part of this century the breed started to become more popular in Austria, Switzerland and Holland. After the Second World War the Boxer became one of the most widely used guard-dogs all over the world, although this has undoubtedly affected its uniformity: for example, there is now an American type, which differs from the German type. The breed produced some excellent dogs for military duties in the Second World War.

TODAY'S BREED

Official classification KC (GB) Working Group; AKC: Working Dogs
Country of origin Germany
Height and weight Males: 57-63 cm (23-25 in); females 53-59 cm (21-24 in). Weight: 25-30 kg (56-67 lb)
Coat Short-haired, close-cropped, shiny, lying smooth; colour: fawn or brindle in various shades from light yellow to dark reddish brown; white markings are admissible as long as they do not cover more than one-third of the body. Black mask obligatory

General appearance A typically Mastiff-like dog, of medium size, at once powerful and elegant
Head Distinctive, striking, with good proportion between skull and muzzle; tip of nose black and slightly pug-like; lips heavy (flews) and distinctively shaped; must never slobber; prognathous, teeth never visible when the mouth is closed
Ears Docked to a specific shape; set well up on the head, movable and upright
Eyes Neither prominent nor sunken; dark brown in colour
Body Gathered, hind-quarters lighter than fore-quarters, chest well set down between fore-legs, belly drawn in
Legs Powerful, muscular, straight; hind legs somewhat angled; feet round, toes close
Tail Docked at the third or fourth vertebra; carried upwards
Gait Supple, elastic at the trot, a good runner

Qualities Good proportions between the head and body, and the fore- and hind-quarters; with an impressive balance between elegance and solidity
Defects Slobbering, white all over, or almost so, black, teeth visible when the mouth is closed, hind-quarters either straight or too angled
Character A warm-hearted dog, good-natured, even over-fond of people, generous, enjoys praise and likes being stroked, but determined and energetic when on the attack. A sincere expression

Uses All the duties of a working-dog, including guiding the blind
Future prospects There is no reason why this breed's worldwide popularity should not continue

The first breed champion, Blanka von Angerthor (opposite, top), won the title in Germany in 1897. Nancy di Valdemone (opposite, bottom) is a fine Italian-bred specimen coming almost a century after Blanka. Two fine specimens, a brindle bitch (above) and a young fawn-coloured dog (below), show the characteristics of the modern Boxer.

BRIARD

This dog was mentioned for the first time in an early 19th-century work entitled **Cours d'agriculture**, which was written by the abbot Rozier.

Later on it found an eloquent and determined champion in Pierre Mégnin, a famous cynologist, and editor of the important magazine **L'Eleveur**. Mégnin was born in Hérimoncourt in 1828, later graduated from the Alfort Veterinary School and began work as a military veterinary surgeon. For many years he concentrated his attention on dogs, and published important books on cynology, zoology and medicine. He was also a good draughtsman. In 1893 he became a member of the Academy of Medicine in Paris.

He died in 1905, leaving a tradition of 'Latin' cynology which was carried on by his son Paul and in Italy by the veterinary surgeon Giuseppe Solaro of Turin, the greatest Italian cynologist in the early years of this century.

The Briard has become a popular dog in France, where it is carefully selected, and invariably encountered at dog-shows.

TODAY'S BREED

Official classification KC (GB): Working Group; AKC: Herding Dogs
Country of origin France
Height Males: 62-68 cm (25-27 in); females: 56-64 cm (22½-25½ in)
Coat Hair long, dry, slightly wavy, supple, with an abundant, water-resistant undercoat; colour: uniform, whatever the colour; preferably dark-haired; white not admissible

General appearance A conspicuous dog because of its full, shiny coat
Head Strong, with plenty of hair (beard, whiskers or moustache, eyebrows, plumes on the ears, eyes half-hidden); tip of nose black; scissor-type bite
Ears Usually with a blunt point, erect, set high on the head; un-docked ears are admissible
Eyes Large, round and dark
Body Ribs and chest broad and deep, belly not tucked up
Legs Strong bone structure, good straight stance; feet rather rounded
Tail Not docked, held low, with an upward hook at the tip. Well covered with hair
Gait Effortless, supple, good at the trot

Qualities The coat is very important – must be full and of good colour; the head must also comply precisely with the standard
Defects Hair that is white, silken, curly or short
Character Keen, playful, bold if necessary. Alert expression

Uses Increasingly rarely used as a sheepdog; has become a guard-dog
Future prospects This rare breed is much appreciated in France, but any future spread will be limited by the attention required to its coat
Similar breeds Cão de Serra de Aires (herding-dog), Portugal: smaller than the Briard, its coat is just as abundant all over the body, and in particular on the head

A pair of black-coated three-year old French champions, Onky des Pierrailles and Onyx des Pierrailles.

BRITTANY
Brittany Spaniel

This dog appeared in the early years of the last century as a tough and rugged companion for the equally tough and rugged hunter in Brittany. There is a fine illustration of such a dog in a painting by Jouy. At the end of the 19th century the breed began to crop up outside Brittany, and specialized canine journals started to pay attention to it, although they frequently confused it with the other Epagneuls (Spaniels) – Picard, Français, de Pont-Audemer and so on. Early in this century the breed was improved by being crossed with Setters. The first Club was founded in 1904, and the first official standard drawn up in 1907.

The breed made its debut at a show in 1892, but it was not until 1919 that it managed to demonstrate its real worth in field trials.

Between 1930 and 1940, the world's greatest expert where this breed is concerned, De Kermadec, drew up the new and definitive official standard.

After the Second World War the Brittany Spaniel began to earn worldwide popularity, especially in trials and as an effective hunting-dog. As the smallest of the Pointer group it is the only one really suited to living in a flat.

TODAY'S BREED

Official classification KC (GB): not recognized; AKC: Sporting Dogs
Country of origin France
Height and weight Males: 48-50 cm (19-20 in); Females: 47-49 cm (19-19½ in). Weight: 14-18 kg (30-40 lb)
Coat Hair fine, fringed but not to excess; colours: orange-white, liver and white, roan

General appearance Small but energetic, compact and lively
Head The skull is rounded, the muzzle quite short; tip of nose matches the colour of the coat; scissor-type bite
Ears Not docked, set high on the head, not long, rounded with a small fringe
Eyes The same colour as the darkest parts of the coat
Body Chest reaching as far as the elbows, back short, belly slightly tucked up
Legs Good stance, muscular, with slight fringes, feet compact with some hair covering them
Tail Docked to about 10 cm (4 in); some specimens are tail-less, others have a short tail
Gait Brisk, lively stride at the trot, swift at the gallop

Qualities Compact, sturdy, medium size, with energetic movements
Defects Height less than 46 cm (18½ in) or more than 51 cm (20½ in); lack of pigmentation in eyelids or tip of nose; 'bird of prey' expression
Character Alert, keen, a busy worker when on the hunt, very devoted to those known to it. Keen expression

Uses An efficient Pointer on any kind of terrain and at all times of year
Future prospects On the increase
Similar breeds Among the French Epagneuls is the Français, which reaches a height of 58 cm (23 in), the Picard, with its blue-grey coat with brown markings and the de Pont-Audemer, which measures between 50-55 cm (20-22 in). Other varieties are confined to local areas

The Brittany has gained popularity in Europe and the United States as a small but highly effective field dog. It is the smallest of the Pointer group.

BULLDOG

The first appearance of the word 'Bulldog' in the English language was in the ancient spelling of 'bulddogge'. The modern name came into use after the 17th century. This extraordinarily distinctive breed has always aroused great admiration or instant loathing: nothing betwixt and between.

The courage of the Bulldog has been spoken of enthusiastically in all historical periods, so much so that the blood of this breed is mixed with that of all those other breeds, including the Greyhounds and the Pointers, required to have tenacity, steadfastness and endurance.

From the 17th century to the early 19th century there was bull-baiting in Britain – contests in which the Bulldog had to seize the bull by the nose. By about 1840 bull-baiting was no longer so popular, and the contests were banned. As a result the Bulldog seemed on the point of dying out, but working-class people in Birmingham and Sheffield made sure that it survived. (In those days, incidentally, it resembled a short, white-coated Boxer.)

The Bulldog first appeared in shows in 1860; the Club was founded in 1864 and recognized by the Kennel Club in 1875. The Bulldog is widely recognized as the British national breed and is the subject of many books all over the world.

TODAY'S BREED

Official classification KC (GB): Utility Group: AKC: Non-Sporting Dogs
Country of origin Great Britain
Weight 22-25 kg (50-56 lb) and sometimes more
Coat Close-lying, dense, shiny; colour: red, fawn, brindle, patched, white, not black all over

General appearance Huge strength contained in a broad, low frame
Head Strikingly large, massive, heavy, square with wrinkles on the skull; muzzle very broad indeed, nose itself quite short and very pug-like (the nose must be conspicuously set back in relation to the round lower jaw that protrudes to the front); tip of nose black; thick, broad and deep lips (flews); must not slobber; when the mouth is closed the incisors can sometimes be seen, but never the canines; very prognathous
Ears Not docked, thin: the term 'rose ear' is applied to them
Eyes Somewhat overhung by the eyelids, and set quite well apart; very dark-coloured
Body Fore-quarters are very large with muscular, conspicuous shoulders, ribs are roundish, the croup is higher off the ground than the withers, hind-quarters are light, the belly well-developed
Legs Short, very powerful, muscular, with a special stance; feet slightly splayed
Tail Not docked, short, known as the 'stern'
Gait Distinctive, unlike that of any other dog, but supple and easy

Qualities All the unusual features peculiar to the breed
Defects Small head, body too light, visible canines, tongue visible, lively tail, difficulty in walking
Character Phlegmatic, calm, 'lazy-bones', patient. A rather unsociable, morose expression

Merriveen-Sno-Wonder (left), at the age of four, a white-coated dog born in Britain, and the print above, dating from 1897, show the maintenance of a consistent type. Zeffira degli Alamandini (opposite, top) is shown at the age of three. The pups (opposite, bottom) are four months old.

Uses This is a dog-lover's dog. It will see off anyone up to no good, and is particularly useful for guarding the car

Future prospects This is a breed for very keen dog-lovers, from all walks of life, and in every country in the world; it will never become commonplace

Similar breeds Staffordshire Bull Terrier, a breed, owing much to the Bulldog, that was developed for dog-fighting. In the United States there has for some time been an American Staffordshire Terrier, which is heavier, more powerful and more aggressive

BULLMASTIFF

This is a recent breed. The first Bullmastiff to be registered in the British Kennel Club records was Farcraft Fidelity in 1921. For registration purposes the specimen must have had four previous documented generations. This means that in 1921 the breed had been thoroughbred selected from about 1910. The creator of the breed is considered to be S.S. Moseley. The Club was founded in 1924. To begin with Moseley crossbred a Bulldog and a Mastiff of the day, hence the name. But the outcome was closer in appearance to that of a medium-sized Mastiff than of a large Bulldog. It seems that it won early support among gamekeepers in their war against poachers, and this was why it was desirable to have a powerful and aggressive dog, but one that was easy to handle. In about 1930 Bullmastiffs were often teamed with night-watchmen, and later with policemen. They have also been used to guard the diamond mines of South Africa. After 1946 the breed developed quite a large following, despite its rival, the Boxer.

TODAY'S BREED

Official classification KC (GB): Working Group, AKC: Working Dogs
Country of origin Great Britain
Height and weight Males: 63-69 cm (25-28 in); females: 60-66 cm (24-26 in). Weight: 40-60 kg (90-135 lb)
Coat Hair short and close-cropped; colour: red, fawn, brindle, mask black extending to the eyes

General appearance A good-sized Mastiff type, slightly larger than average, more substantial than distinguished
Head Striking, like that of a Mastiff; muzzle short; tip of nose black; the upper lips (flews) hang to the bottom of the lower jaw, but are not pendulous; prognathous
Ears Set high on the head, not docked, V-shaped, pricked forward when the dog is on the alert
Eyes Average-sized, hazel-coloured or darker, depending on the colour of the coat
Body Strong, vigorous, ribs deep and well sprung, belly well developed
Legs Very powerful, straight, the hind legs are slightly bent; feet rounded
Tail Not docked, broad at the base, tending to taper, never raised
Gait Steady, solid, loose, easy at the trot

Qualities Strength and nobility, a large upright neck, good balance between fore- and hind-quarters
Defects Thinness, weak musculature, long muzzle, absence of black mask to the areas around the eyes
Character Alert, good-natured to those it knows, suspicious of strangers, a fearsome dog in attack. Confident expression

Uses All the special duties of a guard- and general working-dog, including tracking
Future prospects The breed seems likely to increase its following in English-speaking countries; elsewhere it is in competition with the ever-popular Boxer
Similar breeds One of the most magnificent breeds of the Mastiff group is the Neapolitan Mastiff, which the author has helped rescue from obscurity

The Bullmastiff is a reasonably common breed in Britain and the United States but is not well represented in other countries. The illustration shows a typical British-bred specimen.

One of the most powerful of the European mastiff types is the Neapolitan Mastiff, an ancient breed but one that had nearly died out before World War II. Socrate di Ponzano (above) and the bitch Bice de Ponzano (right) are two fine specimens of the breed.

BULL TERRIER

First the English selected and bred the Bulldog, and various types of Terriers. Then they had the idea of creating the Bull Terrier, a 'gladiator' of a dog, which combined the qualities of the Bulldog and the talents of the Terriers. Fighting dogs were in the process of disappearing in the 1840s, as a result of laws banning their use. In 1860 a Birmingham breeder called James Hinks, who had a soft spot for 'pure white' coats, selected the specimens that were the first to be given the current name of Bull Terrier. At the end of the 19th century this breed had spread beyond the shores of Great Britain, where the Champion Como was ruling the roost. In Germany, in Braunschweig, one famous breeder was Dr A. Wolf. The English Club was founded in 1887.

Excessive stress on selecting white specimens brought about conditions of poor health, deafness and worse. As a result a better-pigmented type was sought, called the 'coloured' Bull Terrier. In the meantime, in Staffordshire a type of Bulldog from the days when dog-fighting was common was still in existence. This was a solid, nimble, pugnacious and fiery creature. It was not actually recognized until 1935, by the name of Staffordshire Bull Terrier. Since then its numbers have increased consistently, so much so that in the United States an American type has been selected and bred, which, it is rumoured, is still used for clandestine dog-fights.

TODAY'S BREED

Official classification KC (GB): Terrier Group; AKC: Terriers
Country of origin Great Britain
Weight 23-28 kg (51-62 lb)
Coat Hair short, compact, flat and shiny; colour: white all over (often with this colouring there is some pink round the nose and eyes); white with black markings or brindle on the head; fawn or brindle with or without white; tri-colour (black, fawn and white)

General appearance Compact, sturdy, with a quite distinctively shaped head – slightly egg-shaped
Head Long, strong and deep; tip of nose matching coat; lips tight and thin; pincer- or scissor-type bite
Ears Not docked, erect, set close together
Eyes Very small, triangular
Body Well rounded, fore-quarters quite broad, chest and ribs rounded, belly not tucked up
Legs Quite short, with strong bone structure, good straight stance; small, compact feet, with well arched toes
Tail Set low, short, carried horizontally
Gait Good at the trot and at the run

Qualities For its small size it must give the impression of the greatest possible strength
Defects Too light, legs too short, poor musculature
Character Reserved, sometimes rather severe, devoted to one master. Inscrutable expression

Uses Guard- and watch-dog
Future prospects Its particular shape attracts only a limited number of fanciers
Similar breeds Guard-dogs and companion dogs related to the Bull Terrier include the Miniature Bull Terrier, weighing about 9 kg (20 lb), the Staffordshire Bull Terrier and the American Staffordshire Terrier

Throughout the nineteenth century specimens of this breed, like many other breeds which were common in Great Britain, had their ears docked so that they stood up erect, as is evident from the print (above). After the ban on docking, British breeders selected specimens with naturally erect ears, as can be seen in the specimen in the photograph on the left.

CAIRN TERRIER

The French word 'terre', meaning land or earth, derives from the Latin 'terra', and the word 'terrier', means an underground burrow or lair with several openings leading into passages all of which in turn lead to a central chamber where various animals – foxes, badgers, rabbits and rats – take refuge with their young. Terrier is a term applied to a dog that hunts such wild animals. There are twenty-four officially recognized English breeds of terrier, many of which have short, straight legs.

The Cairn Terrier is possibly the oldest of them all. There is still some uncertainty about whether the first specimens came from the Highlands and Islands of Scotland or from the Isle of Skye. In its early days the Cairn was used for hunting foxes and badgers.

Its first appearance at an English dog-show was in 1909. After this it became popular, not least because of those first Scottish breeders who turned this small dog into one of the most sought-after breeds in English-speaking countries.

The Cairn is descended from at least four breeds of Terrier: Scottish, West Highland White, Skye and Kyle (the latter is now extinct). The Cairn Terrier was the favourite pet of the Duke of Windsor, later King Edward VIII of England.

In the early twentieth century specimens of the Cairns, such as that shown in the print above, were often kept in farm buildings as ratters.

TODAY'S BREED

Official classification KC (GB): Terrier Group; AKC: Terriers
Country of origin Great Britain
Weight Preferably 6.3 kg (14 lb)
Coat Hair distinctive, abundant, medium length, hard but not rough, with an undercoat that is dense, short and soft, fur-like, and water-resistant; colours: grey, black and white, almost black, sandy, red, with brighter colouring on the ears and muzzle

General appearance This is the smallest of the working Terriers, sturdy but not thickset, and nimble
Head This is shorter and broader than in any other type of Terrier, and is well covered with hair; the nose matches the colour of the coat; scissor- or pincher-type bite
Ears Not docked, small, pointed, erect, with no fringes
Eyes Rather sunken (with bushy eyebrows), chestnut, but the shade – light or dark – matches the coat colour
Body Rather oblong because of the short legs, back straight, belly not tucked up
Legs Short, with plenty of hair, absolutely straight; front feet slightly outward-turned and larger than the hind feet
Tail Docked if not short enough at birth, carried straight and high, but not over the back
Gait Distinctive, dainty and skipping, tireless

Qualities The hair and undercoat are characteristic and the actual hair quality is a sought-after feature
Defects Pale-coloured tip of nose, any resemblance to the Scottish Terrier, small feet
Character Active, full of initiative, good endurance, does not get in the way, enjoys hunting for vermin. Cheeky expression

Uses Underground hunter, good-natured and tough little companion-dog
Future prospects The large variety of short-legged Terriers means competition between them all, so this breed, like others, is becoming less widespread, except in Great Britain
Similar breeds The West Highland White Terrier (Great Britain) is close in general outline to the Cairn

CAVALIER KING CHARLES SPANIEL

The Cavalier is the descendant of the Toy Spaniels of the 16th, 17th and 18th centuries, and was seen in Italy, France and Holland during that time. They have been great favourites with Royalty and noble families of Europe for generations. King Charles II was especially fond of these little dogs, hence their name. Over the years the faces of these Spaniels grew shorter and shorter until they became more like those of dogs known today as the King Charles Spaniel. In 1926 an American, Rosewell Eldridge, was so disappointed in this new type that he offered a prize at Crufts of £25 for the best specimen exhibited in a class for Blenheim Spaniels of the old type. This prize was offered for five years and encouraged breeders to breed back the long noses. In 1928 the Cavalier King Charles Spaniel Club was formed and registration as a separate breed was accepted by the Kennel Club in 1945.

The standards for the King Charles Spaniel (known as the English Toy Spaniel in America), unlike those for the Cavalier King Charles, allow for four varieties according to colour: the King Charles proper is black and tan (considered a solid colour); the Ruby is a rich chestnut red; the Blenheim has red markings over a white ground; and the Prince Charles, a tri-coloured dog, has black and tan markings on a white ground.

Although the King Charles Spaniel was very fashionable earlier this century, more recently the numbers registered have declined. The Cavalier King Charles is a heavy dog among the Toys but it is now much more popular than the lighter King Charles Spaniel.

TODAY'S BREED

Official classification KC (GB): Toy Group; AKC: Miscellaneous Group
Country of origin Great Britain
Weight 5-8 kg (11-18 lb)
Coat Long, silky and free from curl. A slight wave is permissible. There should be plenty of feather. Colours: black and tan, ruby, red on a white ground, tricolour

General appearance An active, graceful and well balanced dog. Absolutely fearless and sporting in character and very gay and free in action
Head Head almost flat between the ears, without dome. Stop shallow. Face should be well filled out underneath the eyes
Ears Long and set high with plenty of feather
Eyes Large, dark and round but not prominent. The eyes should be spaced well apart
Body Short, coupled with plenty of spring of rib. Back level. Chest moderate leaving ample heart room
Legs Fore-legs moderate bone and straight. Hind legs with well turned stifle and no tendency to cow or sickle hocks
Tail The docking of the tail is optional. No more than one-third to be removed. Length of tail to be in balance with body
Gait Gay and free movement

Qualities Very amenable, charming dog with a sporting character
Defects Any tendency to appear snipey in muzzle is undesirable. Light eyes. Undershot or crooked mouth and pig jaws. White marks on whole-coloured specimens. Coarseness of type. Nervousness
Character Friendly and happy with no aggression

Uses Companion-dog
Future prospects Popularity likely to be maintained
Similar breeds The King Charles Spaniel is closest to the Cavalier King Charles but the family resemblance is strong in most of the Spaniels

The Cavalier King Charles (opposite) a large breed among the Toys, has overtaken the King Charles Spaniel (right) in popularity.

CHIHUAHUA

Chihuahua is a city in northern Mexico, after which the breed of dog is named. There are plenty of stories about the origins of this dog, which is the smallest currently in existence. Some say it was the favourite pet of Aztec noblewomen, although archaeologists and palaeontologists maintain that there were no dogs in Mexico before the invasion by the Spaniards.

It seems more possible that the origins of the modern Chihuahua are relatively recent, and that they lie in the Orient, where plants, fish and dogs have been reduced to dwarf-size – bonsai trees are an example. The Spanish Empire traded with China, and it is possible that the forbears of the Chihuahua came from there.

In about 1850 the peasant **indios** in northern Mexico started to sell these small dogs to tourists from the United States. The first specimens made their official appearance in 1895, and the first Chihuahua Club was founded in 1923. Today the breed is one of the twelve most popular in the United States. The British Chihuahua Club was established in 1949. In the 1960s the breed was frequently publicized on television in Europe by the singer Abbe Lane and the conductor Xavier Cugat, who included a Chihuahua in their shows.

TODAY'S BREED

Official classification KC (GB): Toy Group; AKC: Toys
Country of origin Mexico
Weight About 1.5 kg (3½ lb), with some specimens weighing as little as 900 g (2 lbs), and others as much as 3.5 kg (8 lb). As with all miniature or very small breeds, there is a preference for somewhat smaller males, and larger bitches
Coat Hair smooth and close-lying, although there is a variety with fairly long hair; colour: all types of colour, and every kind of mixture

General appearance A tiny dog, somewhat cheeky; typical lap-dog
Head Apple-dome shape, with a small pointed muzzle; tip of nose matches the coat colour; a pink nose is admissible; lips thin; teeth often incomplete, and sometimes prognathous; the teeth should not be visible when the mouth is closed
Ears Not docked, erect, at rest they fall at an angle of 45°
Eyes Full, large, bright, all colours permitted
Body Cylindrical, sometimes a little Greyhound-like
Legs Hocks set well apart, stance average, on account of dwarfishness; feet small
Tail Not docked, long and thin, carried curved over the back or to one side
Gait Skipping and dainty

Qualities Accentuated dwarfishness is required, but with no signs of degeneration. Loose, easy gait is sought after, as is good colouring in the visible mucous membranes
Defects Too delicate; signs of rickets, prolapse of the tongue
Character A typical toy-dog, which tends to amuse people by its cheekiness and arrogance; a keen watch-dog. Saucy expression

Uses Companion-dog
Future prospects Its leading position as a miniature dog guarantees it a safe future with dog-fanciers who have a soft spot for small lap-dogs

The Chihuahua, the smallest dog in the world, has gained a very strong following. The smooth-haired variety (left and opposite, top left) and the long-haired variety, different colourings of which are shown (opposite, right), have the same saucy expression.

CHINESE CRESTED DOG

This is one of several hairless breeds of rather perplexing origins found in various parts of the world. Lack of teeth, characteristic of many specimens, is sex-linked with hairlessness. In 1895 a breeder in Hamburg called Bungartz claimed that his specimens came from Central America and southern Africa. In 1936 the Belgian journal, *L'élevage* (Breeding), referred to a kennels breeding the Chinese Crested Dog near Brussels. In fact the dogs bred there were called Levrette d'Afganistan, and came from Kabul. Some claim that the breed hails from Mexico, and the cynologist F. Beltrán of Mexico backs this up as a thesis, maintaining that the breed reached America from China between 1580 and 1600. In French 18th-century prints it is known as the Chien Turc. Some zoologists have classified it as **Canis africanus**, in view of the fact that the various hairless mammals all come from Africa. The naturalist A. Brehm believes that it is possible to establish the Crested Dog's journey as follows: Africa, Guinea, China, Philippines, America. In spite of all this attention, the breed has always been a rare one, and is possibly of more interest to the teratologist (one who studies malformations in plants or animals) than to the cynologist.

TODAY'S BREED

Official classification KC (GB): Toy Group; AKC: not recognized
Country of origin Mexico, China (?)
Height and weight Approx. 35 cm (14 in). Weight: approx. 5 kg (11¼ lb)
Coat In the so-called Mexican (Hairless) variety there is a total absence of hair; in the so-called Chinese variety there is a topknot of rough hair on the head and often some downy hair beneath the tail as well; the skin is always smooth and soft, not wrinkled, and warm when touched; the colouring may come in a wide range, often grey or slate-coloured, with quite pinkish markings

General appearance A small, lively dog with the dimensions and general appearance of an Italian Greyhound. One distinctive feature is the nervous quivering of the muscles and tendons, as happens with some thoroughbred race-horses
Head Thin, with a long, pointed muzzle; tip of nose matches the colour of the coat; the premolars are often missing
Ears Not docked, large, sometimes rose-shaped, sometimes erect
Eyes Chestnut or yellow, with liver or pink eyelid rims
Body The Chinese variety is usually sturdier than the Mexican type
Legs Greyhound-like
Tail Greyhound-like
Gait Lively and graceful

Qualities A sturdy constitution, with good colouring
Defects Too delicate, signs of dwarfishness, hampered gait
Character Gentle, sensitive, affectionate, good lap-dog

Uses Companion-dog
Future prospects Although at one time this breed disappeared from the dog scene, it has recently achieved some popularity, and is increasingly seen at British shows
Similar Breeds Mexican Hairless, or Xoloitzcuintli, originally from Central and South America. Its flesh was highly regarded as food

The Chinese Crested Dog (left) and the Mexican Hairless Dog (above) have a certain following because of rather than in spite of their curiously nude appearance.

CHOW CHOW

For centuries the Chinese have regarded certain dogs as a source of food, and Chow Chow pups in particular as something of a delicacy. The breed has been selected and bred to have a blue tongue, purely for gastronomic reasons. Before ordering and tasting this choice dish, Chinese gourmets will invariably ask to see the tongue before it is cooked: if it is blue, it is Chow Chow. In northern China the Chow Chow's coat is used as a fur, and various parts of the dog are included in the Chinese pharmacopoeia as medicine (bones, bile and tongue).

In 1880, Queen Victoria's ambassador to Peking sent a pair of Chow Chows as a gift to the Prince of Wales (later to become King Edward VII). In 1894 the British Kennel Club officially recognized the breed and the standard. In those days the most important Chow Chow kennels were run by Lady Granville Gordon, owner of the famous Blue Blood and Peridot. She was also chairwoman of the Chow Chow Club, which had its headquarters in London. There were rival kennels run by J. McLaren Morrison, owner of Chinee, John Chinaman and Tu-Fu. Other famous dogs of the day were Miss E. Bagshow's Chow VII and Miss E. Casella's Bosco.

A Chow Chow is the leading character in Paul Achard's novel **Nous, les chiens**.

TODAY'S BREED

Official classification KC (GB): Utility Group; AKC: Non-Sporting Dogs
Country of origin China
Height and weight Not less than 46 cm (18½ in). Weight: approx. 20 kg (45 lb)
Coat Hair thick, straight, quite long, forming an abundant mane resembling that of a lion; single-coloured black, red, tan (tawny), blue, cream, white, silver-lilac. There is also a Short-haired variety

General appearance A typical, though large, member of the Spitz group, dignified, rather demure and reserved
Head Strong, with a broad, flat skull, muzzle quite short; tip of nose matches the colour of the coat; tongue violet; scissor-type bite
Ears Not docked, small, stiffly erect, mobile
Eyes Small, dark, almond-shaped (slanting)
Body Chest broad and deep, back short, belly not tucked up
Legs Very sturdy, quite short, with a good stance; feet cat-like
Tail Set high, curled over the back
Gait Distinctive, 'stilt'-like

Qualities Violet tongue, lion-like in appearance, almond-shaped eyes, tail plumed
Defects Thin hair, slender bone structure, pink marks on the tongue, patchy coat
Character Likened to a 'mandarin' because of its inscrutable nature; self-confident, disdainful towards strangers, extremely loyal to its owner, easy to train. Eastern expression

Uses Used as a guard-dog and hunting-dog in China. In Europe it is a companion-dog, and can be kept in city flats
Future prospects The breed has always been subject to the whims of fashion, and always will be, but it has a good and faithful following
Similar breeds Another edible dog is to be found in the Philippines. American cynologists call it the Philippine Islands Dog. For centuries the inhabitants of Luzon have regarded this dog's flesh as a delicacy when roasted with a stuffing of rice and herbs

The French champion Jong-Lhi du Sama Khada at the age of six years. The print shows a forebear of the breed, which was imported into Britain in 1896.

COCKER SPANIEL
American

In the United States the smaller Spaniels developed along different lines to the Cocker Spaniel as known in Britain. The breed known in the United States as the Cocker Spaniel is in other countries called the American Cocker Spaniel and the breed that is known in Britain as the Cocker Spaniel is called in the United States the English Cocker Spaniel. The American Kennel Club gave the breeds separate recognition in 1946 but it was not until the 1960s that the American Cocker Spaniel was shown in Britain. Since recognition in Britain, the breed's qualities, long recognized in the United States, have ensured its growing popularity.

For the heavier game that the English Cocker Spaniel is expected to carry the American variety is generally too light. In its home country, however, it is frequently used for retrieving small game such as quail. Its great popularity as a companion-dog owes much to its affectionate nature and the ease with which it can be trained.

The American Cocker Spaniel is a lighter breed than the English Cocker Spaniel and has a longer coat.

TODAY'S BREED

Official classification KC (GB): Gundog Group; AKC: Sporting Dogs
Country of origin United States of America
Height Male: 38 cm (12 in); female: 35 cm (14 in)
Coat Short and fine on the head, medium length on the body. The ears, chest, abdomen and legs are well feathered but not so as to affect performance as a sporting dog. The texture, an important feature, should be silky, flat or slightly wavy and of a kind that permits easy care. The acceptable colour range includes jet black, uniform shades of other solid colours, tan markings on black and parti-colours such as roan

General appearance An active serviceable-looking dog that is sturdy and elegant and shows a friendly nature
Head Neat and rounded with no tendency towards flatness, the muzzle broad and deep and the jaws square and even
Ears Not docked, lobular, of fine leather and well feathered
Eyes Round, full and looking directly forward
Body Short and compact, firmly knit together
Legs Strongly boned and muscular
Tail Docked, set on and carried on a line with the topline of the back or slightly higher
Gait Typical sporting-dog gait, driving with the strong powerful rear quarters

Qualities Alert and active
Defects Refinement at the expense of sturdiness, coat of a texture that is difficult to take care of
Character Affectionate, lively and willing

Uses In the field and as a companion-dog
Future prospects As a companion-dog its popularity is likely to increase
Similar breeds The English Cocker Spaniel

COCKER SPANIEL
English

The Cocker is the oldest member of the large family of British Spaniels. The name derives from the use to which this dog has always been put — the hunting of woodcock.

The history of the modern Cocker Spaniel began on 14 June 1879, with the birth in England of Obo, regarded as the official standard. Four years later, Cocker Spaniels started to make their appearance at dog-shows. In 1899 the first field trials were held. In 1895 the magazine **Chasse et pêche** (Hunting and Fishing) published a famous print of Champion Obo and Champion Miss Obo at work in dense undergrowth. These two dogs belonged to J.F. Farrow of Ipswich in Suffolk. Another champion of the day was Solus, belonging to J. Royle of Manchester. The most important British breeder of this dog in this century was H.S. Lloyd, who established the Ware kennels, which are now maintained by his family.

In the latter half of this century the Cocker Spaniel has earned immense popularity all over the world as a companion-dog. The first Cocker Spaniel Club dates back to 1902. Studies of the breed have been published in many languages.

The English Cocker Spaniel is very popular all over the world, especially as a companion-dog, and it retains a very strong following in Great Britain. It is one of the most effective of the smaller field dogs.

TODAY'S BREED

Official classification KC (GB): Gundog Group; AKC: Sporting Dogs
Country of origin Great Britain
Height and weight 38-41 cm (15-16½ in). Weight: 12.5-14.5 kg (28-32 lb)
Coat Hair is of medium length, with fringes on the ears, chest, abdomen and legs. Colours: liver, red, black, orange and lemon with white distributed all over the body, blue roan, black and tan; in single-coloured dogs white is only admissible on the chest

General appearance A small, good-natured dog, always on the move, combining energy with elegance, and vivacity with agility
Head Conspicuous, muzzle square; tip of nose matches the colour of the coat; scissor-type bite
Ears Not docked, very large, set low on the head, covered with long hair
Eyes Large, not prominent, dark brown
Body Compact, chest deep and well sprung, belly not tucked up
Legs Good stance, with solid bone structure, quite short; cat-like feet
Tail Docked, carried in line with the back and never cocked up
Gait Lively, goodish stride, swift at the gallop

Qualities Must show itself to be a keen working-dog, active, energetic, always on the alert
Defects Muzzle short or pointed, hair short or woolly, eyes prominent
Character Constantly on the lookout and alert, cheerful, keen to be useful whether on the hunt or in the home

Uses As a tracker, and as a companion-dog
Future prospects Its impressive spread all over the world has been somewhat to the detriment of its character in terms of selection, but nonetheless its future seems assured
Similar breeds The Spaniel group is a large one, and includes the Clumber Spaniel, which is the largest, with a long, low body; the Field Spaniel, which is more like the Cocker; and the Sussex Spaniel (selected by the breeder Fuller of Rosehill Park, near Hastings, who died in 1847), which has the distinctive feature of barking while tracking.

The American Cocker Spaniel is smaller than the British variety and quite different in many respects

COLLIE

The Collie was a rather coarse dog living in a state of neglect in the grasslands of Scotland until, one day in 1860, Queen Victoria happened to see one on a journey. She showed a great deal of interest in it, and sang its praises so loudly that it became a dog with a reputation. In those days it was called the Scots Colley Dog, Colley being a breed of black sheep.

The first show was held in Birmingham in 1880. Manchester later became an important centre for dog-fanciers, including A.H. Megson, owner of the Champion Southport Perfection, which was regarded as without rival. Dr George McGill, who was chairman of the Northern and Midland Sheep Dog Club in Manchester in 1895, supervised the selection of a natural Short-tailed Collie, while the Smooth Collie Club, also based in Manchester, was concerned with the smooth-haired variety, with Champion Pickmere as the specimen serving as model.

In the 1930s the breed fell on bad times, and was reduced to show-dogs, which is often the case in Great Britain. It was possibly crossed with the Borzoi, which gave it a certain nobility but also made it somewhat melancholy. Its real revival was due to the highly successful film **Lassie**, in which the female Collie in the story was, in fact, played by a male.

TODAY'S BREED

Official classification KC (GB): Working Group; AKC: Herding Dogs
Country of origin Great Britain
Height and weight Males: 56-61 cm (22½-24½ in); females: 51-56 cm (20½-22½ in). Weight: 18-29 kg (40-65 lb)
Coat Hair long, thick, with a mane; plentiful at neck, tail and on legs; undercoat; colours: fawn, tri-coloured (white, black and fawn), blue merle (blue-grey, splashed and marbled with black); the collar must always be white. The Smooth Collie is short-haired with no undercoat

General appearance A typical wolf-like breed with a fine coat that makes it look heavier than it actually is
Head Wedge-shaped, muzzle not pointed; tip of nose always black; scissor-type bite
Ears Not docked, small, sometimes falling forward; two-thirds erect, with the topmost third tipping forward naturally
Eyes Quite small and almond-shaped; dark chestnut brown (often blue or blue-flecked in blue merle varieties)
Body Ribs deep, back firm with a slight rise over the loins, hind-quarters not very angled, belly not very tucked up
Legs Straight, with oval-shaped feet
Tail Long, hanging, slightly curved when at rest, lively when moving, never straight, over the back
Gait Elegant, slightly skipping, good long stride at the run

Qualities The coat is an extremely important feature of the breed
Defects Poor coat, lack of distinction, ears totally erect, shyness
Character This breed has been called 'the dog with the intelligence of a man and the charm of a woman'; easily trained; avoid shy and nervous specimens

Uses Pet dog, show-dog, trials, guard-dog
Future prospects Too aristocratic to become popular, not least because of the attention required by the coat, but still increasing in numbers
Similar breeds Bearded Collie (guard-dog and general working dog), Great Britain: more like the English Sheep Dog than the Collie, this breed is almost exclusive to Great Britain where, in 1978, there were a number of recognized kennels dedicated to selection procedures. Shetland Sheepdog (pet dog), Great Britain: this is a Toy version of the Collie, but it has different origins

The Collie has remained virtually unchanged in the last century as can be seen by comparing the photograph (above), of two Italian-born champions (left and right) with the print (opposite, top) dating from 1896. The Shetland Sheepdogs (opposite, bottom) resemble toy Collies.

DACHSHUND

References to Dachshund-like forms of dog can be found in ancient Assyrian and Egyptian monuments. Xenophon (430-354 BC) refers to the Agasso, and his description of it certainly brings to mind a Dachshund-like dog. Arrian of Bithynia (AD 95-180) mentions the **Canis castorius**. (Arrian was a cynologist as well as being a disciple of Epictetus and the biographer of Alexander). In German cynological circles the Dachshund is dealt with by, among others, Hohlberg (1701), Döbel (1746) and Reichenbach (1836). It was called the Dachshund because of its skills as a hunter ('Dachs' in German means badger). Its other German name – Teckel – derives from the abbreviation for 'Teckelbeine' or 'short leg' ('teckel' meaning short). The first Dachshund Club was founded in Germany in 1840; an official standard was drawn up in 1879, and the Long-haired variety was officially recognized in 1886. Recognition came to the Wire-haired variety in 1898, and the Deutscher Teckel Club was founded in 1888.

The Dachshund was imported into England in 1850, and it subsequently became the favourite pet of Queen Alexandra. Thereafter German breeders of the Dachshund started to select the breed quite separately.

About 1914 the English successfully turned their attention to the Miniature Dachshund, a Toy variety, whose interests were subsequently championed by the Miniature Dachshund Club, founded in 1935.

TODAY'S BREED

Official classification KC (GB): Hound Group; AKC: Hounds
Country of origin Germany
Weight Standard Dachshunds in UK should not exceed 11 kg (25 lb); Miniature Dachshunds in the UK should not exceed 5 kg (11 lb); Miniature Dachshunds in the USA should not exceed 4.5 kg (10 lb). The Kaninchen (rabbit) variety must not weigh more than 3.5 kg (8 lb) at eighteen months, with the circumference of the ribcage not exceeding 30 cm (12 in)
Coat In the Short-haired variety, the coat is smooth, close-lying, dense, and single-coloured: tan (tawny), yellow with or without black stripes; two-coloured: black, chestnut, grey or white, with rust-coloured or yellow markings; speckled, dappled, striped: a pale brown or grey-to-white ground, with irregular darker coloured markings – brown, tan, yellow and black; there are also other colours. In the Long-haired variety the coat is silky, smooth, flat, slightly wavy, longer beneath the neck, on the ears and on the lower part of the body, with fringes on the lower part of the tail as well. In the Wire-haired variety the coat is rough, dense, close-lying, with a beard, moustache and bushy eyebrows. In both the Long- and Wire-haired varieties the same colours are permitted as for the Short- or Smooth-haired variety.

General appearance A short-legged dog, with an elongated body and plenty of energy; well muscled
Head Elongated, tapering towards the tip of the nose, lean; the colour of the nose matches the coat; lips tight; pincer- or scissor-type bite
Ears Not docked, large, but not too long or curled over, mobile
Eyes Oval and brown. In grey and dappled varieties bluish or pearly eyes permitted
Body The end of the sternum is prominent; back straight; belly slightly tucked up
Legs Seen sideways, the front legs reach the lowest point of the line of the chest; the front lower leg is short, and arched slightly inwards; the feet are closed, and the toes arched
Tail Not docked, carried in line with the dorsal line, with no evident curve
Gait Must not look clumsy, heavy, or hampered in its movements, and, even more important, must avoid looking weak

Qualities The dachshund must have all the qualities required of an underground (burrowing) hunting-dog

Defects Short-chested, very loose
shoulders, metacarpal bones turned
completley outwards, improper shape to
the tail
Character Proud, expressive, keen,
energetic, devoted and loyal. Friendly
expression

Uses Hunting, Companion-dog
Future prospects It is becoming more and
more popular both as a hunting-dog and
as a companion-dog for the whole family

The Short-Haired (opposite) and Long-
Haired (above) varieties of Dachshund are
among the most popular of the
companion breeds. In Britain miniature
varieties – long-haired, short-haired and
wire-haired – are also popular.

DALMATIAN

This breed was once used for hunting. In his **Histoire naturelle** (1749), Buffon calls it the Braque du Bengale (or Bengal Pointer). It subsequently became quite common in Great Britain and throughout the Commonwealth.

In the days of the great Italian naturalist Ulisse Aldrovandi (1522-1605), its existence in Italy was already documented. Linnaeus called it **Canis variegatus** in 1758. Later on in France it was called the Petit Danois (Small – as opposed to Great – Dane), and an Italian cynologist by the name of Faelli saw in the Dalmatian an ancestor of the Harlequin Great Dane.

In the 19th century it spread in England, and tended to lose its hunting skills to become a companion-dog, and was often used as an elegant 'coach-dog', to suit the fashion of the day.

After the Second World War, because of its distinctive coat, it became more and more popular in other European countries and in the United States as a guard-dog and companion-dog.

Cynological circles in Yugoslavia have recently claimed their country to be this breed's birthplace, and the Fédération Cynologique Internationale has backed their claim.

TODAY'S BREED

Official classification KC (GB): Utility Group; AKC: Non-Sporting Dogs
Country of origin Yugoslavia
Height and weight 50-60 cm (20-24 in). Weight: 22.5-25 kg (51-56 lb)
Coat Hair short, hard, dense, fine, smooth and with a sheen; colour: the ground is pure white, with markings which can be liver or black; the markings must be clearly defined, and as round as possible, ranging in size from a one-pence piece to a ten-pence piece; the more markings the better; the markings on the head, muzzle, ears, legs, tail and extremities must be smaller than those on the rest of the body

General appearance A well-balanced member of the Pointer family, with a distinctive and unmistakeable coat
Head A good length, with a flat skull; muzzle long and vigorous; tip of nose black with black markings and chestnut-coloured with liver-coloured spots; lips thin; scissor-type bite
Ears Not docked, set high on the head, long, with rounded tips, and plenty of markings on them
Eyes Round, bright, dark in colour, but matching the markings on coat, as should the rim of the eyelids
Body Ribs deep and well sprung, belly not tucked up
Legs Sturdy, good stance; cat-like feet
Tail Not docked, tapering towards the tip, never ring-like, with a slight curve, preferably with plenty of markings
Gait Free, easy, long stride at the trot, tends of dash into the gallop very fast

Qualities All the features to do with the coat and the markings, as well as their shape and distribution
Defects Hair woolly or silky, off-white, markings that are not round, and set too close together forming splashes
Character Lively, good-natured, very attached to its master, docile. Keen expression

Uses Companion-dog, guard-dog
Future prospects On the increase all over the world, to such an extent that it has become the mascot of firemen in the United States

The pups of the Dalmatian are born white but soon develop the clearly defined black, blue or liver spots of the adult. Vistalba Aumura of Leopoldo (opposite, bottom), champion of Argentina, and the illustration above show the dignity and grace of this attractive hound. The print (opposite, top) dates from 1895.

DANDIE DINMONT TERRIER

The Dandie Dinmont Terrier is a very old Border breed and became known in England through the romance **Guy Mannering** by Sir Walter Scott (1771-1832). In this work the author tells the story of the sporting farmer Dandie Dinmont and his game little Terriers. They are different from most other Terriers as they have no straight lines in their make-up. The first Dandie Club was formed in 1876. It is believed that the Dandie Dinmont was taken to Germany in the last part of the 19th century to be crossed with the Smooth-haired Dachshund to produce the Wire-haired Dachshund

The Dandie Dinmont Terrier, named after a character in a novel by Sir Walter Scott, is an amusing little breed of astonishing energy and endurance.

TODAY'S BREED

Official classification KC (GB): Terrier Group; AKC: Terriers
Country of origin Great Britain
Height and weight 20-28 cm (8-11 in). Weight: 8-11 kg (18-24 lb)
Coat Hair should be about two inches long and from the skull to root of tail a mixture of hardish and soft hair. Hair on the under part of the body is lighter in colour and softer than that on the top. Colour: pepper or mustard. Pepper ranges from a dark bluish-black to a light silvery-grey, the mustards from a reddish-brown to a pale fawn

General appearance A long-bodied, short-legged Terrier with pendulous ears and long curved tail. Differs from most Terriers in having gently flowing rather than straight lines
Head Strongly made and large but not out of proportion to dog's size. Skull broad between ears getting gradually less towards the eye. Forehead well domed. Top of muzzle is generally bare for about one inch from back part of nose. Nose black
Ears Pendulous, set well back wide apart and low on the skull, hanging close
Eyes Set wide apart, large, full, round but not protruding, bright, expressive of great determination, intelligence and dignity
Body Long, strong and flexible, ribs well sprung and round, chest well developed and let well down between the fore-legs. Back rather low at the shoulders having a slight downward curve and an arch over the loins
Legs Fore-legs short, with immense muscular development and bone, set wide apart and chest coming well down between them. Hind legs are a little longer than the front ones and set wide apart
Tail Rather short, 20-25 cm (8-10 in), covered on the upper side with wiry hair of a darker colour than that of the body and on the underside with hair of a lighter colour and not so wiry. Tail should not be twisted or curled in any way but should come up with a curve like a scimitar
Gait Quaint but tireless

Qualities Very amenable, loves human companionship
Defects Any exaggerations in the conformation
Character Likes to hunt. Makes a very attractive family companion

Uses Companion- and guard-dog
Future prospects Steady following

DEERHOUND
Scottish Deerhound

Fallow deer were common in Scotland in the 17th and 18th centuries, but became rare in the 19th century, and more or less died out. As a result this breed of Hound fell on hard times, even though it was the favourite of the writer Sir Walter Scott. In 1820 or thereabouts he owned a handsome deerhound by the name of Maida. He was devoted to the dog, and had it buried in his home at Abbotsford, where the tomb can still be seen.

In 1860 an Englishman, Colonel Inge, took the breed in hand, and entered a pair called Valient and Brimstone at various dog-shows. Sir Edward Landseer painted the deerhound at the suggestion of Queen Victoria. Another English painter, J. Charlton, painted the pair owned by Sir Humphrey Trafford – Lord Randolph and Sheila – in 1890. (Trafford was one of the first people to champion Greyhound racing in Manchester.) In 1897 various shows were dominated by J. Maxwell's Champion Robin Gray and W.H. Singer's Champion Athole. Singer was chairman of the Deerhound Club of Birmingham.

In this century the breed has become rare, although the 1960s saw the emergence of various small groups of Deerhound fanciers in the United States, Canada and Australia.

TODAY'S BREED

Official classification KC (GB): Hound Group; AKC: Hounds
Country of origin Great Britain
Height and weight Males: 76 cm (30½ in) upwards, females: 71 cm (28½ in) upwards. Weight: 30-48 kg (66-106 lb)
Coat Hair long, measuring 8-10 cm (3-4 in) on the neck and legs, where it is harsh and wiry and longer on the other parts of the body; colour: usually grey-blue, sometimes pale grey, brindle, tan or fawn

General appearance A fairly tall Greyhound type, powerful and hairy
Head Long, quite broad between the ears, with plentiful beard and moustache; tip of nose black or blue; lips thin and tight, scissor-type bite
Ears Set high on the head, raised above the head in excitement
Eyes Average size, dark
Body Chest deep, back slightly arched, belly very tucked up
Legs Front legs have a good stance, hind legs are muscular and angled; feet closed and compact
Tail Not docked, long, tapering to tip, slightly curved at extremity
Gait Easy, swift or brisk, very fast at the gallop

Qualities A combination of elegance and sturdiness, hardy, wiry coat, long, so-called 'swan' neck, mane
Defects Ears erect or flat, hair woolly, dewlaps, eyes pale in colour, back straight, tail ending in a ring
Character Affectionate, slightly shy, calm, faithful to owner, not aggressive. Expression usually gentle, piercing when excited

Uses Hunting-, sporting-, companion-dog
Future prospects Gradually on the increase as a sporting-dog (for example, it is used for hunting coyote in the United States) in English-speaking countries

The Scottish Deerhound is not a numerous breed; it requires too much space for exercise to be easily accommodated in a city. However, it is a dog of attractive temperament that is extremely faithful.

DOBERMANN
Doberman Pinscher

From 1863 onwards the Verein zur Veredlung von Hunderassen für Thüringen staged a dog market in the town of Apolda, then a township with a population of 20,000, mainly textile and foundry workers. Among the inhabitants was a certain F.L. Dobermann, born in 1834, something of a jack-of-all-trades, a town-bailiff and tax collector, and possibly the local dog-catcher too. Between 1870 and 1880 Dobermann owned a black bitch with fawn markings called Bisart, who produced another bitch by the name of Pinko, with a natural short tail; Pinko, in turn, bore grey-blue pups. At the same time as this, a certain Dietsch, who owned a sand quarry at Apolda, mated his grey-blue bitch with a black dog with fawn or tawny markings. 'Dobermann took the offspring of this couple and crossbred them with Pinschers', wrote the magazine **Unsere Hunde** in 1898.

Dobermann died in 1894, taking with him the secret of many of his crossbreeding experiments. His work was carried on by Otto Göller who, in 1899, founded the first Dobermann-Pinscher Club. In about 1900 there were a dozen or so clubs in Germany: the breed spread to Switzerland, Holland, Austria and then to France, Poland, Russia, Scandinavia, before finding its way across to the Americas. The French Dobermann Club was established in 1920. The year 1956 saw the founding of the International Dobermann Club, which now has represented in many countries.

TODAY'S BREED

Official classification KC (GB): Working Group; AKC: Working Dogs
Country of origin Germany
Height Males: 67 cm (27 in) (maximum 70 cm [28 in]); females: 63-66 cm (25-26½ in) (maximum 67 cm [27 in])
Coat Hair short, thick, hard, close-lying, and shiny; colour: black with fawn or rust-red markings, brown and tan, blue with rust-red markings

General appearance Powerful, proud carriage, elegant, attractive type of guard-dog
Head From the side resembles a blunt wedge; not heavy; tip of nose black for black-haired varieties, paler in dogs of other colours; lips thin; scissor-type bite
Ears Docked to a specific shape, set high on the head, erect or drooping (preferably erect), alert
Eyes Not large, oval, dark in colour
Body Athletic, ribs deep and well sprung, back short, belly tucked up
Legs Quite long and powerful; feet small and cat-like
Tail Docked at first or second joint
Gait Very free, elegant, an excellent runner

Qualities Good balance between strength and elegance, neither being predominant
Defects Too large, or Greyhound-like
Character Energetic, slight tendency to bite or be vicious; if well trained will prove to be a fine guard-dog. Resolute, striking expression

Uses Personal protection, police and military duties, sporting competitions, anti-crime duties, tracking
Future prospects Very well supported by the various Dobermann Clubs around the world, the breed is constantly on the increase
Similar breeds Kelpie (herding-dog), Australia: smaller than the Dobermann, but no less energetic, and very important in the sheep-farming area of Australia where the so-called Australian Cattle Dog is bred for herding livestock

The Dobermann has acquired a formidable reputation as a guard-dog that is affectionate and loyal to those he knows. Jack vom Dammberg (opposite), the Austrian champion, shown at the age of five, is a fine example of this powerful breed. The print (above) places the Dobermann next to the smaller German Pinscher.

ELKHOUND
Norwegian Elkhound

In the first half of this century fossil remains of dogs from the Stone Age were unearthed in Norway, skeletons almost identical to that of the modern Elkhound. The Norsk Elghund, to give it its Norwegian name, has been an inhabitant of the Scandinavian area for centuries, the companion of the Vikings on their hunting parties and expeditions to foreign parts. The fact that the breed has remained unchanged for so long indicates that it has carried out to perfection the specific tasks for which it was bred: elk- and even bear-hunting. In this century it is used to great effect as a retriever of wild game birds.

It is closely related to the larger Swedish Jämthund. Both dogs share a feature common to several Nordic breeds, in that they do not have a typical dog smell about them; this has to do with their particular sebaceous glands.

In the latter part of the 19th century this breed was already starting to become known in Great Britain where it was called the Scandinavian Elkhound (Skandinavisk Elghund), and in 1895 it even found its way into the royal household. At a much later date President Eisenhower had an Elkhound as a pet.

The first English Club was founded in 1923, and the official standard was drawn up in 1927.

TODAY'S BREED

Official classification KC (GB): Hound Group; AKC: Hounds
Country of origin Norway
Height and weight Height approx. 50 cm (20 in). Weight approx. 23 kg (52 lb)
Coat Coat dense, abundant, rough, water-resistant, forming a collar, longer on the chest, rump and tail; undercoat soft and woolly; colours: all shades of grey, with black-tipped long outermost hair

General appearance A typical larger member of the Spitz group, with a compact body and attractive coat
Head Lean and well defined, broad between the ears, muzzle pointed; tip of nose black; scissor-type bite
Ears Not docked, erect and pointed
Eyes Not prominent, very dark, bright and alert
Body Ribcage deep and well sprung, trunk short and muscular, belly very slightly tucked up
Legs Good stance, sturdy, lean; feet small
Tail Not docked, strong, carried over the back
Gait Quick, easy, very good at the gallop

Qualities The coat is very important, and typical of a dog suited to northern climates; another important feature is the absence of any 'doggy' smell; it is preferable if the muzzle, ears and saddle of the back are darker in colour than the rest of the body
Defects Thin hair and coat; poor undercoat; belly too tucked up
Character Energetic, good endurance, not highly strung, sometimes shows an independent streak; easy to train. Intrepid expression

Uses Elk-hunting, also used for hauling, and as a companion-dog
Future prospects On the increase, especially in English-speaking countries
Similar breeds The Norwegian Buhund and the Finnish Spitz are two 'polar' members of the Spitz group. Another Norwegian breed called the Lundehund. It is used for hunting on islands in the north of Norway: it would appear to have an excess number of toes on its feet, and to be able to close off its ears to prevent water entering

The Norwegian Elkhound, a large member of the Spitz group, has remained little changed over hundreds of years. Outside of Scandinavia it is still not so common, although it has been known in Britain, for instance, since the second part of the last century.

ENGLISH SETTER

The French use the term 'épagneuls' for dogs that are possibly of Spanish origin (often hunting- or gun-dogs), with falling ears (in the words of Larousse, 'with long, silky hair, often curly, but not growing as eyebrows or whiskers'). The word 'épagneul' became 'spaniel' north of the English Channel, and applies to many British breeds. The Setters are related to the Spaniels and the Epagneuls to the extent that they are all used for hunting, have long ears and a similar coat.

The English Setter came into being thanks to Sir Edward Laverack (1798-1877), whose good work was carried on by his successor, Richard Purcell Llewellin (who died in 1925); the kennels were taken over by Sir William Humphrey (1883-1963). Selection has been going on uninterruptedly since 1810.

The Llewellin strain was still highly sought after in the 1970s; it has produced the so-called blue belton coat.

TODAY'S BREED

Official classification KC (GB): Gundog Group; AKC: Sporting Dogs
Country of origin Great Britain
Height and weight 61-70 cm (24½-28 in). Weight: 25-30 kg (56-68 lb)
Coat Hair fine, 5-6 cm (2-2½ in) long, silky, with fringes, undercoat abundant in winter; colours: blue belton (white with black tending to blue); lemon belton (orange and white); liver belton (white and chestnut); tri-coloured (white with black-and-tan markings). There are also single colours including white, liver, orange, black and tan, but these are not greatly sought after; the favourite colour is with a white ground

General appearance An average-sized member of the Pointer family, with elegant lines and brisk, alert movements
Head Long, lean, muzzle quite square; tip of nose black or liver; lips not too large; scissor- or pincer-type bite
Ears Not docked, set low, falling against the cheeks, with fringes
Eyes Dark hazel
Body Ribs deep, back short, belly slightly tucked up
Legs Large, muscular, good stance, thighs long; feet compact with hair between the toes
Tail Not docked, set on the dorsal line, with fringes, never held over the back
Gait Better at the gallop than the trot

Qualities Must combine strength with elegance, with easy flowing movements; hair silky and flat
Defects Too large (taller than 64 cm [25½ in]), hair abundant, head large; lymphatism; lacking freedom of movement (slow), poor endurance
Character Extremely friendly and good-natured. Lively expression, bright and gentle

Uses Good hunter with speed as principal quality backed up by keen scent
Future prospects
One of the most widespread breeds in the world, not least because of its character and its handsome appearance. Future in no danger

The working English Setter (above) and that depicted in the print opposite show the characteristic posture of the breed. It is a popular dog as much for its handsome appearance and good nature as for its reliability in the field.

ENGLISH SPRINGER SPANIEL

The English Springer Spaniel, although not recognized in Britain as a separate breed until 1902, is one of the oldest sporting dogs and has played an important role in the development of all Land Spaniels except for the Clumber. The breed, formerly known as the Norfolk Spaniel, is now used to flush and retrieve game for the gun, as well as making a handsome show dog. The ancestors of the present breed were used to spring game for the net or for falcons or greyhounds to pursue. He is the highest on the leg of the land spaniels and a racy breed that is a fast and wide-ranging hunter that will work tirelessly in the field. When moving slowly he shows a characteristically ambling gait.

There has been a tendency for the show type to be larger that the stocky type favoured for field work. However, efforts have been made to achieve greater uniformity in the breed.

His qualities of temperament, endurance and usefulness in the field make him suitable for the sportsman who can only keep one dog.

The English Springer Spaniel (below) and the Welsh Springer Spaniel (left) are quite distinct breeds but have a common ancestry.

TODAY'S BREED

Official classification KC (GB): Gundog Group; AKC: Sporting Dogs
Country of origin Great Britain
Height and weight About 51 cm (20 in); about 22.7 kg (50 lbs)
Coat The coat should be close, straight and weather proof with a fringe of moderate feathering on ears, chest, legs and belly. Liver and white, black and white or either of these colours with tan markings preferred but any recognized Land Spaniel colour is acceptable

General appearance A symmetrical, compact and strong spaniel built for endurance and activity
Head The handsome head, combining strength and refinement, should be of medium length, fairly broad and slightly rounded. The nostrils are well developed
Ears The ears should be of good length and width without being exaggerated, set close to the head in line with the eye
Eyes Alert, of medium size and well set in
Body Strong and of proportionate length, the chest deep and well developed. The ribs should be well sprung and the thighs well developed
Legs The forelegs straight and nicely feathered, the hindlegs well let down from hip to hocks and the feet well rounded with strong full pads
Tail Set low, following the natural line of the croup, well feathered with a lively action
Gait The forelegs should swing straight forward from the shoulder, the feet being thrown forward in an easy and free manner. The hocks should drive well under the body

Qualities Sturdiness and soundness in motion
Defects Any fault that detracts from the all-round conformation and soundness of an upstanding spaniel that is first and foremost a sporting dog
Character Friendly, eager to please and tireless in the field

Uses Excellent general-purpose field dog, companion-dog and guard-dog
Future prospects Its merits as a gundog are always likely to be appreciated, as are its qualities in the ring
Similar breeds The Welsh Springer Spaniel, which probably has the same origins, is a smaller dog and the coat colour is always dark rich red and white

FIELD SPANIEL

This breed was developed in Britain for sportsmen who wanted a heavier animal than the Cocker Spaniel. This was nearly a calamity for the breed as breeders got the dog so low to the ground and of such a great length that it became unable to hunt. The Field also became very sluggish in his nature. Fortunately this breeding programme was abandoned. In the last fifty years a very much more workmanlike Field has been produced and the breed has become more popular.

In the early part of this century the Field Spaniel was so exaggeratedly long and short in the leg as to be useless in the field. The breed has been rescued from extinction by enthusiasts who have got back to a dog that is longer in the leg than the Cocker.

TODAY'S BREED

Official classification KC (GB): Gundog Group; AKC: Sporting Dogs
Country of origin Great Britain
Height and weight 46 cm (18 in). Weight: 16-23 kg (35-50 lb)
Coat Flat or slightly waved and never curled. Sufficiently dense to resist the weather and not too short. Silky in texture, glossy and refined without curliness or wiriness. On chest, under belly and behind legs there should be abundant feather. Colour should be self-coloured, i.e. black, liver, golden liver, mahogany red, roan or any of these colours with tan over the eyes, on cheeks, feet and pasterns

General appearance A well balanced, noble, upstanding sporting dog, built for activity and endurance, a combination of beauty and utility, of unusual docility
Head Distinctive, giving the impression of high breeding, character and nobility. Skull well developed with a distinct occipital protuberance. Not too wide across the muzzle. Nose well developed with good open nostrils
Ears Moderately long and wide and set low and sufficiently clad with nice Setter-like feather
Eyes Not too full but not small, receding or overhung. Colour to match the coat and markings, except in livers, when eyes may be a light hazel
Body Moderate length, well ribbed up to a good strong loin. Chest deep and well developed
Legs Fore-leg of fairly good length with straight, clean, flat bone. Immense bone is not desirable. Quarters strong and muscular
Tail Well set on and carried low if possible below the level of the back. Nicely fringed with wavy feather of silky texture
Gait Powerful and tireless

Qualities Very steady temperament and makes an excellent companion
Defects Too low to ground or too heavy in head
Character Slow maturing dog, courageous in the field and docile in the home. Needs careful handling as it is maturing

Uses Gundog and companion-dog
Future prospects Will retain its popularity with a limited following

FOXHOUND

Fox-hunting started to become very fashionable in England in the 18th century, when deer-hunting was losing its popularity. The pursuit of the fox required special packs of dogs, which could run with horses. As a result of this, work started on selecting and breeding a dog which would show a combination of endurance and swiftness of foot. In fact, the Foxhound reached the point where it could trot along happily for 20 km (12 miles) or so from its kennels to the meet, and then gallop non-stop for five hours or more, at roughly the same speed as a Greyhound; it would then trot back to its kennels when the hunt was over, and was capable of hunting twice a week virtually all year round.

The first Pedigree records for the breed were established in Great Britain in 1880, and today it is still kept by those with a taste for fox-hunting.

As the English hunting method has gradually spread (hunting on horseback, or 'riding to hounds') with all its traditional rules and regulations, the breed has also found its way to many other parts of the world.

Figures worked out by the Italian cynologist F. Fiorone put the number of officially recognized packs of Foxhounds at 369, in 1975. Of these 212 were in Great Britain, 113 in the United States and Canada, and the rest in Europe.

TODAY'S BREED

Official classification KC (GB): Hound Group; AKC: Hounds
Country of origin Great Britain
Height and weight 58-64 cm (23-25½ in). Weight: approx. 30 kg (66 lb)
Coat Hair smooth, short, hard, with a sheen; tri-coloured (black, white and tan) or any combination of these three colours

General appearance Noble appearance: endurance and courage are expressed in every line of the physical structure of this king of Hounds
Head Well proportioned to the body, skull quite flat, muzzle strong; tip of nose black; scissor-type bite
Ears Not docked, large, lying close to the head
Eyes Round, large and dark coloured
Body Ribs deep and well-sprung, back strong, belly not tucked up
Legs Strong, straight, with an excellent stance, solid and muscular; feet cat-like
Tail Not docked, set high, carried gaily with a slight upward curve
Gait Very good at the trot, and excellent at the gallop

Qualities A fine blend of hunting ability and good aesthetic balance, making it (in the view of the British cynologist, Stonehenge) of one of the most handsome animals in existence
Defects Poor or soft coat, fore-quarters with weak knees, shoulders excessively fleshy, poor musculature, and lack of strength when on the move
Character Well balanced, serious, enjoys kennel-life, very energetic. Keen expression

Uses Fox-hunting; in France it is also used for hunting wild boar, and is regarded as a fair hound for hunting roe-deer
Future prospects Its continued existence will be bound up with the spread of fox-hunting in the English style
Similar breeds Harrier (Hound), Great Britain: the Harrier is a smaller version of the Foxhound. There is also a variety known as the American Foxhound, selected and bred in the United States. In Sweden the most popular Hound is the Hamilton Stovare

The Foxhound is still essentially a pack animal (the coats are sometimes marked in case packs get mixed up) and used for foxhunting.

FOX TERRIER

For more than a century this has been one of the most popular of all dogs all over the world. It is regarded as the monarch among Terriers, all of which are selected in Great Britain, even though the word 'terrier' is a French one meaning lair, hole in the ground, burrow, den, etc. The Terriers are all good 'ferreters', hence the name.

The Fox Terrier made its appearance in about 1830, when fox-hunting was a popular sport. It would often happen that large Foxhounds would force the fox to take refuge in its lair, and the hunt would end there, much to everyone's disappointment. Huntsmen then started to introduce the smaller Fox Terrier into the lair to pursue the fox underground and flush it out.

Fox Terriers first appeared at shows in 1859, and the first Club was established in 1876. The breed soon became so popular that it was chosen to be the emblem for His Master's Voice gramophones.

In Italy it is commonly known by the word **raff**, when it is of the 'Wire' variety, a corruption of the English 'rough'.

TODAY'S BREED

Official classification KC (GB): Terrier Group; AKC: Terriers
Country of origin Great Britain
Height and weight Approx. 40 cm (16 in); approx. 8.5 kg (19 lb)
Coat Hair smooth, thick, and plentiful in the Smooth variety; in the Wire Fox Terrier it is longer, dense, wiry (with a coconut-matting-like texture), with a tendency to become twisted. The 'preparation' involves stripping and trimming. Colour: predominantly white with black and tan markings

General appearance A small dog with a very long head and a very short body
Head Very long; the skull is flat, the muzzle powerful, the cheeks narrow; tip of nose black; scissor-type bite
Ears Not docked, small, set high up on head, V-shaped; with the base semi-erect, and the points drooping towards the eyes; when alert they are turned forward
Eyes Small, not prominent and even sunken, dark in colour
Body Chest (brisket) deep but not broad, back very short, loins short and powerful, belly slightly tucked up
Legs Strong bone structure, hind legs muscular; feet small, round, compact, toes moderately arched, narrow
Tail A three-quarter dock is about right; set high, sturdy, straight, carried gaily but not curled
Gait Distinctive, relatively short but decisive pace, very good runner

Qualities Maximum compactness for its small size, sturdiness, suppleness; contrast between long head and short body is very conspicuous
Defects Absence of 1:1 ratio between skull and muzzle; pasterns not perpendicular; the coat must not be silky, woolly, wavy, or curly
Character Always alert, combative, will chase anything that moves, runs with its feet apparently not touching the ground, with impressive twists and turns

Uses Hunter of vermin, guard-dog and companion-dog
Future prospects The breed is still very popular, but is affected by changing fashions. Requires periodical trimming, like many other Terriers

The Smooth-haired Fox Terrier (above) has always been an enthusiast's dog; between the two World Wars the Wire-haired variety (opposite, bottom) enjoyed a period of great popularity, which has since waned. The breed has changed little since 1895, the date of the print (opposite, top).

FRENCH BULLDOG

The French Bulldog derives from the English Bulldog, and more specifically from the Toy Bulldog, which has a tendency to prick its ears. As early as 1868 it was possible to find small Bulldogs in Paris, where they were popular with butchers in the working-class quarter of La Villette. A certain Hartenstein, who was a famous German fancier of the breed, saw his first Bouledogue on the walls of Paris when it was under siege by the Prussians in 1871. In 1885 or thereabouts the demi-mondaine ladies of the capital fell in love with the little dog, and ensured its popularity.

In due course the Club was founded, under the chairmanship of the Prince de Wagram. The famous American journalist, James Gordon-Bennett, who had greatly encouraged motoring and aviation with large sums of prize-money, also established a Prix Gordon-Bennett for breeders of Bouledogues Français. As a result, this breed found its way to the United States, and then appeared in England, where King Edward VII acquired one. An international French Bulldog Club was founded in Munich to protect the future of the breed.

Between the two world wars Austria was the home of the famous Von Leesdorf kennels, and a very active Club was also set up in Italy.

TODAY'S BREED

Official classification KC (GB): Utility Group; AKC: Non-Sporting Dogs
Country of origin France
Weight 8-14 kg (18-32 lb)
Coat Close-lying, dense, brilliant; colour: brindle (a mixture of black and red hair, with less white), patched (white with brindle markings), or sometimes white all over)

General appearance Powerful, compact
Head Strong, broad, square, skull with wrinkles; muzzle broad with a short nose, pug-like in shape (i.e. with the tip of the 'chin' protruding beyond the tip of the nose, which must be black); lips thick, but not slobbering; teeth never visible when the mouth is shut; prognathous
Ears Not docked, distinctively bat-like
Eyes Large, round, set well apart, dark-coloured
Body Gathered, fore-quarters open, hind-quarters not very angled, belly well developed
Legs Powerful, muscular, with a specific stance; feet slightly open
Tail Not docked, short, set low down, never lively
Gait Distinctive, alert, supple

Qualities Lightness, very strong
Defects Small head, long body, ears not fully erect
Character Good-natured, docile, patient, alert

Uses An indoor dog, also useful for guarding the car, and an elegant pet, good with children
Future prospects A breed for somewhat specialized dog-fanciers, not easy to reproduce, not likely to become popular

In about 1870 prick-eared miniature or toy Bulldogs, were bred in Great Britain. In the print above we see two specimens of the day with the two different types of ears. The breed was subsequently taken up by the French, in Paris in particular. Nowadays the French Bulldog is being bred all over the world. An English-bred bitch, Marisemi Horatia of Bonlitz (left), at the age of four, and the champion bitch Hari Nice (opposite), born in England and taken later to Hungary.

FRENCH POINTER
Braque Français

All the various regions of Europe have their own types of Pointer. The French Pointers (Braques) recognized today, are: d'Ariège, d'Auvergne, du Bourbonnais, Dupuy, Français, de Petite Taille and St Germain.

The commonest variety is the Braque d'Auvergne or Auvergne Pointer (which received a considerable input of English Pointer blood in the 19th century), followed by the Braque Français or French Pointer (a brisk gun-dog, descendant of the so-called Charles X Braque or Pointer). Next comes the Braque St Germain or St Germain Pointer (produced in 1830 by crossing a Braque with a Pointer), then the Ariège Pointer (a rather 'difficult' dog, but good at the trot), the Bourbonnais (often born virtually tail-less, and standardized by Delage in the early part of this century) and lastly the Dupuy variety (selected by Delage). The following text describes the Braque Français.

TODAY'S BREED

Official classification KC (GB) and AKC: not recognized
Country of origin France
Height and weight 56-65 cm (22½-26 in). Weight: 25-32 kg (55-72 lb)
Coat Hair close-lying, dense and somewhat hard (wiry); the most usual colour is white with large pale brown markings, or alternatively a speckled look; specimens that are black and white, white and orange, black all over or brown all over are rarer

General appearance Powerful and sturdily built, with a typical facial structure due to the heavy, square shape of the head
Head Skull oval, slightly convex, muzzle straight and broad; tip of nose usually brown (chestnut-coloured); lips drooping; scissor-type bite
Ears Not docked, large, set at eye-level, slightly curled or rolled
Eyes Large, round, ranging from yellow to brown in colour
Body Chest deep, trunk sturdy, back straight, belly not tucked up
Legs Good stance, straight, muscular; feet compact, roundish
Tail Often shortened, straight, not carried gaily
Gait When on the move prefers the trot to the gallop

Qualities Well known for its brisk gait, and keen efficiency as a Pointer. It is the trusted companion of many hunters in central and western France, who prefer it to other dogs for its good working skills, rather than for its purely physical attributes
Defects Hard bite when retrieving, reluctant to hunt in water
Character It demands a master who can control and direct it, if it is to become totally loyal. Resolute expression

Uses Hunting in the field
Future prospects The breed is limited to certain parts of France, and is stubbornly standing up to the competition from British Pointers and Setters
Similar breeds Other Pointers not recognized by the KC (GB) and the AKC include the Danish Gammel, and the Dutch Drentse or Partridge Hound and Stabi

The characteristic shape (above) of the French Pointer and a typical head (opposite). The Pudelpointer (left) has been selected and bred in Germany and is standing up well to the strong competition from other Pointers.

GERMAN POMERANIAN
Spitz

One artist in particular who painted the Spitz was A. Ludwig Richter (1803-1884), a well-known German illustrator of fairy-tales. The ancestor of the German Pomeranian (allowing for a little science fiction) is probably the Pdauhlbauspitz, the Palafitte or Lake-dwelling dog or Peat-bog dog with the Latin name of **Canis familiaris palustris**.

Early in the 19th century the Spitz was commonly seen on barges plying their way up and down the Rhine. In Belgium it became the Schipperke, and in the Netherlands the Keeshond. It then spread throughout Europe: the French called it the Loulou, the Italians the Volpino, the English the Pomeranian and the Russians the Laïka (the name of the bitch that was the first dog to be launched into space).

In 1897 Henri de Bylandt used the name Laïka for the Chien de Sibérie, and the German artist L. Beckmann made a print of it, depicting the ideal type, in the book entitled **Der Rassen des Hundes**.

Mozart had a Spitz as a pet in the 18th century. This dog was his loyal companion in Vienna while he composed the unfinished **Requiem**, and (so the story goes) the only mourner to follow the composer's coffin before his body was buried in the paupers' grave.

TODAY'S BREED

Official classification KC (GB) and AKC: not recognized
Country of origin Germany
Height Large: 45-60 cm (18-24 in); medium-sized: 40-54 cm (16-20 in); small: 29-36 cm (11½-14½ in)
Coat Hair of average length, straight, never curly or flat, forming a mane round the neck and a large plume on the tail, fringes on the legs: colours: wolf-grey ('wolfsfarbig'), black ('schwarx'), white ('weiss'), brown ('braun'), orange

General appearance Although varying in colour and size, the Spitz group all has the typical features of the Pomeranian family, with its wedge-shaped head, and compact body, plus the distinctive abundant coat, kept straight by the undercoat
Head Elongated and wedge-shaped, tapering to the tip of the nose, which is round, small, and black or brown; scissor-type bite
Ears Not docked, small, triangular, pointed, good and erect, and mobile
Eyes Not large, slightly aslant, dark in colour
Body Chest deep and well sprung, back quite arched, belly moderately tucked up
Legs Quite short, sturdy, fringed; feet cat-like
Tail Not docked, set high, carried over the back, with plenty of hair
Gait Stride short, brisk and lively, nimble at the trot, and good at the gallop

Qualities The coat is an important feature, and should preferably be wolf-grey for large specimens; orange is only permitted for small varieties; if the hair is to stay straight (rather like the spines of a porcupine) the undercoat must be abundant
Defects Apple-shaped head, flesh-coloured nose, ears not erect, eyes weepy
Character Alert, suspicious of strangers, very at home indoors and therefore rarely straying, a keen watch-dog. Sharp expression

Uses Guard-dog and companion-dog
Future prospects Like all the other members of the Spitz group, this breed is assured of its future by its keen following
Similar breeds Among the various national Spitz dogs are the Finnish hunting-dog, known as the Suomenpystykorva and the Japanese hunting-dog, called the Hokkaidō-ken.

Two portraits (opposite bottom, and above) or Irko Vom Elmdorf, German and world champion at the age of three. The print (opposite, top) shows the breed at the end of the nineteenth century, similar to the large Spitz on the right.

GERMAN SHEPHERD DOG
Alsatian

In 1894 the Dutch cynologist de Bylandt said: 'The German, Belgian and Dutch Shepherd Dogs make up a single breed and ought to be called Continental Sheepdogs.' But things have turned out quite differently, and almost a century later the German Shepherd Dog is quite unlike the Belgian Shepherd Dog (or Groenendael) and the Dutch variant.

In a work written in 1897 De Bylandt again makes a reference to a club called the Phylax Spezial Klub für Deutsche Shäferhunde und Spitze. The chairman was M. Reichelmann and the secretary E. Hartmann, and the address was listed as Friesenstrasse 13, Berlin (annual subscription 10 marks).

Until shortly before the turn of the century, the German Shepherd Dog was divided into long-haired, short-haired and coarse-haired types. In prints of the time, the latter has a coat similar to that of the present-day German Shepherd Dog. There were also specimens with large white markings, as can clearly be seen from a contemporary photograph (published by **Der Hunde Sport**) which shows the standard pair, Stoppelhopser and Schäfermädchen, whose owner was, in fact, the Phylax chairman. The activities of Captain von Stephanitz, the real creator of the breed as we know it, were to change the selection procedures of the breed radically, from 1899 onwards.

TODAY'S BREED

Official classification KC (GB): Working Group; AKC: Herding Dogs
Country of origin Germany
Height Males: 62.5 cm (25 in); females: 57.5 cm (23 in) (with an admitted tolerance of 2.5 cm [1 in] either way)
Coat Medium-length, straight hair, thick, close, rain-resistant, never short or long, undercoat thick, mild form of breeching near the thigh; colour: black, black with tawny or fawn markings, grey, grey and fawn, fawn; small white markings on the chest are permitted, but not white overall

General appearance Typically wolf-like, quite powerful and long in the body
Head Muzzle fairly pointed, head lean and clean-cut, quite broad between the ears; muzzle strong; tip of nose black; lips thin; scissor-type bite
Ears Not docked, erect, medium-sized, pointed
Eyes Medium-sized, almond-shaped, quite dark in colour
Body The chest is well developed, good depth of brisket, not too broad, trunk long, belly slightly tucked up
Legs Fore-legs perfectly straight viewed from the front, pasterns have a slight angle; hind-quarters markedly angled, with well turned stifles; good posture; feet short, toes curved
Tail Not docked, well covered, reaching as far as the hock, sometimes forming a slight curve at the tip, hanging in a slight curve at rest, raised when moving, but never higher than horizontal
Gait This breed is a pastmaster at the trot; the motion travels gracefully from rear to front

Qualities A ratio of 8:10 between the height at the withers and the length of the body; angled fore- and hind-quarters; good movement when trotting

Nowadays, the German Shepherd Dog, in the English-speaking world often incorrectly called the Alsatian, has a very precise standard, as the modern specimens on these pages show. The print above depicts a short-haired and docked specimen and a long-haired specimen before the breed was stabilized.

Defects Trot too short paced, tendency to gallop; fringes of long hair; poor undercoat
Character Versatile, faithful and devoted, well balanced, when young may often be slightly difficult and even shy, but this disappears with age and training

Uses All the duties of a general working-dog
Future prospects Becoming more and more popular throughout the world
Similar breeds Charplaninatz Sheepdog (herding [sheep]), Yugoslavia: a powerful wolf-like dog, used by shepherds in Illyria. The Karst Sheepdog (herding [sheep]), Yugoslavia: similar to the above breed, but nevertheless recognized as a separate breed. In Yugoslavia there is also a Croatian Sheepdog called the Hrvatski Ovcar

GERMAN SHORT-HAIRED POINTER

Eighteenth-century German artists painted the earliest Pointers. Among their finest works are two drawings by Ridinger (1722), portraying some specimens with undocked tails and others with docked tails.

The year 1817 saw the publication of a work by a veterinary surgeon named Walter, entitled **Der eigentliche Hühnerhund**, in which there is a good description of the German Short-haired Pointer.

In the meantime the English Pointer was winning over German-speaking hunters, and in 1839 a club was set up in Hanover for the importation of these English dogs with the additional aim of improving the German breeds by crossbreeding. But in 1870 Germany's various military victories heightened the sense of nationalism in the country, and this caused the English Pointers and Setters to be passed over in favour of the thoroughbred German Pointer. In that same year the official standard was drawn up.

The first club was founded in 1891 and the meticulous selection procedures aimed at producing an all-round hunting-dog, capable of switching on command from being a pointer to a hound, and from being a search-and-rescue dog to a pure tracker, able to deal with vermin, such as wild cats and foxes. The German Pointer can even act as personal 'bodyguard' to the solitary hunter, and as a guard-dog in the home.

TODAY'S BREED

Official classification KC (GB): Gundog Group; AKC: Sporting Dogs
Country of origin Germany
Height and weight Males: 62-64 cm (25-25½ in); females never less than 58 cm (23 in). Weight: 25-30 kg (55-66 lb)
Coat Hair short and dense, hard to the touch (somewhat wiry); colours: brown, brown with small white markings or speckling; roan-brown, quite pale; white with a brown mask and brown markings and spots; black with brown or roan-brown; yellow and tan

General appearance A sturdy Pointer, not heavily built, athletic, well-balanced
Head Neither light nor heavy, lean, in good proportion to the body; muzzle quite thickset; tip of nose brown; lips tight, not falling; scissor-type bite
Ears Not docked, quite long, with rounded tips, flat and lying close to the head
Ears Medium-sized and brown
Body Chest deep, back short and vigorous, belly not tucked up
Legs Sturdy, straight, good stance, with closed, roundish feet
Tail Docked to one-third or one-half, set high
Gait Loose and easy, with good endurance at the trot, and very fast at the gallop

Qualities Complete dentition, lines indicating strength and speed, precisely the right size for a hunting-dog
Defects Heavy, slow specimens, dogs with poor temperament and dogs that are too highly strung; narrow chest that is not sufficiently deep
Character Well-balanced and keen, a zealous hunter, ready to both attack and defend, highly devoted to its master, easy to train. A lively expression

Uses All kinds of hunting
Future prospects This breed is permanently on the increase in popularity all over the world
Similar breeds Germany has selected and bred several Pointers apart from the famous Short-haired variety: these are the Drahthaar (Wire-haired), Langhaar (Long-haired), Stichelhaar (Rough-haired), Large and Small Münsterländer, and Pudel-pointer

The German Short-haired Pointer (opposite and above) has had considerable success worldwide, being valued particularly for its practical qualities in the countries of Europe, where wild game is rare. The German Wire-haired Pointer (left) is a less common breed with a very hard coat.

GOLDEN RETRIEVER

The origin of this breed has created a certain amount of controversy, but in 1952 it was generally accepted that in the last century Lord Tweedmouth mated a yellow wavy-coated retriever with a Tweed Water Spaniel. From this mating came four yellow puppies and these became the ancestors of all Golden Retrievers.

In 1918 the Golden Retriever Club was formed in England to look after the interests of this breed, which is now one of the most popular breeds today, both as a show dog and a companion-dog.

TODAY'S BREED

Official classification KC (GB): Gundog Group; AKC: Sporting Dogs
Country of origin Great Britain
Height and weight Males: 56-61 cm (22-24 in). Females: 51-56 cm (20-22 in). Weight: Males: 32-37 kg (70-80 lb). Females: 27-32 kg (60-70 lb)
Coat should be flat or wavy with good feathering and dense, water-resistant undercoat. Colour any shade of gold or cream

General appearance Should be a symmetrical, active, powerful dog, a good level mover, sound and well put together, with a kindly expression, not clumsy nor long in the leg
Head Broad skull, well set on clean and muscular neck, muzzle powerful and wide, good stop
Ears Well proportioned and of moderate size
Eyes Dark and well set apart, very kindly in expression
Body Well balanced, short coupled and deep through the heart. Ribs deep and well sprung
Legs Fore-legs straight with good bone. Quarters strong and muscular with good second thighs and well bent stifles
Tail Should not be carried too gaily nor curled at tip
Gait Free and well co-ordinated

Qualities Very honest well proportioned dog without any extremes
Defects Snipey muzzle. Absence of bone and substance. Lack of pigmentation. White collar, feet, toes or blaze
Character Should always be even tempered

Uses An excellent companion for a family and a safe reliable gun-dog for the shooting man. The Golden Retriever is also much used as a guide dog for the blind
Future prospects The breed's qualities will ensure that its popularity will continue

The Golden Retriever owes its great popularity as much to its lovely temperament as to sturdy build and usefulness in the field.

GORDON SETTER

The Italian cynologist Pollacci, who is an expert on this breed as well as an important breeder, has written in **The Gordon Setter**: 'In that part of Scotland lying to the north of Fochabers, near the River Spey, and just a few miles from the sea, even before the last century shepherds were using dogs which, though trained for herding sheep, could also point game a long way off, and track it slowly but surely, displaying an extraordinary sense of smell and a pointing instinct that was even superior to that of other hunting-dogs then in existence. In fact Duke Alexander IV of Gordon, who died in 1827 at the age of 84, often asked shepherds to lend him these dogs for his hunting parties; among them was a bitch with truly exceptional pointing abilities, and an outstanding sense of smell. It is in effect to this anonymous and humble female that we in all probability owe the familiar and famous requirements as laid down for breeding these so-called Gordon Setters. The Duke in fact mated this bitch with the best of his own Setters, and thus gave rise to the present-day black-and-tan Setter.'

Selection procedures have made this Setter somewhat sturdier and slower than some other breeds of Setters, thus making it suitable for hunting in water as well as on land.

TODAY'S BREED

Official classification KC (GB): Gundog Group; AKC: Sporting Dogs
Country of origin Great Britain
Height and weight 56-64 cm (22½-25½ in). Weight: 22-30 kg (50-68 lb)
Coat Hair 5-6 cm (2-2½ in) long, not wavy, with fringes; colour: coal-black with mahogany-tan markings

General appearance A large, powerful member of the Pointer family, but still quite elegant
Head Skull broad, muzzle elongated; tip of nose black; lips large; scissor-type bite
Ears Not docked, falling close to the head, set quite low on head
Eyes Quite large, dark brown in colour
Body Chest and ribs deep, belly not tucked up
Legs Sturdy, muscular, good stance; feet oval with plentiful hair
Tail Not docked, straight or slightly curved, carried low or at most horizontal
Gait Brisk at the trot, with a short stride, not as happy at the gallop

Qualities Symmetrical shape, well-defined colour; should not resemble the English Setter, and even less the Irish breed
Defects Head large and heavy, body bulky, hair curly, woolly, dull, light-coloured tan markings, feet white, a lot of white on the chest
Character Well-balanced, a thorough worker, not impetuous, but will hunt well at the gallop, although not flat out. Alert expression

Uses All forms of hunting
Future prospects Although in competition with the other two Setters, it is managing to do well, and is winning over new followers

Cleo of Hamburg, a British-bred German champion Gordon Setter at the age of three.

GREAT DANE

The origins of this large hound were the subject of some controversy in 1935, at the International Cynological Congress. The Danish delegation presented a report that showed that the Great Dane's native country is Denmark, where it was called Broholmer and Dansk Hund. This claim was disputed by the German delegate who held that the breed hailed from Ulm, a city on the river Danube between Württemberg and Bavaria. The Fédération Cynologique Internationale, with its headquarters in Brussels, sided with the German viewpoint. The Dansk Hund was a favourite with Frederick VII of Denmark (1808-63), who appointed a certain Klemp, one of his counsellors, to reinstate the Great Dane, which had become rare. From his teenage years onwards, Otto von Bismarck (1815-98) had a soft spot for the Deutsche Dogge. As a student at Göttingen he had a much-loved specimen called Sultan. Later on in his life, when he had become chancellor and founder of the German Empire (1871), he was master to the colossal Tyras. His fondness for the breed made it popular throughout the Empire, and the world. Max Hartenstein was one of the first great breeders. The so-called Harlequin variety came from the Meyer kennels. Gigantism made the Great Dane lymphatic, frail and dull, and it almost disappeared in about 1914. It reappeared, however, in about 1925, in much better shape. It was shown for the first time in Hamburg in 1863.

TODAY'S BREED

Official classification KC (GB): Working Group; AKC: Working Dogs
Nationality German
Height and weight For males, at least 80 cm (32 in) at the withers; females, 72 cm (29 in). About 60 kg (135 lbs)
Coat Short, close, smooth and shiny; colour: buff, tawny, tawny striped, black, blue, black patches on white for harlequins

General appearance A sturdy giant, powerfully-built, well-proportioned, with pleasing lines
Head Large, with 'chiselled' features, elongated and narrow; muzzle black; lips large and hanging; teeth level
Ears Smallish, pointed and upright, specific to the breed; in Great Britain they may not be clipped
Eyes Round, with the colour varying with the colour of the coat, preferably dark; in harlequins blue is permissible
Body Deep and square, with the ribcage lower than the knee; belly slightly drawn up
Legs Muscular; stance natural; feet rounded
Tail When relaxed slightly curved at the tip; when active, carried scimitar-like; but it must remain above the dorsal line; unclipped
Gait Supple, long strides, back firm

Qualities Look for good proportions, where the height does not give an appearance of thinness, and the muscularity does not appear cumbersome. The supple movements are appreciated
Faults Inelegance in the body, gauche head, clumsy gait, hollow back, poor natural stance
Character Generally calm, self-controlled, rarely aggressive. Erratic specimens are dangerous. Affectionate to the point of forgetting how large it is, and regarding itself as a lap-dog. Not used for training because of its excessive size, but quick to learn, and 'gifted' dogs are suitable for training. A fine guard-dog, with an alert, good-natured look

Uses An impressive guard-dog because of its size and loud bark; also used as a 'beast of burden', which it enjoys; not suitable for hauling
Future prospects Lovers of Great Danes go for its size, although this threatens to limit its future spread. It seems destined to remain a rather heraldic and aristocratic hound which will not become a functional

or commonplace breed. Sought after as a show-dog

Related breeds Fila brasileiro, Brazil: A large mastiff from Brazil, possibly descended from Molossian hounds brought to the Americas by the Spanish conquistadors, used for guarding and as a workdog. Its standard requires an ambling gait

An Italian-bred champion bitch, Deborah della Dragonara (opposite), and a German-bred harlequin dog (above) of this large but graceful breed belonging to the mastiff-type. The Fila Brasileiro (right) is another large breed of the mastiff type.

GREYHOUND

As breeds of dog have continued to change, the English Greyhound is possibly the only one that has retained its original shape and character. It is, in fact, depicted on Egyptian tombs dating back some 4000 years. Leonardo da Vinci wrote of it: 'On the hunt the pointers put up the beast, and then the greyhounds catch it.' In fact, the word Greyhound refers to **Canis leporarius**, hunter of hares. In Germany it is known as the Windhund. In England it is used for 'coursing': a sport that entails chasing hares, based on a set of rules drawn up by the Duke of Norfolk during the reign of Queen Elizabeth I, at the end of the 16th century. A time-honoured tradition has developed into what is known as Open Coursing, which culminates every October in the Waterloo Cup, with impressive prizes. The Greyhounds are set after live hares and classified on the basis of their behaviour by judges on horseback.

In addition, Greyhound racing, using mechanical hares, became a popular sport, and large sums of money changed hands on the race tracks and in betting shops, although the sport has declined in recent times.

The Greyhound is the racing-dog par excellence particularly in the English-speaking world, where it has been selected and bred over many years for the racing track.

TODAY'S BREED

Official classification KC (GB): Hound Group; AKC: Hounds
Country of origin Great Britain
Height Males: 71-76 cm (28½-30½ in); females: 68.5-71 cm (27½-28½ in)
Coat Short and fine; colour: black, white, tan (or fawn), brindle, blue, with or without white, sometimes with markings

General appearance The most typical of the large members of the Greyhound group, with close-lying coat
Head Long, skull flat, muzzle sturdy; tip of nose matches the colour of the coat; lips tight; scissor-type bite
Ears Not docked, small, rose-shaped, set towards the back of the head, semi-erect when the dog is excited or in motion
Eyes Large, expressive, bright, preferably dark
Body Chest very deep, trunk long, slightly arched, belly very tucked up
Legs Front legs long and straight, hind legs muscular and longer than the front legs, markedly angled; feet are cat-like with very hard pads
Tail Not docked, long, thin, carried low, slightly curved at the level of the hocks
Gait Easy, supple, good stride, very fast at the gallop

Qualities An essential feature is the anatomical line which enables the dog to fulfil its racing role
Defects Head not long enough, musculature weak and not in relief
Character Keen, well-balanced, a zealous hunter, responds well to all types of training. Shrewd expression

Uses Unrivalled as a Hound
Future prospects Its increase is closely bound up with dog-racing tracks, and the keen efforts and loyalty of a handful of Greyhound-fanciers
Similar breeds Magyar Agár (Hound), Hungary: similar to Greyhound, appears to be still in use for hunting in its homeland

GRIFFON BRUXELLOIS
Brussels Griffon

Early in the 19th century stable-dogs were much sought after; they did away with rats and mice, and got along well with horses. Types of dog deriving from the stable-dog include the German Schnauzer and Pinscher, and in Belgium, a small Griffon. This latter turned into a little pet-dog towards the end of the last century. Prints dating back to 1890 show specimens of the day with long, thin muzzles of the Schnauzer type. In about 1910 this dog was crossed with the Pug. This had the effect of altering the shape of the head, and brought the breed popularity. In 1910 in Brussels there were some 2000 brood-females living in workers' homes, small shops and greengrocers' shops.

In 1883 the breed was officially recorded for the first time, and in 1905 the Club drew up the official standard. The German occupation of Belgium in the First World War brought about the virtual disappearance of the Griffon Bruxellois, but it reappeared as a result of being bred in Great Britain, and also because of its extremely likeable and good-natured character. The French cynologist Lafond has described this little Griffon as follows: 'as inquisitive as a journalist, as affectionate as a lad from Provence and as beloved as an inventor'.

TODAY'S BREED

Official classification KC (GB): Toy Group; AKC: Toys
Country of origin Belgium
Weight Males: 3-5 kg (6½-11 lb); Females preferably slightly more
Coat The Bruxellois and the Belge have long, hard hair, with whiskers and a beard; the Brabançon has a short, smooth, soft coat; colour: red with whiskers and beard often black; Belge black, black with tawny markings, mixture of red and black; Brabançon as the Belge

General appearance A small, compact dog, with the facial expression of a small monkey
Head Round, muzzle Pug-like; tip of nose black; teeth slightly prognathous
Ears Not docked, or docked at the tips; thin
Eyes Large, protruding, very dark
Body Ribs quite deep, belly well developed
Legs Strong with a good, straight stance
Tail Docked to two-thirds of its original length
Gait Brisk, elegant

Qualities A small lap-dog, distinctive and well proportioned
Defects Hair soft and silky, six-toed feet, muzzle not Pug-like
Character Very affectionate, devoted to a single owner, lively and alert. Loving expression

Uses A good companion, and watch-dog in the home
Future prospects This breed is very much subject to the ups and downs of fashion, so it may be popular one day, and neglected the next
Similar breeds Affenpinscher (pet dog), Germany: halfway between the Brussels Griffon and the German Schnauzer; the Americans call this dog the Monkey Pinscher

The Griffon Bruxellois is an alert watch-dog that has been bred with particular success in Belgium, France and Italy. As is clear from the print (above), it originally had a long narrow muzzle. The present-day very short muzzle is the result of crossing with the Pug.

IRISH SETTER

The first pedigree record for this breed dates back to 1859. The history of the breed can be traced through its famous stud dogs: Bob (1859), Ranger (1864), Plunket (1868), Dak (1870), Champion Garryowen at Dublin in 1895, and Champion Ruby Glenmore in New York. This abundance of champions was nevertheless to have sinister results. After the First World War Champion Rheola Bryn, son of Didona, became famous, although his mother suffered from retinal atrophy, a congenital illness which caused her to become blind. In 1930 or thereabouts it was impossible to find a single Irish Setter that did not have at least one connection with the Rheola Bryn pedigree: so this dog handed on to hundreds of his children and grandchildren his mother's hereditary illness, although he himself was not affected by it. All that was needed was for two of Bryn's offspring to mate to transmit progressive blindness to their offspring.

The disease was incurable, usually ending in blindness by the age of three: at first only night-blindness, then daytime blindness, and lastly total blindness. The efforts of cynological circles all over the world to combat this danger started in earnest several decades ago, and concentrated on breeding dogs which would not transmit the disease. The results have been extremely satisfactory.

TODAY'S BREED

Official classification KC (GB): Gundog Group; AKC: Sporting Dogs
Country of origin Great Britain
Height and weight 54-64 cm (21½-25 in)
Coat Hair 5-6 cm (2-2½ in) long, silky, flat, with light fringes; single colour bright mahogany red, with small white markings permitted on the chest, forehead and toes

General appearance A nimble member of the Pointer family, lean, with a fine bone structure
Head Lean, long, with a long muzzle; tip of nose black; scissor-type bite
Ears Not docked, tending to be triangular, falling, with fringes
Eyes Open, iris from dark hazel to chestnut
Body Chest quite narrow, ribs deep to below the elbow, belly not tucked up
Legs Normal stance, thighs muscular, fringes on the legs, feet compact and oval
Tail Not docked, tapering, fringes, carried low, or horizontal at most
Gait Best at the gallop

Qualities The colour is important, as is its intensity and sheen; handsome fringes are sought after; athletic agility is another important feature
Defects Hair short, wavy, curly; colour brown or liver; wrinkles on the head; dewlaps; paler fringes
Character Lively, energetic, freedom-loving, stubborn if not well controlled. Bright, gentle expression

Uses Hunting requiring a fast dog with a keen scent
Future prospects Very good because of its incomparably handsome coat, its elegance and hunting abilities

Hartsbourne Engar, an English-bred German champion. The attractive Titian-red colouring has made this a popular companion-dog. Work continues on eliminating the genetic weakness that has caused blindness in many specimens.

IRISH TERRIER

Breeds of dog native to Ireland are for the most part red-haired. Like the famous Irish Setter, the Irish Terrier is also red. The first Irish Terrier Club was founded in Ireland in 1879, with the initial aim of prohibiting and then banning ear docking, common for this breed in those days.

Towards the end of the 19th century the Irish Terrier started to become a popular entry at the Dublin dog-show. The first champion went by the name of Spuds, and was the great rival of the famous Champion Erin, regarded as the living official standard. The breed was improved by the Breda kennels, with Breda Miner and Breda Madler, out of the stud dog Poor Pal.

In old Gaelic manuscripts this dog is described as 'the friend of the peasant, the sentinel of the poor, and the favourite of the rich'.

Jack London, who often used dogs as the heroes of his novels (**White Fang, The Call of the Wild**), chose an Irish Terrier as the leading character in his books **Jerry of the Isles** and **Michael, Jerry's Brother**,

Apollo von der Lichtenbeide, a German champion at the age of two. Owners and fanciers of the Irish Terrier maintain that, despite a superficial resemblance to the Fox Terrier, the breeds are very different, especially in character and behaviour.

TODAY'S BREED

Official classification KC (GB): Terrier Group; AKC: Terriers
Country of origin Ireland (Eire)
Height and weight: Approx. 45 cm (18 in). Weight approx. 12 kg (27 lb)
Coat Hair hard, wiry and stiff, not soft at all, not long enough to blur the shape of the body, thick and close enough not to reveal the skin when the toes are parted; never curly; undercoat soft; the preferred colours are bright red, golden-red and yellowish red; a small white speck on the chest is permitted

General appearance A lively, slender Terrier, full of vitality, sturdy and muscular, not heavy
Head Long, quite narrow between the ears, jaw strong and muscular; the hair on the muzzle is shorter, except on the chin, where it forms a beard; tip of nose black; scissor-type bite
Ears Not docked, small, V-shaped, set well on head, drooping forward closely to the cheek
Eyes Small and dark, not prominent
Body Longer than that of the Fox Terrier, back therefore moderately long, loins arched, belly tucked up
Legs Very good stance; muscular; feet round
Tail Docked to about three-quarters of its length, covered with close, rough hair, carried gaily, straight, not over back or curled
Gait Supple, easy; a very good runner

Qualities A small, supple, athletic dog in its overall shape; texture of the coat is important; appreciated for its bright colouring; black toe-nails desirable
Defects Anything that may make it look like a Fox Terrier, from which it must remain quite distinct; long, wavy hair is a serious fault, as are a broad head and pale-coloured eyes
Character Fearless to the point of recklessness, it is nevertheless very affectionate, always shy, even with its owner or master, constantly offering faithful companionship and devoted service. Very fiery, lively expression

Uses In Ireland it is used for hunting rabbits and foxes, and for getting rid of vermin; good watch-dog in the car and the home
Future prospects Rivalry from the Fox Terrier is affecting the spread of this breed, but it is still an unforgettable companion-dog. It requires periodical trimming

IRISH WATER SPANIEL

This breed which has the most distinctive appearance of any member of the Spaniel family, belongs to the group somewhat informally known as the 'Irish Reds'. It includes Setters, Spaniels, Terriers and Irish Wolfhounds.

The selection and breeding of this dog got under way in about 1834, and the reasons for its popularity have been aptly summarized by the breeder J. S. Skidmore in his book **British Dogs**. He points out that the Irish Water Spaniel is ideal for the hunter who can afford only one dog, given that it acts as Pointer, Setter, Retriever and Spaniel, and also that it is particularly well suited to working in water, where it is in a class of its own.

It made its first public appearance at the Birmingham Dog Show in 1862. One of the major breeders and showers of the Irish Water Spaniel was McCarthy; the first Club dates back to 1890. In those days the top breeding kennels were those run by Colonel W. Le Poer Tench of Buckinghamshire. He raised four generations of champions, including the famous Champion Shaun.

The Irish Water Spaniel is not common outside the British Isles. Where it is known it is appreciated for its intelligence when working and its comical good-humour when off duty.

TODAY'S BREED

Official classification KC (GB): Gundog Group; AKC: Sporting Dogs
Country of origin Great Britain
Height and weight 51-58 cm (20½-23 in). Weight: Males: 25-30 kg (55-65 lb); females: 21-26 kg (45-58 lb)
Coat Hair oily, consisting of tight, dense curls, not woolly, with plentiful fringes; long curls on the skull; undercoat water-resistant; colour: rich dark liver, sometimes referred to as 'puce liver'

General appearance Unusual, both facially and generally because of the distinctive curly coat
Head Quite large, with a strong, long muzzle; lips conspicuous; tip of nose dark liver coloured; scissor-type bite
Ears Not docked, large, set quite low on the head, falling against the cheeks, covered in long curls
Eyes Quite small, brown
Body Ribcage deep and well sprung, carried well back, belly slightly tucked up
Legs Good bone structure, vigorous, good stance; feet large and covered with plenty of hair
Tail Not docked, short and straight, tapering, set low, with curls at the base, and almost hairless towards the tip
Gait Distinctive, specific, quite like that of the Poodle

Qualities Important features include the coat, fringes, curls, and undercoat, all those things that help to make this dog a tireless worker in water
Defects White markings, timid or lazy temperament
Character Keen, active, a good working-dog with plenty of stamina, a tireless retriever, happiest of all in water

Uses It will tackle the most arduous of hunting duties in thick marshland, and deep, icy water
Future prospects Rare, will only ever have a small, special following
Similar breed American Water Spaniel (Retriever, Gun-dog), United States: a tracking breed, also used for flushing out game in water and for retrieving it; specializes in hunting at sea

IRISH WOLFHOUND

In olden times this dog, or more precisely 'hound', was the natural enemy of the wolves that roamed the countryside of Britain during the reign of King Henry VIII. It was Henry's lord great chamberlain, Thomas Cromwell, who banned these dogs from being exported in the year 1539.

One story has it that in 1689 King James dispatched to his ally, William of Orange, Irish troops accompanied by thousands of hounds. These, instead of dying of hunger, destroyed nearly all the hares in France, with the result that all similar kinds of hunting were then banned.

When the wolf disappeared from Britain, there was a risk that the Wolfhound would also die out. Luckily, however, towards the end of the 19th century, a certain Captain G. Graham of Dursley devoted his life to restoring the breed – a task that cost him the princely sum of £20,000 in gold – literally a small fortune. But his endeavours were successful, and he used as a prototype a famous dog, who bore the name Scott.

TODAY'S BREED

Official classification KC (GB): Hound Group; AKC: Hounds
Country of origin Ireland
Height and weight Males: 81-86 cm (32½-34½ in); females: slightly less. Weight: males: 54 kg (120 lb); females 40 kg (90 lb)
Coat Hair rough and tough, with long eyebrows, moustache and beard; colours: white, black, red (resembling the colour of deer), grey, grey-yellow, red and grey, brindle

General appearance A powerful Hound, sturdy and hardy, shaggy, very tall
Head Long and moderately pointed; tip of nose matches the coat colour; scissor-type bite
Ears Not docked, small, Greyhound-like in carriage
Eyes Dark
Body Chest very deep, belly tucked up
Legs Very good stance, thighs long and strong; feet round and quite large
Tail Not docked, long, slightly curved towards the tip
Gait Graceful with a long stride, good at the trot, excellent at the gallop

Qualities Impressive in both size and structure; this is the most powerful of all the British Greyhounds
Defects Head and neck carried low, height at the withers less than 80 cm (32 in), weight less than 54 kg (120 lb) for males, and 40 kg (90 lb) for females
Character By nature the Wolfhound is not a vicious guard-dog. It will warn of the presence of a stranger without attacking him. If taught how to attack, can be dangerous. Thoughtful expression

Uses Guard- and watch-dog, companion-dog
Future prospects Will only ever have a small following

Eagles Crag Fingal, an exceptionally fine specimen and champion of the breed, at the age of four.

ITALIAN GREYHOUND

Known in French as the **levron** or **levrette**, and by the Germans as the **italienisches Windspiel**, this small version of the English Greyhound also resembles the Sloughi.

From earliest times it has been depicted in works of art. At the end of the 18th century it found a patron in no less a person than Frederick the Great, King of Prussia, who had his own tomb built in the midst of the tomb of all his Italian Greyhounds; and in the various portraits and sculptures of him, he is invariably surrounded by these dogs. In 1857 it is said that Flaubert gave Madame Bovary 'une petite levrette d'Italie', and in 1865 the novelist Paul Duplessis was buried with his own Italian Greyhound, Littaud. The year 1923 saw the establishment of the Solcio kennels in Italy (run by the lawyer, E. Cavallini) and the Peltrengo kennels (run by Marchioness G. Montecuccolli), with the expressed aim of reviving the breed. In the period following the Second World War the Italian Greyhound found plenty of support in both Europe and the United States. Nowadays it is used in some countries for hunting hares, and in pheasant-shoots. The official historian of the Italian Greyhound is Maria Luisa Incontri.

TODAY'S BREED

Official classification KC (GB): Toy Group; AKC: Toys
Country of origin Italy
Height and weight Minimum 32 cm (13 in), maximum 38 cm (15 in). Weight: 5 kg (11¼ lb), preferably less
Coat Hair close-lying, fine; single-coloured: black, slate-grey, 'isabella' (yellowish to light brown); white on the chest and feet permitted

General appearance A small Greyhound, graceful and lively
Head Skull flat, same length as the muzzle, which is pointed; tip of nose matches colour of coat; scissor-type bite
Ears Not docked, set high on head, small, rose-shaped
Eyes Large and dark
Body Chest deep, almost reaching the knees, back arched, belly very tucked up
Legs Good stance, straight and lean (front), with longer and more muscular hind-quarters; feet oval
Tail Not docked, set low, tapering to the tip
Gait Elegant, skipping

Qualities Lines reminiscent of those of the Sloughi, but with the added refinement of being a miniature version; elegance of movement, very distinctive postures
Defects Height at the withers exceeding 38 cm (15 in) or less than 32 cm (13 in) in males; less than 31 cm (12½ in) in females; not single-coloured; tail not tapered
Character Though a small dog it is an energetic watch-dog, quick to warn of strangers in the vicinity; indoors it is lively; it enjoys going on long walks and has good endurance; very affectionate. Bright expression

Uses As a small Hound, for hunting hares, putting up pheasant, and as watch-dog in the home
Future prospects It has a loyal following of admirers and faithful breeders, but does not seem likely to become popular

The Italian Greyhound has remained unchanged over a long period.

ITALIAN HOUND
Segugio

The cynologist Angelo Vecchio, who lived in the early part of this century and devoted much of his energy to Italian breeds of hunting-dog, maintains that the birthplace of the Italian Hound or Segugio is ancient Gaul, and more precisely the region lying between the River Saone and the River Rhône – an area once occupied by a people known as the Segusians, hence the dog's name.

This author likens the Segugio to a beggar mournfully asking for alms, and he describes a pack of Italian Hounds baying in pursuit of its victim as if it were expressing its own sympathy for the fleeing game.

Perhaps the breed did come originally from Gaul. It is known for sure that in the 16th century a certain Erasmus of Valvasone called it the 'Ségugio di Bergamo' or Bergamo Hound. The cynologist Ferruccio Faelli, whose writings after the First World War covered such a wealth of canine subjects, agrees with this, and states quite definitely that the Rough- or Hard-haired variety comes from Piedmont, and is known in the local dialect as the Ceravin.

In byegone days the Italian Hound was used in packs for hunts involving horsemen. In this century it has become quite popular in its homeland, where it is usually used for hunting hares, either on its own, in pairs, or in a small group.

TODAY'S BREED

Official classification KC (GB) and AKC: not recognized
Country of origin Italy
Height and weight 48-58 cm (19-23 in). Weight: 18-28 kg (40-62 lb)
Coat Two varieties: Smooth-haired – dense, smooth, fine and with a sheen; Rough-haired – rough, not more than 5 cm (2 in) in length, never drooping over the eyes; colours: all shades of tan or tawny; black and tan (if there is a white star on the chest the coat is defined as tri-coloured)

General appearance As elegant member of the Pointer group, of medium height and build, with a well-balanced physical appearance
Head Lean, muzzle long and pointed; tip of nose prominent and black; scissor-type bite
Ears Not docked, falling, triangular, flat and very wide
Eyes Large, bright, almond-shaped, dark ochre in colour
Body Ribcage deep and well sprung, reaching to the elbow, belly tucked up
Legs Quite long, lean, solid where they meet the body, with oval feet and hard pads
Tail Not docked, elegant and slender, with a fine, slightly curved tip
Gait Gallops well when hunting

Qualities Strong and solidly built, symmetrical, lean in appearance, with no sign of fat, well muscled
Defects Ears short, colouring slate-grey or chestnut or liver, or with white dominant; wrinkles on the head, presence of dewlaps
Character Rather self-contained, courageous, great endurance, a very keen worker. Bright expression

Uses Tracking small game with a shrill baying sound
Future prospects Popular in its native country
Similar breeds Hamilton Stovare (Hound), Sweden: for hunting large game, this breed was developed by the breeder A.P. Hamilton, after whom it is named

In its native country this distinctive hound is highly regarded. It is often used in pairs or small packs for hunting hares.

ITALIAN POINTER
Bracco Italiano

The term bracco first was first used in the 13th century by Dante and Boccaccio. The art of pointing or setting was described by Lorenzo de' Medici:

> The hare and the pointer lie in a bush
> the latter does not bark, and the former is not moaning yet.

Italian Pointers were much praised in the Renaissance, and often exchanged as gifts by sovereigns, popes and princes; they were also frequently exported to France and Spain. Towards the end of the 19th century the breed seemed to disappear. This was due to a preference among hunters for the faster British Pointers and Setters.

The breed was defended, extolled and brought back into the arena by the cynologist and breeder, Ferdinando Delor, author of **I Cani da ferma italiani e esteri** (Italian and other Pointers and Setters) (1886) and of other works. He was also editor of the **Rivista cinegetica** until 1912, promoter of the first Italian dog-show in 1881 and of the foundation of the Italian Kennel Club in 1882. In 1882 he set up in Milan the Hunting Kennels (Canile della Caccia). Its primary aim was to breed Pointers, and, later, Griffons (Spinone) as well. With all the authority at his disposal he unfailingly drew attention to the qualities of the Italian Pointer and the Italian Griffon, and was the first to describe the various features of these dogs in 1887.

TODAY'S BREED

Official classification KC (GB) and AKC: not recognized
Country of origin Italy
Height and weight 55-67 cm (22-27 in). Weight: 25-40 kg (56-90 lb)
Coat Hair close-lying, dense, and shiny; colours: white, orange-white, brown and white, brown-roan, white with small pale-orange markings (honey-coloured)

General appearance An energetic Pointer, with very distinctive features
Head Very typically Pointer-like, with a squared muzzle; lips well developed; tip of nose ranging from chestnut to flesh-coloured, matching the coat; fierce-looking teeth
Ears Not docked, curled, set quite well back, falling, long enough to reach the sides of the nose
Eyes Open, ranging from ochre to yellow in colour
Body Chest broad and full, deep, trunk sturdy, belly never tucked up
Legs Good stance, muscular and straight; feet large and roundish
Tail Docked, leaving 12-15 cm (5-6 in)
Gait Loose and easy; long, nimble stride at the trot

Qualities Lean limbs, prominent muscles, generally distinguished air
Defects Prognathous teeth, or the reverse, double nose, flabby lips, small ears
Character Serious, docile, gentle, diligent when seeking out prey, good endurance as a Pointer, suitable for all types of hunting. Kind expression

Uses Hunting in the field
Future prospects It has a large following in Italy. Little known in other parts of the world
Similar breeds Perdigueiro Português (Pointer): this is the national Pointer of Portugal. The Perdiguero de Burgos fulfils the same role in Spain; both dogs possibly have origins similar to those of the Italian Pointer

Toro del Rossendola (left), an Italian champion at the age of five. Current breeding in Italy emphasizes the type known as the 'Gonzaga Pointer' illustrated in the nineteenth-century print (above).

JAPANESE CHIN
Japanese Spaniel

Theo Marples writes of the first Japanese Chin (or Spaniel) to be shown in England towards the end of the 19th century: it was called Ming Seng, and had been brought over on a ship from Japan with a cargo of tea. It weighed about 6 kg (13 lb) and was awarded a prize at the Crystal Palace Show in London by the judge, the Reverend F. Hodgson, who was an authority on breeds from the Orient. In Japan, in those days, there was a preference for very small dogs, weighing about 1 kg (2¼ lb); they were so highly priced and so fragile that they never survived the journey to England. Nevertheless, various kennels started to select and bred the Toy Spaniels. At the turn of the century the champions of the day were Day Butzn owned by Mrs J. Addis of Liverpool and Sasaki owned by Mrs McLaren Morrison of London – as far as can be deduced from the magazine, the **Ladies' Kennel Journal**. The Empress of Germany had a pair called Itti and Kuma.

The Japanese Chin is quite delicate when it comes to breeding, and its colours are tricky to select. It was pushed somewhat into the wings by the huge success of the Pekingese, which was a sturdier little dog, with all types of colouring permitted. The Japanese call the Chin the Tchin, and in France it is known as the Chin-chin.

TODAY'S BREED

Official classification KC (GB): Toy Group; AKC: Toys
Country of origin Japan
Height and weight Preferable when kept small: 20-30 cm (8-12 in); Weight: 2-5 kg (4½-11 lb)
Coat Hair long and abundant, with no waves or curls, and a tendency to stand up straight, especially on the mane; colours: white and black or white and red (with shades of orange, lemon and sand): there is a preference for pure white and colours distributed evenly on the head (rather like a mask) and over the body, too

General appearance A small lap-dog, pretty and fragile, but with a strong bone structure
Head Large, roundish, skull broad, practically no muzzle as such, with the result that the tip of the nose (whose colour matches the coat) is situated right between the eyes and at eye-level; teeth are often incomplete, with signs of prognathism
Ears Not docked, falling beside the head, with very long hair covering them
Eyes Very large, prominent, almond-shaped, dark, with a moist look about them
Body Square-shaped, ribcage sturdy, black short, belly slightly tucked up
Legs Very small-boned, slender in appearance, with large fringes; feet small and long
Tail Not docked, long, carried over the back to right or left, with plenty of very long hair
Gait Gives the impression of walking on tiptoe

Qualities Muzzle broad and short with the upper lip well rounded on both sides of the nose; distinctive habit of cocking the head, as if it wanted to look at you with just one eye
Defects Pekingese-like member of the Dachshund group, with bent front legs, thin coat, with few fringes
Character Aristocratic attitude, quite dignified, even rather disdainful towards anyone ruffling it. Distant expression

Uses Pretty lap-dog, enjoys attention
Future prospects Rare and sought-after by a handful of connoisseurs

Tora no Suke, a Japanese-born specimen and champion in its own country.

KEESHOND

The Keeshond, historically speaking, has been the faithful companion of Dutch boatmen and sailors. After the French Revolution in 1789 it became the national dog of the Netherlands in the struggles that ensued between the sovereigns of the House of Orange and the insurgents under the popular leadership of Kees de Gyselaer, who was invariably seen with a Spitz-like dog, which was then named after him – hence Kees-hond, or Kees's dog.

After various fluctuations in popularity the Keeshond seemed to become a forgotten breed. In fact, it was in the process of becoming bastardized on Dutch barges when Baroness Van Hardenbroek began to select and revive the breed in the 1920s. For all her efforts, however, the Keeshond once again fell on hard times in Holland after 1950, and was subsequently classified with the German Wolfspitz.

It is worth mentioning that the Keeshond's extremely handsome coat keeps on growing until the dog is three years old, and does not really look its best until then. This is a feature of other members of the Spitz group as well.

Before its revival in Holland, the Keeshond had been made very welcome in Great Britain, thanks to the activities of Colonel Wingfield Digby and his wife, early this century. It was officially recognized by the British Kennel Club in 1927, and is still being bred successfully in Great Britain, where, in 1978, there were three important kennels specializing in breeding Keeshonds.

A British-born champion of the Keeshond, an intelligent and lively breed that makes an ideal companion-dog.

TODAY'S BREED

Official classification KC (GB): Utility Group; AKC: Non-Sporting Dogs
Countries of origin Holland, Great Britain
Height and weight Approx. 46 cm (18½ in). Weight approx. 28 kg (62 lb)
Coat Hair thick and hard, straight, with a large mane round the neck and a large plume on the tail, fringes on the legs; undercoat thick, soft, pale yellow; colours: wolf-grey, silvery-grey with darker colouring; white or black coats are not permitted

General appearance A typical larger member of the Spitz group, with a wolf-like head, compact body, and brisk movements
Head Skull broad, muzzle tapering towards the tip, which is always black; lips thin and tight; scissor-type bite
Ears Not docked, small, pointed, erect and mobile
Eyes Very sunken, with dark rings round them, known as spectacles, very dark in colour
Body Short, compact, back straight, belly slightly tucked up
Legs Short, sturdy, muscular; feet compact and cat-like
Tail Not docked, carried in a tight curl over the back, with a pale-coloured plume
Gait Brisk and lively, with a distinctive stride; quick at the trot, fast at the gallop

Qualities Long, dense, hard fur-like coat, with hair emerging straight from the undercoat; important features are the large mane and the large plume on the tail
Defects Inadmissible colours, tail carried wrongly, prominent eyes
Character Always on the alert, a fine guard-dog, which will bar intruders with threatening barks until its master returns. Bright expression

Uses Guard- and companion-dog
Future prospects Popular, particularly in the countries along the Rhine, and in the English-speaking countries
Similar breeds The Akita, the national dog of Japan, is an excellent hunter, a good guard-dog and is easy to train. Another large member of the Spitz group is the Karelian Bear Dog of Finland

KERRY BLUE TERRIER

County Kerry, in Ireland, lies at the south-eastern tip of the country, and is named after the wild and picturesque Kerry Mountains.

The Kerry Blue Terrier has been used for herding both sheep and cattle, for hunting vermin, as a watch-dog in homes and, more particularly, on pig-farms.

Although these dogs were entered in shows in the latter years of the 19th century, the breed was not officially introduced to London until 1922, the year that saw the foundation in England of the first Kerry Blue Terrier Club. The Irish Club was established soon after. The breed's attractive colour and wavy coat have earned it a good following. When Ireland became a Republic, the Kerry was adopted as the national dog and was renamed the 'Irish Blue'.

The attractive blue coat is a distinguishing feature of the modern Kerry Blue Terrier, which has changed considerably from the original type. The style of dressing has been very successful.

TODAY'S BREED

Official Classification KC (GB): Terrier Group; AKC: Terriers
Country of origin Ireland (Eire)
Height and weight 45-48 cm (18-19 in). Weight: 15-17 kg (24-28 lb)
Coat Distinctive, soft and silky, plentiful and wavy; colour: all shades of blue, sometimes with white points on the chest. The breed is black at birth, and does not acquire its blue colouring until the age of about 18 months. In puppies there are sometimes tan markings that subsequently disappear

General appearance A compact Terrier, powerful yet graceful, with an attractive coat
Head Long, quite narrow, skull flat; tip of nose black; scissor-type bite; palate and gums dark coloured
Ears Not docked, tending to be smallish, V-shaped, carried forward with the upper part hanging close to the head
Eyes Not large, quite dark in colour
Body Chest and ribs deep, ribs well sprung, belly tucked up
Legs Straight, strong bone structure, hind legs muscular, good stance; feet small and round, toenails black
Tail Docked to fourth or fifth joint, set high, carried erect
Gait Easy, hind-quarters free when moving; a good runner

Qualities The silky coat is an important feature and must be neither woolly nor wiry, but dense and wavy. Trimming (required in Great Britain and the United States, but not permitted in Ireland) must leave the body well covered with hair, apart from the ears, cheeks and head, where moustache and beard must remain. The tuft on the head hangs between the ears. The preferred colouring ranges from silvery to steely grey. Black on the muzzle, head, ears, tail and feet is permitted
Defects Height exceeding 48 cm (19 in); light-coloured eyes; black colouring in adults
Character Courageous, sometimes impetuous, but always in control, while remaining alert and determined

Uses Companion-dog, show-dog and guard-dog
Future prospects Like so many breeds for which periodic trimming is obligatory, this breed is not spreading fast; its attraction, like that of all blue dogs, lies in its coat

KOMONDOR
Hungarian Sheepdog

The Magyar **puszta** – the treeless, uninhabited steppes of Central Europe with their flocks of sheep roaming more or less wild, and their herds of cattle and horses – have produced various specific breeds of dogs. These include the Komondor (the largest of the Sheepdogs, spending its life out-of-doors, protected by its tasselled white coat from head to tail), the Pumi (whose name comes from Pomerania where the Pumi was crossbred with Pomeranian dogs), the Puli (medium-sized, with a coat like that of the Komondor, but dark in colour), and the Kuvasz (whose name, which comes from the Orient, means watch-dog; in fact, the Kuvasz is used for general farm duties rather than for sheep-herding). Recently a fifth breed has been internationally recognized, the Mudi. Late-19th-century cynologists also refer to the Lompos and the Jahasz. These have possibly died out; in any event, they are not known at the present time.

The most important breed is the Komondor, a very distinctive dog that has aroused the interest of many dog-fanciers outside Hungary.

TODAY'S BREED

Official classification KC (GB): Working Group; AKC: Working Dogs
Country of origin Hungary
Height and weight Males: 65-80 cm (26-32 in); females: 55-70 cm (22-28 in). Weight: 40-60 kg (90-132 lb)
Coat Distinctive: tasselled, corded and felty, long, woolly and dense, reaching a length of 27 cm (11 in) and more in some cases; colour: white

General appearance A large, powerful dog, enveloped by its thick coat
Head Broad, with the skull longer than the muzzle; tip of nose black; lips tight-fitting and black; scissor-type bite
Ears Hanging U-shaped; not docked
Eyes Dark in colour
Body Chest broad, ribs well sprung, belly tucked up
legs Strong and powerful; feet large
Tail Not docked, hanging, slightly curved at tip
Gait Very good at the trot

Qualities The main feature of this breed is the coat, with its dense, corded, and felty qualities; it must be capable of protecting the dog in the harshest of climates and the most violent of weather conditions
Defects Hair not long enough, tail too short, poor undercoat
Character Active, good-natured, friendly towards people known to its master, suspicious of strangers. Its facial expression is not visible

Uses Herding both sheep and livestock, watch-dog
Future prospects This is a rare breed that has been bred for a particular purpose and in a remote part of the world. Fairly limited popularity
Similar breeds Polski Owczarek Nizinny (Berger Polonais de Vallée) (herding), Poland: this Sheepdog is similar to the Komondor, but smaller in size. Owczarek Podhalanski (Polish Tatra Herding-dog), Poland: this Tatra herding-dog calls to mind the Maremma Sheepdog and the Pyrenean Mountain Dog, as well as the Hungarian Kuvasz. (Tatra is a region of the Carpathian Mountains.)

The Komondor, the breed illustrated on these two pages, is probably the best-known of the four major types of Hungarian herding dogs and has remained very little changed over many centuries.

LABRADOR RETRIEVER

One reliable theory maintains that this breed is descended from a small dog from the island of Newfoundland that was highly regarded as a retriever and particularly suited to hunting wild duck. It was known as the St John Water Dog. It was mainly black in colour and the size of a Pointer. In the 1930s the third Duke of Malmesbury brought some of these hounds to England and selected them, with a careful eye on retaining their typical features and character. He was also responsible for the name Labrador being given to the breed, which was recognized by the British Kennel Club in 1903.

For many years retrievers were given the task of bringing in game in forms of hunting dominated by Pointers and Setters, which were so skilful and so suited to their particular roles that they more or less turned up their noses at mere 'retrieving'.

At first the Labrador Retriever had a secondary place, but it earned itself a more important role when people began to realize that it was a highly efficient hunter when working on its own, as well as a shrewd and thorough seeker and retriever of game that had either been shot or lost.

More recently it has come into its own as a guard-dog and a police-dog, and is used in particular for detecting drugs concealed in luggage and parcels.

TODAY'S BREED

Official classification KC (GB): Gundog Group; AKC: Sporting Dogs
Country of origin Great Britain
Height 54-57 cm (21½-23 in)
Coat Hair short, close, not wavy, with good weather-proof qualities, and a very efficient undercoat; single colours: black, liver, yellow (ranging from cream to red), with no white areas except for a small white marking on the chest

General appearance A sturdy member of the Pointer group, solidly built, alert and active
Head Quite large, skull broad, muzzle stocky; tip of nose wide, matching the coat in colour; scissor-type bite
Ears Not docked, set quite well back, not too large, falling and lying close to the head
Eyes Average size, ranging from hazel to chestnut in colour
Body Sturdy, with wide ribs, deep and well sprung, belly not tucked up, back straight and solidly built
Legs Good stance, muscular, with round feet
Tail Not docked, distinctive, defined as 'otter-like', conspicuously round, covered with plenty of hair, but not fringed, carried gaily but not curved over the back
Gait Supple and free, good at both the trot and the gallop

Qualities Well developed nostrils, broad in the rib, solidly built, very active
Defects Poor undercoat, head with wrinkles, heavy ears
Character Well balanced, energetic, likes being put to work, a natural retriever, easy to train. Alert expression

Uses A versatile hunter, and guard-dog; used by police and drug squads
Future prospects Seems destined to be increasingly used by police forces and in the war against drug smuggling

The coat of the modern Labrador Retriever, a breed of exceptional qualities, is close and weather-proof, as in the black specimen (left) and black and cream (opposite, top) illustrated on these two pages. The forerunner (above) of the modern breed had a longer coat, similar to that of the Golden Retriever (opposite bottom).

Similar breeds Golden Retriever (Gun-dog), Great Britain: similar to the Labrador Retriever, its coat ranges in colour from cream to golden. The main breeder of the Golden Retriever, a century or so ago, was Lord Tweedmouth. Another type of English Retriever is known as the Curly-coated variety, with a black or liver coloured coat.

In the United States there are two Retrievers which deserve a mention: the Chesapeake Bay Retriever that originated on the coast of Maryland after a brig had been shipwrecked there: two Newfoundland pups were saved from the wreck and subsequently mated with Otterhounds; and the Flat-coated Retriever with black hair, slightly longer than that of the Labrador Retriever

LEONBERGER

This breed is named after the German town of Leonberg, in Swabia. It was selected in about 1870 by the Stadtrat Essig, a town-councillor who was so fond of his little town and its new citizen that, struck by the resemblance of its tawny colouring to that of a lion, he used the new breed heraldically on the municipal coat-of-arms. For many years specimens of the breed were not permitted to spread beyond Heidelberg and Apolda (the birthplace and home of the Dobermann in that same period of the 19th century). The newly arrived Leonberger aroused envy, backbiting and jealousy, especially when it began to be in demand abroad, even sought after by the royal family of Japan. The First World War could have signalled the end of the Leonberger, but its fortunes revived after the conflict, and the breed was improved. Where Councillor Essig came by his first specimens is not known, but he used as mates for them the Newfoundland of the Landseer variety (with a lot of white in its coat), the large Pyrenean Mountain Dog (which in those days often had large fawn markings) and, in particular, the St Bernard (which at that time did not have its present huge and rather round head).

A comparison of the photograph of Chipsy vom Theresienhof (below) a German and world champion aged three years, and the print above shows how the breed has changed little in the last century.

TODAY'S BREED

Official classification KC (GB) and AKC: not recognized
Country of origin Germany
Height and weight Males: 72-80 cm (29-32 in); females 65-75 cm (26-30 in), with preferred heights of 76 and 70 cm (30 and 28 in) respectively. Weight: about 50-60 kg (110-132 lb)
Coat Fairly long, quite coarse, loose, with an abundant mane round the neck and chest; colour: various shades of fawn, with a black mask

General appearance Sturdy and massive, powerful, with an air of grandeur
Head Well-proportioned to the body; tip of nose black; scissor-type bite
Ears Set high on the skull, drooping and flat
Eyes The colour depends on the coat, ranging from dark brown to hazel
Body Ribs deep to well below the elbow, belly deep
Legs Quite powerful and straight; feet round
Tail Thickly coated, curved in shape; it should never rise above the dorsal line; it is not docked
Gait Tends to trot briskly rather than gallop

Qualities Strength, height and elegance of posture. A particularly sought-after feature is the plentiful name and the long-haired tail
Defects Insufficient height, dewlaps, curly coat, tail curling over the back
Character Selected from the outset for its alert intelligence, its affectionate nature, and its fondness for children. It has a docile look

Uses Stern guard-dog; will carry good loads and can be trained for haulage purposes
Future prospects The limited number of Leonberger-fanciers and the competition from similar breeds (Newfoundland and St Bernard) will restrict its spread
Similar breeds Mastín de los Pirineos (Pyrenean Mastiff) (guard-dog and general-purpose working-dog), Spain: akin to the Leonberger in size, and in having a full coat; found in the areas around Léon and Navarre

LHASA APSO

The Lhasa Apso comes from Tibet where it is known as Abso Seng Kye, which translated means 'Bark Lion Sentinel Dog'. It was thought to bring good luck. They were first introduced into England by the Hon Mrs Bailey in 1928 and accepted in the American Kennel Club Stud Book in 1935.

TODAY'S BREED

Official classification KC (GB): Utility Group; AKC: Non-Sporting Dog
Country of origin Tibet
Height Ideal 25 cm (10 in)
Coat Top coat heavy, straight and hard, not woolly or silky, of good length. Dense undercoat. Colours golden, sandy, honey, dark grizzle, slate, smoke, parti-colour, black, white or brown

General appearance Should give the appearance of a well balanced, solid dog.
Head Heavy head furnishings with good fall over the eyes, good whiskers and beard. Skull moderately narrow falling away behind the eyes in a marked degree, not quite flat but not domed or apple shaped. Straight fore-face with medium stop. Nose black. Muzzle about 4 cm (1½ in) long but not square. Length from tip of nose to be roughly one-third the total length from nose to back of skull
Ears Pendant, heavily feathered. Dark tips an asset
Eyes Dark. Medium-sized eyes to be frontally placed, not large or full, or small and sunk. No white showing at base or top of eye
Body Length from point of shoulders to point of buttocks greater than height at withers. Level topline. Strong loin
Legs Fore-legs straight, heavily furnished with hair. Hind legs well developed with good muscle. Heavily furnished. Hocks when viewed from behind to be parallel and not too close together
Tail High set, carried well over back and not like a pot-hook. There is sometimes a kink at the end. Well feathered
Gait Free and jaunty in movement

Qualities Sturdiness and dense coat
Defects Any variation from the standard of points
Character Gay and assertive although can be rather wary of strangers

Uses Make excellent companion-dogs and good house-guards
Future prospects Increasing popularity

This gay and sturdy breed of Tibetan origin makes an attractive companion-dog.

LÖWCHEN

The Löwchen is often referred to as the Little Lion Dog because the body is clipped in the traditional lion clip and the tail, also clipped, is topped with a plume, thus giving the dog the appearance of a small lion. The Löwchen is a member of the Bichon family and has many of the distinctive features common to some of the French Toy breeds. Sufficient registrations were obtained in Britain in 1975 for the breed to qualify for Kennel Club Challenge Certificates in 1976.

TODAY'S BREED

Official classification KC (GB): Toy Group; AKC: not recognized
Country of origin France
Weight 3.5-4 kg (8-9 lb)
Coat Fairly long and wavy but not curly. Fine and silky. Clipped in the traditional lion clip. Any colour

General appearance A strongly-built, active, well balanced and alert little dog whose presentation gives the 'little lion' appearance
Head Short, fairly broad skull, flat between the ears, head carried proudly and high. Well defined stop. Short, strong muzzle
Ears Long and well fringed, set on level with the eye, close hanging
Eyes Round, large and intelligent; dark in colour
Body Short, strong, well proportioned. Level topline. Ribs well sprung. Strong loin with moderate tuck up
Legs Fore-legs straight and fine boned. Hind legs well muscled with good turn of stifle, straight when viewed from the rear
Tail Of medium length, clipped with a tuft of hair to resemble a plume. Carried gaily on the move
Gait Free, parallel movement fore and aft

Qualities Very intelligent little dog that makes an excellent companion
Defects Any departure from the standard points
Character Intelligent, lively and affectionate

Uses Companion-dog
Future prospects Popularity likely to grow

The Löwchen, or Little Lion Dog, is a boisterous and playful breed that has gained considerably in popularity in the last ten years.

MALTESE

Like its brother, the Bolognese, and its cousin, the Yorkshire Terrier, the Maltese is included in the Spitz group not so much because of its conspicuously 'Pomeranian' features, but more because of the problem of putting it with any other group. It cannot be included among any of the other five groups described in this book, so it has been included in the Spitz family, with which it has certain features in common.

Despite the name, the Maltese does not come from the island of Malta, nor has it ever been specifically bred there. The name is thought to come from the Latin word **melite** – referring to the island of Meleda in the Adriatic, close to the Dalmatian coast.

In the 19th century the Maltese was immortalized by painters and poets alike. This in effect was its 'golden age', and it was popular throughout Europe. In 1890 and thereabouts it was being successfully bred in England, France and Germany. In those days Maltese dogs of a larger than usual size were known as Chiens de la Havane. In this century the breed has regained a firm footing in Italy. The Electa kennels run by Nadya Colombo in Varese in the 1950s and the famous Gemma kennels in Genoa, run for the past thirty years by Bianca Tamagnone, have produced some thirty national and international champions. Bianca Tamagnone is the author of an important work about the Maltese breed.

The Maltese was the favourite of the great Italian financier, Riccardo Gualino, who wrote about this dog in glowing terms.

The beautiful white coat of the Maltese and the fact that it is so easily trained make it a delightful and distinctive dog for showing.

TODAY'S BREED

Official classification KC (GB): Toy Group; AKC: Toys
Country of origin Italy
Height and weight Males 21-25 cm (8½-10 in); Females: 20-23 cm (8-9 in). Weight: preferably 2-3 kg (4-6 lb)
Coat Hair dense, bright, with a good sheen, heavy, very long, silky, never curly, about 22 cm (9 in) in length; the coat, which must be pure white (pale ivory is also admissible), must reach the ground, with no clumps or tufts

General appearance Very elegant, conspicuous, an affectionate lap-dog
Head Sturdy, completely covered with long hair; tip of nose black (although there may be decoloration at certain times of the year); lips covered with long hair forming a moustache; scissor-type bite
Ears Not docked, lying close to the sides of the head, completely covered with long hair, dense to the top of the shoulder
Eyes Large, round, quite prominent, black rims round the eyelids, deep ochre-coloured iris
Body Long and narrow, ribcage reaching the elbow, trunk stocky, belly not very tucked up
Legs Quite short, covered with plenty of hair; feet roundish
Tail Not docked, carried over the back, with a large fringe
Gait A rolling type of trot

Qualities Heavy, plentiful coat, reaching the feet, pure white in colour
Defects Males measuring more than 26 cm (10½ in) and less than 19 cm (7½ in); females measuring more than 23 cm (9 in) and less than 18 cm (7 in); tip of nose not black; bluish eyes
Character Inquisitive, lively, keen, sometimes cheeky, has all the qualities designed to win the hearts of adults and children alike, of both sexes. Lively expression

Uses Lap-dog, and watch-dog
Future prospects Successfully bred in several different countries, it has quite a solid following
Similar breeds Tibetan Terrier (Companion-dog), Tibet(?): this dog is said to be the father of the various small Tibetan dogs (Shih Tzu, Lhasa Apso, Tibetan Spaniel) successfully bred in Great Britain

MANCHESTER TERRIER

This breed was originally known as the Black-and-Tan Terrier. It existed as far back as the end of the 18th century, and the creation of the breed is attributed to the breeder John Hulme who, together with other dog-fanciers, had a soft spot for a small dog that would be efficient at rabbit-hunting. This sport was particularly common around Manchester, and this was why the breed's name was eventually changed.

The custom of docking the ears came to an end when the Kennel Club laid down that specimens of any breed with this type of docking, born after 31 March 1895, would not be allowed to appear at dog-shows. The breed has declined in Great Britain also because of the very strict official standard, which lays down a rigid adherence to the form of the tan markings, and makes successful showing and breeding difficult.

There are very specific standards for the black-and-tan markings of the Manchester, which has made for difficulties in breeding this terrier of great charm.

TODAY'S BREED

Official classification KC (GB): Terrier Group; AKC: Teriers
Country of origin Great Britain
Weight Males: preferably 8 kg (18 lb); females: 7.7 kg (17½ lb)
Coat Close, smooth and glossy; the distribution of the colours is of great importance; these include dark tan (mahogany) and black (like brown coal), which must not overlap with one another but form clearly defined and distinct areas. There must be small tan markings above the eyes, on each cheek, and at each side of the chest above the front legs. The edges of the lips are also tan coloured, as is the inner part of the ears and the area beneath the tail

General appearance A fairly small dog, with quite well-balanced lines, and an attractive, glossy coat
Head Long, wedge-shaped, without the round shape peculiar to miniature dogs; muzzle fairly long; scissor-type bite
Ears Not docked, small, V-shaped, set high, hanging close to the eyes
Eyes Small and dark, oblong in shape, not prominent, not sunken, bright and sparkling
Body Brisket narrow and quite deep, flanks hollowed, belly tucked up
Legs Straight, with a good stance; foot small and somewhat oval-shaped
Tail Not docked, broad at the base and tapering to a tip, never carried over the back
Gait Supple and easy, lively and brisk, a good dog at the trot, and very good at the gallop

Qualities Close attention must be paid to the brightness of the tan colouring, and how it is distributed
Defects All signs of miniaturism (dwarfishness), such as a short muzzle, prominent eyes, poor stance of legs
Character Lively, keen, impetuous, but at the same time cautious; a fierce hunter. Bright expression

Uses Hunter of vermin, good as a small guard-dog
Future prospects An increasingly rare breed which has been outdone by other breeds competing for popularity (Pinschers and other Terriers)
Similar breeds The English Toy Terrier, known in America as the Manchester Terrier (Toy), is a miniature variety, perhaps with an admixture of Italian Greyhound blood

MAREMMA SHEEPDOG
Maremma-Abruzesse

This breed takes its name from the Maremma, the coastal lowland area of Tuscany and northern Latium (Lazio) that stretches from Pisa to Grosseto and on towards Rome. In ancient times there was already a similar white herding dog here. The Italian Kennel Club did not acknowledge its existence for about twenty years. The first record in the Italian Book of Origins at number 3172, is the bitch Maremma di San Clemente, born in October 1915 of non-registered parents. In Genoa, in 1922 there was a short-lived Italian Sheepdog Club. After the Second World War the British founded a Club for the promotion of the Maremma Sheepdog in London. In 1950, the National Association of Italian Cynophilia (ENCI), based in Milan, failed even to declare a champion for this breed, and that year a specimen imported from England won the prize at the Florence show. In 1951 Professor Giovanni Pischedda founded in Aquila the Circolo del cane da pastore abruzzese (Abruzzese Sheepdog Club), making a distinction between the Maremma and the Abruzzese on the basis of the latter's larger stature and longer, looser coat. But the ENCI opposed the idea and merged the two varieties into a single breed, known as the Maremma-Abruzzese. Sheepdog trials have never been encouraged, however, although they would have promoted the selection and spread of the breed

TODAY'S BREED

Official classification KC (GB): Working Group; AKC: not recognized
Country of origin Italy
Height and weight Males: 65-73 cm (26-29 in); females: 60-68 cm (24-27 in). Weight: males: 35-45 kg (77-100 lb); females 30-40 kg (67-90 lb)
Coat Quite long, full, close-lying, coarse, plentiful on the legs and tail; colour: white, a few ivory, lemon or pale orange markings are admissible

General appearance Good height and bulk, but not over-large, powerful
Head Conical, tip of nose black; lips smallish; scissor-type bite
Ears Relatively small, V-shaped, set high up, drooping
Eyes Almond shaped, colour ranging from dark brown to ochre
Body Ribs well sprung, belly well developed
Legs Powerful, muscular, straight; front feet rounded; hind feet slightly oval
Tail Abundant, curved at the tip, well-covered all over, not docked
Gait Loose, long, rapid trot

Qualities White coat is sought after, black mucous membranes, abundant hair, fine undercoat
Defects Pale yellow colour, many-coloured, brown marks, small stature, insufficiently powerful
Character Docile, balanced, generally quiet, reserved towards strangers, tireless worker. Alert expression

Uses Bred for herding sheep, it can also deal with cattle and horses. Guard-dog
Future prospects Its future is bound up with its selection as a Sheepdog. As a guard- and watch-dog it has rivals in other Sheepdogs (German, Belgian)
Similar breeds Tchouvatch (herding-dog), Czechoslovakia: like the Maremma Sheepdog, the Kuvasz and the Pyrenean Mountain Dog, it has been recognized as a breed since 1964

A fairly typical Maremma bitch and pup, bred in England. At a certain stage British-bred specimens were used to improve the breed in Italian kennels.

MASTIFF

Since the Middle Ages the terms Mastiff (English), **mâtin** (French and **mastino** (Italian) have been used to describe a large type of dog, but one that was certainly not a thoroughbred. Nevertheless, English dog experts are clear that some aristocratic families kept certain thoroughbred lines of Mastiffs for four centuries, and that the present-day Mastiff is derived from one such stock. At the battle of Agincourt, in 1415, it was a Mastiff that saved the life of the nobleman Piers Leigh, and it was his family that became guardians of the breed. In the 16th century, together with the Bulldog of the day, the Mastiff was used in contests with bulls, bears and even lions – such spectacles being very popular in those days. When laws were passed to ban such bloodthirsty events towards the end of the 19th century, the Mastiff breed, like the Bulldog, was threatened with extinction, had it not been for the efforts of certain Mastiff enthusiasts who set about the task of restoring the breed. The two world wars reduced the numbers of the Mastiff to a mere handful: 14 in 1945, and little more than 50 by 1950. The revival of the breed was helped by specimens being imported into Great Britain from the United States, where this breed has always been well tended.

In the early part of this century the St Bernard was used in breeding to increase the Mastiff's size. The formidable appearance hides a friendly temperament.

TODAY'S BREED

Official classification KC (GB): Working Group; AKC: Working Dogs
Country of origin Great Britain
Height and weight Males: 75-80 cm (30-32 in); females slightly smaller. Weight: 73-90 kg (160-220 lb)
Coat Short and close-lying; colour: from apricot to dark reddish-brown (tawny), also silver, or dark fawn-brindle, with a black mask on the muzzle and black around the ears

General appearance Large, massive and powerful; slow-moving
Head Skull large and wrinkled; muzzle quite short; tip of nose black; lips large; pincer-type bite, or slightly prognathous (lower incisors projecting beyond the upper)
Ears Small, thin, set well apart and on the highest part of the sides of the skull
Eyes Small, dark brown, showing no haw (white)
Body Powerful, ribcage arched and deep; flanks very deep
Legs Strong and straight, although in many cases the pastern is slightly bent rather than upright; feet round and broad, toes close together
Tail Large, hanging straight at rest, forming a curve when moving; tapering
Gait Slow but supple when at the trot

Qualities Good height, powerfulness, bulk, a dark mask, strong bone structure
Defects Insufficient height, making it more like a Bull Mastiff; feet open; gait clumsy
Character Calm, placid, well-balanced, but fearsome if roused. A gentle look about the eyes

Uses Watch-dog, whose size alone tends to discourage trespassers
Future prospects This rare and highly prized breed has few fanciers, and that situation seems sure to continue
Similar breeds Tosa (a fighting breed), Japan: used for fights (but not to the death) in Japanese villages, with clear-cut rules and regulations; very popular

Comparison of the modern British-bred specimen (opposite) and that depicted in a nineteenth-century print shows how little the Mastiff has changed. The puppy (left) is 65 days old.

MINIATURE PINSCHER
Zwergpinscher

The German Zwergpinscher or Miniature Pinscher is a close relative of the English Toy Black-and-Tan Terrier, and both breeds have often been interbred. The only real difference between the two is the fact that the German breed has docked ears and a docked tail, which is not the case with the British dog.

In the first half of the 20th century the Miniature Pinscher showed conspicuous features of dwarfishness: a round head, prominent eyes and a pointed muzzle, calling to mind the head of the Chihuahua. Between 1925 and 1935 the Von Glan and Von Kirchberg kennels carried out careful selection to get rid of any defects of this sort. The concern of German breeders has been, first and foremost, the breed's distinctive appearance, and then its small size. As a result a small and good-looking breed has come into being, and has found its way all over the world: it looks somewhat like a miniature Dobermann.

Tan (fawn) specimens have also been selected and bred. They are called Rehpinscher.

The Miniature Pinscher Club of America has been very active since 1950. The Zwergpinscher has become as widespread as the Toy Black-and-Tan Terrier in Great Britain in recent years.

TODAY'S BREED

Official classification KC (GB): Toy Group, AKC: Toys
Country of origin Germany
Height 25-30 cm (10-12 in)
Coat Hair short, dense, glossy and close-lying; colour: black and tan, tan all over, chocolate coloured with tan markings, grey-blue

General appearance A very small dog, but athletic nonetheless; no degenerative signs
Head Long, sturdy, conical muzzle, not pointed; tip of nose matches the colour of the coat; scissor-type bite
Ears Docked to a point, set high, erect and alert
Eyes Oval and dark
Body Brisket not broad, reaching to the knees; belly moderately tucked up
Legs Good straight stance, hind legs angled; cat-like feet
Tail Docked to the third joint, carried high
Gait Confident, slightly mincing, quick at the gallop

Qualities Small but well-balanced, athletic
Defects Any sign of dwarfishness; muzzle narrow and short; eyes prominent, poor tooth formation
Character Affectionate, gentle, a keen watch-dog, capable of deep attachment, an ideal indoor dog. Cheeky expression

Uses Companion-dog, watch-dog
Future prospects This breed is becoming increasingly popular among people with a special liking for miniature dogs

Thanks to the selection processes carried out by German breeders, the Miniature Pinscher is no longer a mere lap-dog of delicate appearance as it was in the nineteenth century (see the sketch above). It is now a powerful little dog capable of acting as a watch-dog in the home.

NEWFOUNDLAND

Named after the island of Newfoundland, off the eastern coast of North America. The island was discovered in 1497 by John Cabot, and was apparently uninhabited. The first description of the breed has come down to us from Bewick in 1789; he described it as a strong and keen swimmer and diver. It may well have originated from Arctic dogs of the Labrador region, crossed with dogs introduced in the 17th and 18th centuries by English and French fishermen. The Newfoundland had the good fortune to inspire various artists: among the poets, both Byron and Burns sang its praises; the painter Landseer, among others, portrayed it, and even has the black-and-white variety named after him. In the 19th century it was the favourite companion of the Swiss naturalist and dog-lover, Heim, who bred Newfoundlands. The breed earned great fame and respect for rescuing many people from water, and in the 19th century was used in the so-called 'River Brigades' which were set up in Paris by the Chief of Police, Lépine. A similar organization was established along the canals of Belgium and the Netherlands. The French Republic awarded a medal for peacetime valour to a Newfoundland that saved three people who were on the point of drowning at Cherbourg. In Great Britain hotels near rivers and lakes invariably had Newfoundland house-dogs for rescue purposes. The Newfoundland club was founded in England in 1886.

TODAY'S BREED

Official classification KC (GB): Working Group; AKC: Working Dogs
Country of origin Canada
Height and weight Males: 70 cm (28 in); females: 65 cm (26 in). Weight: 50-67 kg (110-150 lb)
Coat Long, flat, fairly coarse in texture, oily and capable of resisting water; colour: dull jet black with blue highlights; white and black, with tinges of bronze; other colours are also permitted

General appearance Powerful, sturdy, alert, supple movement
Head Large and heavy, broad; muzzle short and square, with conspicuous eye sockets; tip of nose black; scissor-type bite
Ears Small, set high up on the skull, lying close to and towards the back of the head, unfringed
Eyes Small, rather deeply set, dark brown in colour
Body Well ribbed up with broad back and muscular loins, belly not drawn in
Legs Strong, muscular and fringed; dew-claws should be removed; feet are sometimes webbed
Tail Of fair thickness, curved – never straight
Gait A typical swaying motion

Qualities Good, thick coat, with an oily texture to make it water-resistant; height is important
Defects Insufficient strength in the body, thin bone structure, tail curving up over back
Character Affable, alert, docile, dangerous if annoyed. An affectionate expression

Uses This is a water dog, used for life-saving, and invaluable to fishermen, sailors and life-guards. An impressive guard-dog, too
Future prospects Currently slightly in decline as a breed; its future relies on a limited but committed number of Newfoundland-fanciers and breeders
Similar breeds Landseer (guard-dog, general purpose), Northern countries: closely akin to the Newfoundland, except for the colour of the coat, which, instead of being black all over, is largely white

The Newfoundland, a large and powerful breed, has been used, among other things, to rescue people from water.

NORWICH TERRIER

The Norwich Terrier has been known for many years, and during the 19th century some of the sporting undergraduates at Cambridge owned these little dogs and used them for ratting or rabbiting. In 1932 they were recognized by the English Kennel Club and at that time they were permitted to have either drop ears or prick ears. In 1964 the Kennel Club agreed to make two separate breeds and the Norwich became the breed with the erect ears and the Norfolk with the drop ears. The Norwich Terrier was first taken to America in 1914 by Mr Strawbridge and the breed was recognized by the American Kennel Club in 1936.

TODAY'S BREED

Official classification KC (GB): Terrier Group; AKC: Terriers
Country of origin Great Britain
Height Ideal 25 cm (10 in)
Coat Hard, wiry and straight, lying close to the body with a thick undercoat. Longer and rougher on neck forming a ruff to frame the face. Hair on head and ears short and smooth, except for slight whiskers and eyebrows. Colour: all shades of red, wheaten, black and tan, or grizzle. White marks are undesirable

General appearance One of the smallest Terriers. Small, low, keen dog, compact and strong with good substance and bone
Head Muzzle wedge-shaped and strong. Length about one-third less than the measurement from the occiput to the bottom of the stop, which should be well defined. Skull wide, good width between the ears and slightly rounded
Ears Erect, set well apart on top of skull. medium-size with pointed tips. Held perfectly erect when aroused
Eyes Small and oval shaped, dark, full of expression, bright and keen
Body Short back, compact body with good depth. Rib cage should be long and well sprung with short loin. Level topline
Legs Short, powerful and straight with elbows close to body. Quarters broad, strong and muscular with well turned stifle
Tail Medium docked. Set on high to complete a perfectly level topline. Carried erect
Gait Free movement despite short legs

Qualities Tough little terrier and a demon for his size
Defects Untypical head, long in back, too big in size
Character Lovable disposition with a gay and fearless temperament. Never quarrelsome

Uses Companion-dog
Future prospects Popularity as a show-dog likely to continue
Similar breeds The Norfolk Terrier is like a drop-eared form of the Norwich. In America the two varieties belong to the same breed

In the United States drop-eared and prick-eared varieties are considered as one breed but in Britain only the prick-eared variety is classed as the Norwich Terrier, the drop-eared variety being known as the Norfolk Terrier.

OLD ENGLISH SHEEPDOG
Bobtail

This breed (known as the Bobtail on the Continent) is often born tail-less, as the nick-name implies, or else the tail is docked. An Old English Sheepdog appears in a portrait by Gainsborough (1717-1788).

According to the cynologist Watson, the breed dates back to 1800 when some British dog-fanciers crossed an Owtchar (a Russian Sheepdog from the Caucasus, with a long coat, akin to the Bobtail) with local herding-dogs. This mixture apparently gave rise to today's dog, although a contribution was made by the Mastiff, which increased the size.

A specimen was shown for the first time in 1865 and from that time this dog, with its unusual appearance, has enjoyed its own 'fan-club'. The breed's Club, founded in 1888, has as its aim the conservation of the qualities of not only the original type, but also of the breed as a whole, in its capacity as a working-dog.

The breed earned its high reputation in the early 20th century.

TODAY'S BREED

Official classification KC (GB): Working Group; AKC: Herding Dogs
Country of origin Great Britain
Height and weight Males: preferably more than 55 cm (22 in); females: slightly less. Weight: 28-35 kg (62-80 lb)
Coat Hair abundant, hard, not curly but wavy; undercoat water-resistant; colour: all shades of grey, blue, with or without white markings

General appearance Large, but more because of the effect of the coat than the actual body
Head Roundish in appearance, wide skull; tip of nose black; scissor-type bite
Ears Small, close-lying, quite hairy
Eyes Preferably dark, sometimes pale blue
Body Compact, ribs well developed, back strong, belly deep and capacious; rump higher than withers
Legs Powerful, muscular, hairy; feet round
Tail Absent or just a couple of centimetres (1 inch) or so in length when docked
Gait Distinctive, often ambling, loose at the run

Qualities Height, abundant coat, preferably with white well distributed among the grey. Long neck
Defects Too thin, poor coat, weak bone structure
Character Its main virtue is its patience, and tolerance with children. Bark is typically loud — often preferred for herding-dogs that have to control livestock. Although hidden by the coat, the expression is a gentle one

Uses Guard-dog (for farm animals), guide-dog and watch-dog
Future prospects The long coat that protects this dog from harsh weather conditions in the open makes it unsuitable for indoor or city life. It will remain quite rare as a breed
Similar breeds Otter Hound (hunting-dog), Great Britain: in size, coat and colour this breed resembles the Old English Sheepdog. However, as the name implies it was used for hunting otters

A nineteenth-century print shows that at one time the working Old English Sheepdog had a shorter coat than the modern show-dog (above). Reenwijk's Dew Fantasy (left), a world champion and Dutch champion at the age of three.

PAPILLON

French cynologist Pierre Mégnin sees this as a pure French thoroughbred dog. There is also an English theory that it is an Italian breed, which was presented as a gift by a certain Giovanni Filipponi of Bologna to Louis XIV, (1638-1715). The king was so delighted with it that he appointed a special 'valet de chambre des petits chiens'. Fifteen years later, Madame de Pompadour (1721-64) fell in love with this little dog, and had a portrait of herself painted with a Papillon. The same dog featured in the slightly melodramatic paintings of Jean-Baptiste Greuze (1725-1805). Before Greuze's time, this variety of Epagneul (Spaniel) had been immortalized by the Flemish artist Rubens (1577-1640).

The Belgian cynologist, Baron A. Houtart, claims in his excellent book **The Miniature European Spaniel** that the origins of the breed are to be found in Italy; from there, according to him, it made its way to France and Spain, and finally to Belgium, where, nevertheless, the Fédération Cynologique Internationale regarded it as French. To appease Italy, Spain, France and Belgium, Houtart coined the term 'Continental' for the breed. In the past there was a preference for it to have drooping ears (as in the 'Phalène'), whereas nowadays there is a preference for the variety with erect ears, known as the 'Papillon'.

TODAY'S BREED

Official classification KC (GB): Toy Group; AKC: Toys
Country of origin France
Height and weight Maximum 28 cm (11 in). There are different weight categories: (1) less than 2.5 kg (5.5 lb) (minimum 1.5 kg [3½ lb]); (2) 2.5-4.5 kg (5½-10 lb) for males and 5 kg (11 lb) for females
Coat Hair abundant, bright, shiny, wavy and not curled, with no undercoat, forming a collar down to the chest, fringes on the ears, and fore-quarters, and very plentiful fringes on the hind-quarters; tail covered with plenty of hair, up to 15 cm (6 in) in length; all colours permitted

General appearance A small lap-dog, pretty to look at, with distinctive markings on the head, which is shaped like a moth or butterfly
Head Distinctive, with short, pointed muzzle; tip of nose dark; teeth sometimes incomplete because of dwarfish tendency, and sometimes slightly prognathous
Ears Not docked, set well apart from each other. In the Phalène variety the ears are drooping, set high on the head with long hair that is wavy and attractive. In the Papillon variety the ears are erect, never parallel as in the Pomeranians, but forming an angle of 45°, with long hair in quite abundant fringes
Eyes Quite large, broad, almond-shaped, with the eyelids showing pigmentation, dark in colour
Body Slightly elongated in shape because of the hair; ribcage quite deep, back straight, belly moderately tucked up
Legs Good stance, fringed; feet oval
Tail Not docked, with a handsome plume, the tip sometimes carried over the back, but not curled over or actually resting on the back
Gait Proud, nimble and elegant

Qualities A plentiful coat, well balanced physique, lively appearance

Germissimo Fo Gerlil (left), a Belgian champion Papillon at the age of two. There are strong similarities between the English-bred specimen (opposite, top) and the animal depicted in the nineteenth-century print above. The Tibetan Spaniel (opposite, bottom) is a breed of great character and delightful temperament.

Defects Tongue visible, ears semi-erect, hair straight, with undercoat, dew-claws (these are best removed when the dog is young)
Character Active, affectionate, courageous, bright expression

Uses Lap- and watch-dog
Future prospects After moving from Belgium (where it was a national dog) to France (where the national companion-dog is the Poodle or Ceaniche), it seems to be going through a difficult patch
Similar breeds Tibetan Spaniel (Companion-dog), Tibet(?): the very 'oriental' head of this dog puts it in a class with the Chin-chin, the Mops and the Pekingese

PEKINGESE

This dog has been bred for centuries all over China, and specifically in the Imperial Palace. It was first brought to London by Lord John Hay and Lord Algernon, who had both had introductions to the Peking Court, hence the name Pekingese. It was a favourite of Queen Alexandra. In the latter years of the 19th century the Pekin Palace Dog Association was founded, and its energies were directed towards selecting and breeding smaller and smaller versions, which cost up to £1000 each. At the beginning of this century kennels run by Mrs. G. Kingscote of Headington were called the Pekin kennels, and they produced Pekin Ping, Pekin Prince and Pekin Peter. Before long the breed found its way to the Continent and in 1897 Henri de Bylandt christened it the Pekingese Spaniel or the Tientsin Spaniel.

For at least fifty years the Pekingese was one of the favourite Toy breeds, routing many that had been popular in earlier times. After the Second World War selection was no longer focussed only on the small size of the breed, but also on the many other qualities which it has always possessed, including its extraordinary character and charm.

TODAY'S BREED

Official classification KC (GB): Toy Group; AKC: Toys
Country of origin China
Weight 2-8 kg (4½-18 lb); even though it is short, this dog can weigh quite a lot
Coat Hair long, smooth, falling, never curly or wavy, with long fringes, plentiful on the thighs, legs, toes, with a luxuriant mane extending round the neck to beyond the shoulders; plenty of hair on the tail. All colours are permitted (combined or uniform); black rims round the eyes, resembling spectacles, are a sought-after feature, as is the mask

General appearance A rather grotesque-looking little dog because of its short legs, but it is nevertheless extremely dignified
Head Very large, broad and flat between the ears; nose very short, set very nearly right between the eyes; tip of nose broad and black; teeth and tongue not visible when the mouth is closed; muzzle broad; teeth often incomplete, prognathous, or with pincer-type bite
Ears Not docked, heart-shaped, never so long that they extend beyond the muzzle, falling and covered with very long fringes
Eyes Large, dark, protruding, the marked distance between the eyes produces the typical so-called 'oriental' look
Body Fairly short and compact, with a large chest which narrows towards the rear, bringing to mind the shape of a lion
Legs Legs short, the front legs turned outwards, the hind legs lighter and straighter; solid shoulders
Tail Not docked, conspicuous, set on high, slightly curved over the back, with a large fringe
Gait Sometimes described as resembling that of a 'sailor ashore'

Qualities The head, first of all, with the proper proportions between the skull and muzzle, followed by the coat, which must be abundant
Defects Spherical skull, long nose; tongue visible when the mouth is shut; thin coat
Character Proud, scornful of anything that does not directly involve it, only just condescends to acknowledge the existence of human beings in general, but is affectionate, even fawning, towards those near and dear: fears absolutely nothing. Bright expression

Uses A gracious companion-dog
Future prospects Its large following means that it will become even more popular in the years to come

Similar breeds There are two types of small English drawing-room Spaniel: the King Charles and the Cavalier King Charles. The Japanese Chin is of somewhat similar style but is higher on the leg

The two Pekingese champions illustrated on these two pages are fine specimens of a breed that has been consistently popular among the Toys.

PHARAOH HOUND

A number of prick-eared hounds found in the Mediterranean region, including the Pharaoh Hound, the Ibizan Hound and the Sicilian Hound, are strikingly similar to the hunting dogs depicted so vividly in the art of Ancient Egypt. It seems highly probable that, more than many other breeds for which extravagant claims of antiquity are made, the Pharaoh Hound and its allies are genuinely very old breeds. They are 'sight' hounds but, unlike the Greyhound, have a good sense of smell.

Despite the antiquity of the breed, its popularity is a very recent development. It is only since the 1970s that the Pharaoh Hound has been widely shown and recognized as a dog of striking appearance and attractive temperament (it was not until 1975 that the breed was granted championship status by the Kennel Club in Great Britain).

The Pharaoh Hound's rise in popularity is very recent but this and related breeds in the Mediterranean area have a long history.

TODAY'S BREED

Official classification KC (GB): Hound; AKC: not recognized
Country of origin Different origins
Height Males: 46-63 cm (22-25 in); females: 53-61 cm (21-24 in)
Coat The hair is short and glossy, fine and close to slightly harsh with no feathering, and tan or rich tan in colouring. The following white markings are allowed: white tip on tail (highly desirable), white on chest ('The Star'), white on toes. A slim white blaze on the centre line of the face is also permissible but fleck or white other than as described is undesirable

General appearance A graceful yet powerful hound of medium size
Head The long well-chiselled head, which is a blunt wedge shape with only a slight stop, is carried proudly on a long muscular and slightly arched neck. The powerful jaws have a scissor bite
Ears Medium high set, fine and large, broad at the base, very mobile and carried erect when alert
Eyes The oval, moderately deep set and intelligent eyes are amber coloured, blending with the coat
Body Lithe with almost straight topline, with a slight slope down from croup to the root of the tail. The ribs are well sprung
Legs The forelegs straight and parallel with strong pasterns; the hindquarters strong and muscular, limbs parallel when viewed from behind
Tail Medium set and tapering, carried high and curved when the dog is in action
Gait Free and flowing movement that is apparently effortless

Qualities Streamlined muscular build, remarkable elasticity of movement
Faults Any departure from the standard points, including variation from the colour standard
Character An intelligent, friendly and affectionate breed that is playful and alert

Uses Formerly for hunting, now largely a companion dog
Future prospects The recent dramatic increase in its popularity is likely to level off but its qualities will ensure that it retains a keen following
Similar breeds Other Mediterranean prick-eared hounds are the Ibizan Hound (Podengo) and the Sicilian Hound (Cirneco dell'Etna)

PINSCHER

The true Pinscher is halfway between the large Dobermann-Pinscher and the tiny Zwergpinscher or Miniature Pinscher. Schnauzers are Pinschers with a wiry coat as opposed to a smooth coat. There is a similarity between the Toy Manchester Terrier and the Miniature Pinscher. At first (like the Manchester Terrier in Great Britain) the Pinscher was selected and bred in Germany to hunt vermin.

Towards the end of the 19th century it was known as the Deutsche Kurzhaarige Pinscher while the Shnauzer was called the Deutsche Rauhhaarige Pinscher. In 1897 there was a Pinscher Club with its headquarters in Erfurt, and a Württemberger Schnauzer Club with its headquarters in Stuttgart. The official 'portrait-painter' of the breed in those days was the German artist, J. Bungartz, who drew the ideal models of the breed. In recent decades the prospects for the Pinscher have been on the decline: in fact, nowadays, it is rare outside certain parts of Germany.

The worldwide reputation of the Dobermann has hampered the spread outside Germany of the Pinscher proper, although this latter might well be a better and no less energetic guard-dog for city apartments, country homes and cars.

TODAY'S BREED

Official classification KC (GB) and AKC; not recognized
Country of origin Germany
Height 43-48 cm (17½-19 in)
Coat Hair short, smooth, glossy; colour: black and tan, or fawn
General appearance A medium-sized to small dog, compact yet elegant, well built and lively
Head Long, wedge-shaped, without wrinkles, muzzle shaped like a truncated cone; lips tight; pincer-type bite
Ears Docked to a tip, set high, alert
Eyes Oval-shaped and dark
Body Brisket narrow, just the right depth, flanks slightly concave, belly quite well tucked up
Legs Good straight stance, with small, compact feet
Gait Very easy, good at the trot, very good at the gallop

Qualities Its physical features are like those of the Dobermann, on a small scale. An important feature is the solid neck, clearly defined, with its elegant, arched shape
Defects Too thin, brisket not sufficiently deep, poorly defined colouring
Character Liveliness, vitality, alertness, capable of being aggressive. Keen expression

Uses Companion-dog, good guard-dog for cars and homes
Future prospects Halfway between the large Dobermann and the Miniature Pinscher, as it is, its future looks a little bleak
Similar breeds Harlekinpinscher (Harlequin Pinscher) (companion- and guard-dog), Germany: this belongs to the group of dogs with a white coat and black markings (Harlequin Great Dane, Dalmatian) that are much sought after by many dog-fanciers; the Harlequin Pinscher is not common outside Germany. Österreichischer Kurzhaariger Pinscher (Austrian Short-haired Pinscher) (companion- and guard-dog), Austria: this breed has only recently appeared at dog-shows; some regard it as more of a Terrier than a Pinscher

POINTER

Wherever this breed's origins may lie, the increase and standing of the Pointer are due to those British hunters who started to select it early in the 19th century. In 1899 the Pointer Club was founded. The first Pointer breeders were almost invariably game-keepers, and among those who should be mentioned are James Graham, Thomas Gaunt (who greatly improved the black Pointers of Scotland) and John Simpson.

The official historian of the breed is William Arkwright, author of **The Pointer and its Predecessors**. There are also important studies of the Pointer by the veterinary surgeon G. Solaro, of Turin.

At the beginning of this century the breed started to be exported from England. With its exceptional speed in the hunt, it managed to revolutionize first the hunting practices of Frenchmen, then of Italians, and ended by influencing hunting throughout Europe. Pointers also won the hearts of the aristocracy of the day. The Conte de Beauffort of Brussels was the proud owner of Champion Wagg; the Prince of Braunfels owned Luck of Hessen; and the King of Italy, owned Grace of Strasbourg.

In this century the Pointer is one of the favourite dogs of hunters the world over.

TODAY'S BREED

Official classification KC (GB): Gundog Group; AKC: Sporting Dogs
Country of origin Great Britain
Height and weight 61-69 cm (24-27 in) UK; 53-63 cm (21-25 in) USA. Weight: 20-35 kg (45-77 lb) USA
Coat Hair, close-lying, smooth with a decided sheen. Colours: white, black, black and tan, orange, fawn, red, shades of red with or without some white

General appearance An elegant member of the Pointer family, with a well-balanced body, a distinctive head, and slender, powerful lines
Head Muzzle fairly concave, square, with tip of nose raised; lips soft and well developed; scissor-type bite
Ears Not docked, set quite well up and close to the head, average length
Eyes A slight depression beneath them; from hazel to brown in colour
Body Chest broad, brisket descending to the elbow and sometimes further; back muscular, belly lean
Legs Perfect stance, thighs with prominent muscles; feet oval
Tail Not docked, broad at the base, tapering fine at the tip
Gait Tireless at the gallop, with a steady gait, swift, brisk and light

Qualities Highly prized for its lightning speed when pointing, tracking in bursts, with the fine scent of a swift hound
Defects Not tall enough, or too tall, tendency to work at the trot, dew-claws, non-admitted colouring (brindle, slate-grey, lead-coloured), bluish eyes
Character Alert, expressive, neither arrogant nor insolent, an extremely keen hunter, also a good retriever if properly trained. Hard, keen expression

Uses The archetypal pointer
Future prospects The breed has a worldwide following of friends and admirers who invest a great deal of effort in ensuring that it will continue to spread
Similar breeds Braccopointer (Gun-dog, pointer), Italy: this breed has a good reputation in Italy among hunters; it is not a pure breed but a cross between the two breeds; some subjects have performed well in field trials

A print of 1890 (opposite, top) shows that by the end of the ninteenth century the Pointer was much as it is in conformation and manner of working to the specimens illustrated on this page. A breeding pair (opposite, bottom) seen at one of the great British shows, the Windsor Dog Show.

POMERANIAN

Pomerania is a huge region in central-northern Europe, with a colourful history. After the Second World War it was largely part of Poland, with a small area included in East Germany. The climate in this area is a harsh one; for centuries the mainstay of the region's economy has been farming geese and sheep. This led in turn to the selection and breeding of long-haired dogs, used as guard- and watch-dogs. It seems to have been the birthplace of this small dog, probably known as the Pomeranian right from the start.

In Great Britain it is regarded as a national breed. It was officially recognized by the Kennel Club in 1871, more than a century ago. Twenty years later the Pomeranian Club was founded. This gave rise to a considerable increase in selection and breeding, with a special emphasis on handsome colours and the Miniature or Toy form. One of the results was the splendid orange colour, which began with Champion Prince of Orange and Champion Ruffle. Another fine champion, in 1895, was Prince Ginger. The finest sandy-coated dog in those days was Champion Sable Mite and the best blue dog was Champion Dragon Fly.

TODAY'S BREED

Official classification KC (GB): Toy Group; AKC: Toys
Country of origin Great Britain
Height and weight Approx. 15-20 cm (6-8 in). Weight: approx. 1.5-3 kg (3½-7 lb)
Coat Hair straight and loose, with no waves, curls or tufts, longer beneath the neck and on the thighs, with fringes on the legs; colours: sandy (originating from black-brown), dark chestnut, orange, white, black (a diluted version of the black coat produces blue; sandy and blue gives orange; orange and blue gives blue). English breeders concentrate a great deal on the colours

General appearance A small Toy dog with a magnificent coat and very dainty movements
Head Skull rounded, muzzle small; lips thin and tight; nose matches the colour of the coat; teeth incomplete because of dwarfishness
Ears Not docked, erect, small and mobile
Eyes Large, round and dark
Body Compact
Legs Normal
Tail Not docked, carried over the back with a large plume
Gait Skipping, dainty, distinctive, attractive

Qualities Sandy, dark chestnut and orange colourings are all sought after; abundant coat, and good stance
Defects Degenerative signs of dwarfishness, drooping tongue
Character Lively, dignified, self-satisfied. Keen expression

Uses Small lap-dog and watch-dog
Future prospects Successfully bred and widespread in Great Britain and the United States, it would seem to be set for a promising future
Similar breeds Small members of the Spitz group include the German Spitz, the Japanese Spitz and the Volpino of Italy

The Pomeranian as it looked in 1870 (above), and how it looks today (left). This dog can boast of having been the first astronaut in space: the bitch Laika, who was sent into space in 1957 was a Pomeranian. The Italian Volpino (opposite) is another small member of the Spitz group.

POODLE

Caniche to the French, Pudel to the Germans, and Poodle to the English: this breed derives from the 'Barbet', a 19th-century hunting-dog, used in water, in France.

The word 'caniche' is derived from the French word 'canard', meaning duck; in German, 'pudeln' means to swim like a dog (i.e. paddle), and the Old English word 'puddle' means to splash about.

In the 18th century the Poodle left marshes and swamps behind it and made its way into fashionable salons and, in its much smaller version, even into the royal palace of Louis XVI. Fashionable once more in the Second Empire, it began to be trimmed to look like a lion-cub, and bedecked with ribbons and bows.

The breed fell on relatively hard times in the early part of this century, then re-emerged in some style, in three different sizes with varying shades of coat colour, in about 1950, clipped and trimmed once again, but this time in a German style.

There was then a bitter cynological struggle between France and Germany to establish which of the two was the birthplace of the breed. Italy also became involved in the controversy, calling black and tan, or fawn Piedmont.

TODAY'S BREED

Official classification KC (GB): all varieties, Utility Group; AKC: Standard and Miniature, Non-Sporting Dogs; Toy, Toys
Country of origin France
Height (Three sizes): Standard: 38 cm (15 in) and above: UK and USA; Miniature: 25-38 cm (10-15 in) USA; 27.5-38 cm (11-15 in) UK; Toy: 25 cm (10 in) or under USA; 27.5 cm (11 in) or under UK
Coat Hair curly (there is a Straight-haired variety), plentiful, thick, woolly, of even length (the Poodle is best with the so-called lion, or the modern clip, also known as the 'karakul'); colours: black, white, cream, brown, silver, blue and apricot

General appearance An elegant companion-dog, with a well-balanced physical build, very active
Head Well proportioned to the body, muzzle not pointed; tip of nose black with coats that are white, silver, black, blue; brown with brown coats; with an apricot coat it matches the colour of the coat; lips of average size; scissor-type bite
Ears Not docked, long, falling onto the cheeks, set low on the head, with round tips
Eyes Depending on the coat, the colour ranges from dark amber to black; slightly slanting
Body Ribcage good and deep, as far as the elbow; back straight; belly slightly tucked up
Legs Good stance, thighs muscular; feet small and oval
Tail Docked to one-third, set high, raised at an angle when moving; (it may be undocked in straight-haired variety)
Gait Skipping, or dainty and light

Qualities An important feature is a good balance between the various parts of the body, plus the distinctive hair, and the typical gait; the proud, lively appearance is also important
Defects Dull or soft hair; white on the feet (some white hair on the chest is admissible); eyes with reddish highlights; prognathous teeth, or the reverse; long or ambling gait and stride
Character The Poodle has an exceptional capacity for learning, and is very easy to train; an alert, keen and active dog. Keen expression

Uses Companion-dog, sometimes used for finding truffles
Future prospects This breed has suffered considerably from the ups and downs of fashion; after the Second World War the

large demand for it hampered careful selection as far as its character was concerned, and as a result its traditional characteristics were not always in evidence. This might possibly affect the way the breed spreads in years to come **Similar breeds** Portuguese Water Dog (used for fishing); this dog is similar to the old French Barbet, and has long been the helper of Portuguese fishermen, retrieving things that have fallen into the water, taking mooring-lines ashore and guarding boats. It is similar to the Poodle, and is often given the 'lion clip'. It has recently been recognized in America

Flower Flit ans der Spielzengschatel (top, left) is a particularly fine example of an apricot-coloured Poodle. The 'lion-clip' (top, right) and the 'karakul clip' (left) are two recognized ways of trimming and presenting Poodles. A good specimen of the Toy Poodle (opposite) shows the very fine coat that is an attractive feature of this breed.

PUG

Known at one time as the Dutch Pug or Dutch Dog, it was taken for granted that it was of Dutch origin. It does indeed seem likely that it was brought to Europe, and to Holland in particular, by Dutch sailors and merchants returning from the Orient, specifically from China. It became popular in Paris where it was known as the Carlin; it was then adopted by the English and called the Pug, which means imp, or little devil, as well as 'snub-nose', although some maintain that the term derives from the Latin word **pugnus**, meaning a fist, because of the facial resemblance to the human clenched fist. The Germans called it Mops which means grumbler or moaner.

The first specimens in Europe had a silver coat with a black mask and black stripes on the back: the fawn colouring eventually developed from this combination. Black specimens (bred in London by Miss M.D. Robinson as early as 1895) all owe their existence to an English traveller by the name of Lady Brassey, who brought a black Pug back with her from China.

TODAY'S BREED

Official classification KC (GB): Toy Group; AKC: Toys
Country of origin Great Britain
Weight: 6-8 kg approx. (13½-18 lb approx.)
Coat Close-lying, soft and fine; colour: silver, apricot, pale fawn (dun), black; mask extending to the muzzle from the forehead and ears; sometimes a black line from the back of the head to the croup

General appearance A small dog, at once powerful and compact
Head Striking, round but never 'apple'-shaped, muzzle squared and short, large deep wrinkles; tip of nose black; lips well defined; teeth slightly prognathous
Ears Not docked, thin, small, drooping or 'rose ear' type
Eyes Very large, round, lustrous, very dark
Body Fore-quarters strong, well ribbed; belly well developed
Legs Short, strong, good straight stance
Tail Not docked, curled over the back as tightly as possible, preferably with a double curl
Gait Easy and supple

Qualities Small in size, very compact
Defects Absence of mask, tail not carried properly, few wrinkles, small eyes
Character Calm, obedient, affectionate. A bright expression

Uses A typical pet, often preferred by women and children; a good watch-dog in the home
Future prospects This breed will only ever have a small and specialized following

During the belle époque in France, the Pug was very popular among the ladies of Europe. It was also known by the German name Mops. After half a century of dwindling fortunes, it returned to favour in the 1970s. A print (above) dated 1895 and a present-day specimen (left) bred in Britain.

PYRENEAN MOUNTAIN DOG
Great Pyrenees

This is a typical mountain dog (similar to the St Bernard or the Maremma-Abruzzese Sheepdog), which has adapted to the high upland plateaux of the Pyrenees, where it has reproduced as a thoroughbred for centuries.

The Court of Louis XIV in Versailles (where numerous breeds of dogs were kept, from large Deer-hounds to small lap-dogs, called this dog the 'seigneur de la fourrure blanche' (literally, the white-furred lord).

With the end of the monarchy, this breed found an admirer in General Lafayette who, during his American exploits, introduced it to the New World. In 1824 he gave a pair to a friend in the United States, when the breed was still something of a rarity.

It was introduced into England in the early 20th century, after very careful selection processes that produced the very best specimens of all. Lady Sybil Grant became the great promoter of this breed in 1911.

It is particularly common in the Andorran region, and is often confused with the Spanish Mastín de los Pirineos (Pyrenean Mastiff).

TODAY'S BREED

Official classification KC (GB): Working Group; AKC: Working Dogs
Country of origin France
Height and weight Males: 70-80 cm (28-32 in); females: 65-72 cm (26-29 in). Weight: 44-55 kg (100-125 lb)
Coat Profuse, long and soft with a slightly wavy mane round the neck and fringes on the legs; colouring: white, sometimes with yellow or grey patches on the body and more often on the head and rump

General appearance A congenial giant of a dog, attractive to look at and well balanced
Head Not massive or heavy, skull convex; muzzle broad and long; tip of the nose black; lips close fitting, drawn back; scissor-type bite, sometimes pincer-type; not much dewlap
Ears Small, high, lying flat as a rule
Eyes Small and amber-coloured
Body Ribcage extending well to the rear, and deep
Legs Strong, straight, with dew-claws
Tail Long, thick coating, with a slight curl at the tip. When the dog moves the tail rises high above the back
Gait Unhurried, supple, with a long stride

Qualities Strength and good lines, ease of movement, tip of nose and lips black
Defects Insufficient height and size, thin coat, head too heavy (this comes from the St Bernard's influence)
Character A gentle giant, affectionate, with a gentle expression

Uses Suitable for herding cattle rather than sheep, since it is too heavy for running over long distances. A good guard-dog
Future prospects Because of its size this breed is totally unsuited to urban life: it will therefore only ever have a few fanciers
Similar breeds Mastín español (Spanish Mastiff) (guard-dog and general purpose working-dog), Spain: a sturdy country Mastiff popular with herdsmen and farmers in general. Another guard-dog of the mastiff-type is the Anatolian (Karabash) Dog, which is recognized in Britain

Top: two ideal specimens of the breed (above) and a specimen bred in Great Britain, where the Pyrenean Mountain Dog has been the object of careful selection for some fifty years.

PYRENEAN SHEEPDOG
Berger des Pyrénées

A print from the first French dog-show in 1863 shows the eighteen best entries. The first prize, worth 500 francs (offered by His Highness the Imperial Prince)m was shared by a **Grand-Danois** (Great Dane) and a Sheepdog (**Chienne de Berger**) named Charmante; the latter was a fairly typical Pyrenean Sheepdog (Berger des Pyrénées). This breed did not appear again at the Paris dog-show until 1910. It aroused a certain interest during the First World War, as a result of the activities of the Service des Chiens de Guerre, which was keen to find courier dogs and dogs for sentry duty. The Club was founded in about 1920, and the official standard was approved in 1921. The Société Centrale Canine recognized the breed in 1936.

This small Pyrenean dog is still to be found in the region lying between Gavarnie and Lourdes, with the varieties differing from valley to valley. In Azun it is black; in Bagnères its coat is more abundant; in St Béat it resembles a small Old English Sheepdog.

The Pyrenean Sheepdog is a small, cocky, lively and intuitive dog, suspicious of strangers, and inseparable from its master. Present-day breeders have maintained the breed's qualities of temperament that make it such an affable companion-dog.

TODAY'S BREED

Official classification KC (GB) and AKC: not recognized
Country of origin France
Height 38-50 cm (15-20 in)
Coat Medium length hair, bristly, slightly shaggy, dense, woolly and slightly wavy, halfway between that of the goat and the sheep, thicker on the croup and the thighs. Although long on the muzzle, the hair goes back from the face and leaves the eyes uncovered; colour: fawn or tan, grey, with black markings. Sometimes harlequin, black

General appearance A small, nimble dog, quite powerful for its size
Head Skull almost flat, roundish at the sides, muzzle conical and short; tip of nose black; scissor-type bite
Ears Usually docked short, sometimes left undocked, in which case they should not be erect
Eyes Small, dark, black-ringed; sometimes bluish with a pale grey or harlequin coat
Body Brisket barely reaching the knees, back slightly arched, belly not very tucked up
Legs Fore-quarters have a good straight stance and are fringed; hind legs often have double dew-claws; feet oval
Tail Not docked, and not long – in fact, sometimes quite short, with a good covering of hair; ending in a hook
Gait Easy, brisk, good at the trot and the run

Qualities Must be small in size, nimble, light, very alert, covered with hair for good protection, with a very expressive head
Defects Ears erect (sign of crossbreeding), hair not dense, hair on the muzzle hiding the eyes, awkward gait
Character Astute, attentive, alert, suspicious, devoted to its master, good memory, capable of unselfish acts, respectful of poultry, good with horses, very easy to train. Somewhat like a small bear. Sharp expression

Uses Herding sheep and cattle, general working-dog
Future prospects Where it is known, its following is on the increase
Similar breeds Perro de Pastor Catalán (Catalan Sheepdog or Gos d'Atura), (herding), Spain: akin to the Pyrenean Sheepdog, but often taller. Cão de Serra da Estrela (Estrela Mountain Dog) (guard-dog), Portugal: a large Iberian wolf-like dog, but little known outside its own native territory

ROTTWEILER

Rottweil is a small town in western Germany. It has an ancient history (the Romans called it Arae flaviae), and has been famous since the 16th century for an explosives factory, which is still working, and for a Cistercian monastery. The breed is named after the town.

In the region around the Jura (both Franco-Swiss and German) several breeds of dog have been selected which have in common a black or dark coat with tawny markings and their qualities as guard-dogs: Rottweiler, Dobermann, Beauceron, Sennenhund (Swiss Bouvier), German Pinscher and Hovawart. It is almost possible to say that these are all varieties of one and the same breed, altered by different selection processes, based on geographical distribution. In the 19th century the Rottweiler was a powerful Mastiff, popular with butchers and cowherds. It was a common sight at the large livestock market in the town.

However, by the early 20th century it had become a rarity: it is only recently that it has been selected with great care, and has earned an important place in German cynology. It is well represented in the United States.

TODAY'S BREED

Official classification KC (GB): Working Group; AKC: Working Dogs
Country of origin Germany
Height and weight Males: 60-68 cm (24-27 in); females: 55-63 cm (22-26 in). Weight 40-50 kg (90-110 lb)
Coat Short-haired, close-lying, compact with undercoat; colour: dark with tawny markings

General appearance Powerful, sturdy, noble and well proportioned
Head Large, skull broad, muzzle strong; tip of nose black; scissor-type bite
Ears Not docked, set high up, triangular, drooping
Eyes Almond-shaped, dark brown
Body Ribs deep, belly well developed
Legs Strong, muscular, hind legs slightly bent; feet round
Tail Docked short
Gait Supple, lively at the trot, a good runner

Qualities Strong and powerful, but not overmuch, very well proportioned
Defects Too slender, lack of proportion between fore- and hind-quarters
Character Balanced, spirited, alert. A calm expression

Uses Guard-dog, police duties, tracking
Future prospects Although in competition with other dark-tawny breeds of the Mastiff type, it has its own special place as a smaller Mastiff, which seems to offer some hope that the breed will spread
Similar breeds Hovawart (guard and general duties), Germany: dark with tawny markings, similar to a long-haired Rottweiler; beginning to become known outside Germany

The Rottweiler is an intelligent breed and of a really solid build that inspires a degree of caution in those who do not know it. It has a growing reputation in America and in Europe as an excellent guard-dog.

ST BERNARD

This dog has a colourful history, often bordering on the legendary. It was possibly being reared as long ago as the 12th century, at the Hospice of St Bernard, where it was kept by the monks belonging to the hospitaller community of Great St Bernard. The hospice is situated on the well-known mountain pass in the western Alps, just to the east of the Mont Blanc massif, at an altitude of 2467 m (7895 ft). The border running between Italy and Switzerland puts the hospice actually in Swiss territory, which is why the breed is regarded as Swiss. The community is also Swiss. For centuries the hospice has run a kennel, next door to the library and the museum of Roman relics found nearby. The passes in this part of the Alps were used by Hannibal, the Gauls, the Romans and the Saracens; they were crossed by Pope Stephen II, Pope Leo IX and by Napoleon with his armies. So much human – and military – traffic, in which the dogs always played a part, made it difficult to keep the breed pure, and this situation was complicated still further by the fact that in the 19th century the hospice also became a hostelry.

The best selection procedures have been practised by Swiss breeders, concentrating on a type that differs from the dogs kept at the hospice. In the 19th century, the English tried to boost their own particularly heavy type.

TODAY'S BREED

Official classification KC (GB): Working Group; AKC: Working Dogs
Country of origin Switzerland
Height and weight There is no maximum height: the absolute minimum is 70 cm (28 in) for males, and 65 cm (26 in) for females. Weight: 65-80 kg (145-175 lb)
Coat In Rough-coated specimens hair should be dense and flat, rather fuller round the neck, thighs well feathered. In Smooth-coated specimens hair should be close and like that of a Hound, slightly feathered on the thighs and tail

General appearance The largest of the large dogs, impressive, powerful and massive
Head Large and massive, with a broad and slightly convex skull; tip of the nose large and black; pincer-type bite; dewlaps
Ears Quite high on the skull, drooping without feathering
Eyes Quite small, dark brown
Body Ribs deep, roundish, belly quite high
Legs Powerful bone structure and musculature. Dew-claws not desirable. Feet quite closed
Tail Heavy, long with a large tip; should not be curled over the back
Gait Heavy but not clumsy; tends to trot

Qualities The lines and bulk of a very large dog, vigorous and supple in its movements. Handsome mask desirable
Defects Curly, crimped or tangled coat; coat of just one colour or with no white included; light head
Character Solemn and out-going, sometimes stubborn. Has a good-natured expression

Uses Because it is too heavy it is no longer used for rescuing avalanche victims. A reliable guard-dog
Future prospects Only of interest to confirmed and enthusiastic St Bernard-fanciers
Similar breeds Rafeiro do Alentejo (guard-dog and general purpose working-dog), Portugal: similar to the St Bernard, but short-haired; used for herding cattle or other livestock

Barry (above), who belonged to the Hospice of St Bernard and is one of the most famous of the breed, and a close-up (left) of a modern St Bernard. The breed is now rarely seen as the bringer of help in the mountains (below) and more often as a fine but not common show-dog (above).

SALUKI
Gazelle Hound

The poets of Persia have described the Saluki as being 'as old as time and as swift as a split second'.

The breed has been bred and thoroughbred for centuries. Persian custom did not permit the Saluki to be sold, but only presented or donated on grand occasions, or, at the most, exchanged for other valuable items. The birth of a Saluki puppy was regarded as a joyous family event.

The first Salukis arrived in Europe at the time of the Crusades.

At the end of the 19th century Count von der Schulenberg devoted himself to the breed. He was attached to the German Embassy in Teheran, where the most handsome of all dogs, called Mesjed, belonging to the Persian dog-fancier, J. Isfahan, reigned supreme at the time.

In 1895 the **Jardin d'acclimatation** in Paris imported a pair called Kuva and Grumisch.

The first English Club was founded in 1912, and the breed was officially recognized by the British Kennel Club in 1922. In 1980 there were 10 Saluki breeding kennels in operation in Great Britain.

TODAY'S BREED

Official classification KC (GB): Hound Group; AKC: Hounds
Country of origin Iran
Height 58-71 cm (23-28½ in)
Coat Hair smooth, close-lying, soft, with long hair on the ears that is silky and sometimes a little wavy; legs are fringed, as is the tail; there is one variety in which the coat is close-lying all over; colour: all colours

General appearance A graceful and nimble member of the Greyhound group
Head Long, narrow, lean; tip of nose black or brown; scissor-type bite
Ears Not docked, large, set high on the head, falling close to the skull, with long silky hair
Eyes Oval, with black rims, quite large, brown, not prominent
Body Brisket deep and flat, back straight, belly tucked up
Legs Straight and muscular; feet long; good stance
Tail Not docked, long, broad at the base and then tapering to the tip, plentifully fringed, may be ring-like at the end, carried naturally in a curve
Gait Loose, free, elegant, good at the gallop

Qualities An important feature, aesthetically speaking, is the proper distribution of short hair and the parts of the body with fringes; functionally speaking, the dog must look like an agile, swift racing-dog, capable of pursuing fast prey. (It is also known as the Gazelle Hound)
Defects Thickset neck, fat trunk, sluggish gait
Character Dignity and calmness; rather distant expression, but inquisitive when the dog is alert

Uses Hunting, sporting, and as a companion-dog
Future prospects As it is in competition with the Afghan Hound on the one hand and the Sloughi on the other, its spread is somewhat limited

Iran has now been superseded by Great Britain as the main breeding-centre for the Saluki. A French champion bitch, Oraya de Treville (left), aged two, and an English-bred pair (opposite).

SAMOYED

The Samoyeds form a so-called 'pre-Mongoloid' ethnic group living in a vast area of Russia in the Arctic zone. Nowadays the economy of these people is based on rearing reindeer, but this is a recent development. In earlier times the economy was based on the dog, which was used for hunting, fishing and hauling, and as food and clothing. The dog is also an important feature of the mythology of these people.

At the end of the 19th century the various polar expeditions introduced this most handsome of dogs to Europe. It is said that the first Samoyed puppy was acquired in 1889 by the explorer Robert Scott (1868-1912). In 1897 it found its way to England, although it was still confused with other polar breeds such as the Laika and the Husky. Famous Samoyeds were Obo and Bosko, belonging to Captain J. Wiggins of Kara.

A Samoyed by the name of Ross was presented to the Duke of Abruzzi (Luigi Amedeo of Savoy, 1873-1933) who undertook several important expeditions in his ship the **Stella polare**. In 1909 a group of breeding dogs was brought to Great Britain, and this marked the start of a methodical selection of the Samoyed, as it came to be known by both the organizations dealing with it: the British Samoyed Club and the Samoyed Association. There are now several Samoyed kennels in operation in England. In America team racing is still popular.

TODAY'S BREED

Official classification KC (GB): Working Group; AKC: Working Dogs
Countries of origin Nordic countries
Height and weight Males more than 52.5 cm (21 in), females more than 45.5 cm (18 in)
Coat Hair of medium length, straight, never curled, with a short, thick undercoat; colour: pure white or biscuit coloured

General appearance A working member of the Spitz group, sturdy, with a distinctive coat
Head Powerful, wedge-shaped; tip of nose and lips preferably black; scissor-type bite
Ears Not docked, small, erect and straight, rounded at the top, mobile
Eyes Small, oval, dark, and deepset
Body Ribcage broad and deep, well sprung, back muscular, belly not tucked up
Legs Quite short, with strong bone structure, muscular, with fringes; feet oval
Tail Not docked, carried over the back, with plenty of hair and a plume
Gait Elegant, lively, good at the trot and the gallop

Qualities Pure white is the preferable colour; it is important that the coat be abundant, with a mane, and that the eyes are 'oriental' or slanting
Defects Hair not straight, or curly, tail carried incorrectly, eyes too large
Character Unexcitable, with good endurance, sociable, good-natured, patient. Eastern or oriental expression

Uses Originally used for pulling sledges, guarding and herding reindeer, and giving protection from bears and wolves. In more temperate countries it is used as a guard-dog and companion-dog
Future prospects Its coat makes it particularly well suited to cold, wet parts of the world, where it has developed a good and loyal following
Similar breeds Nordic dogs used with reindeer and for hunting elk: Lapinporokoira (Finland), Lapphund (Sweden), Grähund (Sweden), Jämthund (Sweden). Another similar dog is the Japanese Kyushu, which is used by fishermen and hunters, as well as by herdsmen and farmers

Like several of the Nordic breeds, the Samoyed enjoys a flourishing world-wide reputation as a handsome and sturdy breed.

SCHIPPERKE

This tail-less dog owes some of its good fortune to this particular feature. Well known since the 18th century for its invaluable assistance to Belgian bargemen, it was adorned with collars made of crafted leather, sometimes studded with silver and gold plaques. Some people maintain that the word 'schipperkee' in old Flemish means 'small shepherd', while for others it means 'little captain', after the much travelled Captain Renssens, who did so much to improve the breed, which was first admitted to dog-shows in 1882, at Spa. Three years later the Queen of Belgium acquired a pair at the Brussels Show and the dog became very much à la mode. The Belgian cynologist Charles Huge traces the breed back to a black-coated forbear by the name of Leuvenaar, who was also the forefather of the Groenendael, but there is no substance to such hypotheses.

The English took a great fancy to the Schipperke, founding a Club as early as 1890, and calling the dog a Schip. It seems likely that it was crossed with Pomeranians, which gave different coats (sandy-coloured, chestnut, and even white) to the traditional black.

TODAY'S BREED

Official classification KC (GB): Utility Group; AKC: Non-Sporting Dogs
Country of origin Belgium
Height and weight Height in UK: 30-33 cm (12-13 in). Weight in UK: 5.5-7.5 kg (12-16 lb); in USA up to 8 kg (18 lb)
Coat Hair abundant, hard to the touch, longer round the neck (mane-like) and on the thighs; black all over. In Great Britain other self colours are permitted

General appearance A small member of the Spitz group with plenty of energy; tail-less
Head Very fox-like, with a tapering muzzle; small black nose; scissor-type bite
Ears Not docked, small, traingular, set high on the head, erect and mobile
Eyes More or less oval in shape, dark brown in colour
Body Ribcage broad and deep, well sprung, back straight, belly moderately tucked up
Legs Fine bone structure, good stance; feet round
Tail None
Gait Numble and brisk

Qualities Abundant mane that stands on end when the dog is excited. Fox-like muzzle; no tail
Defects Weight less than 3 kg (6½ lb) or more than 9 kg (20 lb); dullish black colour of coat, or other colouring
Character Very interested in what is going on around it, suspicious of strangers, keen protector of anything put in its charge, inquisitive, with a rather shrill bark, likes horses and children. Keen, piercing expression

Uses Guard- and watch-dog, companion-dog; hunts moles
Future prospects Although the breed has only a small following, it is well thought of in cynological circles

The distinctive mane has been a sought-after feature of the Schipperke at all stages in its development.

SCHNAUZER

Throughout the 19th century this breed was used in cowsheds, stables, courtyards and on farms in the fight against vermin (mice, rats, weasels and foxes). It was known as the Schnauzer, Rattler or Schnauzer-Pinscher.

The names are self-explanatory: 'Schnauze' in German means snout or muzzle, 'Schnauzbart' means mustache or whiskers, 'schnauzbärtig' moustachiod or whiskered, as well as rustic or coarse, 'schnauzig' gruff or grumpy, and 'Schnauzer' itself means a scolding or telling-off. This is a good name for a breed of dog with a rather rough-and-ready look about it, which is both moustachioed and gruff, and always ready to give voice to its bark. 'Rattler' from 'Ratte', meaning rat, and is close to the French word 'ratier', meaning rat-catcher or exterminator. 'Pinscher' is a word used in German cynology for a variety of breeds: the real Pinschers, the Dobermann-Pinscher, the Affenpinscher and the Schnauzer-Pinschers. 'Pinscher' is of English derivation (pinch = nip or bite). In a word, this is a type of dog that is good at chasing, seizing hold of things, and biting.

In varying shapes and sizes, the Schnauzer started appearing at shows in about 1890. The year 1895 saw the founding of the Schnauzer and Pinscher Club.

TODAY'S BREED

Official classification KC (GB): all varieties, Utility Group; AKC: Giant and Standard, Working Dogs, Miniature, Terriers
Country of origin Germany
Height Giant: 60-70 cm (24-28 in); Standard: 45-50 cm (18-20 in); Miniature: 30-35 cm (12-14 in)
Coat Hair coarse, thick, wiry, forming moustache and beard; colour: black and white or black

General appearance Varying in size, but always compact and hairy, with the coat trimmed in a specific style
Head Narrowing from the ears to the eyes and the muzzle; the muzzle ends in a point, but is made to look square by trimming; tip of nose black; scissor-type bite
Ears Docked and erect (Continent); neat, V-shaped, set high and drooping forward (UK)
Eyes Average size, oval and dark
Body Trunk sturdy, hind-quarters angled, belly slightly tucked up
Legs Strong, good straight stance; round feet
Tail Docked to three joints, set and carried high
Gait Easy, supple, elegant, good at the trot, a very good runner

Qualities The coarseness of the hair is important, as is solid build; good mobility
Defects Hair silken, especially on the skull, beard soft and too long, defective or poor bone structure, pale eyes
Character Extra-large specimens are reliable, courageous and affectionate, requiring long periods of training to become good working-dogs; medium-sized specimens are very lively and alert, sometimes with a tendency to be vicious, and are easy to train; miniatures are quite energetic, very attached to their owners, good watch-dogs, and very suspicious of strangers. Lively expression

Uses Guard- and watch-dog, companion-dog
Future prospects This breed is on the increase, but nevertheless somewhat held back by its coat, which needs frequent attention and trimming
Similar breeds Cão de Castro Laboreiro (herding), Portugal: a robust wolf-like dog the same size as a large Schnauzer, with a less wiry coat, greyish in colour; a sturdy mountain dog

A comparison of modern specimens and those depicted in nineteenth-century illustrations shows how the Schnauzer is much the same as it was when it won the hearts of German dog-fanciers in the early twentieth century with its moustachioed, rather rough and gruff look.

SCOTTISH TERRIER

Theo Marples was known in the first half of the 20th century as the 'grand old man of the canine British Empire'. In his book entitled **Show Dogs** he mentions that, in the dog-shows held between 1860 and 1880, there was much confusion between Skye Terriers, Yorkshire Terriers, Dandie Dinmont Terriers and Scotch Terriers. The year 1882 saw the establishment of the first Club for the present-day Scotch Terrier; its chairman was J.B. Morrison, who drew up the official standard. In 1887 another Club was founded that changed the name from Scotch to Scottish.

Marples laid down that the Scottish Terrier shared the same origins as the Yorkshire Terrier, but their selection meant that within just a few decades they had become quite different, in terms of both their physical appearance and their character.

Among the various breeders at the end of the last century who must take the credit for creating the breed of today were W.W. Spelman (owner of Champion Bradstone Loma), W. McLeod (Champion Alister) and H.J. Ludlow (owner of Champion Kildee), who was the secretary of the English Scottish Terrier Club.

Between 1920 and 1940 the Scottish Terrier became popular in many parts of the world. More recently it has experienced a certain decline.

TODAY'S BREED

Official classification KC (GB): Terrier Group; AKC: Terriers
Country of origin Great Britain
Height and weight 25-28 cm (10-11 in). Weight: 8-11 kg (18-24 lb)
Coat Hair compact and bristly, with a short, dense and soft undercoat; colour: black, sandy or grizzled in varying shades

General appearance A small dog, but one that is strong and agile. The way it is clipped greatly affects its overall appearance
Head Carried high, it is long, but in good proportion with the body; tip of nose black; scissor-type bite with large teeth
Ears Not docked, erect, covered with short, velvety hair
Eyes Almond shaped, dark chestnut in colour, set well apart, framed by the eyebrows as a result of proper clipping
Body Ribcage appears to be slung between the front legs; back quite straight and short
Legs Front legs short and straight, hind legs sturdy, with broad thighs
Tail Not docked, quite short, carried on high, with a slight curve
Gait Nimble, flowing and easy

Qualities As with many dogs that have become companion- and show-dogs, the coat of the Scottish Terrier is very important, as is the sturdy quality of the body and the strong jaw
Defects Ears semi-erect, eyes light in colour, cheeks prominent
Character The British regard this as the jack-of-all-trades dog. It has a bold expression

Uses Hunting (underground), but now more often a guard- and companion-dog
Future prospects It is still popular throughout the world, but seems likely to become slightly less so
Similar breeds Australian Silky Terrier (Silky Terrier in the US) is akin to the Scottish Terrier, with a silky coat; it was officially recognized in 1933. Although it is called a 'Terrier', it is and has always been a companion-dog

Over the last hundred years or so the Scottish Terrier has changed considerably in appearance. It remains, however, an active and alert breed that makes an attractive companion-dog.

SEALYHAM TERRIER

This breed came originally from the same county as the Corgi. Its originator was Captain John Edwards, an Englishman who died in 1870; he lived in a rural part of Pembrokeshire called Sealyham.

Captain Edwards was a tireless hunter of foxes, rabbits, badgers, rats, otters and, in particular, of polecats, which used to infest his land. He therefore set himself the goal of owning a Terrier that would be of a suitable size to allow it to get into underground burrows and lairs, and bold enough to confront the wild animals it found there without flinching.

It would appear – although this is not in fact documented – that Captain Edwards was the first person to crossbreed a Pembrokeshire Corgi with a Dandie Dinmont Terrier; this was followed with the West Highland White Terrier, the Bull Terrier and the Rough-haired Fox Terrier. Whatever the breeds used in subsequent combinations, there is no doubt that Edwards managed to obtain the type of Terrier that he had set his sights on: it had short legs, was a keen hunter, intelligent, and had an attractive appearance.

The work started by Captain Edwards was carried on by one of his grandsons, and the breed subsequently became quite popular; in fact it became so popular that the Sealyham Terrier Club was founded in 1908 and the official standard was duly drawn up.

The breed made the most of the popularity that surrounded all the English Terriers between 1920 and 1940, but since then it has been less fortunate.

TODAY'S BREED

Official classification KC (GB): Terrier Group; AKC: Terriers
Country of origin Great Britain
Height and weight Not more than 30 cm (12 in). Weight: 8-9 kg (18-20 lb)
Coat Hair long and bristly; usually white or white and lemon, or with brown markings on the head. The hair must be clipped

General appearance A lively, game little dog, very active, should be clipped with an eye to humour
Head Skull slightly domed and broad between the ears, muzzle square; scissor-type bite with particularly strong canine teeth; tip of nose black
Ears Not docked, lying against the cheek, rounded
Eyes Round and dark
Body Trunk stocky, but supple, so that the dog can dig its way into burrows
Legs Short, sturdy, straight, hind-quarters longer than fore-quarters, perfect stance; cat-like feet

Tail Docked by one-third; carried erect
Gait Supple and brisk, typical of a Terrier

Qualities Hair 'wiry'; undercoat dense and soft; body compact and sturdy
Defects Heaviness, clumsiness, nose not black, a lot of black in the coat, eyes light
Character Good-natured, cheerful, playful, affectionate. Inviting expression

Uses Once a hunting-dog, nowadays a companion-dog
Future prospects Becoming increasingly rare in Great Britain, as a result of competition from other similar breeds of Terrier
Similar breeds Ceský Terrier (Terrier), Czechoslovakia: this dog has been selected by Franta Horák in Bohemia and recently received its official international recognition

The Sealyham (left) was bred in the nineteenth century by a keen fox-hunting gentleman. What role was played by the four types of terriers (above) associated with various regions of the British Isles is not certain.

SIBERIAN HUSKY

'Husky' is the name commonly given to all breeds of dog used for pulling sledges. These include the Siberian Husky (United States), the Alaskan Malamute (United States), the Grünlandshund (Nordic countries), the Lappland Spitz (the north of Sweden, Norway and Finland) and, lastly, the Canadian Eskimo Dog, which is widely used by the Royal Canadian Mounted Police to help with their duties in northern parts of Canada, a country in which it was recognized as a breed before the turn of the century. Before the end of the 19th century there was a group of them at London Zoo and others were already being entered in dog shows.

The modern breed of Siberian Husky is said to be descended from dogs kept by the Chukchis, a group of people living in north-east Siberia. It was used by Russian travellers exploring their own country and played a part in the polar explorations of Peary and Nansen.

It is a lighter and faster dog than the Alaskan Malamute, which takes its name from a tribe living on the shores of Kotzebue Sound in Alaska.

Prince Igor (left) a United States champion Siberian Husky at the age of three. The nineteenth-century print (top) shows a rather lighter dog than the 'Husky' breeds of today. The Canadian Eskimo Dog (above) is a rugged and powerful breed of Husky.

TODAY'S BREED

Country of origin North-east Asia
Height and weight Male: 53-59 cm (21-23½ in); female: 51-56 cm (20-22 in). Weight: male: 20-27kg (45-60 lb); female: 16-23 kg (35-50 lb)
Coat Double and of medium length, the undercoat soft and dense, the outer coat never rough or shaggy; all colours admissible

General appearance A moderately compact working dog that is quick and graceful in movement
Head Medium in size, finely chiselled, muzzle of medium length tapering to rounded nose; scissors bite
Ears Triangular in shape, erect, set high on head and well furred
Eyes Almond-shaped, set slightly obliquely
Body Back straight and strong; ribcage deep and strong but not too broad
Legs Moderately spaced and parallel when viewed from front and back; medium-sized feet that are well furred and slightly webbed between the toes
Tail Well furred and generally carried over the back in a graceful curve
Gait Smooth and seemingly effortless

Qualities A strong well-made dog that has a hardy constitution and an affectionate nature
Defects Excessive weight or bone; constricted or clumsy gait
Character Intelligent and eager disposition; alert and outgoing

Uses W   g dog, guard-dog, companion-dog
Future prospects Hardiness and good temperament likely to ensure a reasonable following

SKYE TERRIER

There is a description of this dog in a work written in the 16th century by John Cajus, which certainly points to its ancient origins. It did not, however, really become part of the official cynological world until 1860, when it was still called a Scottish Terrier, although this name was subsequently given to another breed of dog. It was first called the Skye Terrier in 1864 at a show held in Manchester. At the end of the 19th century there were two Skye Clubs, the first in Edinburgh (where the honorary chairman was the Duke of Roxburghe), the second in Oxford (under the chairmanship of Viscount Melville, whose secretary was the Reverend Thomas Noland, owner of Champion Thurkill). In 1895 the artist Maud Earl painted six Skye Terriers belonging to Mrs. W.J. Hughes, owner of Champion Wolverley Duchess, the great rival of Mrs. E.M. Williams's Champion Old Burgundy. One of the famous London breeders at that time was D. Cunningham, owner of Champion Monarch. This breed was originally used for hunting foxes and badgers, and the fringe that hangs over its muzzle helped to protect its eyes from attack. Later, its luxuriant coat earned it a place of honour in fashionable drawing-rooms, and it even made its way into the Court of St James early in this century. As a result, it became popular as a companion-dog in the British Empire and in the United States.

Today, as in the nineteenth century, the Skye is a breed of quaint and endearing appearance. The coat, a distinctive feature, requires careful attention.

TODAY'S BREED

Official classification KC (GB): Terrier Group; AKC: Terriers
Country of origin Great Britain
Height and weight Approx. 25 cm (10 in). Weight: approx. 11 kg (24 lb)
Coat Hair long, straight, hard, flat, with no curliness or waviness, and a fringe on the skull and over the eyes; large fringes on the ears and tail; undercoat short, dense, soft and woolly. The colour is light or dark blue, or alternatively grey, cream, dove-coloured or tan, but always with black ears

General appearance A long-bodied dog with a long coat and ears with quite full fringes
Head Long, broad in the forehead, and narrowing towards the muzzle; tip of nose black; scissor-type bite
Ears Not docked, may be either erect or falling
Eyes Set close together, chestnut coloured
Body Very long and low, sturdy, with broad shoulders
Legs Short, straight, muscular; feet large
Tail Not docked, never carried gaily or upright
Gait Typical of a short-legged dog

Qualities The coat is important, as is the bright colouring; other important points are the large fringes, and the hair reaching to the feet
Defects Tail carried over the back, yellow eyes
Character Extremely loyal to its master, suspicious of all strangers, but will not usually bite. Bright expression

Uses Companion- and show-dog
Future prospects Its demanding coat has reduced its popularity somewhat, but its very distinctive appearance may bring it back into fashion
Similar breeds Soft-coated Wheaten Terrier (Terrier), Great Britain: this dog first appeared at shows in 1933, but has always been fairly uncommon

SLOUGHI

This breed was produced by Arab nomads. It has survived in a pure state in North Africa, Arabia, Egypt and Ethiopia, and in a somewhat bastardized state in the Sudan, between the Sahara Desert and the area known as Tripolitania.

The Arabs call this dog **el har** (the noble one), and will readily allow it into their tents. It is treated with respect by women, who make decorative ornaments for it; some will even offer orphaned puppies their breast to suckle. On journeys the Sloughi is carried on the backs of camels so that it does not become tired.

For centuries it has defended and protected encampments and villages from jackals, hyaenas and leopards, keeping watch all night long. The Arabs do not regard the Sloughi as a dog, ('kelb', Arabic for dog, is a term used pejoratively in the Koran).

As a hunting-dog the Sloughi is not common in Europe, and some countries even put a ban on it: in France, for example, there is a law which prohibits hunting with Greyhounds.

In the 1960s various countries in Europe and in the Americas established Clubs to promote both Greyhounds and Greyhound-racing, and their efforts embraced the Sloughi.

TODAY'S BREED

Official classification KC (GB): Hound Group; AKC: not recognized
Country of origin Algeria, Morocco
Height 60-70 cm (24-28 in)
Coat Hair smooth and close-lying; colour: all shades of tan (or fawn), black and tan, brindle, off-white, sometimes with a black mask

General appearance A well-defined member of the Greyhound group, with accentuated bone structure
Head Quite striking and large, skull flat, muzzle cone-shaped; tip of nose brown or black; lips thin and tight; scissor- or pincer-type bite
Ears Not docked, triangular, drooping to the sides of the head
Eyes Large, usually dark, but topaz-coloured with light-coloured coat
Body Chest not particularly deep, back straight, croup bony, belly tucked up
Legs Clearly defined, lean, with conspicuous tendons; feet thin and oval-shaped
Tail Not docked, thin, lean and with a slight curve at the tip
Gait Brisk, supple and easy, good at the gallop

Qualities A very distinguished dog, with a fine build, no fat, and bone structure tending to be more important than the musculature; very dark, almost gazelle-like eyelids
Defects Ears erect or rose-shaped, coat patchy, depigmentation or poor colour of nose or eyelids, teeth prognathous
Character Alert, reserved, willing. Gentle, almost nostalgic expression.

Uses Hunting-dog, guard-dog, sporting-dog
Future prospects There is a faithful and constant number of Sloughi-fanciers to guarantee the breed's future, even though it seems destined to remain quite rare outside the Arab countries.

Each of the Greyhound breeds has distinctive ears. The Sloughi (left) has plain hanging ears; the Saluki (above, right) has hanging fringed ears and those of the Greyhound (above, left) are sometimes described as rose-shaped.

SPINONE
Italian Griffon

The first document giving reference to the existence of the Spinone is possibly a fresco by Mantegna (1431-1506) in the Ducal Palace in Mantua, which shows the dog at work. Between that time and the 19th century the breed was often described by dog-loving writers, painted by artists, and greatly appreciated as a fine hunting-dog in every Court in Italy. In 1886 F. Delor gave a good description of the breed, and in 1887 the official standard was drawn up, although this was modified in 1897 by the Società Braccofila (Pointer Club). In 1904 the dog-expert and author Angelo Vecchio produced a drawing of the ideal type of Spinone, which still applies to this day. This drawing was inspired by a painting by G.B. Quadrone (1844-1898), an artist from Piedmont who was particularly well known for his hunting themes. In this century the breed has been selected and improved by the work of Dr Paolo Brianzi. The official historians for this dog are Adriano Ceresoli and Manlio Matteucci. In 1953, the editor of the Milanese magazine **Andando a caccia**, F. Ceroni Giacometti, organized a referendum among the hunting fraternity to establish which dog was considered the most suitable for hunting purposes in Italy. The Spinone came out top, followed by the Pointer, the Italian Pointer and the English Setter.

TODAY'S BREED

Official classification KC (GB): not recognized; AKC: Miscellaneous Breeds
Country of origin Italy
Height and weight 58-70 cm (23-28 in). Weight: 28-37 kg (62-82 lb)
Coat Hair hard, dense, 4-6 cm (1½-2½ in) long, with moustache, beard and eyebrows; colour: white, orange-white, white speckled with orange (honey-coloured), white with chestnut markings, roan-chestnut with or without chestnut markings

General appearance Solid, rugged, energetic member of the Pointer (Griffon) family, with a distinctive coat
Head Impressive, with a distinctive muzzle; tip of nose pink in white specimens, darker in orange-white specimens, brown in roan specimens; scissor-type bite
Ears Not docked, long, falling with an inward spiral form
Eyes Large, roundish, from ochre to yellow in colour
Body Ribs broad, brisket extending to below the elbow; back sturdy and solid, belly not tucked up
Legs Good stance, with strong bone structure, muscular; feet round
Tail Docked to 15-25 cm (6-10 in) from the base, not carried above the horizontal
Gait Distinctive at the trot with a long, flowing stride

Qualities An important feature is the thick skin, which is both fatty and leathery; the coat is also important and must be quite close-lying, and cover the body all over, with a fine, dense undercoat
Defects More than 72 cm (29 in) in height or shorter than 56 cm (22½ in); tip of nose black; bluish eyes
Character Gentle, docile, friendly, strong-willed, brave. Very gentle expression

Uses All types of hunting at all times of the year, particularly in woodland and marshland; a good swimmer and retriever
Future prospects Increasingly popular and sought-after in Italy, the Spinone may also acquire a name for itself in other countries
Similar breeds Ceský Fousek (Gun-dog, Pointer), Czechoslovakia: a typical Rough-haired Pointer, popular in its native country, where interest in it has recently been revived

The Spinone has a long history as a gun
dog in Italy, where it is still highly
esteemed. A handsome group of roan-
brown Spinones (top) includes Ticinella
del Restore and Bice di Morghengo,
successful champions in Italy, and a
young breeding dog, Nator.

SWISS HOUNDS

Ten types of Hound have been selected and bred in Switzerland, four of them small in size, and one wire-haired. Some of them are named after their birthplace: Berne, Lucerne and Jura, for example. The large varieties are called Laufhund and the small ones Niederlaufhund.

French cynologists agree that the origins of all these breeds are to be found in the French Briquet, and in fact there are marked similarities between the Lucerne Hound and the variety from Gascony, the Bernese (Mountain Dog) and the Saintongeois, and the Schweizer Laufhund and the Porcelaine. The Swiss cynologist Tschudy takes the opposite view: the French Hounds, he maintains, derive from the Swiss.

The official standard for the Schweizer Laufhund was eventually laid down in 1933. It is worth pointing out that after the Second World War, Swiss breeders managed to retain and reproduce conspicuously native types of dog, and never resorted to crossing them with English Hounds, such as the Foxhound, Harrier or Beagle.

TODAY'S BREED

Official classification KC (GB) and AKC: not recognized
Country of origin Switzerland
Height 40-55 cm (16-22 in)
Coat Hair close and plentiful, close-lying (there is also a Wire-haired variety); colour: white with orange markings, and sometimes small reddish markings

General appearance An average-sized Hound, elongated in the body, energetic and alert
Head Long and narrow; lips quite tight; tip of nose black; pincer- or scissor-type bite
Ears Not docked, large, set low on the sides of the head and well back, very long and curled over
Eyes Dark
Body Ribcage deep and well sprung, back straight, belly slightly tucked up
Legs Good stance, strong bone structure, muscular, no dew-claws; feet rounded
Tail Not docked, tapering, never carried erect
Gait Very good at the trot and gallop

Qualities Most important of all are this dog's hunting skills – a fine sense of smell, reliability, loud bark, and physical prowess, which enable it to hunt well over difficult terrain
Defects Dew-claws, poor stance, weak hind-quarters, shrill or strident bark
Character Lively, alert, good endurance, a very keen hunter, and loyal. Gentle expression

Uses An excellent tracker of hares
Future prospects A typically Swiss dog, popular and common in areas where it is bred
Similar breeds Slovensky Kopov (Hound), Czechoslovakia: very much a national dog, specializing in hunting wild boar. Erdelyi Kopo (Hound), Hungary: average size, black and tan, also known as the Transylvanian Hound

The Lucern Hound has changed very little in the last century, the type having been bred true over many years.

VIZSLA
Hungarian Vizsla

This breed is the National Dog of Hungarian sportsmen and the only shooting dog of Hungary. Between the two world wars the breed almost died out and it was only thanks to a few loyal supporters that it survived. After the Russian occupation in 1945 many Hungarians fleeing into Austria took their dogs with them. The Vizsla combines the duties of Pointer, Setter and Retriever on land and water. It is related to both the Pointer and the German Pointer.

TODAY'S BREED

Official classification KC (GB): Gundog Group; AKC: Sporting Dogs
Country of origin Hungary
Height and weight Males 57-64 cm (22½-25 in); Females 53-60 cm (21-24 in). Weight: 22–30 kg (48½-66 lb)
Coat Should be short and straight, dense and coarse and feel greasy to the touch. Colour russet gold. Small white marks on chest and feet, though acceptable, are not desirable

General appearance Should be a lively and intelligent medium-sized dog of distinguished appearance, robust and not too heavily boned
Head Gaunt and noble. Skull should be moderately wide between the ears with a median line down the forehead and a moderate stop. Muzzle a little longer than skull and should be well squared at the end. Nostrils well developed
Ears Moderately low set, proportionately long with a thin skin and hang down close to the cheeks
Eyes Neither deep or prominent, of medium size and a shade darker in colour than the coat. A yellow or black eye is unacceptable
Body Back should be level, short, well muscled, withers high. Chest moderately broad and deep with prominent breast bone. Ribs well sprung and belly should be tight with a slight tuck-up beneath the loin
Legs Elbow straight, pointing neither in nor out and the forearm should be long. Quarters should be straight when viewed from rear, hocks well let down
Tail Moderate thickness, rather low set, with one-third docked off. In movement the tail should be held horizontally
Gait Far-reaching, light-footed

Qualities Bred for hunting for fur and feather on open ground or in thick cover, pointing and retrieving from both land and water. Very affectionate and easily trained
Defects Any over exaggeration of the standard points
Character Lively and intelligent, but sensitive. A very graceful gun-dog with a lively trot and ground-covering gallop

Uses Gundog
Future prospects The breed's popularity is likely to increase

The Vizsla has an increasing number of admirers, who recognize his qualities as an all-round dog.

WEIMARANER

The earliest specimens of this breed were selected and bred towards the middle of the 17th century in the kennels of the dukes of Saxony-Weimar, where they continued to be bred until the 19th century. Their typical coat, with its silver-blue colouring, may be due to an intense blood relationship over many generations: the blue and silvery colour is a diluted version of black, and there is no doubt that the black Pointer was used in the 19th century to improve the qualities of the Weimaraner.

The spread of the Weimar Pointer to the other parts of Germany began about 1920, but there were already detailed references to it in the work by Count Henri de Bylandt, **Les races des chiens**, published in 1897; in this the author claims that the breed came originally from Thuringia.

Bred for many decades as a pure thoroughbred, it differs from the German Pointers not only because of its handsome colouring, but also because of the shape of its head and body. Long-haired specimens are sometimes born among short-haired litters. In the period after the Second World War the breed started to become very popular in the United States, where it has found a loyal and enthusiastic following.

TODAY'S BREED

Official classification KC (GB): Gundog Group; AKC: Sporting Dogs
Country of origin Germany
Height 57-70 cm (23-28 in)
Coat Hair short and fine (some specimens, though these are rare, have long hair); colours: silver-grey, kid-grey, mouse-grey, with intermediate shades; often with a darker dorsal line; sometimes there may be small white markings on the chest and feet

General appearance A typical member of the Pointer group, elegant, proud, alert and lively
Head Lean; muzzle long; tip of nose ranging from greyish to dark pink; scissor-type bite
Ears Not docked, broad and long, tips rounded
Eyes Amber-coloured; sky-blue in puppies
Body Chest extending to the elbows, trunk quite long, belly slightly tucked up
Legs Quite long, muscular; feet rounded and compact
Tail Docked, left sufficiently long to cover the genitals
Gait Graceful, swift, good for trotting with a long stride, and for full gallop

Qualities The distinctive nature of the breed requires grey colouring in any one of the permitted shades; preference for intense colours tending to blue; among its working qualities are docility, tenacity, love of water and confident retrieval
Defects Excessive heaviness, making it resemble the German Pointer
Character A very keen hunter, aggressive with vermin, capable of picking up scents and tracking. Inquisitive expression

Uses All forms of hunting
Future prospects This breed is progressively gaining in popularity

Two champion Weimaraners, Palacky du Lac de L'Emprunt, a two-year-old male bred in France, and Sir Jmar of the Three Turnips, a British-born specimen at the age of five.

WELSH CORGI CARDIGAN

The Cardigan Welsh Corgi is thought to be the oldest of the two varieties of Corgis and one of the oldest breeds in the UK. These dogs have been used as heelers by the Welsh farmers for centuries but it was not until 1925 that they appeared at dog shows for the first time. The breed is thought to have originated from a dwarf dog brought to England by Flemish weavers about the year 1100. Some of the weavers moved to the south-west corner of Wales and crossed their dogs with the native dog as in Cardigan and particularly in Pembrokeshire. Cardigan and Pembrokeshire Corgis were interbred until early in this century but since the English Kennel Club gave separate classification in 1934 this has been stopped.

TODAY'S BREED

Official classification KC (GB): Working Group; AKC: Herding Dogs
Country of origin Great Britain
Height 30 cm (12 in)
Coat Short or medium, of hard texture. Weatherproof with good undercoat. Preferably straight. Any colour with or without white markings but white should not predominate

General appearance Sturdy, mobile and capable of endurance. Overall silhouette long in proportion to height, terminating in a fox-like brush in line with the body
Head Foxy in shape and appearance, skull wide and flat between the ears, tapering towards the eyes above which it should be slightly domed. Moderate stop
Ears Erect, proportionately rather large for the size of the dog
Eyes Medium-sized, clear, giving a kindly, alert but watchful expression. Eyes preferably dark or to blend with coat. One or both eyes pale blue, blue or blue flecked, permissible only in blue merles
Body Chest moderately broad with prominent breast bone. Body fairly long and strong with deep brisket, well sprung ribs and clearly defined waist. Topline level
Legs Fore-legs short but body well clear of the ground, fore-arms slightly bowed to mould round the chest. Hind-quarters well angulated and aligned with muscular thighs and second thighs, strong bone carried down to feet, short legs
Tail Like a fox's brush set in line with body and moderately long. Carried low when standing but may be lifted a little above the body when moving, but not curled over the back
Gait Free and smooth

Qualities Good balance
Defects Any departure from the standard points
Character Alert, active and intelligent with steady temperament

Uses Good guard-dog and family pet
Future prospects Likely to retain a small but keen following

Arablue di Castel Martini, a world champion Italian-bred Cardigan bitch, at the age of five.

WELSH CORGI PEMBROKE

In 1934 the original Welsh Corgi split into two varieties: the Pembroke and the Cardigan. The two types had already been recognized in the 19th century and both were, in fact, present at the first show to include this breed, held in a village in South Wales in 1896.

For many years, the Corgi stayed in its mountainous birthplace. In 1925 the Corgi Club was founded to promote the Pembroke variety, the prime movers being Captain G. Checkland Williams, Captain Jack Howell and Adrian Howell. In 1930 Miss Thelma Evans set up the Rozavel kennels, which greatly improved the Pembroke type and began to make it more widespread. A few years later King George VI gave his elder daughter Elizabeth (later to become Queen Elizabeth II) a pair of Pembrokeshire Corgis, and since that day the breed has been part and parcel of the royal household, and is often seen with the Queen, even on official journeys. This has made the Corgi extremely popular both in Great Britain and abroad. In the period from 1970 to 1980 at least ninety out of every 100 Corgis were of the Pembroke variety.

TODAY'S BREED

Official classification KC (GB): Working Group; AKC: Herding Dogs
Country of origin Great Britain
Height and weight 25-30 cm (8-12 in). Weight: 8-11 kg (18-24 lb)
Coat Medium-length hair; colours: red, sandy, tan, black and tan, often with white on the chest, neck, feet, tolerated on the head and muzzle, but only a little

General appearance A stockily built, though small (compact) member of the Dachshund group
Head Brings to mind a fox's head, with a pointed muzzle; nose black; pincer- or scissor-type bite
Ears Not docked, straight, slightly splayed
Eyes Round, hazel-coloured, the shade matching the colour of the coat
Body Oblong because of the short legs; sturdy, ribcage broad and deep, back straight, belly not tucked up
Legs Front legs short and as straight as possible, knees close together, strong bone structure, good stance; hind-quarters sturdy and with a good stance; feet oval with the two middle toes set further forward than the others
Tail Short, docked if too long at birth
Gait Supple stride, active and brisk

Qualities The movement is important: the front legs must move forward without being raised too high, in time with the thrusting movement of the hind-quarters; the ratio between the muzzle length and the length of the skull is 3:5
Defects Knees too close together, ears floppy, body short or Terrier-like
Character Bold and alert, gives all its attention to its master. Questioning expression

Uses Used originally for herding, is now an excellent guard- and companion-dog
Future prospects In the near future it seems set to remain popular
Similar breeds Västgötaspets or Swedish Vallhund is quite like the Welsh Corgi, even as a herding-dog, and just as amusing to look at, hence its development as a companion-dog

The Pembroke is the more popular of the two varieties of Welsh Corgi, partly, perhaps, because of its association with the British royal family.

WHIPPET

Dogs belonging to the Greyhound group have often been kept, selected and bred along pure lines in aristocratic circles, from the Pharaohs to the Tsars.

One exception to this rule is the small English Greyhound known as the Whippet. It became popular as a racing dog in the latter part of the last century in the mining towns of north-east England, where people needed an inexpensive sport.

The first breeder, at work between 1870 and 1880, was John Hammond, although an earlier attempt had been made in 1845.

Miners called the dog the 'snap-dog', because of its lightning acceleration when it set off in pursuit of rabbits. Eager betters raced the Whippet over the 180 m (200 yd) distance, and so made the breed what it is: the fastest dog in the world over short distances.

In the cramped race-tracks that sprang up in towns and cities throughout Great Britain people began to show a preference to the Whippet's bigger brother, the Greyhound. After the Second World War the Whippet spread in Germany and Switzerland, where it is raced over grass, for purely sporting purpose, which did not involve betting.

TODAY'S BREED

Official classification KC (GB): Hound Group; AKC: Hounds
Country of origin Great Britain
Height Preferably about 47 cm (19 in) for males and 44 cm (17½ in) for females
Coat Hair smooth and close-lying; colour: all colours

General appearance A smaller version of the Greyhound
Head Long, skull flat, muzzle sturdy; tip of nose matches colour of coat; lips tight; scissor-type bite
Ears Not docked, small, rose-shaped, semi-erect when alert
Eyes Large, expressive, bright, preferably dark
Body Chest deep, trunk long, slightly arched, belly very tucked up
Legs Good stance, front-legs long, hind legs muscular and angled; cat-like feet
Tail Not docked, long, thin, carried low, with a slight curve at the end
Gait Good stride, supple and loose, very swift at the gallop, with a lightning burst of speed at the start

Qualities The lines of a fast sprinter are vital
Defects Signs of dwarfishness, erect ears, humped (the arching of the back starts at the withers)
Character Alert and calm, neither vicious nor combative, affectionate, obedient. Keen expression

Uses Sporting-, companion-dog
Future prospects Although an excellent companion-dog, and a good watch-dog, its increase and spread has mainly to do with the growing number of small dog-racing tracks

Weon of Neve Dith, at the age of four, a British-bred French, Spanish and international champion.

WIRE-HAIRED POINTING GRIFFON

From 1872, the Dutchman, E.K. Korthals, who was in the employ of the Prince of Sohns, selected a wire-haired variety of Griffon at Biebesheim in the Grand Duchy of Hesse. He found the original pair in France among the many Griffons which were then in that country. In fact some of Korthal's first seven breeding specimens were given names such as Partout, Mouche and Nitouche. Later there was considerable and heated debate surrounding the birthplace and homeland of the breed, as the German Griffon Club, the Belgian Griffon Club and the Dutch Nimbrod Club all vied with one another. In the end the Dutch Club acknowledged that the breed's origins lay in France, and the breed is now internationally recognized as having originated there.

Among the finest Korthals Griffons of the late 19th century were those belonging to the Dutch breeder G. Leliman, to G. van der Elst of Brussels, to the Grand Duke Constantine of Russia, and Champion Kate-Bella belonging to Baron A. de Gingins of Kronberg. The Baron continued the good work begun by Korthals.

An early specimen (right) of the breed selected by the Dutchman Korthals in the nineteenth century, and modern specimens, (below). The breed has a strong following in France.

TODAY'S BREED

Official classification Gun-dog, Pointer
Country of origin France
Height and weight 50-60 cm (20-24 in). Weight approx. 25 kg (56 lb)
Coat Hair hard and 'boar-like', never curly or woolly, with water-resistant undercoat; colours: grey with brown markings, roan, white and chestnut, white and orange

General appearance A sturdy, rugged Griffon, well protected all over by its hard, wiry coat
Head Large and long, with conspicuous moustache, eyebrows and beard; skull broad, muzzle long and square; tip of nose brown; scissor-type bite
Ears Not docked, not curled over, flat
Eyes Large, not hidden by the eyebrows, ranging from brown to yellow in colour
Body Sturdy, strong, ribs deep, trunk compact, belly not tucked up
Legs Quite sturdy and strong, muscular, good stance, with dense hair; toes together, feet round and solid
Tail Docked by one-third or one-quarter, with no fringe
Gait Loose and easy, free, brisk at the trot with a short stride, and good at the gallop

Qualities The coat is an important feature, and must protect the dog even in the very worst weather conditions, in all climates, whether hunting in marshland or thick undergrowth; other important features are the dog's sturdy quality and its gait
Defects Hair soft and woolly with silky areas, or else curly, or with a poor undercoat, which must be dense and protect the whole body
Character An energetic, alert dog, swift to react, brave and faithful. A questioning expression

Uses All forms of hunting
Future prospects Becoming increasingly rare

YORKSHIRE TERRIER

Theo Marples credits the improvement of this breed to the activities of Miss M.A. Forster of Bradford, and in particular to the acquisition by her kennels of the stud dog Ben Huddersfield (1865-71), produced by W. Eastwood. Ben is the forefather of the present-day Yorkshire Terrier. For decades this little dog was bred by clerks, shopkeepers, greengrocers and ordinary working people: they would select and breed their dogs by keeping them in their large kitchens, under the watchful eye of all the family, who would lavish on them all the attention they needed. For kennels these people would use a chest, with its bottom drawers removed and the space split into three cubicles or more by brass partitions.

The floor would be covered with a woollen blanket, which had to be frequently washed. As the pups started to wander away from their mother, they would be fitted with 'bootees' to stop them spoiling their coats by scratching. They would be rubbed with the finest olive oil and a drop of paraffin, which would stop the coat from becoming tousled, and stimulate its growth.

These Yorkshire Terriers enjoyed all this attention, and readily joined in all the different family activities; and when they were sold, it was invariably for a profitable sum, to the advantage of small-time breeders.

A nineteenth-century Yorkshire Terrier (above) and a German-bred modern champion, Quadri von Friedheck (below).

TODAY'S BREED

Official classification KC (GB): Toy Group; AKC: Toys
Country of origin Great Britain
Weight Up to 3.5 kg (8 lb)
Coat Puppies are born with a black coat; between three and five months a blue coloration starts to appear at the root of the hair; by the age of eighteen months at the most the coat must have taken on its permanent colour: steely blue (as opposed to silvery blue) from the occiput to the tip of the tail, whereas the 'tumbling' hair, which reaches the feet, is a bright tan colour, although darker at the root and paler at the tip. Hair dense, shiny, heavy, very long, silky, never curled, with no tufts or ringlets

General appearance Although small, this dog is every bit a Terrier, and exudes all the lively qualities of the family
Head Quite small, muzzle not elongated; tip of nose black; scissor-type bite
Ears Not docked, small, V-shaped, erect or semi-erect, covered with bright tan-coloured short hair
Eyes Dark, black rim round the eyelid; the hair covers the eyes
Body Compact and strong, especially the hind-quarters; artificial parting running along the back, dividing the hair into two 'halves' which reach the ground
Legs Straight, and covered with much hair
Tail Docked to half, carried slightly higher than the line of the back, well covered with bluish hair, which – at the end of the tail in particular – is darker than that on the rest of the body, coming close to black
Gait An upright bearing, giving the dog an air of importance, dainty at the trot with an easy stride, and fast at the gallop

Qualities Colour and length of the coat are the main features
Defects Hair that is tawny, or bronze or black; coat that is too thin
Character Always on the move, very alert to the world around it, affectionate, faithful

Uses Lap-dog
Future prospects The breed is likely to suffer from periodic decline of physical qualities following spells of being fashionable
Similar breeds Two Australian breeds, the Australian Silky Terrier (Sily Terrier in the US), and the Australian Terrier show similarities to the Yorkshire Terrier

DOGS: THEIR PSYCHOLOGY AND USES

Four young Bearded Collies.

THE MODERN DOG

Dogs are still essential for a variety of tasks, just as they were in the past.

Hunting uses: pointing; setting; tracking; flushing out prey underground; retrieving in all types of terrain, and in water; locating lost game (large and small); guarding game – and anything else that the hunter may need to entrust to the dog's care; finding objects that the hunter may have lost; protecting the hunter; carrying out anti-poaching duties and so on – not forgetting more specialized activities, such as truffle hunting.

General working duties: guarding and tracking (for the police and the military); protecting people and property; rescue work; pursuit of criminals and escaped prisoners; identification of suspects; mine, weapon and drug detection; messenger and sentry duties; herding sheep and other livestock; guiding the blind; finding people buried in snow or rubble, or trapped in buildings damaged by bombs or earthquakes; carrying out fire and parachute duties; hauling loads, packwork and sledge-pulling; taking part in shows and competitions, such as sheep-dog trials.

As a rule, authors writing about hunting dogs tend not to concern themselves with working dogs, and vice versa. This is a serious oversight. Only comparative studies of dogs can enable us to gain a real knowledge about these creatures, how they can be used, and what the features of the varius breeds are. Anyone who regards a Setter or a Sheepdog as different in nature from a Mastiff or a Pekingese is neither a dog-expert nor a dog-lover. Anyone who teaches a hunting dog to point to perfection, but fails to teach it how to retrieve game will only ever have a dog working at half-pitch, when with a little foresight, he could have a fine, all-round animal. Anyone who owns a valient guard dog that does not know how to use its nose only has half a guard dog, which is not being used to the full.

All dogs are a combination of guard dog, hunting dog and companion, but they will only use all their capabilities if

they are trained to do so. Once you have taken your own dog through the whole course of training, you can develop the most appropriate qualities.

When you embark on the training, the first thing you need is a 'dictionary' – a dictionary of dog language. If you do not understand what a dog is saying to you, how can you possibly talk to it, or train it? People and dogs can (and must) talk to each other.

A DICTIONARY OF DOG LANGUAGE

In the context of this book 'language' implies a system of signs that are visual and auditory as well as oral, and that can also involve the senses of touch and smell. By means of these signs one living creature can communicate its state of mind to others. The language of dogs is based on bodily attitudes, sounds, smells, physical contact. Many people have no idea how to interpret it, and consequently do not deserve the company of a dog. This 'dictionary' will provide a basis for a real understanding of dogs, an understanding that lies at the root of good and successful training for all purposes: hunting, guarding, tracking, racing, companionship and shows.

If an owner or trainer is not acquainted with the language used by dogs, or does not understand it, or fails to interpret it properly, his dog – essentially a social creature – will feel shut up in an alien world and unable to be content or useful. Any dog that is not properly understood will first become anxious and ill-at-ease, then unbalanced and finally useless.

By contrast with humans – omnivorous bipeds that walk upright on the soles of their feet, have prehensile hands, quite a large brain, and keen vision, dogs are quadrupeds that walk on their toes in a horizontal position, have quite a small brain, an excellent sense of smell, and are predominantly carnivorous. They live in a world that is different from the human world but that coincides with it, and that they experience in their own way. They have, for example, absolutely no grasp of the value a human being may attach to an arm-chair, a tie, or another piece of clothing, to a rosette or a razor. We

need determination to understand any animal acting as our companion or helper. Co-operation between people and dogs is therefore based on an ability to communicate.

There is no suggestion in this book of turning dogs into people, of claiming that dogs talk, or that human beings can talk to dogs. The language of dogs is altogether different from ours: it expresses mood, not ideas. Dogs do not understand words, only intonation. If you say in a kind voice to a dog, 'Bad boy! Bad boy!', it will wag its tail; if you say in a stern voice, 'Good dog! Good dog!', it will put its tail between its legs. For dogs the human voice is a source of sounds, acoustic signals – not words.

A dog's exceptional sense of smell is of great use to man, for hunting and other general duties.
Opposite: A Pointer a work some distance from the game, which the hunter himself cannot see at all.

Below: Two dogs getting to know one another. In this ceremony dogs use their sense of smell to glean information.

Soul/mind: Do dogs have a soul? A mind? This is the same as asking if dogs have a body. It is quite obvious that dogs have both a physical existence and a mental or spiritual one, and in their upbringing and training, their mental characteristics have to be taken into account before their physical ones. Dogs think a form of 'non-verbal' thought of the kind we have all known as children. Dogs have memory, will (and therefore desires), intelligence, a whole range of feelings and emotions, including love, devotion, loyalty, joy, fear, grief, despair, anger, jealousy, shame, pride, and the capacity for imagination, curiosity and perplexity. Not only do dogs have a 'soul' or 'spirit' in this sense: they have a fairly rich and complex one.

Ano-genital investigation: Man's most important sense is sight. People look at one another in their most expressive area – the face. The dog's most important sense is the sense of smell, so dogs sniff each other in their most expressive area – the ano-genital region. Here there are cutaneous glands secreting substances that smell, and that are of great interest to other dogs. When a dog sniffs at the ano-genital region it establishes the sex of the other dog, as well as its approximate age, its state of health, and its mood. What is more, when dogs sniff at one another, the process indicates their position in the hierarchy. A senior or superior dog is entitled to check the ano-genital region of all junior or inferior male dogs, bitches and young dogs. A meeting between two dogs follows an invariable pattern which resembles a ritual 'ceremony': (1) mutual nose smelling, (2) coat contact, usually at shoulder level, (3) ano-genital investigation, which rounds off the process of mutual acquaintanceship. All dogs, of either sex, frequently check their own ano-genital region, and keep it clean by careful licking. This is a natural and hygienic thing for dogs to do, and it should not be disapproved of or scolded. When a dog sniffs its own anal region more than usual, this may well mean that the animal is not well and has some digestive upset.

Panting and sweating: Just as human beings sweat to keep their body temperature at a constant level, so other animals pant to get rid of any surplus heat; they do not have sweat glands in their skin, only in the soles of their feet (the pads). When one dog follows another along a track, it naturally searches the ground for traces of sweat from the first dog's feet. This natural tendency gives rise to some of a dog's typical attitudes and postures, and its ability to follow the scent of wild game or of human beings, depending on whether it has been trained as a hunting dog or a tracker.

Tail: The tail comes in a variety of shapes and sizes, according to breed. As has already been mentioned, wild dogs invariably carry their tails low; one sign of domesticity is a tail carried towards the front of the body (the head); this applies in the case of Pomeranians, Huskies, some mountain dogs, and the Chow Chow. Some dog-experts – technically known as cynologists – regard this as a sign of special familiarity with people, and a healthy attitude towards training. However, every breed of hunting-dog, from Pointer to Dachshund, carries its tail low, never curled over the back, and this has to do with the length of time they have been domesticated, and with their gentle nature.

The movements of the tail are bound up with the sense of smell (see **Sense of smell**, p.212), and the special anal glands that give each individual dog its own specific scent. A happy dog will wag its tail to spread its own smell; a frightened dog will cover up its anus and genitals to smother its smell. There are some dogs in the Dachshund group that express their happiness by wagging their tails not just from side to side, but with a spiral motion, too. The rate at which a tail is wagged indicates the degree of well-being or happiness. From the tails of dogs in the Pomeranian group it is possible to identify a whole range of different states of mind and varying moods. While hunting-dogs are at work their tail speaks volumes.

Conditioning: I. Pavlov, the Russian physiologist, was the first person to define conditioned reflexes. From a study of the gastric and salivary glands of dogs, he noticed that the saliva varied in both composition and quality depending on the food that the animal in question was about to eat. If the food was meat, the saliva was thick; if the food was not tasty or to the dog's liking the saliva was watery (any dog owner recognizes the watery saliva secreted when a dog is reluctant to swallow medicine). This salivary modification is caused by the senses of smell and taste and is known as a simple reflex.

Immediately before offering a plate of food to his subject, Pavlov set a metronome in motion. He observed that, after a while, the dog learned to associate the metronome with the imminent arrival of a meal. At the sound of the metronome the dog's ears stood erect, and it began to salivate. The simple reflex thus became a conditioned reflex: in other words, the response to the sound of the metronome replaced the senses of taste and smell. The same thing happened if the dog became accustomed, not to sound, but to the appearance of lights, or to vibrations, immediately before the meal was offered to it. This is known as Type 1 Conditioning, where the dog stays passive. It weakens if, for a given period of time, the sound of the metronome, for example, is no longer followed by the food.

Later, in the United States, B.F. Skinner defined what is known as Type 2 Conditioning, where the animal is active. It is, in effect, persuaded to make a certain movement, and as soon as it has done so, it is rewarded. Type 1 Conditioning is quick to take hold, whereas Type 2 is slower but increases in intensity as time passes. The training of all animals – and of dogs in particular – is based on Type 2 Conditioning.

Opposite: Dogs and cat by the fireside. The common smell of animals that live together in the same house makes them accept one another.
Right: A young German Shepherd offering its paw to its owner.

These types of conditioning are not, however, altogether mechanical. There is more to dogs than that. In Pavlov's time (about 1903) it was observed that very clever dogs salivated well before the metronome started up. When they were first brought to the laboratory they would start to salivate a little; when they were put on the table the amount of saliva increased; and once they were tied up, they salivated even more in their impatience for the metronome to begin. Was their behaviour a conditioned reflex or rather a matter of memory, perception and intelligence? Another interesting feature of 'controlled' conditioning was discovered during experiments carried out in America in 1960. It was observed that although the conditioning experiments were carried out with uniform precision, not all the experimenters obtained the same results; some did much better than others. It could therefore be supposed that the individual experimenter exerted psychological influence over the animal in question.

Curiosity: Throughout their lives dogs are driven by an intense curiosity, evident at all times, but particularly so when they are in any new surroundings. It is this curiosity that enables dogs, young and old, to enjoy the process of learning, and if a dog is to be trained in any special way, it is crucial to maintain – and encourage – this natural joyousness.

Even when a young dog is no more than a fortnight or so old it generally starts to display intense curiosity about everything around it, by sniffing and smelling. Going for walks – something all dogs love to do – not only provides them with a chance to run about and take exercise; it also gives them a chance to explore, and thus stimulate mind as well as body. (A lot of dogs enjoy travelling in cars for the same reason.) A dog's curiosity can be defined as exploration.

Visual curiosity is also important. A dog's sight is, however, the sense that can most easily trick it. It is worth mentioning that a dog's alert, attentive expression (commonly described as

its 'intelligent look') is the over-all result of the keenness of its sense of smell and of hearing, which provide the dog with a correct sense of direction, in spite of its inherently weak eyesight (see **Sight**, p.216). Visual curiosity should not be linked with a dog's facial expression, which differs a great deal between one breed and another.

'Shaking hands': Shaking hands (actually, offering a fore-paw) is something dogs quickly learn to do, but it has no connection with the way in which human beings shake hands, as the famous ethologist, Konrad Lorenz, has suggested. It is, on the contrary, an instinctive gesture that young puppies make towards their mother and other adult dogs, as a sign of affectionate submission. It also occurs between adult dogs, as a sign of affection and an invitation to play or to mate. It is not so much 'shaking hands' or 'offering paws' as a way of reaching out with a paw to touch another dog, usually on the muzzle or the neck.

Defecation: A dog's faeces, like its urine (see **Urination**, p.215), represent an indication of territory. A dog will spend a long time seeking out the most suitable and appropriate spot, and this will be frequently changed. Cats tend to hide their faeces in the ground with painstaking care, so as to cover their tracks, but dogs have defecatory habits more like those of the fox, which will deposit its faeces on tree-trunks so that these mark its territory. Once a dog has found the right spot, had a good long sniff, pirouetted about as if it were pinpointing the right movement of air, and finally deposited its faeces, it will often disturb the earth around the place. The amount of earth it disturbs depends on circumstance and terrain. If the earth is powdery, the dog will dig at it quite a lot, not to obliterate its own tracks, but to add the smell of the sweat from its feet to the smell of its faeces (see **Panting and Sweating**, p.204) and **Threatening behaviour**, p.209). A dog will never, in fact, cover up its own faeces. Defecation is part and parcel of its language.

ESP Present-day para-psychology deals with, among other things, the extra-sensory perception (ESP) of living beings. There are some indications that all animals, including dogs, communicate by means of telepathy. In order to have a proper grasp of dog language it is necessary to take into account the extra-sensory world that, as it were, envelops all living things, animals in particular. The relationships between dog and dog, dog and man, and dog and wild game have their own kind of radiation: the sending and receiving of messages that either replace or complete sensory messages, which become to some extent secondary.

Good examples of ESP are to be found among members of the Greyhound family belonging to the peoples of southern Africa. When these people cross arid areas, they make their dogs thirsty by giving them salt, then put them on leads, and the dogs lead their owners without delay or detour to far-off sources of water undetectable by the senses alone. The

dogs thus become rather like dowsers or water-diviners.

Perhaps another example of ESP is the observed fact that dogs can sense earthquakes and volcanic eruptions before they happen. It is possible that ESP also governs a dog's sense of direction and its ability to find its way back home over very long distances, and it may well come into play when a trained dog carries out a command even before its master has made a single gesture or spoken a single word but has simply thought the command.

It is, incidentally, common knowledge in dog-training circles that some trainers are capable of obtaining first-class results from the dogs in their charge, using precisely the same techniques as other trainers whose success rate is far lower. An unexplained 'magnetism' can certainly be established between a human and a dog working together which makes it appear that thoughts and feelings can be transmitted directly to hunting dogs, trackers, show-dogs or companion dogs. The famous French cynologist Jean Castaing puts this notion plainly: 'When I want to make myself clearly understood by the dog I am training, I look at it straight in the eyes and think hard about what I want the dog to do. I then get the impression that a kind of current is created between the two of us.'

Cats: Dogs tend as a rule to behave in a hostile way towards cats. This can irritate the hunter who sees his 'right-hand' chasing after a cat instead of responding to his orders. It may well annoy the animal-lover, too, who simply wants to live in peace with both his dog and his cat.

The underlying hostility that generally exists between dogs and cats stems from the profound differences between them. Dogs are social creatures; cats are solitary. Dog language differs considerably from cat language, and dogs adapt more readily than cats to human partnerships.

A mother cat with a litter of kittens to look after will show phenomenal spirit, boldly attacking even a large dog that happens to get too close: it is in her nature to do so. A dog that sees a cat running away will go in pursuit of it because the cat suddenly turns into prey: that is in the dog's nature. Most dogs will, however, accept the presence of a kitten in the home, and the chances are that the animals will become firm friends, as cats will with puppies.

To make for a good-natured co-existence between the two creatures, do not feed them together or make them compete for food; avoid occasions for jealousy (if the cat is sitting on your lap, give the dog a biscuit to compensate); and encourage them to play with one another from an early age (this is an excellent solution, with long-lasting results).

Above: When a dog licks the corner of another dog's mouth, it is showing affection. Dogs will sometimes show affection to humans in a similar way. Opposite: Cats and dogs can live together without hostility, particularly if brought together at an early age.

Hierarchy: Dogs are gregarious by nature: in other words, dogs live in the wild in packs and will readily adapt to the hierarchic structure of the pack, like other members of the **Canidae** family, such as wolves and jackals. The hierarchy takes in subject and ruler alike. In litters, in kennels, among wild dogs (such as the dingo), and among dogs living together in villages

or town suburbs, a social scale develops that is dominated by a 'head dog' – usually the oldest male. The 'head dog' is entitled to check the ano-genital region of every other dog (see **Ano-genital investigation**, p.204) and to urinate as it pleases (see **Urination**, p.215). If for some reason – for example, the right to eat first – the 'head-dog' snarls at another inferior dog (see **Threatening behaviour**, p.209), the inferior dog will snarl or growl at a dog that is in turn inferior. This type of behaviour also occurs among human beings – when the captain is rebuked by his colonel and gets his own back on a junior.

Dogs have an ever greater need than people to contain, control and get over conflicts with the society in which they live. For this reason a dog may often prefer to live in kennels (where everything is straightforward, and where the other dogs understand his language) rather than in someone's home (where in many cases everything is incomprehensible, and the dog himself is not understood). Certain

gestures acknowledge the hierarchic superiority of another male: allowing ano-genital inspection, without reciprocating (see **Ano-genital investigation**, p.204); not urinating over the urine of another dog; wagging the tail while another dog is growling; turning the head away; becoming playful; backing away; sitting or lying down; staying put while the superior or senior dog walks away; allowing the other dog to mount (see **Mounting**, p.210); lying prostrate on the ground and displaying the undefended belly (see **Threatening behaviour**, p.209), and yelping (see **Vocal sounds**, p.216). As soon as hierarchic superiority is acknowledged, hostilities cease and the dogs will start to become friends. A dog adopts similar attitudes to his master, whom he sees as 'head dog'.

Play: Throughout their lives dogs are playful animals. This is why they can be trained through games. A puppy will play at fighting and hunting; it will chase its own tail, and seize things in its mouth. Puppies start to become

playful at the age of three to four weeks, and then play is a learning process. It is a good idea to play frequently with any puppy that you intend to train later. Make your hands into the shape of a muzzle so that you can push the puppy, tip it over, and cuff it gently. In the pack, the parents and other adults teach the puppies and the young dogs how to behave by playing with them, rewarding and reprimanding them, showing your authority, and playfully altering any kind of inappropriate behaviour. In this way the young animals learn how to deal with situations that they will encounter in the future. An adult dog at play often releases impulses which have become too bottled up by living constantly with people.

Playing with people (and working with them) is a great pleasure for any puppy. It will soon learn that it cannot get the better of its master, and as a result will readily and happily accept him as 'head dog'. Puppies belonging to more defenceless breeds, once they realize that they can intimidate their owner, even if only at play, may well end up ruling the roost and adults, because it is in the nature of all dogs to take on the role of head dog or 'top dog' if it is vacant (see **Hierarchy**, p.207). A puppy will good-naturedly accept its master – or its parents – suddenly breaking off a game, for any reason, but it will be bewildered if a game is suddenly followed by some form of punishment; this will give rise to a feeling of insecurity.

If, for example, a puppy nips its master's hand with a little too much enthusiasm (because it has still not learnt that human beings do not have the same kind of coat or skin as its own parents), it is good to put a stop to that particular game, but you should never hit the puppy. You can say a firm but friendly 'No', but without shouting or mistreating the puppy. In this way it will soon learn to tone down its natural aggressive instincts and as an adult, when it has been trained, will become an extremely useful companion. Puppies particularly enjoy 'hunting' one another and so do adult dogs. One will play the part of the hunted, and make off with others in pursuit. When two animals play together, one will lie in wait, quite motionless while its companion plays the part of the prey, and when it takes to its heels, it is chased, caught and held firmly. Hunting is the best game of all for dogs, and no general purpose or working dog, no matter how well trained, will ever experience the joys of the well-trained hunting dog on its hunting expeditions with its master and trainer.

Taste: In dogs, as in people, the senses of taste and smell are quite different; the sense of smell is much more sensitive, and much more capable of distinguishing variations. Dogs are carnivorous and tend to gobble their food too fast to really taste it. Food is simply swallowed, with scarcely any appreciation of the flavour, unless it is associated with scent. Dogs, like people, have just four basic tastes: sweet, bitter, salty and acid.

Imitation: Although dogs are capable of learning by watching the behaviour of other dogs, they are not imitative creatures, unlike sheep in flocks, certain birds, and certain fish in shoals, which will all change direction together. Dogs make greater use of their experience. In other words, they will repeat what past experience has shown them to be pleasant or enjoyable, and they will not repeat what has turned out to be the reverse. To some extent dogs behave as Galileo did: they test something, and then test it all over again. This is why it is easy to train them.

A dog's imitative faculties must also be based on deep-rooted impulses. If one dog sees another unlatching a door, it will not do the same, but a young dog will swiftly imitate the movements and methods of an efficient sheep-dog. The hunting or herd-ing instinct is deeply implanted in many breeds of dog.

Licking: Dogs are licked from the moment they are born. They lick one another affectionately, and clean themselves by licking any dirty or injured parts of their body. Licking is an affectionate, friendly gesture (see **Ano-genital investigation**, p.204) and a method of cleaning.

Threatening behaviour and fighting: Imitation threatening behaviour starts with the tail. It becomes erect, straight and hard, like a flag-pole. At the same

Opposite: A mother always licks her pups.
Below: Fights between dogs usually take the form of a precise ceremony.

210

time the legs seem to stiffen at the joints, and the brisk movements usually made by the dog seem almost awkward. A dog in a threatening pose seems to want to appear larger than it actually is, in both breadth and height; it lifts up its trunk, and raises the hackles on the back of its neck, and on its back. If it is threatening another dog, it will stare at it with piercing intensity. Even when the two contestants do not move, they appear to be intently involved in a trial of mental strength. At a given moment, one of the two often makes itself smaller and 'throws in the towel' by turning its head away, lying on the ground, backing off, or moving right away, with its tail between its legs.

If this trial of mental strength is not enough to establish which dog of the two is superior, the threatening pose and appearance will become more intense: the ears flatten over the back of the head, the nose becomes wrinkled or creased, there is menacing growling and snarling, the lips curl back and bare the teeth, and the jaws start grinding together. In some cases, one of the two dogs will paw at the ground with its hind-feet, possibly to spread sweat (see **Panting and sweating**, p.204). The tails of the two 'duellists' will be positioned so that they cover the genitals. The two dogs will then move closer to one another, their bristling coats will touch, as if an electric current is running through them, and this contact only serves to heighten the tension. By now they will be shoulder to shoulder, and all of a sudden their threats will cease and they will start biting one another. In some cases, and in particular if they are not being held on leads by their owners, fighting dogs rear up on their hind-quarters and one will try to sink its teeth into its opponent's throat or place its front legs round the other dog's neck to force it to the ground. In most cases fights between males do not last very long, and no blood is spilt: the biting does not go further than the coat. It is extremely rare, and almost always accidental, for one dog to kill another. A small, but spirited dog may end up dead, and the larger dog in the fray may be responsible for

killing it, but only because its sheer strength and size have overpowered the smaller aimal. In an encounter between males of the same size one of the two will soon acknowledge the superiority of the other, and make a gesture of surrender: the clearest and swiftest acknowledgement of the other dog's superiority is to lie on the ground and display the belly, as if offering the most defenceless part of the body. This is a frequent gesture among puppies.

If a dog acts in this way when its master has raised his voice, it is important to treat it at once in a kindly way. The dog is saying 'I surrender': in dog society, the superior animal will always accept surrender and stop behaving aggressively; people should behave in the same way, so that the dog can see that its language is being understood.

When two dogs are snapping at or biting each other, their respective owners must firmly pull them apart either by grasping them by the hindlegs, or by picking them up in their arms. As a rule the two dogs involved will be only too pleased to be separated. Make sure, however, that both dogs are pulled apart at the same time. If only one dog is pulled away, the other may well bite it with renewed vigour, and a serious wound could result. Remember, too, that a dog that is restrained by its master or owner and is still bitten by the other dog, will instantly lose all trust in its master, and that trust will be extremely hard to win back.

Bitches tend not to be content, as males are, with gestures of submission, or territorial surrender: their fights are rarer, but they can also be more unexpected, with little advance warning; and they may also be quite bloody. A bitch does not defend a territory as a male does; nor does she defend a hierarchic position or status; in theory a bitch is only concerned with the defence of her litter (even if she does not actually have one to defend). This is why she will suddenly start to snap at and bite her rival without any warning. On the other hand, plenty of bitches live together quite happily and peacefully all their

lives, feeding their own puppies and those of other mothers, sometimes even in a shared basket. Proper fighting between dogs and bitches does not really exist. At most an irritated male might push a bitch, and get on top of her, but he will never bite her seriously; in fact, it is more likely to be the bitch that will leave some sign of the fight on the male's coat.

A clear sign that two dogs are on the point of having a fight is that each one will raise its tail high and move it about slowly – each saying, in other words, that it is the superior. If one of the two gives in, it lowers its tail and wags it busily as a sign of submission; it will stop staring its opponent straight in the eye and start looking somewhere else. Even though it has submitted, it will not run away so that it does not trigger off the other dog's impulse to chase it. At most it will back away slowly. Dog-breeders would do well to remember that aggressiveness is hereditary; it is therefore a good idea to select animals in order to increase the level of aggression in some breeds where it is required or appropriate, and to get rid of it in others where it is not needed.

Mounting: When one dog mounts another, the action is not solely connected with mating, which may only occur during the few days or even hours when the female is on heat. Mounting is a gesture which can be seen between puppies, and as such it is regarded as being playful (see **Play**, p.208), although a kind of playfulness that for a moment involves the genital area. In dogs it is often influenced by affection. We have all seen a dog develop an embryonic erection when its owner returns after an absence: this is a manifestation of joyous affection, and has no sexual implication as such. Two males at play often simulate copulation, although no erection is involved. In such cases it is a matter of one dog attempting to establish superiority over the other. The second dog will often refuse to accept this and start growling, and then it in turn will try to assume the male mating position. Some males raise no objection, and thus accept a rung low down on the hierarchic ladder (see **Hierarchy**,

211

p.207). Dogs are extremely aggressive when it comes to defending their own territory, but they will not fight when a bitch is on heat, and will accept being mounted. Males will court the bitch by rubbing against her, lining up and allowing her to make her choice. Sometimes she will pretend to run off, take a few steps, then sit down with her tail raised. Some bitches will accept several different males in quick succession, but as soon as a bitch feels that she has been fertilized, she will reject any further suitors, sometimes snapping and biting at them. In fact the males realize that she is no longer on heat – simply by sniffing her – and will wander away. A bitch's flirtatious behaviour may include rubbing herself tenderly against the dog, standing still with her tail raised high, and, most provocative of all, mounting the male to encourage him to mate with her. Mounting between members of the same sex is also a feature of other mammals, for example grazing cows.

Nuzzling and stroking: Touching with the muzzle is a gesture of tender affection. To win its mother's affection or attention, a puppy will prod the corner of her mouth with its nose and lick her. When a dog does the same thing to its owner, it too is asking for affection. If this tender gesture is rejected the animal will feel very bewildered and be unable to understand its human companion. This in turn will make it harder to train, because it will feel that its language is not being understood. During weaning the bitch regurgitates food which she has partly digested; she then offers it to her young, and they will happily eat it. (Regurgitation happens also in female wolves, jackals, African hunting dogs, and many species of birds.) To get their fair share of the regurgitated food the young push at the corners of their mother's mouth with their muzzles. This is precisely why a dog will push against its owner when he is eating, asking to share the food. If you stroke a puppy two to three weeks old on the corner of the mouth, it will yawn loudly. If a dog that has been scolded for some reason tries to touch the corner of its owner's mouth with its muzzle and

lick it, it is simply seeking to re-establish an affectionate relationship, and make it clear that it recognizes its owner as the head dog (see **Hierarchy**, p.207). A dog tends to jump up to greet anyone of whom it is fond, to make its ritual nose contact with the corners of the mouth. If the person stoops down, the dog will stop jumping at once. The best thing is to lay a hand on the dog's mouth and let it have a good lick (and then wash your hands afterwards): once the dog has expressed its welcome in its own instinctive way and with its own ceremonial ritual, it will calm down. If a dog is punished or mistreated when it jumps up, it will regard the person

All dogs will show a preference for some visitors over others. The reasons for their likes and dislikes are difficult to understand. In this photograph a handsome Great Dane warmly greets a friend with almost overwhelming affection.

who punishes it as someone beyond comprehension, with weird reactions, and find it hard to work with them. In order to train a dog you must make it very clear that you understand its language. Whenever a dog gives you an upward tap with its nose, it is expressing some desire or other, and is encouraging you to satisfy it. A dog may even ask to be stroked: it will stop

Sense of smell: Smell is a dog's chief sense (in other mammals, such as monkeys, for example, the sense of smell is weak and of only secondary importance), and this should be borne in mind if we are to understand fully a dog's attitudes and postures, and interpret them in linguistic terms. A new-born puppy is straight away capable of picking up smells. A dog's entire life can in fact be likened to a succession of olfactory impressions, just as a human being's life might be defined as a succession of visual impressions, and a dolphin's a succession of acoustic impressions. A dog has a typical carnivore's sense of smell, which explains why it is more receptive to animal than to vegetable scents. This in turn explains many canine attitudes and postures, and gives us a better possibility of coming to grips with a dog's particular language. In a dog's nose the network of olfactory nerves occupies an area equivalent to 160 sq cm (25 sq in), whereas in a human being it only takes up 5 sq cm (.75 sq in). This anatomical feature explains why a dog is at heart a 'sniffer' or 'smeller' of things, and also why a dog's behaviour (and thus its actual language) is, as a rule, nasal. Unlike human beings, who interpret with their eyes and see the world as a complex combination of colours, forms and perspectives, a dog interprets with its nose, and perceives the world in terms of lines, tracks, currents, spirals, volutes,

prodding with its nose and simply manoeuvre your hand up over its head with its muzzle. These are all signs of love, devotion and a desire to help, and it is very important to respond to these expressions of affection with similar gestures. Dogs with drooping ears (including Dachshunds, Greyhounds, Mastiffs, Poodles and Spaniels) particularly like to have their heads stroked, whereas dogs with erect ears (Sicilian Hounds, Sheepdogs, Pomeranians, etc.) prefer being stroked on the neck, throat, chest and back. Dogs belonging to the same breed will often take each other affectionately by the muzzle with their bare jaws, and pretend to bite each other, and an affectionate dog will do exactly the same thing with its master's hand: it is merely a warm invitation to play. If it not only takes your hand, but then pulls on it, this is an invitation to go for a walk.

A dog also has an affectionate way of saying 'good morning' to the people it cares for: it goes up close, wagging its tail, with its body moving all askew.

Above: a dog will normally direct its look straight at its owner, unless it is scolded, when it will look elsewhere. The Spinone has a gentle expression.

Below: The facial expression of the Bulldog is rather gruff.

combinations of smells and scents, scented tracks, exciting whiffs laden with meaning, places surrounded by specific smells, sweet-smelling things, animal and vegetable scents, and human scents – each one distinctive and specific. The tip of a dog's nose is moist which enables the dog to retain the scent-bearing particles in the air more effectively. As a result, it can pick up the scent of wild game at a distance of 200-300 m (220-330 yd), and human scent at a distance of up to 400-500 m (440-550 yd). It can also pick out a particular pebble, in a whole pile of stones, that has been held in a person's hand for only a couple of seconds. Our eyes present us with the world at the actual moment of visual perception, whereas the dog's sense of smell enables it to sniff out the past as well. By smelling its master's gun, clothing, suitcase or car-tyres, a dog will know where he and his gun and his suitcase have been, as well as the terrain over which he has driven his car.

Young dogs in particular greatly enjoy rubbing their neck, muzzle and shoulders against strong-smelling substances, and will often roll in them, too. Some dogs only roll on grass, but others choose animal faeces. This behaviour, which comes quite naturally to dogs, is not viewed too kindly by human beings. It can be remedied by careful training.

The most exciting experience of scent occurs when a bitch is on heat. Her state can be smelt several kilometres away, and a dog may travel day and night to find her.

The French ethologist J. Goldberg maintains that the acuteness of a dog's sense of smell is 100 million times greater than that of a human being. It is this sense that is at the root of any dog's role as man's right hand.

Expression: A dog's facial expressions contain a wealth of meanings. If a dog looks at you candidly, straight in the eye, this indicates a relationship of understanding and security. If a dog never looks you straight in the eye, this means that you have not managed to understand its language or establish a good working relationship with it. If a dog constantly shifts its gaze from place to place, this means that it is not fond of you, and may even be afraid of you. If a strange dog comes towards you looking rather menacing, with a particular staring look, this means that it may well bite you if you make the slightest movement: it is advisable to keep still.

Sympathy (liking): Dogs show signs of sympathy (liking) towards some people, and antipathy towards others. Not only will a dog allow some people to stroke it but not others: it will even bark at certain passers-by, and wag its tail at others.

Sociability: The sociability of a dog depends largely on its first contact with people, when it is between three and seven weeks old. This is the period when what Lorenz calls 'imprinting' takes place. If there is no contact with people during this time, a dog will never become particularly sociable. If dogs spend the first two months of their lives alone with their parents and other dogs, without getting to know or being with people, they will stay aloof from human beings all their lives, and be reserved and difficult to train. The very opposite happens if, from birth, they have been stroked by people, and become familiar with human smells. When you are choosing and training a dog it is important to take this imprinting process into account. The ideal situation is when a puppy realizes in its imprinting period that people are friends and companions with whom it can play and work. Do not, however, try to achieve this by keeping the puppy apart from other dogs – its brothers and sisters, and its parents – with which it can play. If you do, it will become resentful, snarling at other dogs, and this may well affect its hunting and other abilities when it inevitably comes into contact with other dogs with whom it must work. Natural sociability is easy to observe in dogs in villages, where they often form small groups and roam around the area together. In a similar way, town- and city-dogs often gather in the street and only return home in the evening, to eat and sleep. Dogs are often ready to befriend other domestic creatures such as cats, horses, poultry and rabbits. In the United States, V.C. Stanley and his colleagues have shown that young dogs have such a degree of sociability towards people that they consider themselves rewarded by the mere presence of a human being close by, even if the person remains passive and does not speak. A puppy that has no people around will quickly grow sad. For dogs in general, and for young dogs in particular, the absence of people is tantamount to a shortage of mental and spiritual nourishment.

Sleep: When an adult dog is asleep it does not want contact: it prefers to be quite alone. Puppies, on the other hand, invariably need to be close to something that is hairy, soft and warm (in the absence of their mother, or their brothers and sisters). If they are not, they will whine and whimper continuously. When a dog prepares to sleep it curls up in such a way as to protect its most sensitive parts: ribs, abdomen and genitals. Huskies sleep in this position beneath the snow. Some dogs – various types of Spaniel, Bulldog and Pekingese, for example – prefer to sleep flat in the position of the newborn pup: the hind-quarters splayed out, the belly flat on the floor, and the head resting on the front legs: in that posture they often look like a furry ring.

Dogs dream while they sleep. Young puppies will twitch their ears and move their legs; adult dogs will stir, yelp and even growl while they dream. If a dog is awoken from a dream, its eyes will have a bewildered look, and it will take some time to rouse itself – just like a human being. Dogs probably dream of smells, just as we dream of images (see **Sense of smell**, p.212). One certain fact is that when they are asleep all dogs make noises which have to do exclusively with dreaming, and have no equivalent in their waking hours. When it dreams a dog possibly experiences a world that differs from the 'real' world.

Before settling down to sleep in its basket a dog that sleeps curled up will turn round several times in its bed. For some time this gesture was regarded as instinctive, a throw-back to those remote days when a dog that wanted to go to sleep would flatten a bush or a patch of grass to make itself a comfortable 'bed'. Darwin based one of his many arguments for evolution on this phenomenon. Other observers have noted that the more a dog has walked, the more it will turn about in its basket before settling down and going to sleep.

One explanation of this turning round habit is that it is designed to find the right curvature of the backbone. If the latter is tired and stiff or sore from a long walk, the dog will have to seek the right position for some time before it finds it, just as human beings, when they go to bed exhausted, shift about for a while before getting comfortable. A dog tends to sleep with its head turned towards the entrance to its basket, or the door of the room, or the front door of the house.

Touch: Touch has to do with sensations of contact or pressure that occur in a dog's hair, skin and mucous membranes. The various tactile sensations include itching and tickling. Each one is intense on each single hair, especially close to the follicle. Touch is stimulated by electric currents, thermal conditions, and possibly by the earth's magnetic field as well, and may last for a certain period after the stimulus has disappeared.

It seems that the human sense of touch is considerably diminished by our actual living conditions, by our clothing, and because we use it infrequently, whereas in dogs the sense of touch is of great importance. In fact, dogs live all the time close to the ground, which is constantly providing them with countless clues. A dog's body is covered all over with hair that transmits various vibrations with different meanings. In addition dogs have a deep-seated tactile sensitivity emanating from the muscles, tendons, bones and internal organs. Because touch is so important for a dog, and for a dog's language (in the form, for example, of scratching, rolling and licking) it is worth remembering how essential it is to stroke a dog when in the process of training it.

Time: Dogs have a clearly defined sense of time, which is like a rhythm. If you feed a dog at precise times, you will see that it starts to grow excited as the moment draws near. The same thing can be observed even if there is nothing of direct interest to the dog — such as food — at stake. A mountain dog will take the flock out to pasture and fetch it back again on the dot. The same is true for a companion dog that is used to going to meet the children of the family from school, or for a dog living in kennels whose training programme is at fixed times. Some even maintain that dogs' sense of temporal rhythm follows a weekly pattern.

Territory: Like many other creatures (including birds, the members of the cat family, and rodents, dogs have a sense of territory. This is why they will guard a flat or home, or patrol a garden or watch over property in general. Dogs will not allow people into their territory. They position themselves at a central point, marking the edge of the territory with their own scent and frequently renewing it (see **Urination**, p.215). Birds sing, lions roar, and dogs bark to indicate their own territorial supremacy. A territory may belong to just one dog, or a pair, or a whole pack. If a dog happens to find itself on another dog's territory it will behave warily and with respect, avoiding fight with the other dog, the 'boss around here'. If the owner arrives, the intruder will not look at it, and pretend to be busy doing something else; then it will move off in a dignified manner. A territory is often surrounded by an area which the dog uses, but does not defend. For village-dwelling dogs this area will be where they make their forays, and go for walks with their owners; for urban dogs it will be a public park or a field at the edge of town. This area — known as the 'living space' — may also be where the dogs habitually hunt. It is in the 'living space' that a dog puts its 'street signs': not signs denoting territorial ownership, but fixed points along the dog's usual routes. This is why, when a male dog is out for a

walk, it will almost always urinate by the same trees, street-lamps, and corners. A female canary chirrups, but does not sing, and a bitch does not demarcate territorial borders with her urine or provide 'street-signs', except when she is on heat, when she will urinate much more often to tell neighbourhood dogs that she is available. (It is worth mentioning that male dogs mark out their territory somewhat less when it is very cold or snowing.)

The constant aggressiveness of a dog kept on a short leash is due to the fact that its territory has been reduced to an absolute minimum. In time a chain will cause a dog to become unbalanced, and therefore unable to obey its natural impulse to live in harmony with man. However, a chain or leash used intelligently can be extremely useful when it comes to house-training a puppy.

Herbivorous and non-aggressive animals also mark out their territory — the roebuck, for example, by rubbing the scent-producing glands in its head against branches, the beaver with the glands beneath the tail. There is even a sense of territory in certain types of fish.

Hearing: For dogs the sense of hearing is next in acuteness to the sense of smell. Because of this a dog moves its ears a great deal and, as the movements are often a sign of its feelings, they make its language easier to understand. It is important not to expose very young puppies (born with their ears closed up) to excessive noise, bangs and shouts. A fright of this kind suffered in its earliest days can cause a dog to be permanently scared of certain noises, such as gunfire, with serious consequences for its usefulness when it is trained. A dog's sense of hearing is sixteen times more acute than our own. A sound that we hear faintly at 100 m (110 yd) can be picked up by a dog at a distance of 1.5 km (1640 yd). A dog is more efficient than a human being at pin-pointing the source of a particular noise, and can calculate its exact distance more precisely, too. A dog will often appear to go on the alert or bark for no apparent reason; it may well be that it is picking

up one of the many ultrasounds inaudible to human beings. It is possible to train a dog for specialized tasks by means of the so-called 'silent whistle'; a useful technique for frontier duties, film work and so on.

Urination: When a dog simply wants to urinate it will produce an even, regular flow of urine; when it urinates little and often, in short jets, it wishes to indicate the limits of its own territory to other dogs — and other animals in general: it is, in effect, leaving them a message. If a male dog finds itself outside its own territory (as urban dogs often do) it marks its route by urinating, where it can, over smells left behind by other dogs. When a dog cocks its leg (a deliberate action, because it can, if it wants, urinate without doing so), it is also indicating its own size and strength. Scents can communicate a lot to one dog about the territory, sex, age, state of health and so on of another. Bitches and puppies to not need to assert their strength in this way: in fact, for them it is prefer-

Above: When sleeping, some breeds, such as the Bulldog, sleep flat out. Opposite: More commonly, sleeping dogs curl up in the manner of this German Shepherd.

able not to reveal too much about themselves to a possible adversary. This is why they urinate in just one spot (three or four times a day, in the case of a female), preferrring places where their traces will not be very obvious, and will disappear before very long: in sand, grass, leaves, etc. When males of different sizes urinate at the same territorial border point — the corner of a wall, or against a pole or tree, for example — it is interesting that a small dog will try to cock its leg as high as possible to hit the mark left earlier by a larger dog. If a very large male passes by the same spot later, it may well try to urinate lower down than normal, over the mark left by the little dog. It is possible to recognize an energetic dog by the way it urinates — in short, strong bursts — and use this information for training purposes.

When weak, timid dogs live in a pack, they will either not even dare cock a leg to urinate, or will only do so reluctantly. An energetic male will urinate with plenty of exhibitionistic jets where a female on heat has left her scent. Some bitches will cock a leg to urinate, or sometimes even both their hind legs, assuming an almost vertical position. A puppy quickly learns to urinate outside the house, before it has reached the stage of leaving territorial marks. An adult dog, living in kennels or in the country, which has always marked its territorial borders, finds this less easy to learn. An adult dog that is otherwise always clean will sometimes leave its mark if a visitor brings another dog to the house, and the problem may get worse if the visiting dog is a bitch on heat: she should be left at home.

Sight: The eyesight of dogs is mediocre when compared to that of human beings and birds (three times better than ours). A dog lost in a crowd and searching for its owner glances anxiously hither and thither, heads for a passerby and when it is only a few metres away, realizes that this is not the person for whom it is looking. Dogs apparently do not see colours. On the other hand, they do distinguish degrees of brightness. When guide-dogs for the blind are in training they cannot tell the difference between red and green traffic lights, but they can distinguish the position of the colours in the top light and the bottom light. However, some breeds of dog see better than others, and some hunt by sight rather than smell – Greyhounds are one example. Their eye detects game as it moves, but has trouble doing so when the game is stationary. Twilight and broad daylight are much the same to dogs, and they see better at night than human beings. A dog's total visual field is 250°, compared to man's 180°, but the binocular field of vision is lower: 90° in the fox terrier, and 140° in man, although some other breeds (smaller Griffons, Pekingese) have the same level of binocular vision as human beings. It is interesting that even though a dog's sight is mediocre, it will look at anyone to whom it is attached straight in the eye. The response to this expression of devotion should be a direct, sincere and warm look. For human being and dog to look at one another in an affectionate and attentive way is regarded as the best form of bond – almost a psychic 'leash' – between trainer and trainee.

Vocal sounds: Dogs make many different vocal sounds with various meanings. Below is a list of the main ones. All other dogs understand them quite easily, but in many cases the same cannot be said of owners.

Barking The type of bark corresponds to some extent to the breed to which the dog belongs; but it is also, in some measure, individual and peculiar to each dog. A trained ear can, for example, tell whether a bark comes from a Setter or a Boxer, male or female. The tone of the bark is more or less hereditary. Each individual owner can recognize the bark of his own dog, and attach a dozen or so meanings to it: a warning that strangers are approaching, or that a strange animal is present, greeting members of the family returning home, playing with a child or friend, challenging passing dogs, expressing fear because of a danger, asking for water (this is a specific, rather whimpering bark), asking for food, asking to play, and signalling in similar ways.

There are dogs given to barking, such as Terriers, and taciturn dogs such as Greyhounds, and dogs that do not bark at all such as Basenjis; there are howling or yelping dogs, such as Hounds, and dogs that are excellent at warning such as Pomeranians and Poodles.

Yelping A yelp is always a request for help, where it is uttered by puppies or adult dogs.

Growling: There is the playful growl (short and distinct) and the threatening growl (prolonged, hostile, menacing, deep and hoarse, uttered between the throat and the teeth). A dog may sometimes grind its teeth when it growls.

Whimpering This is a sign of pain or injury, and may also be a form of protest or a request for help.

Yapping This is forceful, hostile and prolonged barking, often to be heard in the country at night.

Whining This is a sort of moaning sound, low in pitch and prolonged. It indicates a lack of well-being, discontent, impatience, and is a plea for pity or attention. Sometimes it may be a way of saying 'Open the door, please', or 'Let's go', or 'I'm fed up here, let's go home.'

Howling A loud, sad noise, made by day or by night, sometimes as a reaction to music or to bells ringing. Other dogs may join in. It is common among some Hounds, and habitual in the Dingo.

Puffing A sort of warning sneeze, a repressed bark with the mouth shut, the first indication that a stranger is approaching, or that there is a suspicious noise somewhere; when a dog 'puffs' or snorts in this way, it will always aim its head at the source of the noise.

When hunting, dogs make various vocal sounds (depending on their breed and use), each of which has a meaning for the hunter. The same is true of dogs used for tracking human beings, for guarding and rescue work.

INSTINCTS AND IMPULSES

The word 'instinct' is ambiguous and is often incorrectly used. Instincts are automatic impulses that have a purpose; and they are innate, not learned, because they are inherited. But from whom does the worker bee inherit its skills, if it is the offspring of a queen and a drone, neither of whom has done a stroke of work? All the members of any given species always carry out their instinctive actions in precisely the same way: the spider weaves its web perfectly each time, the bird builds its nest to perfection the very first time it embarks on the task, and does not improve its technique over the years. Conversely, the hunting instinct in a puppy or its defensive instinct improve considerably as time goes by, and with training. There are imperfect or 'mistaken' instincts, too: for example, that of the newborn elephant that sucks its mother's tail instead of her teat, and dies as a result. Dogs have an innate instinct to bury

any surplus food; this is an automatic action and the dog burying the food does not know why it is doing so; in a similar way a mole will store earthworms in autumn for winter food, removing their heads, which does not kill them but prevents them from burrowing, and thus getting away. A good knowledge of a dog's instincts helps to create a better understanding of its language, but it does not have a great deal of importance when it comes to training. A dog is not a slave to its instincts and this is precisely why it has plenty of personality. A dog can overcome powerful and compelling instinctive feelings: it can, for example, hold back its bodily functions so as not to soil the home, whereas parrots, which are highly intelligent, cannot do this; a dog can stop chasing prey and go to ground on a simple order from its master; the cat, which is so highly domesticated, will not do this. The training of a dog is based not so much on instincts as impulses and for the most part these are inherited, and only rarely acquired.

It is generally easy to distinguish between the short growl of a dog that is playing and the deep hoarse growl of a dog that is hostile and menacing.

Inherited impulses:

(1) **The food impulse** This gives rise to the impulses to do with hunting, tracking, digging, violently shaking prey held firmly in the mouth; it is also linked with retrieving, and, of course, a dog's greediness, very useful in training.

(2) **The movement impulse** Connected with pursuit, searching, herding; and slightly less with retrieving, and the enjoyment of play, also very useful in training.

(3) **The fighting impulse** Connected with combativeness, readiness to bite, determination when hunting and guarding.

(4) **The defensive impulse** The opposite of (3), and closely linked with the individual's status in the hierarchy. The defensive impulse is stronger in females than males. It sometimes leads to surrender, or flight, or even to an apparent readiness to bite, which is why some dogs will bite out of fear. It can be quite useful in training.

(5) **The power impulse** Makes a dog want to hold the highest possible position in the hierarchy of the pack. Since it regards its human company as a sort of pack, if it has a strong power impulse, and if its owner or owners are easy-going or indecisive, it will show a tendency to disobey, or become stubborn or rebellious. Properly used, the power impulse will produce excellent results in training.

(6) **The impulse to know** Connected with a dog's curiosity and keenness to explore.

Acquired impulses:

(1) **Direct experience** The teaching provided by life; it can give rise to both positive and negative impulses. In training it is sometimes necessary to modify or bolster the dog's negative or positive impulses (defects or qualities) which may have resulted from previous experiences – frightening experiences to do with the noise of a gun, or enjoyable experiences to do with retrieving, and so on.

(2) **Training** In the training processes human beings supply dogs with direct experiences, designed for some useful purpose, by taking into account the dog's innate impulses.

THE THREE MEMORIES

To complete our exploration of a dog's psychology, we should know how its memory works. A dog remembers smells and sounds just as human beings remember images and words. We can, in fact, talk in terms of three memories: mechanical, affective and associative.

The mechanical memory is that very conspicuous faculty in a dog for retaining the experience of movements it has made, and thus being able to reproduce them mechanically, with less and less effort. For example, a trained Pointer will lie down on the ground as soon as it hears a shot; a trained guard-dog will sit as soon as its master stops walking.

The affective memory is the ability to reproduce previous states of mind associated with certain particular conditions whenever these present themselves. For example, a hunting dog's face will show its pleasure as soon as it sees its master go for his gun; the companion dog will bark boldly as soon as it hears the doorbell ring; a dog trained to react to the command 'Bark!' reproduces in itself the excitement which makes it bark.

The associative memory is the ability to understand the gesture or word of command of the trainer, and to carry out the desired action. At first the trainee dog does not grasp the meaning of the command 'Down!' or 'Sit!' or of the raised arm; but in time it associates the voice and the gesture with the movement which it is meant to convey to the animal.

The associative memory is vital to a dog: without it training would not be possible. However, some associations are useful, while others are certainly undesirable.

Undesirable associations: If we give commands, such as 'Sit!', 'Lie down!'; 'Sit!', 'Lie down!' at regular five-second intervals, the association that will form in the dog's mind will no longer relate to the command but to the time involved, and the dog will change positions after five seconds without waiting for the command. The most talented dogs tend to be the ones that develop undesirable associations, although

these are invariably caused by the trainer's mistakes. It is enough, for example, to give commands at irregular intervals for the undesirable association not to form. Another example: when teaching a dog on a lead how to retrieve game, watch that it does not pull at the lead; if it does this two or three times, it will carry on doing so. To get rid of this undesirable association, make the job of retrieving an enjoyable one, and stroke the dog, and give it a reward. Undesirable associations can be spotted quickly and nipped in the bud. With regard to rewards, make sure that they do not become monotonous (always the same sort of stroking, or always the same titbit).

The mechanical aspect of association may also be harmful in other ways. When a highly trained trial dog or a terrier used for underground prey has always worked in a certain place or under certain conditions, it will not work efficiently elsewhere. The trial dog may well turn out to be rather mediocre when it comes to the real hunt; the Dachshund used to the artificial burrow will not have much idea how to flush out a real fox before it wreaks havoc in the chicken-coop; a guard-dog will attack someone wearing protective clothing, but not a real villain wearing normal clothes. It is therefore important to avoid this mechanical aspect and its dangers.

DISTRACTIONS

During training it is advisable to make use of distractions all the time. Do not train a dog for too long in an enclosed area (a room, yard or garden): there will only be few distractions, and they will always be the same. As soon as the dog leaves the enclosed space, all the novel things in the world outside will distract it, and everything gained in terms of obedience will be lost. If you change places, circumstances, times and conditions frequently you will soon manage to reinforce the results achieved by the dog, and give them a solid foundation. A dog is useful when it adapts its skills to a wide range of practical requirements that may crop up on the hunt, during guard duties, while tracking, and so on.

Developing the lively intelligence of a dog calls for a sympathetic understanding of the animal's psychology and an ability to combine firm discipline with warm affection throughout the training period.

Hounds, or with just one dog that has all these skills 'under one roof', as it were.

To the dog-lover whose particular liking is any dog used for personal protection, guarding, attacking, rescuing and tracking – and who wants at his side a faithful and alert helper, ready to protect him against dangers of all sorts.

To those who require a good working dog: for looking after sheep and cattle, for hauling and pack-work, for pulling a sledge, for film and television work, for police and military duties (sniffing out and detecting mines, weapons and drugs), for fire duties, for anti-burglar duties, for rescue work when buildings are demolished, and for duties on board ship.

To anyone who is handicapped – the blind, the deaf, or the crippled – and who needs a dog to give guidance, warning and help.

To those who are fond of dogs' sporting skills at shows, competitions, trials, and racing.

To those who want the companionship of a dog, who want their home to include a devoted animal with centuries of understanding of human beings in its make-up. To those who live in modern towns and cities at such a distance from nature. To those for whom trials and tribulations are made up for by the presence of a faithful friend. (It is well established that the friendship of a dog gives elderly people not only greater mobility, but also greater strength to come to terms with solitude, or loneliness, a sense of safety in the home, and a knowledge that someone still needs them and loves them, and will not criticize them.)

This book is intended for all these people. In the following pages everyone will find appropriate hints and words of advice. With a little effort and commitment, anyone can enjoy bringing up and training his or her own favourite dog.

CONCLUSION

In our Dictionary we have delved into the secrets of dogs of all sizes. We have understood a dog's language, based as it is on the senses of smell and hearing. We have grasped the dog's sense of hierarchy and its need for a society (or pack) in which the man (master) or woman (mistress) is the 'boss'. We have understood how a dog expresses its intentions, or wishes, with its whole body, from eyes to tail. We have seen how dogs enjoy playing. We have learnt about their strength of will and their sense of territory; their many and varied impulses; their ways of 'talking'; and how they sleep. We now know about their memory and the associations deriving from it, both desirable and undesirable. In fact we now know who this creature – the dog – is, and so we can ask it to work – and live – in harmony with us. In this modern world, with all its problems and burdens, training a dog can give you hours and days of relaxation and fun. In a word, a dog is (and should remain) a thoroughly enjoyable friend and companion.

But to whom are we speaking? To the hunter, who is quite sure that there is nothing finer, more thrilling and more fulfilling on earth than hunting with expert Pointers, trackers, Retrievers, Setters, with dogs that work underground, in water, or in a pack of

TRAINING

A pair of Afghan Hounds. The popularity of this breed has grown considerably in recent years.

TRAINING A PUPPY
Choosing your puppy
Some readers may not be too sure what to do when choosing a puppy. What kind of dog to choose? A pedigree or a mongrel? and what breed? Should you buy the animal, or get a friend to give you one? A dog or a bitch? A puppy, a young dog, or an adult?

What kind of dog?
This certainly depends very much on what it will be used for: hunting, general working duties, sports, or as a companion. The hunting dog may belong to breeds which are specially good at pointing or tracking or retrieving, working underground, or pursuing; some breeds can be trained in all the different hunting skills. In order to choose the most suitable breed, it is important to know whether the dog will be kept in the home or in a kennel, in the town or in the country; the type of hunting you intend to do; the number of dogs you may have and – if you have several – whether you want them all for a certain type of hunting, or one for pointing and one for retrieving, one for tracking and another for underground work, and so on. An all-purpose dog can be useful for personal protection or for human rescue work, as well as for police and border duties, working in films and so on; or you might choose a dog for a special ability.

If the sporting dog is wanted for racing, a Greyhound will be the obvious choice; if it is wanted for shows, the choice could as easily be a Chihuahua or a St Bernard; a dog intended for trials could be a sheepdog of some kind, a mountain dog or a Dobermann. The companion or family dog must be chosen on the basis of the size of the home and the type of household (basically whether there are children or not): a toy or miniature breed or type for a city flat or apartment, and a very large dog for a farm or large country house. This book has already described the major breeds and discussed their personalities and the uses for which they can be trained. The choice is yours, once you have taken the various relevant factors into consideration.

Pedigree or mongrel?
The pedigree or thoroughbred breeds are the result of selection over a very long time in such a way as to produce specimens with standard physical and mental features. In the case of a thoroughbred dog purchased from a good breeder (and not from someone who happens to have a litter of puppies, or from a shopkeeper who buys and sells dogs like any other commodity), there will be no surprises. For the practical reasons outlined above, it is advisable to choose a thoroughbred dog belonging to a breed suitable for the purpose or purposes you have in mind; and it is well worth going to a breeder who does not restrict himself to selecting just the most handsome of dogs for showing, but one who also selects sound dogs for working purposes as well. If the choice lies between a good working dog and a good show-dog the author would tend to choose the former. Another advantage of the thoroughbred dog is that it has a financial value that is lasting, whereas a mongrel may cost nothing or next to nothing, but has no market value either. Furthermore, by selecting a pedigree dog you will also be improving that particular breed and reducing the number of strays. For many years the author has bred only thoroughbred dogs, 'producing' show champions and working champions, and even

'creating' a breed, the Neapolitan Mastiff. But there are perhaps other considerations besides these.

The 'purists' may protest, but it must be said that the author has known mongrel dogs (of all shapes and sizes and ages) who were not only truly fine and beautiful, but also gifted in hunting, protection, hauling and film work, as well as being excellent family companions. Of course they were excluded from taking part in sporting events requiring pedigrees, but in all other respects they were useful all-round dogs.

So, if you cannot afford a thoroughbred dog, you may well find a great deal of satisfaction in training a mongrel. Dogs have a moral worth that must be respected and defended, regardless of whether or not they have a pedigree.

Opposite: Choosing a puppy from a litter of German Shepherds.

Right: Many mongrels are physically attractive and good-natured and can make good pets.

Four stages in the growth of a pup

4 days

28 days

56 days

156 days

Breeders

Do not buy from anyone who breeds and deals in all kinds of animals. For these breeders a dog is just an animal from which to make a profit; they are not qualified or competent. Do not buy, either, from dealers who deal in all kinds of dogs – small, large, medium-sized, thoroughbreds and mongrels. And do not put too much trust in vets: they tend to recommend the dogs owned by their clients. Most are excellent at their job – looking after dogs – but as a rule they are not knowledgeable about the temperaments of different breeds. Never buy a dog from someone who has a box in the bathroom containing a mother and her pups: he has probably had the bitch mounted by the first dog to appear on the scene and is now desperate to get rid of the results, which are making the house dirty.

Do not buy on a sudden impulse because you happen to feel like having a dog on that particular day. Remember that you are choosing a helper, a colleague, a working companion, a

tended use of the dog you are after. Any good breeder has rivals, and he will take pains to preserve his reputation: you can have confidence in him. Make sure, however, that you go in person to fetch your dog: it will be well worth the trouble.

Choosing a puppy

Here you are with a breeder showing you four or five pups between 50 and 60 days old. Do not take any puppy from a litter of more than seven: the mother will not have been able to suckle them properly. (Another thing to consider here is whether the breeder has given the excess puppies a good 'wet-nurse'.) So, how do you choose the right one? (1) First and foremost, have a good look at the parents. (2) Rule out any puppies that are clearly much smaller than the others, any thin puppies, and any that are trembling even if it is warm; do not bother with any puppies that lack liveliness, stay in a corner, or look sad. (3) Of those that remain, do not choose one with a large, taut belly

pupil, a friend, a member of the family, an animal to be proud of, and an animal that will, it is to be hoped, provide a lot of pleasure. You will have the companionship of your dog in enjoyable times and in sad ones.

The good breeder of dogs is an enthusiast, like you, the potential purchaser. He or she usually aims to improve just one or two breeds. This will often be simply a pastime, and it usually costs money, sometimes a good deal. However, breeders enjoy their work, and go to shows, trials and competitions, in the hope of winning a prize. A few breeders actually manage to live off their kennels, but not many of them; the majority simply breed dogs for the love of it. Having chosen the breed of dog you want, go to an expert, and preferably a local expert. Rule out any breeder who is breeding four or more breeds: he is likely to be a dealer in disguise. Dealers do not select their dogs in the same way as a proper breeder, and if a breed is not properly selected, it will decline.

If you have to write to a breeder, specify precisely the sex, age and in-

(indicating round-worm), even though it has not yet eaten solid food at this stage; reject any puppy with its back arched like a camel's (unless it is a Greyhound you are buying); with signs of diarrhoea; any with large rhachitic swellings on the front legs, or with markedly bent legs (unless you are buying a Bulldog); do not consider a puppy that eagerly gobbles up faeces dropped by its brothers and sisters. (4) Pick up the puppies that have passed all these tests. Take a close look at the almost bare skin on the belly: if you see any small pimples, reject the dog, since these may indicate distemper or enteritis. Make sure the eyes are not affected by catarrh; the nose must be cold and moist (although if a puppy has just woken up its nose may stay dry for a while). Do not take any puppy that has an obvious swelling round the navel, which may mean a hernia. (5) Now you are left with the pick of the bunch, the liveliest and sturdiest pups. You can let your heart do the choosing from now on. (6) It is now time to pay the breeder the price

Opposite, top: A Bulldog bitch with a pup. To make the right choice of a puppy it is advisable to see it with its parents or at least with its mother. Opposite, bottom: Liveliness in a puppy is a good sign, as with this Corgi.

Right: An Italian Greyhound with pups suckling while she stands.

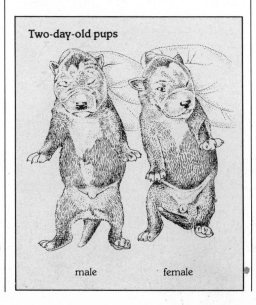

Two-day-old pups

male   female

he is asking. Do not haggle. If you cannot afford the asking price, say so quite openly, and offer the most you can manage. Remember, the breeder is a dog-lover just as you are: he will try to come to the best possible arrangement.

Dog or bitch?
A male dog will usually have a stronger personality and physique; females are more adaptable. A dog is more impetuous, energetic and combative; a bitch is gentler, more sensitive and more intelligent. Bitches are preferable for certain forms of training (as guide-dogs for the blind, for example). A bitch will be more affectionate, a dog may be somewhat rough. It is only the inexperienced who think of male dogs when they think about dogs in general. A bitch comes on heat twice a year, but a dog may wander off and roam all year long if it picks up the scent of a bitch on heat, even if she is some way away.

A dog and a bitch can live quite happily together without ever mating. A large male dog may become a stud and be in demand, earning quite sizeable fees for each mounting: and a fine bitch may give birth to pups that will be booked in advance by knowledge-able dog-fanciers. So what is it to be: a dog or a bitch? First-time trainers will have more success with a bitch, but

Puppy, young dog, or adult dog?

Buy a puppy 50 to 60 days old if you have the means and the time to train it from the word go. Take a young dog of 7 to 12 months if you are after a show-dog and you want to avoid the risk of buying a puppy that may or may not become a prize-winning champion. Choose a young dog if you do not manage to find the right puppy. As far as training is concerned, you can train any young dog between the ages of six months and two years, just as you can train a two-, three- or five-year-old adult dog. Some dog-lovers prefer adult specimens, either semi-trained, or trained for hunting, guarding or sporting uses. Remember that a dog that works perfectly with a professional trainer will rarely work as well with a master lacking the same skills. When you buy an adult dog you must get used to it and it must get used to you, so you will have to be very firm to begin with so that the necessary understanding between the two of you is established.

Advice: Before buying a puppy, think about whether you are in a position to rear it properly. A puppy is a delicate young creature that cannot be farmed out here, there and everywhere. It needs you to look after it, and it needs a happy household. If you cannot feed it four times a day, buy a young dog of up to two years of age. Do not believe the absurd notion that a dog aged one or two will not grow fond of you. If you

expert and seasoned trainers often prefer a dog that requires a firm hand. You must make your own personal choice, depending on the type of life the dog will lead, where it will live, and how, and on your own personal preferences.

Dogs as gifts?

The financial value of a dog ranges from nil to astronomical sums. It is often difficult to give away an ordinary, undistinguished dog as a present, but a pure-bred, beautiful and perfectly trained dog can be worth a fortune, and will always find a buyer. With very few exceptions, anyone who gives a dog away simply wants to get rid of it as easily as possible.

All dogs are suitable at one and the same time for guard duties, hunting and companionship. A Poodle will turn into a hound when it sees a hare, act as a guard and also companion. Opposite, top: The Wire-haired Pointing Griffon has been bred for pointing but it can be trained as a guard and is a fine companion-dog. Opposite, bottom: The Schnauzer, bred for ratting, is a good general dog.

buy your young dog from a kennel, it will become your friend for life from the very first.

Let us suppose you have chosen a young dog, and that you are about to take it home, with every intention of training and house-training it in the best possible way. These are some of the things you ought to know.

The right time
During this century, in Europe in particular, methods of training dogs for hunting or for general work have frequently changed, as a result of detailed studies of animal psychology. People are increasingly aware of the importance, in training, of abiding by the various cycles which correspond to the nature, and the physical and spiritual growth of the dog. Ethology (**ethos** = custom, **logos** = science) is the study of the natural habits, customs and behavioural patterns of animals. In the training of dogs, the first lesson to be learnt from present-day ethology is that it is no longer possible to write treatises or training manuals and handbooks by separating the various breeds on the basis of their particular speciality or expertise: hunting, guarding, companionship. All dogs are at once hunting dogs **and** guard-dogs **and** companion dogs. Nowadays we must take into account the whole range of canine psychology if we want to achieve the best results as quickly as possible.

Present-day ethology has a second lesson. From birth to the age of 50 days, the puppy needs both its mother's care and human imprinting. In all creatures imprinting occurs at a precise moment in the first cycle of infancy, and does not last long. Once acquired, the imprinting is irreversible, and irrevocable: it will be instrumental in the dog's future behaviour. Lorenz says that it is because of imprinting that the very young animal recognizes the members of its own species. Man must make sure the very young puppy knows him (at the age of 20 days or slightly more, but no more than 50) if he is to be regarded as a friend and fellow-being, a trainer and a master (see **Sociability**, p.213).

At between 70 and 90 days the puppy can fend for itself, survive outdoors, run away from any enemies, join a pack and become aware of the attitudes and postures of its father, and other senior animals. In a word, it can learn about hierarchy.

When it is four months old it starts to co-operate, in its puppyish way, with adults, who become its teachers: they teach it how the pack behaves, and about collective tasks, tracking, hunting, defence and attack and collaboration. These foundations of collective life are consolidated by the age of six months. During this period the puppy is by its nature open to this type of teaching.

At ten months the individual is regarded as an adult by the pack. The parents, with whom the puppy has lived for most of the time throughout the preceding months, now reject it. the pack no longer looks on it as an

apprentice, but as a free agent. By this time the puppy-turned-adult has learnt the essential things: it is time to set to work.

Given that a puppy that is to live with people does not live in a pack any more, its nature will expect from this human society everything that the canine pack would have given it. This is why a puppy is easily trained between the age of 50 and 90 days; trained for some special task between three and six months; and prepared to do work from the age of six months onwards. This quickness to learn conforms to the animal's own pattern of development and will produce the best results.

It is possible to train dogs for all uses and at all ages, be it after ten months or five years. It is up to you. It is simply easier, more profitable and rewarding, and more convenient to start with a young puppy. Among other things it has the advantage of creating empathy, and training cannot work without empathy, the capacity to identify oneself with another living creature. Without a merging of heart and mind (human and canine) there can be no training.

Advice: Some puppies are reared on a bottle and deprived of their mother's natural tender loving care, for particular reasons. As adults, such dogs will often be timid, unadaptable, and even depressed. Similarly, puppies that are removed from their mother pre-

Above: German Shepherd puppies following their master. The first impressions made on a puppy will determine its future behaviour.

Below: A Norfolk Terrier puppy with a rabbit. If a dog is to live with other animals, the sooner the better.

maturely (i.e., before 50 days) may be quite disoriented for some time.

First Puppy Programme
The First Programme applies to puppies between 50 and 90 days old, of any type and breed, to be used for hunting, general duties, or for sport. The psychology of the dog is at one and the same time the psychology of a hunter, a guardian and a companion.

The Programme for the puppy of this age involves seven instructions: (1) Imprinting (which begins at three weeks). (2) The order 'Basket!' (3) Calling by name, and by whistling. (4) The command 'No!' and cautioning when the puppy growls. (5) The commands 'Lie down!' and 'Come here!' (6) Cleanliness in the house. (7) The command 'Fetch!'

If this Programme is used with a certain sense of fun, you will soon be won over by the co-operation and good will of your diminutive pupil, just a few weeks old, but already striving hard to understand and obey you. Keep in mind at all times the need for

empathy: without it, without identification, understanding and affection, all you will end up doing is dominating a poor little creature that is already very attached to you and wants to be loved. If you cannot identify with it, stop trying to train your puppy – in fact, give up dogs altogether.

Advice: Never over-burden your young pupil when you start the training programme. Stop as soon as a particular exercise has been carried out successfully just once. The puppy needs a rest once it has understood what you mean by a new command. Do not be sparing with praise and kindly words – if anything, overdo them. Of all animals the dog is the most sensitive to reward in the form of praise.

Another word of advice: Make sure the rewards you offer are not monotonous – always the same sort of stroking, the same words of praise, or the same tasty titbit; rewards must be varied: a small pat on the head, then another small pat on the back; a simple 'Well done!', followed by an enthusiastic 'Well done! Good dog! What a good dog you are!'; a familiar titbit, followed next time by an unfamiliar morsel. Variation in the rewards keeps the puppy's level of keenness sharp, increases its good will, and speeds up the whole training process.

And a third word of advice: in its formative period a puppy needs to be surrounded by a calm and happy environment. In the words of an English expert, Cofield: 'Angry voices, which can be raised in the happiest of households, have a harmful effect on puppies. If crying babies are shouted at, a dog will cower away as if the reproach were addressed to him.'

20-50 days

Although the puppy is still with its mother and its brothers and sisters, it must live in an environment where it will quickly acquire familiarity with human beings, learning to identify them by smell, and enjoying being stroked by them. This is what Lorenz means by imprinting. And the sooner it happens the better (see **Sociability**, p.213). If the litter is put out of the way, and there is a possibility that the

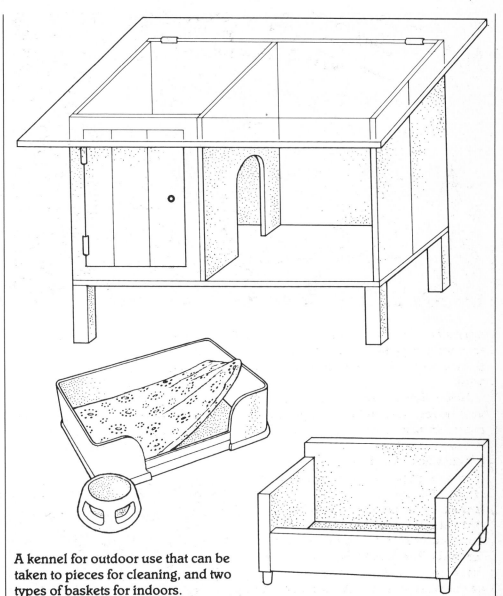

A kennel for outdoor use that can be taken to pieces for cleaning, and two types of baskets for indoors.

young puppy will be isolated for more than 50 days with no chance of getting acquainted with people, the future owner/trainer must visit the litter as often as possible, with small titbits; he or she should spend some time with the litter, befriending the mother, and playing on the ground with all the pups, but particularly with the one that will become his or hers. If the puppy is bought after the 50-day period, be sure that it has already had a chance to be among people.

By 20-30 days it is a good time to put a light cord around its neck: it will soon get used to it, and this means that there will be no problems when it reaches the stage of wearing a proper collar.

50-90 days

The selected puppy is removed from the litter and taken to where it will live with its owner or family (flat, garden, terrace, courtyard, kennel, etc.). The closer the relationship between puppy and master (or mistress), the better the results will be.

Basket

In its new home the young puppy must first of all get to know its basket, wherever it is. For any puppy, the basket is a place of refuge.

If the puppy is to live in an apartment or flat, give it a type of basket or box that will make it feel that it is in a den. The best way to achieve this is to choose a basket with some kind of lid or cover, or to stand it under a table. It should be big enough for the puppy to be able to stretch out, but it should also be cosy. Cover the bottom with some washable fabric or a thin washable mattress. Never put covers over a dog. Put the basket or box in a sheltered corner, free from draughts, well away from the kitchen, stoves, chimneys and radiators, but in a place that people or other animals constantly pass. The puppy should feel safe and sound in its corner. This is its place, where it can retreat when it wants and sleep undisturbed. Both puppies and adult dogs need to sleep during the day. A shortage of sleep can cause a dog to become ill, and may even cause death. Put the basket outside once a day, and make sure it stands in the sun once a week.

It is most important to fit a 1-2 m (3-6 ft) light chain close to the basket (either in the basket itself, or to a ring in a nearby wall) to which the puppy can be attached if necessary – and it will be necessary in these early days. When the puppy is on the chain, it should not wear a collar but a harness. This is very important.

If the puppy is to spend time outdoors (in a garden or courtyard, or on a terrace), it will need its own wired-in enclosure, large enough to allow it to run about and play. Inside there should be a dry kennel. The best kennels are made of wood; they should be easy to dismantle so that they can be cleaned properly; they should be painted outside and in to keep parasites away. They should be raised at least 30 cm (1 ft) off the ground to avoid damp. The bottom should be covered with a washable blanket or thin mattress. Fill in any cracks between boards. The roof must be waterproof, set at a slight angle, and easy to remove and replace. Take it off frequently to let in the sun. Make the entrance quite small, but not so small that the dog finds it tricky to use. In winter make a curtain from a piece of heavy blanket and hang it across the doorway; this will prevent the cold night air from reaching the sleeping dog. A dog that usually lives outdoors will be healthier and live longer than one that always lives indoors.

Make sure that the basket quickly becomes a pleasant place for the young newcomer. Put a water-bowl close by and keep the water fresh. Feed the puppy close by the basket. Every so often you can put the odd tasty morsel inside the basket, with the simultaneous command 'Basket!' As soon as the puppy goes to its basket, praise it and stroke it. (Dogs with erect ears do not like their head stroked: they prefer to be touched on chest and back.)

Commands should always be given in a quiet voice, and not authoritatively but in a friendly way. Remember that a dog's sense of hearing is very acute and that the young dog is at an age when all it wants to do is learn: all you have to do is make yourself understood. Frightening the puppy is harmful and cruel. Anyone who is incapable of gentleness and kindness should give up any ideas of training dogs. Dogs – and young dogs in particular – should never be mistreated or punished: at most they should be corrected. This is the only way to train them.

If the young dog is living outdoors, visit it as often as possible in its run: in the morning before leaving home, at lunchtime, in the afternoon, and for a good long session in the evening. It will need feeding four times a day. Greet it with plenty of fuss, stroke it, and talk to it. Play with it, too, and give it various playthings to gnaw and to wrestle with when it is alone. The ideal is for any puppy to spend at least a few hours each day with a dog of the same age. Perhaps a neighbour will oblige. When the puppy is in its run you should also sometimes order it into its basket, encouraging it to go in with titbits. As soon as it obeys, praise it and stroke it while it stays inside. If, once the titbit has been eaten, you see that it wants to come outside again straight away, step back, call it by name, and as soon as it approaches give it another titbit, stroke it, and praise it (again in a quiet voice). This is the way to instil in it the rudiments of being called. Do exactly the same thing if the basket is indoors: your call is essential.

As time passes (towards about 80-

90 days) the order 'Basket!' must be obeyed: as soon as the young dog hears it it must go there briskly, and stay there. As it goes, clap your hands, and when it is in the basket, praise it warmly.

The name

Choose a short, clear name that is easy to say. Choose an unusual name, too, or else, on future occasions, when you are hunting with others or at a group training class, there may well be several dogs with the same name, and three or four will come running up whenever you call your own dog.
Advice: Do not call your dog (puppy or adult) by name all the time. The dog will cease to pay attention, and the call will go unheeded.

The first days

Without its mother and its brothers and sisters, and away from the place where it was born, the young puppy will feel lost and bewildered in your home. To speed up the adaptation process, bring with it something which smells of its mother and its siblings: a piece of material, or even some straw, to make it more comfortable in its basket.
Advice: A few days before you go to fetch your new puppy, take to the kennels the blanket or mattress that will be used in its basket, so that it becomes impregnated with the smells of the place where the puppy has lived so far. Take it home again with the puppy, so that it will be like taking the puppy's own smell home with it.

It has already been said that in the absence of the mother or siblings puppies need to be close to something hairy, soft and warm or they will whine and whimper rather than sleep. There is a good reason why a puppy whines, too: it is, in fact, complaining so as to obtain its mother's aid. If you make it feel safe and secure with you, it will not whine.
Advice: For the first few days put a small clock inside the warm, soft mattress: its tick will remind the puppy of its mother's heartbeat.

One of the first things to teach a puppy is its own call.

Calling

A dog that cannot be called is of no use. A good response to a call depends not on the dog, but on you. When the dog has learnt that it has a name, it must learn to react to it by coming happily to its master or mistress, so its name must be associated with something positive: rewards, stroking, words of praise. If you call a puppy to you to scold it or worse, the point of the call will be lost. If you have to correct a mistake made by the puppy, never use its name when doing so. The dog should equate its name with positive, enjoyable things. It must come to you readily, wherever it may be. And is this easy to achieve? Of course — as long as you do not make any mistakes. Call your puppy in particular when it is hungry and when you actually give it its food. Call it also when you see that it is already coming towards you. Greet it with warm words and lots of stroking. Make it very clear that coming to you when called will always be to its advantage. Tell yourself over and over that 'A dog that cannot be called is of no use', and that a good response to a call depends not on the dog, but on you. Tell yourself, too, that it is useless and harmful to say the dog's name if you are going to shout at it or correct it: this will undermine the effectiveness of the call.

If you do not make any slips, you will soon see your young trainee, wherever it may be, running up to you, tail wagging, at the first call.

At the 80-90 day stage, alternate calling by name with calling using a whistle of the type that makes a shrill but not piercing sound. Give short, sharp blows on the whistle, and keep whistling until the dog is by your side.

'No!'

At the first order the dog must stop whatever it is doing. If the young puppy is about to climb into an armchair or is trying to nibble a piece of furniture, or venturing into an out-of-bounds room (the kitchen, for example), or doing something that it should not be doing, put things right with the command 'No!', uttered clearly, but not shouted. To begin with the puppy will fail to understand, of course. It will stop doing whatever it is up to and look at you with curiosity. Call it to you: give it a titbit, some warm words and a good stroke. To begin with, only actually say 'No!' when the puppy is close by you so that the 'No!' coincides with your direct action in stopping it from doing something that is not allowed. Remember that in a pack puppies of about 60 days start fighting among themselves to establish their own hierarchy and supremacy.

Later on you can back up your 'No!' by throwing a bunch of keys (or a small chain). While the dog is doing what it should not be doing, keep your distance and simply throw the keys or the chain, without a sound. Throw them quite high, in a good arc, so that the puppy will think they have dropped out of the sky. Just as the keys or chain are about to land near the puppy, say your 'No!'. The young dog will stop short in amazement; it will sniff at what has landed so close to it and you should go to it at once, calling it cheerfully by name, reassuring it, rewarding it and stroking it. The 'No!' corresponds to prohibitions that, in the pack, would be taught by the mother, father and other adults, by growling at the young offender.

If you do not make any blunders you will soon see your young trainee stopping whatever it is doing as soon as it hears your 'No!' and coming trustingly to you.

If the puppy understands your 'No!' and, later on, your correction (between 50 and 90 days it is still too early to 'correct'), if it understands and accepts the command, it will not lie prostrate on the ground, or on its back, showing you its belly; it will come towards you, head held high, and nuzzle you and touch you with its paws.

This means that it is keen to cooperate, and that it recognizes you as the 'head dog'.

Advice: After achieving your first suc-

An unhappy dog kept day and night on a short chain and forced to urinate and defecate where it lives will soon become vicious.

The 'Down!' position with the head raised and between the legs.

cessful results you can alternate your 'No!' with a growl (yes, a low growl from the throat, as a mother would make to discourage her puppy from some action). You will be amazed how effective this will be. At a certain stage you can limit yourself to a very brief growl, and only use 'No!' if the dog is a long way off.

If your 'No!' (or your growl) is not effective and the situation is a serious one, behave just as the puppy's parents would in a similar situation: when the puppy carries on doing the very thing that the command 'No!' was meant to stop, take it by the scruff of the neck, give it a sharp shake (but not too sharp), lift it up high and at the same time repeat in a severe voice 'No! No! No!' (or else growl loudly). Then put the dog back on the ground and watch it closely: if it appears to have got the message, praise and reward it. Your success depends not on controlling your dog by force, but on getting it to understand you.

In the pack the puppy at the learning stage is every so often made to go through disciplinary exercises: the head dog (or mother) will growl at it while it is preparing to eat. You can do the same at about the 60-day stage. Make the puppy lie down right in front of its meal with a 'No! Lie down!' and leave it there for a few moments (15 seconds, then 30 seconds, then, later on, 45 seconds at the most), before allowing it to eat. While it is lying still on the ground, touch its tail and its hind-quarters. This is what the head of

the pack (or its mother) does: sniffs it and then allows it to eat. The puppy will understand instinctively what this adult gesture means, and accept it readily.

A strong-willed puppy may growl at you if you get too near it while it is eating. Don't worry: a strong character means an excellent future companion and colleague. Take the dog in a kindly way by the scruff of the neck, growl, remove it a little from its food, stroke it and then let it eat again.

In large litters it may be that the weakest puppies do not manage to get any food, if the litter is fed from one large bowl. It is better to give each puppy its own bowl and make sure that the dominant members of the litter do not eat anybody else's food.

Chain
A dog living in an apartment or flat must have its own special place – i.e., its basket – as a place of refuge. This is the only place where it can sleep soundly (not on sofas or beds or in armchairs), gnaw at the odd bone to soothe its teeth (these change when it is about four months old and the bone will step it gnawing at shoes or furniture), drink water when it is thirsty, and eat four times a day. The puppy should stay in its basket while its owners are eating (never let it stay close to the table: it will beg and scrounge, constantly drooling at the mouth, and be a bother to all and sundry). It should also stay in its basket whenever you feel like a moment without its company. What is more, it must be made to go to its basket, so that it can learn to be clean.

There are just two ways of making the puppy go to its basket: you can either shut it in (in a flat or an apartment, the basket could be a small kennel with an entrance that can be closed off), or you can attach it to a light chain, 1-2 m (3-6 ft) long, fixed to the wall (or to the basket itself if it is sufficiently heavy). When you use the chain, do not attach it to the puppy's collar, but to its harness (a good leather one of the right size); this will mean that it does not spend long, and maybe harmful, hours trying to free its neck from the chain.

If properly used, a chain is a good and swift means of training, and helps to build that important harmony between man and dog.

Advice: The first time you attach the dog by the chain to its basket, or shut it inside its kennel-type basket, do so only when it has eaten and evacuated its faeces, or when you have tired it out in a long session of play. In other words, choose a moment when the dog feels a natural desire to have a nap, then its protests will be short-lived, especially if you present it with a new bone to gnaw.

You should soon have the satisfaction of seeing your young dog happily spending an hour or so on its own, without making a fuss. But not longer than an hour and, if anything, somewhat less. At first leave it alone for just a few minutes, and then gradually increase the period. You should, of course, never keep your puppy chained or shut away in a confined space for hours on end. This would soon dispose of any ideas you have about training it. (There is obviously no need for a chain if a dog usually lives outdoors in its own run.)

'Lie down!'
This is the main command, and it is a vital one. It is the beginning of a process that will eventually make the dog perfect at whatever special skill you have in mind for it – from pointing to rescue work to being in films. With the command 'Lie down!' you can turn a Dobermann into a pointer, and a pointer into a guard-dog. A dog will become **your** dog when you have got the 'Lie down!' command taped and not before. It is not very difficult: in fact, it corresponds to a natural and spontaneous position for a puppy in a pack.

After a few days the new young puppy will have got accustomed to you, to your flat or apartment, or to its run, and to its basket. Wait for a moment when you are playing with it and it looks a little tired, and about to lie down on the ground of its own accord; offer it and then give it a titbit, and while it is close to you hold it gently but firmly in the lie-down position, repeating the order 'Lie down!' several times in a no-nonsense tone of voice.

The lie-down position is the sphinx position, but with the head also resting on the ground or floor, between the front legs.

Keep the puppy in this position for a couple of seconds, and then suddenly let go of it, releasing it from the lying position with the command 'Go!', spoken in such a way as to encourage it to move. Repeat the procedure at various times, but only when the puppy is close at hand and you can make it stay in the lie-down position. Never give the command when it is some way off and you cannot make it stay in the right position. When you say 'Lie down!' the response should be immediate and precise (head on the ground), the position should be held for just a short time, followed by the releasing command 'Go!'

After the first attempts, extend the period during which the puppy must remain lying down: keep it there for 3, then 5, then 10 seconds. Then let it go with a 'Go!', praise it and show that you are pleased with it. Do not prolong the lie-down position too long, because this might make the puppy lose its eagerness and initiative.

This stage of training is rounded off with the command 'Lie down!' right beside the dog's food, before each of the four daily meals. Mealtimes are excellent for reinforcing the training that has been given. The young dog is hungry: call it, holding its bowlful of food in your hand. It will come running up, and this in itself develops a good response to the call; put the bowl close to the dog's basket and as it darts forward to eat its fill, give the command 'No!', and prevent it physically with your hands from throwing itself on the food. At the same time give it the command 'Lie down!' (again in a low voice), and if need be make it lie down by the gentle pressure of your hands; leave it there for 5 seconds, then gradually increase the period to 10, 15, and finally a maximum of 40 seconds; while it is there touch it round the base of the tail: and last of all give it the command 'Go!', letting it free.

If the puppy is to be trained as a hunting dog, police-dog or guard-dog, and needs to become used to fire-arms, while you are giving the command 'Lie down!' by its food, accustom it at the same time to hear a shot fired some way away (from a child's cap-gun, for example, so that the dog will associate the pleasure of eating with the sound of gunfire). If it is to be a hunting dog, it must lie down when it hears a shot.

If everything goes well – and if you make mistakes, put them right straight away – you will soon have the satisfaction of seeing your 60-day-old dog carrying out the main part of the First Programme just as it should, responding to the commands: 'Basket!', 'Call!' 'No!', 'Lie down!' and 'Go!' All that now remains is house-training and the command 'Fetch!' Both these stages are simple and enjoyable.

House training

To make sure that a puppy stays clean, it is easiest to make use of two of his basic impulses: (1) he does not foul his own den, (2) he will readily foul a place that he has fouled before.

In the pack, as soon as a puppy can walk, it will leave the den where it was born of its own accord to evacuate its urine and faeces. It prefers to do this where it can smell the odour of previous urine and faeces.

If the puppy lives outdoors, in a run with its basket, the problem is a simple one: the puppy itself will choose where it will defecate and urinate.

Advice: Put some earth or plant some grass in part of the run; the puppy will soon chose this area as its 'lavatory'.

If the puppy is to live in a town flat, a little special attention in the first few days should do the trick. Use the moment when it has just finished eating and will feel like relieving itself. Take it straight away in your arms out into the garden, or on to the terrace or balcony, or into the bathroom, or wherever you have placed a good-sized box filled with earth and old leaves – the 'toilet' in other words. When the puppy has relieved himself, lavish praise on it,

A serious training mistake is to raise the hand threateningly to punish the dog. Use it to inspire trust.

take it into the living-room for a while, play with it, and then put it down to sleep in its basket. Take it to the 'toilet' every couple of hours or so. In three or four days, as soon as you let it off the chain or leash, it will run straight to its toilet, and then come and play with you. In about 10 days, with a little discreet supervision, you will be the proud owner of a thoroughly house-trained puppy.

Another method: This is an excellent method for very young dogs. Take a box the right size for the puppy, cover the bottom with a piece of turf that should have roots – the best type is the kind used for garden lawns. Place the box right by the basket after meal-times and when the puppy wakes up. It is better still if the piece of turf smells a little of the puppy's previous urine and faeces. The dog will feel at home in this type of 'toilet', which should be moved gradually further away from the basket each day – a few centimetres at a time. This is a reliable method even for those rare cases when a puppy that is upset for some reason or other has a tendency to foul its own basket. As time passes and the puppy grows bigger, the toilet box should be changed for a larger one, and gradually moved right outside to the terrace or balcony, if there is one.

Another method: For anyone who has a small spare room, or a box room or other area in their flat in which to put the basket. Cover the whole floor of the room with newspapers spread out flat. The puppy will have to relieve itself in one or more places where there is newspaper; as soon as it has finished, remove the dirty paper and replace it with clean. Every morning remove a newspaper near the basket and leave the floor there uncovered. The puppy will not foul the visible area of floor (which should be disinfected), but will choose a place covered with newspaper, with a preference for places where there is still some scent of its previous urine. If you remove a newspaper every day, deodorize the area of uncovered floor, and make the increasingly small area covered with papers well scented, the puppy will relieve itself only where you have left the newspapers.

Wrong method: In the first few days after the puppy has arrived, letting it foul the house or flat wherever it likes, then changing your tune, smacking the 'dirty little beast', rubbing its nose in its urine and faeces, spanking it and then banishing it to the balcony to cry. The puppy does not understand why on earth it has been hit for having relieved its bladder as nature intended; it does not understand why it should be shut away from the owners to whom it wants to show affection, and from whom it wants help and protection; and it will end up thinking that there is some association between its bodily needs and being hit. This will give rise to confusion and a lack of understanding that will have an adverse effect on training and on the future relationship between owner and dog. As well as doing harm in this way, the nose-rubbing method may encourage a nasty tendency in the puppy to eat faeces. However, if you steer well clear of this method you will soon be the owner of a thoroughly clean and house-trained pup.

'Fetch!'

Dogs 'think' with their noses, but a dog that lives from its puppy days in a human household – where people 'think' with their eyes – will end up by making less use of its sense of smell than if it were a member of a pack, where all the other members use their sense of smell all the time. So it is a good idea if the young dog soon becomes accustomed to trusting in its own nose. The modern method involves getting the puppy to find its own meal bowl, using a trail that should be made as difficult as possible. When the puppy has had ten days or so to get used to the house or flat, its basket, its bowl left by the basket, you can hide the bowl, without warning, a few feet from where the puppy usually expects to find it. Lay a trail of small scraps of food or drops of water to the new place. The puppy will put its nose down and soon find the place where its food is hidden. On the following days gradually make the trail more and more complicated and less obvious. As the puppy is about to start following the trail, give it the command 'Fetch!' in an encouraging tone of voice. A puppy nine to twelve weeks old can follow accurately a trail of 54 m (60 yd) or so over varied terrain (earth, grass, cement, etc.), with two corners, and find its meal at the end. The trail could change direction every day and became more difficult, but the puppy still should manage to follow it, wagging its tail, not putting a foot wrong, and enjoying itself immensely.

A word to hunters: It is wrong to think that a pointer or setter should never put its nose to the ground, because if it does it will lose its skills as a pointer. This is one of the many hunting superstitions. A good pointer should use its sense of smell from the word go, gaining confidence in it and improving it. German hunters, who have a fine tradition of training, teach their dogs to point nose in the air, or to fetch nose in the air, depending on the situation. The way to achieve this is explained below. Puppies that will eventually become pointers will benefit a lot from learning the meaning of the order 'Fetch!'

Any dog trained by you as a puppy will be, as it were, moulded by your affection and your guidance. As time passes it will understand every move you make, and at a glance it will carry out whatever command it is given. At the end of the 90-day First Programme there will already be a state of mutual understanding between teacher and pupil, and the solid foundations of a firm future partnership will have been laid.

Watch out for your hand!

The trainer's hand must always be used to stroke the puppy: never to punish or threaten or hit it. A puppy (and a dog, for that matter) must regard your hand as a source of pleasure – nothing else. When it sees your hand stretched towards it, it must head for it of its own accord – even, and above all, when it has been scolded for some reason. It must be fond of your hand, seek it out, sniff at it, and rub its muzzle against it. Confidence and trust in your hand will be of very great importance and a major factor in success when the dog starts to work with and for you.

Watch for undesirable associations

We have already mentioned the subject of 'undesirable associations' (see p.218). Make sure that your dog does not become mechanical. As soon as it is responding to your first commands, change the circumstances a little, or the place, or the conditions: in this way the dog will learn that commands are all distinct, each and every time. Re-read the section about 'distractions' (see p.218), and adapt it to the First Programme, but bear in mind that you cannot demand too much of your young puppy.

Food and feeding

Each case is different, but all dogs are thoroughly omnivorous creatures. Huskies live on dried fish; some dogs living in the tropics eat insects, others eat fruit and vegetables, others just meat or milk and related products, or simply bread and cereals. The following notes apply to dogs living in Europe and America.

Water: This must be clean, fresh and always available. Keep a bowl and a supply of fresh water in your car and on journeys offer your dog a drink from time to time.

Meat: Dogs ae carnivores (this is evident from their teeth and their digestive apparatus) and meat is their ideal food. However, down the ages, through living with people, dogs have gradually become omnivorous. For puppies and young dogs, and for pregnant and nursing bitches, meat is essential; for adult dogs too much meat may cause poisoning or eczema. Give a hard-working dog plenty of meat – e.g., after long hunting or tracking expeditions, hauling or pack-work, and so on. Do not give much meat to a dog that sleeps a lot in the home or garden. Mix a little meat with other types of food. Some dogs, no matter how hungry, will refuse poultry. Offal – tripe, liver, heart, etc. – is excellent but lung is not very nutritous. Always cook offal. Horse-meat and beef are both excellent; pork, however, is not so good.

Coprophagy: This is the technical name for the tendency in an animal to eat its own or other faeces. It is quite common in puppies and young dogs.

TABLE OF FOOD CONSUMPTION IN DOGS

	Growing Dogs		Adult Dogs	
	Dry Food	Moist Food	Dry Food	Moist Food
% Water	9	72	9	72
Live weight of animal	grm/oz per day	grm/oz per day	grm/oz per day	grm/oz per day
2.3/5	182/6	592/21	90/3	292/10
4.5/10	300/10	975/34	150/5	468/16
6.8/15	382/13	1240/43	191/7	620/22
9.1/20	493/17	1600/56	245/9	800/28
13.6/30	682/24	2215/78	340/12	1080/38
22.7/50	1137/40	3690/129	567/20	1850/65
31.8/70	1590/56	5170/181	794/28	2585/90
50/110	2400/84	7800/273	1200/42	3900/137

Some studies maintain that coprophagy has to do with poor digestive enzymes. Boston Terriers often look for cats' faeces; German Shepherd Dogs often look for cow-dung or sheep's droppings. Almost all young dogs regard horse droppings as a delicacy. Breeds with round heads and short muzzles may suffer from enzyme deficiency. Coprophagy may be remedied by a course of B-complex vitamins, with pancreatin and papain (also known as vegetable pepsin). A good remedy is to feed the dog consistently with nutritious meat such as heart and liver.

Fruit: Most dogs eat fruit.

Milk: Cow's milk causes diarrhoea in all dogs that are not used to it, and in puppies in particular. A dog that is used to it can live on nothing but milk and milk products, including whey, which is excellent as a remedy for eczema (give the dog nothing but dried bread and whey for a week). Goat's milk is more suitable for young dogs. Dog's milk is four times richer in protein that cow's or goat's milk, or the milk of any herbivorous animal. A bitch's milk does not curdle in the stomach; cow's milk separates at once into rennet and whey. Whey is extremely useful for adult dogs suffering from eczema, but will cause stomach upsets in puppies, with a risk of enteritis. Cheese and processed cheese is excellent for dogs.

Number of meals At the age of two months, five meals a day. After three months, four meals a day. After four months, three meals a day. After twleve months, two meals a day. Never leave the bowl on the ground: once you have offered the dog its meal, take the bowl away after five minutes, whether the meal has been eaten or not. A single meal a day can be harmful. If the dog eats it in the evening, it will fall asleep as it digests the food, and be useless as a guard-dog. It is a good idea to feed your dog in the morning when it wakes up, and towards dusk. In this way, throughout the day the dog can stay on its own or travel with you, without needing to be fed. Meals – and especially a puppy's meals – should be given at regular times. An adult dog will be the better for fasting one day a week.

Bones: Some people say that bones are the perfect food, and others that they are fatal. A world-wide study has been carried out in universities and veterinary laboratories to find out how many accidents involving bones have occurred. The result is quite astonishing. Everyone had heard bones described as harmful, but no one had observed any cases of actual damage, or any fatal accidents – not even caused by those famous dog-killing chicken or rabbit bones, which tend to splinter most easily. A dog's very nature gives it a liking for bones; its teeth enable it to grind them; its gastric fluids break them down quickly into a pulp that can easily be digested. Bones are also useful for keeping the teeth strong and clean. Many kennels only ever give dogs boiled poultry heads; these are full of bones and have never caused any trouble. It is as well to avoid giving your dog very hard bones that might splinter, but otherwise give it as many bones as you feel like, from an early age, both cooked and uncooked.

Bread: Best if dry and hard. Some dogs prefer this to any other type of food. Fresh bread is not so good: it is best to dry it in the oven first. Dry bread goes well with broth or soup, but as a rule a dog's food should not be too liquid. Bread cooked with meat and bones is excellent. Note that mouldy bread is poisonous.

Noddles and rice: Rice is preferable, and is even better than bread. Too much rice can cause intestinal upsets, however. Cook it thoroughly. Do not give your dog noodle leftovers because they can often be acid.

Left-overs: All left-overs are fine, and dogs tend to like them: in other words, a dog will enjoy what its owner eats, but this is not to say that your dog should be close at hand while you eat, unless you want to turn it into an undisciplined and annoying scrounger.

Eggs: Always a good idea, raw or cooked.

Green vegetables: Uncooked, a dog will not digest them. Cooked, they may often cause fermentation. The same is true of potatoes.

Sugar: Harmful, causing fermentation, making it hard for the dog to digest other food. Also causes obesity. The same goes for sweets, chocolates, and so on.

Second Puppy Programme

The Second Puppy Programme applies to puppies between 90 and 120 days old, of all types and breeds to be used for hunting, general working duties or for sporting purposes and as companion dogs. The idea that training can be neatly divided into compartments is now regarded as a mistaken one – i.e., hunting dogs, working dogs, and companion dogs. It is important to grasp the fact that a Pekingese is also a hunting dog (a pack of these dogs at work can be very efficient at hunting rabbits), that a Pointer is also a guard-dog (in many countries the Kurzhaar, or Short-haired German Pointer is used as a police dog), that the Setter is also a tracker (there have been many fine examples of Setters tracking people), that the Labrador Retriever is a world-renowned retriever on the hunt, and also excellent at sniffing out drugs and illegal firearms, and, finally, that all dogs, of all breeds, from the Newfoundland to the Chihuahua, are marvellous companions for people all over the world. For this reason this Second Puppy Programme for the 90-120 day period should be used for all puppies, whatever the use or uses you have in mind for them.

If you acquired your puppy at the age of 50 to 90 days, and have finished the First Puppy Programme, you can now embark on the Second Programme. If you got your puppy at the age of 90 to 120 days, start on the Second Programme only when you have finished the First Programme, which you should adapt to the greater age of the dog. As far as imprinting is concerned, if your puppy has an open friendly nature, wags his tail and has plenty of self-confidence, you can reckon that between 20 and 50 days it had a chance to get to know about, and enjoy the company of, people. If this was not the case, let your new puppy be among people (in homes, streets, and with children), but be sure that you stay close at hand. Comfort it if it becomes frightened and pick it up out of harm's way if necessary. If it goes on looking frightened and timid, take your time, take things step by step and introduce it gradually to crowds and traffic. A few minutes a day will be enough at first, starting off in isolated spots, and gradually increasing. (See **First walks** below p.239). When you use this Programme, bear in mind the dangers of 'undesirable associations' (p.218).

'No!' 'Basket!' 'Lie down'

Develop what you have done in the First Programme. Continue to give your commands in a quiet voice, little more than a murmur, so that the dog will always be on the alert, and looking at you straight in the eye. Anyone who raises his or her voice or shouts will make the dog hard of hearing, or only capable of obeying shouted commands. Some hunters in various European countries use the English 'Down!' or 'Lie down!' and some trainers of police-dogs prefer the German word 'Platz!'

If the dog is rather slow to obey, you will have to repeat the command and this involves the risk of an 'undesirable association'. The dog will only obey when you have said the words two or three times, not at the first command, which is when it should obey. When you give the command 'Down!' always make the dog take up the 'sphinx' position with its head between its front legs. The word 'Down' should immediately root the dog to the spot. This is important for the hunter (forcing the dog to the ground when he shoots, or when the game is roused, and so preventing it from giving chase); it is important for the guard-dog (forcing it to the ground, and so stopping it from attacking the assailant who has surrendered); it is also important for the companion dog (stopping it in its tracks when it is dangerous for it to cross the road or when it is frightening a child). It is worth repeating yet again that 'Lie down!' or 'Down!' is the main command, and the essential one. It lies at the basis of everything that comes next. But why does the dog have to have its head on the ground between its front legs? Because this reduces the temptation for the dog to get up again and run off, chase the game, bite an assailant or wrongdoer who has already been put out of action, or frighten a passer-by. To disobey, the dog will have to transgress three times by (1) raising its head off the ground, (2) sitting up, and (3) running away. If you allow the dog to keep its head off the ground, there will be only two rules to break. It is natural for the young member of a pack to lie with its head on the ground and in the sphinx position: the position indicates its acceptance of the supremacy of the adult, or head-dog. You are the head-dog as far as your puppy is concerned. In the Second Programme, too, the command 'Down!' must always be followed by the releasing command 'Go!'. It is so important that it must be given in three different ways, so that it fits the situation in question: (1) 'Down!' (spoken quietly), until the dog is close by, or if it is on a lead or a long leash – i.e., under your close control. (2) Whistle: in the First Programme, when discussing the call, the use of a training whistle with a high pitch, shrill but not loud, was recommended for summoning the dog with a series of short sharp whistles; the same whistle is used as an alternative to the command 'Down!' but the sound must be prolonged and constant; the whistle can be used in the future to give the command 'Down!' when the dog is some way off. (3) Raised arm: this is the visual signal for the command 'Down!', when you want to give the command without making a noise, whether the dog is close to you or at a somewhat greater distance.

Important point: at the command 'Down!' the puppy should not turn to its owner or trainer, but stay facing the direction in which it was already facing.

For the hunting dog there is a fourth command, 'Down!' when you are shooting. This is vital, and obedience to it must be developed very slowly: start by firing the gun at a distance from the dog, at meal-times, giving plenty of praise and reward, so that the noise of the gun is associated in the dog's mind with food and the command 'Down!'

With a nervous and timid dog, be very gentle when it comes to firing a shot, and make sure the animal's head is firmly on the ground.

To make sure that the dog drops straight to the ground on the various commands, give them all together to begin with: 'Down!', arm raised, and continuous whistle, or arm raised and gun fired by a helper at a good distance from the dog. In the dog's memory a useful association will be created and it will start dropping straight to the down position on the three different commands. These are given together for a time and then increasingly in separation, until they alternate, in different places and circumstances, always being followed by the release command 'Go!'

Compulsory call

You will have instilled in the puppy, during the First Programme, that running to you when called by its name or by a whistle is an enjoyable thing to do, and to its advantage in the form of strokes and titbits. Now it must be taught that the call is also unavoidable. Earlier on you were advised to attach a light cord round the puppy's neck when it is 20 to 30 days old, to accustom it to wearing a collar later. If it was not possible to do this, do it when you take your puppy home with you. When it has grown used to the cord, repalce that with a small, light collar, not too tight. In the meantime you will also have accustomed it to wearing a harness as well as a light collar (see discussion of the basket p.229).

For the compulsory call, choose a moment close to the dog's feeding time when it is minding its own business. Call it. It will come running. Stroke it and give it a titbit. While it is eating, attach to the harness a light cord about 2m (6 ft) long, doing this as unobtrusively as possible. With the command 'Basket!' send it back to its basket where, without its knowledge, you have put a juicy bone for it to gnaw, or some other tasty morsel. While it is busy eating, call it again, hoping that it will not come, because this is the only way you can start to teach it to make a correct response to the compulsory call.

If it goes on gnawing at its handsome bone, keep on calling it and, by means of the cord, start to pull it towards you, not roughly and not too hard. Meanwhile, talk kindly to the dog, which will probably start rearing up like a wild horse. Once it has arrived at your feet, stroke it, and say plenty of kind words, as if it has achieved something special. Start playing with it, getting down on the ground (dogs like you to do that) and make it forget about being pulled out of its basket. After a while send it back to its basket and its bone (not straight away, or else the basket will become like a refuge from you). Repeat the whole exercise after 10 minutes or so. On the following days, repeat the exercise at intervals.

It will be surprising to see how, by the fifth or sixth time, the young dog will respond immediately to the call, leaving its games or bones or food, and even deserting someone of whom it is fond while it is being stroked. These exercises should be repeated as often as circumstances permit.

The call must be absolutely clear and quick, not only in the home, but also in the garden and elsewhere outside, where there are a thousand and one things to distract the puppy. Up to 90 days the puppy will have stayed in the house or garden. Now the time has come to take it outside to get to know the 'big bad world'.

In the car

The first walks should be taken in isolated spots, which is why it is a good idea to accustom the puppy to a car. You can also carry it in a basket on your bicycle or motorcycle, putting a cloth which smells of the dog's basket in the bottom and making sure that the puppy is not in a draught.

Young dogs often suffer from car sickness (they drool and vomit). This

is easy to cure. Put the dog enthusiastically into the car, but do not drive away: stroke it, give it a few titbits, and then take it home. Repeat this four or five times in the following days. When the dog is happy to get into the car, get someone else to drive, and keep the puppy on your lap, stroking it: drive for two or three minutes, then go back home.

Extend the time a little each day, driving the car yourself, and before long the dog will sleep soundly. If things do not work out in this way, give the puppy a travel sickness preparation half an hour before leaving on a car journey.

Do not let the puppy poke its head out of the car window: it may get otitis or conjunctivitis. Always leave the window open a crack, so that it can get some fresh air, and establish where it is with its keen sense of smell.

Do not leave the car with the dog inside it parked in the sun: even if the windows are open a little, the inside temperature in summer will sometimes cause dogs to die (especially Bulldogs, Pekingeses and short-muzzled breeds). Even if it is not sunny, a dog left in a car with the windows all closed may also die from lack of oxygen. There are instances of hunters putting three or four Pointers or Setters in a car, forgetting to open the windows a little, going to have a meal and finding all the dogs dead when they get back.

If you spend all day travelling in the car, do not feed the dog, but have a bowl and a container of water handy and give it a drink every so often. Let it get out to urinate and stretch its legs every 100 km (60 miles) or so.

In winter, if the dog stays in the car out of doors, cover it with a blanket. If it is raining or snowing, a hunting or working dog may stay soaked through for hours on end. Before it goes back into the car, put it into a sack filled with a little hay or dry straw, tying the sack round its neck so that only its head is free. No matter how wet and muddy the dog is, by the time you get home it will be almost completely dry.

Opposite: In the car the dog should have its spot, separate from people.

First walks

At the 80 to 90 day stage the dog will have got used to its light collar (as long as it is not too tight), and can now be taught to go for a walk with you outdoors. If there is nowhere quiet and secluded near your home, go somewhere that is.

For a leash use a piece of strong string or light cord (at least 2 m (6 ft) long), attached to the collar (it is sometimes a good idea to have a whole ball of string with you). The length of the string will give the dog a chance to move away and come back to you, without pulling on the lead or being pulled by it. Imagine you are like a fisherman, playing a fish in relation to

It is a mistake to keep a puppy on too short a leash. The puppy will be encouraged to pull on it and will turn into a poorly trained adult.

its movements: never force the pace. Short leads teach a dog to pull and should be banned. The first walk must be very brief: five minutes at the most.

The new world with its new smells will interest the young dog quite a lot. It will often forget all about you and dash hither and thither, smelling everything with amazement. It will sometimes give itself the odd fright, too. Sometimes it will pull on the lead, prancing like a foal; it will refuse to follow you, and lie with its legs in the air (remember that offering its belly is a gesture of surrender and requires a gentle response from you). Bend down to it, talking softly, and comfort it with the odd titbit.

You must get the puppy to follow for a few dozen metres, keeping the lead slack, so that it does not have the impression of being forced too much. After five minutes, get back into the car, and make a great fuss of your dog when you get back home. Take the first walks when the dog has an empty stomach.

On the following day, go for another walk, stretching it out to seven minutes; in under a week the puppy will be used to following the trainer for about ten minutes. Until the puppy is six months old, restrict these walks to a maximum of fifteen minutes; when it is between six and nine months, this can be extended to half an hour; when it is between nine and twelve months, 45 minutes will be enough. Remember that a dog on a leash is normally on your left, so as to leave your right arm free.

Get the dog to follow you, but do not expect it to become a slave, tagging along at your heels. Dogs are inquisitive creatures, as all dog-owners know. Their curiosity is useful during training; do not discourage it. Lengthen the lead when your dog darts off to smell something, when it falls behind, when it runs ahead, and do not let it get used to pulling on the lead; call it to you every now and then; divert its attention from the world around it back to you, but do not dampen its interest in what it comes across. You must mould or form your puppy — not deform it. When walking has become a regular pastime, when the dog can walk calmly on a lead, use this development to test its obedience outside the home, in different places and circumstances, and at the precise moments when it is most distracted.

'Down!'
On your walks, at unexpected moments, but only when the young dog is close to you and on a lead, practise with the command 'Down!', the whistle, the raised arm and the release command 'Go!'

Call
While the dog is thinking of other things, and when it is a little way off — but still on the lead — call it by its name and with the whistle; if it does not obey at once, pull it towards you with the lead, and then stroke it and give it a reward. Increase the dog's distractions as time passes, and avoid any 'undesirable associations'.

You can let the dog off the lead during your walks, when it is about 120 days old but not before, and only for a short time and only in safe places, where there is no traffic and where the puppy cannot run out of sight and get lost. Even though the dog is off the lead, call it to you with a bribe of tidbits. If it does not come, do not shout at it (it might run away once and for all), but wait until it comes close of its own accord; then put it back on the lead and practise some compulsory calling.

Advice: Every time you call the dog, move back with brisk short steps as it gets close to you. After a walk, and all the interesting things in the outside world, the puppy may well not have urinated, and as soon as you get back home, it may well relieve itself in the first place it comes across. This also happens because a young dog is afraid of leaving its own traces in an unknown place. So, as soon as you return home put the dog in the place where it usually relieves itself.

Assistance
An assistant will often come in useful during training sessions. He or she is usually a friend whom you have helped in the same way. Get someone to help you on your walks, when your dog is about 120 days old. This is the time when the call tends to be less effective outdoors. Act at once: a dog who does not obey a call is worthless. Call it, hoping that it will **not** come to you, while it is playing somewhere. This is precisely when the assistant must throw the chain or bunch of keys. The puppy will be a bit bewildered or even a little scared; without pulling on the lead, call it very gently and offer it protection, with plenty of stroking and patting, and the odd titbit; it will come to you to take refuge and find comfort. The assistant should move away at this point. Repeat this a few times and the call will work every time, wherever you are.

The one-owner dog
If you want to have a dog of your own, which spends all its time with you, and not with a family — a private dog in other words, one that hunts only with you, or acts as a guard-dog only for you, or which wants only you for company — make sure that no one else at all strokes or pats it, fondles it, feeds it, plays with or looks after it. Everyone else must act either hostilely or indifferently towards it. If this is what you want, it is quite possible, and you will have your very own dog. There are some breeds that by nature, tend to have just one master or mistress (several types of Pointer, Collie, Bulldog and Pug, for example).

To round off the Second Programme you should improve the responses outdoors to the commands 'No!' (again with some help if necessary) and 'Find!', teach the basic rudiments of retrieving and the command 'Bark!'

'Find!'
During your walks, take the dog's meal for it to have at the usual time when it is hungry; get someone to hold the dog and, using bits of food, make a simple trail at the end of which it will find the food-bowl. Make the trail on grass or earth, not on the road or footpath. Gradually increase the distance from 18 to 64 m (20 to 70 yd). The dog will be quick to learn and will find this exercise fun (and so will you). Make straight or curving trails, with a few corners to be negotiated, exciting trails that will not disappoint the young dog, and so give good results. This is a game: real trails and tracking are dealt with on p.273.

'Fetch!'
When it is about 80 days (and sometimes as young as 60) your dog will of its own accord bring you a rag or a stick or one of its playthings, such as a slipper or shoe. Do not scold it; do not stifle this natural tendency: if anything, encourage it with approving words and praise. The term 'natural tenden-

cy' is used here because all dogs are natural retrievers and it is up to you to use this instinct in the right way. Here is one way of going about it: (1) Encourage the young dog to fetch things, throwing a stick or rolling a ball which it will instantly want to chase. (2) Do not ask the young dog to bring back the stick or ball: when it has let go of it, pick it up and throw it again. The dog of its own accord will bring it back close to you as soon as it realizes that you will throw it for it again. Do not play this game for too long, as it will tire the puppy out: stop (by hiding the stick or ball) when the dog is still full of energy. Make the process of learning and co-operating an enjoyable one, as if the puppy were one of a pack. (3) When the dog starts to be quite good at fetching things, and comes back to you with the object in its mouth, take short steps backward, calling the dog to come close to you, and then command it sharply to lie down. (4) Go up to it, stretching out one hand towards the object and offering the dog a titbit with the other. The dog will spontaneously let go of what is in its mouth (which you must take at once) in order to swallow the food.

At this stage you will be three-quarters of the way towards the training of a 17-week-old dog and all done with two basic commands: the call, the command 'Down!'. Improve the exercise with two new commands 'Fetch!', and 'Drop!' You must always give the command 'Fetch!' as you actually throw the object, repeating vigorously but in a quiet voice, 'Fetch! Fetch! Fetch!' As the dog comes towards you, holding the object in its mouth; give the command 'Down!' and just as the dog opens its mouth to let go of the object and take the titbit give the command 'Drop!' In this way the dog's 'mechanical' memory will repeat the movements it has learnt (fetching the object and dropping it) when it associates them with the commands 'Fetch!' and 'Drop!'. At the same time its 'affective' memory will enable it to enjoy the exercise because of your words of praise and the titbit at the end of it all. Here again, beware of 'undesirable' associations.

Note that good retrieving depends on you, not on the dog; all dogs retrieve or fetch of their own accord, but must not be made nervous about doing so, or find it an unpleasant experience, or be shouted at. It is quite easy to get a puppy to fetch things, and it is enough to improve its performance a little at a time to make it a fine retriever, all because of the four basic commands, by now well instilled in the dog: the call, and the commands 'Down!', 'Fetch!' and 'Drop!'

Bark

A dog should bark — and stop barking — when it is told to do so. For the hunter, barking can be very useful and for any working dog barking is a vital part of guard duties and of retrieving. A family or companion dog must be quietened when it barks too often and without any good reason.

A puppy's first lesson in barking can be given when you are about to put its food-bowl on the ground. If you keep it waiting, it will whine and yelp and bark. At that precise moment give the command: 'Bark!' With a little patience it will be easy to make the dog understand what is wanted of it at its next meal-time. Its appetite will sharpen its wits; it will soon get the message and bark whenever you want it to: before you give it a titbit, before you put on its collar for the walks it likes so much, and so on.

In order to bark a dog has to put itself in the right mood. It does not bark in the same way that people talk; a dog's bark is like a bird's song. If a dog turns wild it will no longer bark.

When a puppy is barking of its own accord because it has heard a suspicious sound or seen a stranger, teach it to bark by giving it the command 'Bark! Bark!'

To stop the barking, give the command 'No!' then 'Down!' and close the dog's mouth with your hand. Calm the dog down by stroking and patting it, and generally distract it. Outdoors drop a handful of earth on its muzzle with the command 'No!' This will work wonders.

This is the end of the Second Programme for the 90 to 120 day-old puppy. This is the period when the young dog in the wild grasps the hierarchic structure and establishes its own position of subordination. The two Programmes help the trainee pup to put its natural abilities at the disposal of human beings, and this will be of benefit to it and to them. In fact, for a dog to be fulfilled and balanced it needs to express itself with people just as it would express itself in the pack. Its good training and 'upbringing', useful for us, is vital for the young dog. In the pack, in fact, the puppy will have learnt all its lessons by the time it is 90 days old and will now start to work with the adults.

Character and personality

A few words about the main features of a dog's character and personality. These will help to clarify the duties to which the puppy may be best suited, once it has gone through both Programmes, and will also help in the appraisal a slightly older young dog, or even an adult to be used for some practical purpose.

Courage: A dog may be described as courageous or brave when in particular circumstances it forgets itself and spontaneously and readily confronts a danger. Hunting-dogs and guard-dogs must all be courageous. A courageous dog will behave in front of its 'community' (the pack, the human family, its master, or people who happen to be there) in such a way that its own interests become subordinate to the collective interest: it will attack an animal that might well wound or blind it, or a vicious person who might even kill it. The natural fighting spirit towards other animals in a courageous dog can actually be a defect, in human terms — just as it is a 'defect' in a courageous bitch when she prevnts all and sundry from coming near her litter. The whole aim of training is to remedy such faults.

Visual curiosity: When a dog is being trained this is an important indicator, because a very keen expression certainly points to good training potential. It is possible that this type of curiosity is more active in females than in males. Every breed includes particularly 'alert' dogs, even those breeds that appear to be rather 'dopey': Pointers and Mastiffs, for example, with keen, lively eyes, full of curiosity and eager to understand and learn. Visual curiosity is usually most evident in puppies and young dogs.

Defence: The defence impulse will make a dog rush to the aid of any friend (animal or human) in the face of a threat. Even dogs that are timid and weak-willed have this impulse.

Good judgement: This is the ability to do the right thing at the appropriate time, and it is a hereditary ability, which is why young mountain dogs or sheepdogs know at once how to behave with sheep or other livestock, and why a young Hound can instantly scent a hare. Good judgement is also the ability not to make the same mistake twice, to learn from previous experience, to behave in different ways towards different types of game when hunting, to attack an intruder in different ways, depending on how the latter behaves.

Docility: The feature that enables a dog to become part of a human group, just as it would a pack, and allows a human being to play the role of head-dog. Do not confuse docility (or obedience) with a weak character. A weak-willed dog will behave solely to avoid the unpleasantness of being told off; a docile or obedient dog will behave so as to adapt to your wishes. Some dogs are srong-willed and docile, others weak-willed and not docile at all.

Fighting: The fighting impulse has been well defined by the American Thorndike as the 'enjoyment of becoming excited'. The Austrian Menzel called it the 'taste for a skirmish' — tantamount to a 'sporting' instinct. A marked fighting impulse may be a drawback. A hunting-dog may prefer fighting with other dogs and neglect its duties as a result. A guard-dog may attack another dog instead of an intruder. This impulse can be dealt with by proper training and turned to good use.

Tendency to bite: A dog's hostile reaction when faced with unpleasant stimuli. Many German Pointers have a tendency to bite, so do many Dachshunds, some Setters and Cocker Spaniels, many Dobermanns and Mastiffs, and a few Boxers and Bulldogs. Some dogs are cowardly but tend to bite,

while others may be brave but will not bite. 'Fear' and 'courage' should not be understood in human terms or in a 'moral' sense. Fear is the root of self-preservation: it may tell a dog to run off at the right moment, and thus save its skin. A species that does not know what fear is will not last long. The most courageous dog of all is the Pekingese: it is not afraid of elephants or lions, but as it lives indoors, it is not in danger of meeting either of them!

Endurance: This enables a dog to summon up energy, both physical and mental, as required in order to remain 'on the job' (hunting, tracking, carrying out guard duties, for example) for as long as possible.

Character: This determines how a dog will react to unpleasant external things. According to character dogs can be divided into strong- and weak-willed groups, with a host of intermediate stages. A dog with a strong character that hurts itself jumping will make another jump straight afterwards. A dog with a weak character, in the same situation, will wait for some time

before jumping again. A strong-willed dog requires a firm hand, a weak-willed dog does not. A cause of failure in training may well lie in a weak-willed trainer choosing a dog with a strong character, and a strong-willed trainer choosing a dog with a weak character. A good trainer will be able to improve, and to switch from being firm to pliant, depending on the dog and the particular circumstances. Which is better, a dog with a strong character or one with a weak character? Both have their advantages. The best dog is one with a character suited to the tasks it will be asked to carry out. If your weak-willed hunting-dog tends to chase birds when they take to the air (or attack cats or chickens), a few rebukes will soon stop it. It is harder to correct a strong-willed dog. Strong-willed dogs have short memories, and weak-willed dogs have longer

Puppies waiting to be fed. The natural behaviour of young dogs in differing circumstances makes it possible to assess their character and qualities.

ones. A dog with a very strong or a very weak character cannot be trained well.

Vigilance: Reaction to a strange stimulus. Vigilance shows in the way the tail is carried, in the ears, and the kind of bark used when a hunting-dog, say, becomes aware of something unusual or when a guard-dog growls or barks. Vigilance is the swift reaction to stimuli involving smell, hearing and sight. All dogs, including hunting- and companion dogs, show how vigilant they are when they are in their own territory, whether this is a flat, or a garden or even a balcony. Some dogs bark when a stranger approaches, and will attack him if he ventures into their territory. Others will bark, but not attack, when their territory is entered; instead, they will circle round the intruder, looking fierce. Others will look suspicious until they manage to sniff the stranger; then their hostile attitude will either increase or decrease. Some dogs will retreat warily as a stranger approaches, barking all the time with their hackles up, others will take to their heels and bark from a safe distance. Last of all, there are dogs that will bark for a time and then wag their tails at the stranger as soon as he or she is close to them. The more afraid or timid a dog is, the more suspicious and alert it will be, and vice versa. Miniature and toy dogs are more vigilant than very large breeds, and bitches are more vigilant than males.

TRAINING YOUNG DOGS AND ADULTS

Buying a young or adult dog

The term 'young dog' refers to a dog between 10 and 24 months old. The term 'adult' applies to dogs two years old and upwards, mature animals that are fully developed physically.

How does one go about choosing a young or adult dog? Below are some hints that may be useful to anyone who is buying a puppy (who should have a good look at its parents, too). They may also be helpful when it comes to assessing whether the puppy has grown into the sort of adult dog you wanted. They concern working-dogs, not show-dogs, which are required to have special qualities peculiar to their specific breed.

In the case of the working-dog (used for hunting, general duties and sport), it is important to bear in mind what it will be asked to do. Will it live outdoors or indoors? If the breed you choose is short-haired and the dog will have to put up with bad weather, make sure that the coat is good and dense: when you spread it with your fingers it should not be easy to see the skin beneath it.

The colour also is important. White all over, due to a lack of pigment, often indicates physical weaknesses. Abundant pigmentation is invariably a sign of a high degree of vitality: the highest degree of pigmentation is found in dogs which are black, or which have a

A dog's eyes are a useful indicator of its health. You should watch them carefully for any abnormal signs. The eyes, too, are a sign of the animal's nature and temperament, whether, for instance, it is timid or bold.

great deal of black, but black dogs have poor endurance in the sun. The same can be said of dark brown dogs. If your dog will be expected to work for long periods in the sun, in warm or hot climates, choose one with a coat of another colour.

External examination: First of all, look at the skin of any young or adult dog. When it is touched it should be pliable and have no scabs or scurf. Have a close look at the hair, which should be shiny and feel almost oily when you run your fingers through it. Look at the eyes; they should be bright, and expressive, with pink, not reddish, conjunctivas.

Next, inspect the mouth. Open it carefully, keeping the jaws together and raising the lips. The teeth of a dog about a year old must all be snow-white. The shape of the incisors will enable you to assess the dog's age. Next, lift up the two side flaps of the lips; have a good look at the condition of the premolars and molars; check to see if any teeth are actually missing or in bad shape; this might be a sign of some ailment. Yellow or brown teeth in a young dog usually indicate distemper that has been cured.

Look at the feet; make sure the pads are sound and hard, and that the skin between the toes is healthy and strong.

Back examination: After these preliminary checks it is advisable to put the dog in question on a lead and make it move ahead of you, first walking, then trotting and last of all galloping. The gait is a crucial factor for any working-dog. It can reveal qualities and defects not detectable when the dog is standing still. While you are walking the dog, take a close sideways look at its back. If it is saddle-backed it will have poor endurance. (Up to a point this defect can be overlooked in a puppy of eight to ten months or in an ageing bitch that has delivered her fair share of litters.)

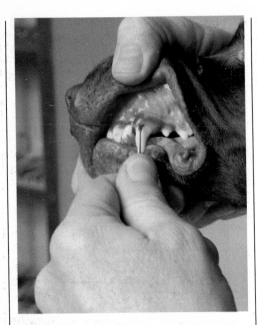

Above: While the 'baby' teeth are being shed, have a good look for excess teeth; also remove any tartar. Opposite: A long programme is needed to train a dog to this standard.

The opposite defect is the hump-back – a back that, when viewed from the side, does not have a concave line, but a convex one.

These two back defects are very serious and can affect the dog in practical ways; they may indicate a deformation of the skeleton that will greatly reduce the dog's endurance when it is working. The first of them, which also points to a general weakness of the muscles and tendons, is undoubtedly the more serious of the two.

Sometimes an anatomical defect can be made up for by an exceptionally good character that will enable the dog to become a good colleague. However, dogs with defects do not have a long active life. In a few years they are worn out by the difference between their good nature and their inadequate physical make-up. Any dog-owner wants to have a dog that will be a companion for many years.

Examining stance and posture: Having taken a sideways look at the dog, look at it now, walking towards you head on. Watch the knees with special care: they must not be visibly outward-turned. Check that the two front legs are properly parallel (or that the stance is correct for that particular breed) and that the feet are aligned with the legs, and neither inside nor outside the line. Make sure also that the feet are properly closed.

After looking at the dog head-on, take a good look at it from behind. The hindlegs must also be parallel, not turned inward or outward. These two defects, being 'cow-hocked' or 'bow-legged', mean that the weight of the body is not properly borne by the bones used for movement, and this seriously affects a dog's endurance.

Examining the gait: So far the dog has only walked; this makes it possible to see if there are any physical deformities. These are of practical rather than aesthetic concern, because they can seriously affect the essentially practical purpose for which the dog may be intended. The next thing is to get the dog to trot and gallop.

A good trot depends, first and foremost, on a well-built back. It must be free and easy, with a long, supple stride, not short, brisk, skipping steps. Short-legged people – children, or short men and women – take two steps to the normal person's one. They tire more quickly than taller people over a similar distance. The same goes for a dog with a short stride. The ideal is a dog that is a good walker, not one that skips along daintily and becomes exhausted after a few kilometres. A good stride is made possible by a strong, well-shaped back.

A good gallop depends not only on a well-built back, but on good hind-quarters, too. The swift, light gallop of a well-built dog, or the half-gallop that can go on hour after hour without causing fatigue, only occur when the fore- and hind-quarters are well balanced. The rump ro croup is also of considerable importance, because, at the gallop, the movement of the hind-quarters reaches the fore-quarters via the rump and the back. A well-built rump must be roundish and about 2.5cm (1 in) lower than the withers. Last of all, it is a good idea for the dog to have a thorough veterinary check-up.

What to make of these examinations
The hints listed above do not apply to all breeds. A hump-back is a quality in the Bulldog, as is a curved stance in the Pekingese. A Neapolitan Mastiff will never have fore-quarters like a Setter's, or the hind-quarters of a German Shepherd Dog; a sheep-like nasal bridge is a quality in the German Pointer, but a defect in the English Pointer; the harmonious proportions of a Foxhound do not exist in Dachshunds, and the build of a small Greyhound is the very opposite of that of a Pug. What has been said here is broadly applicable to most ordinary breeds of dog, but get some advice from an expert on a specific breed before you choose your young or adult dog.

When it comes to looking at the character of the young dog, take good note of what is described for the basic tests for all breeds, and all types of dog.

When you have bought your dog
Once you have made your choice, take the dog home with you. From the beginning treat it with affection and understanding. For a short time it will feel lost and bewildered. Help it to understand where it is, and to understand you. If you show it love, it will quickly return it. Remember, above all with regard to adult dogs, that the nobler a dog's character (in temperament, courage and so on), the longer it will take to become comfortable in its new home. If you can, go yourself to collect the young (or adult) dog from the kennels or owner who has sold it to you. If the dog comes to your home straight from an aeroplane, train or truck, put the cage in an enclosed place before opening it, so that the dog will not be able to run away. Open the cage yourself, and have a little food (meat and/or cheese) and a bowl of fresh water at the ready. Let the dog have a bite to eat and a drink if it feels like it – at first it may not. Put it on a lead and let it smell you all over, starting with your hands; move gently, and speak softly; and stroke the dog all the time. Its lead should be at least 2 m (2 yd) long. Do not fasten the collar too tightly or too loosely. Take the dog out of doors to an open space where there are trees and earth, so that it can relieve itself, while it is still

on the lead. Walk it for about half an hour, talking to it quitely every so often, not in a silly, babyish way, but in a friendly tone of voice. It is a good sign if it keeps looking you straight in the eye: this means it is a docile dog. If it has plenty of character, it will behave quite boldly as soon as it is in your home. If it is frightened, comfort it: it wants your protection, and if it does not have a strong character, it will be an easy dog to control.

After its walk, take the new dog back home, where its basket, kennel or run should already have been prepared.

Rewards and restraints

Now training can start: one of the most enjoyable pastimes bringing man and animal together. The hints given below apply to all breeds of dog, no matter what their function is to be. They apply to young and adult dogs that have never been previously trained, and to part-trained or badly trained animals.

The following exercises can also be used for older puppies – over 120 days old – that have already gone through the First and Second Programmes (see pp.228-42). They will be at an advantage and should progress quickly.

A word about rewards and restraints. A restraint is an action designed to persuade a dog to do something against its initial intention. There is no form of training – human or canine – that does not include restraints. They are like the rule of law. There can be no shared working arrangement, nor even simple co-existence, without a law that clearly defines what is good and what is bad. Training might be defined as the communication to the dog of this law or rule, enabling it to know what it can and cannot do.

Restraints

It is crucial that restraints are instant and 'alternated' and neither too soft nor too severe. 'Instant' means that the restraint is applied at the precise moment when the dog is doing some-

thing it should not be doing, ceases as soon as the dog desists, and is changed straight away into a reward, i.e., praise, stroking and a titbit. There is nothing more futile than 'sulking' with a dog: and it is absurd to think that a dog can achieve moral assessments of bad and good in a human sense. To make the rule of conduct quite plain to the dog, show it that the restraint, which is not to its advantage, changes swiftly into a reward, which is to its advantage, as soon as it stops doing what it should not be doing. Before long, what is undesirable in your view will become undesirable to the dog as well.

Restraints must fit the nature of the undesirable act, and so must not be used after it, although in some cases they may precede it. It is, in effect, easier to stop the dog getting used to doing something wrong than to get rid of an entrenched habit. If, for example, you have good reason to think that your dog has a tendency to jump up on the couch, or chase chickens, it is possible to nip this in the bud with an appropriate restraint. Once you have brought the dog (on its lead) close to the couch or the chickens in question, set the restraint in motion (pull on the collar, admonish it verbally, threaten it with a crop, depending on the circumstances and the dog) so that the desired association is implanted: going near the couch or the chicken-coup is not a good thing to do. This amounts to prevention rather than cure.

This example shows what a mistake it is to regard a restraint as a punishment, in the human sense. It would not be considered fair to punish a person for something before he or she had done it – i.e., before a sense of guilt could be felt. A dog does not know what guilt or blame is. As far as the aims of training are concerned, there are only associations of favourable ideas, made or unmade in the dog's mind.

A restraint is effective more quickly if it is applied using the 'alternated' method. This consists in establishing a quick alternation of restraint/reward. If the dog in question shows an undesirable aggressive or fighting tendency ards other dogs, try this way of

getting rid of it. Take your dog, on its lead, close to several other dogs and apply the restraint, to the relevant degree, which will depend on the degree of the dog's aggression. As soon as the tendency appears to have gone away, go somewhere else and have a good romp with the dog. Return to the place

where the other dogs are, get close to them, and apply the required restraint, when the aggression appears to have faded again, move away and play with your dog once more. The use of this 'alternated' method will make it easier to implant in the dog the next association: getting close to other dogs in

order to fight with them is not a pleasant thing to do.

It is very unwise to apply a restraint for too long, and too short an application will also have adverse effects.

At the start of training the restraint used should not be harsh, but it can become harsher (if necessary) as the training programme progresses. A novice trainer should choose mild restraints rather than harsh ones, because these, if not properly applied, will do damage to even the most gifted of dogs.

Early in training make absolutely sure that the dog cannot escape from the restraint by simply running away. If this happens, it will always try to take to its heels and your task will become much more difficult. This is why you must to begin with, always work with the dog on its lead; do not leave it alone, without any control.

This is a typical scale of restraints: (1) the lead; (2) compulsory positions (a mechanical method to compel the dog to make a certain movement, such as to sit; some compulsory positions can be enforced by special means; (3) a tight collar (quick tugs, of varying degrees, on a tight collar are the most usual form of restraint; despite the collar being called tight, it does not actually bother the dog); (4) the crop (if properly used this method can overcome problems that appear to be insurmountable; as we shall see, the whole secret lies in making the dog think the crop is a threat rather than a real punishment).

Golden rule 1: To stop your dog from doing something it should not be doing, apply the restraint at precisely the same time as the dog has the impulse to commit the 'offence'.

Golden rule 2: While the restraint is in force the trainer should, as far as possible, stay in the background and be seen as a source of comfort rather than punishment. Here is an example. The dog is on a tight collar with a 10-15-metre (yard) lead. With the help of a friend, flush a hare or rabbit out of

Opposite: The driving force behind training is praise, uttered in a soft voice and in a kindly tone, accompanied by patting and stroking.

a bush. The dog will give chase; let it run the full length of the lead, but when it reaches the end pull it up short and, at the same time, while it is yelping, call it, praise it, stroke it and offer it a titbit; give it plenty of comfort and have a game with it. After several tests like this, when you give the dog the command 'Lie down!' as the hare breaks cover, the dog will obey without any trouble, and will soon stop chasing other creatures when it should not; in fact, it will eventually lie down as soon as it sees a hare.

Golden rule 3: A well-used restraint turns duty into what the dog wants to do, in its own mind. If the dog is an adult and has a long-established habit of chasing hares, the process of getting rid of the habit will take longer, but it will work in the end.

Golden rule 4: Restraints are most effective when they are used to prevent the formation of bad habits, or when they can nip bad habits in the bud. This is yet another reason why it is an advantage to start training a dog as a puppy.

Golden rule 5: The use of tiredness is effective with all 'trainees' that are lively and usually display a certain degree of disobedience during the exercises aimed at instilling submission, because they are fresh and brimming with energy. Give the dog a good run before starting on the exercises.

Rewards

The opposite and the complement of restraints. With no rewards training would not be possible. A good trainer always needs to reward his pupils, and rarely needs to restrain them. It is important that the dog moves from doing what it has to do (restraint), to what it wants to do (complying with what you, the trainer or owner, wants), to what it really enjoys doing (in other words, and thanks to the reward system, happily carrying out the tasks that it has been taught to carry out). Never be afraid to reward your dog too much; in fact be lavish with your attention in both actions and words. A dog likes to see its master or mistress in a good mood; it wants to play; it enjoys being stroked and patted; and in order to get what it wants it

will do its best to please you. In short, the dog's own nature will help to establish in it those pleasant associations that will make it possible to achieve through training all the desired results.

Restraints can be almost completely done away with if, during training, you bear in mind the dog's natural impulses and do not demand the unreasonable. The really good trainer uses restraints as little as possible and only with gentle firmness.

Training tools and training places

Below you will find a list of the main tools used for dog-training. These tools make the job less tiring, and ensure that you will achieve the goal you have set yourself and avoid making countless mistakes.

(1) **Normal collar**: A simple one-piece metal chain. If the lead is attached to the outer ring the collar becomes tight; if it is attached to the inner ring, it stays in one position.

(2) **Training or choke-collar**: There is a German saying that says 'The training collar is vital for a dog, just as spurs are vital for horses.' The saying has got it wrong. Training collars have ruined many more dogs than they have helped to train: they may come in useful for a few special dogs, for certain special exercises, but they must be used sparingly and removed quickly. They can be helpful, for example, with certain stubborn dogs that have to be discouraged from attacking other dogs. They should never be used in obedience exercises, because they will make the dog depressed and bored in its work and will hold up the end result.

(3) **The lead or leash**: the best kind is made of supple leather, or fairly stout cord, about 1.8 m (6 ft) long, with two tough clips, of the type used for a horse's harness. Never use a short leash even on walks; it will teach the dog to pull. A lead should normally be at least 1.3 m (5 ft) long.

(4) **Collar and loops for the commands 'Down!' and 'Fetch!'**: Very useful tools that will give you quick results.

(5) **Retrieving 'dumb-bell'**: A simple wooden type, used for the initial retrieving exercises.

sausage, with cotton-wool filling and cloth or leather outside, and hard bristles in the middle.

(15) **Pistols and crackers**: Used to accustom the hunting-dog, as well as police and guard-dogs, to gunfire. Start off gradually, first from a distance and then getting closer to the dog, with one or two people to help you while the dog is in a good mood, or eating, or playing with other dogs. Well-balanced dogs soon become used to the noise.

Suitable training sites

A training room, quiet, with no strangers or other distractions in it, is an ideal place to get the dog to concentrate. But it is most important that it remains a place where the dog enjoys itself and does not turn into a kind of 'torture chamber'. If it does, the dog will turn in on itself in the room and instead of being alert, curious and fun-loving, will become frightened, listless and unenthusiastic, in no condition to learn anything.

The training room should be alternated as often as possible with an outdoor site, to keep the dog fit and healthy and to boost its morale after a tiring lesson indoors.

Golden rule: The dog will work well and understand everything, and then repeat perfectly the lessons taught it with a sense of fun, light-heartedness and playfulness. But its intelligence will be in a sense paralyzed, and it will not see eye to eye with you, whenever you have to act with force.

The training room can be any shape, but should be at least 3 m (10 ft) wide. The bigger it is the better, however. It should not have any furniture in it, or other objects which the dog might use to hide behind; a bare room is best. You can hang your training tools on a wall. You might also place a fairly high table against one wall; this will come in useful while you are at work. Lastly, fit a large metal ring into an end wall, about 40 cm (16 in) from the floor. This will also come in useful on many an occasion. In fact, this last item is so vital that even if you do not have a training room at your disposal you should still set up some kind of ring in any available wall or outside fixture.

(6) **Crop**: A thin bamboo cane, very light and whippy, which you can find in any cane-brake. It should not be used to hit the dog, only to admonish it.

(7) **Whistle**: The best type has a changeable pitch – soft when the dog is close by, and loud when it is some way off. It should not be too noisy or piercing, to avod the dog becoming 'hard of hearing'.

(8) **Harness for tracking**: a large harness, to be used when the dog starts learning how to track.

(9) **Long cords or light ropes**: Similar to the lead, but 4.5, 9 and 14 m (5, 10 and 15 yd) long or even longer, de-
ⁱⁿg on the exercise to be done.

(10) **Gloves**: When training a dog, it is always a good idea to wear a pair of tough leather gloves; this will prevent you from getting scratched and make for better working conditions.

(11) **Small gate and length of fencing**: Not vital, but can definitely come in useful. They can be replaced by other similar obstacles, such as hedges or walls, for example.

(12) **Light chain or bunch of keys**: Used to pull the dog up short; the chain should make plenty of noise when it hits the ground; and the bunch of keys should be quite a sizeable one.

(13) **Sling**: Use a boy's ordinary catapult, and load it with gravel.

(14) **Hard tooth pouch**: Resembles a

The reason for having a disciplined dog

Training your own dog is a fine way of ridding your mind of day-to-day problems. The exercises described here have helped thousands of dog-lovers to make their canine friend into a really satisfying colleague and helper, for the owner and for his or her friends.

ON THE LEAD
Commands: 'Heel!' 'Back!'

The Second Puppy Programme gave some hints about how to start using the lead. If your 120-day-old is doing well, you can now move on to the real lead exercise, but keep the following things in mind: (1) Up to the age of six months a puppy should not walk for more than fifteen minutes in all; from six to nine months not more than half an hour, and from nine to twelve months not more than 45 minutes. (2) The younger the puppy the less you should demand of it. Below we give some words of advice for exercising a very well-behaved dog on the lead – a competition dog, in other words. But good competition dogs will be aged two years and upwards: this is why you should not ask too much of your puppy, still not even a 'teenager'.

As far as young dogs are concerned – and adult dogs, too, for that matter – they should be regarded as untrained, even though they may know one or two things. In any event, the dog must adapt to its master or mistress, and this is why the exercise must start from scratch.

Golden rule: The first lessons should never last more than 10 minutes at most. The dog should never work on a full stomach or on a completely empty one.

The aim of the exercise: The dog has to learn the technique of being on a lead, to the point where its owner can walk with it with complete freedom. It must follow every movement of the

Opposite: When the dog is on the lead, it must stay level with its trainer and the lead must be slack. Trainer and dog must walk in step. Give the order 'Heel!' quietly.

Right: The 'Sit!' exercise.

trainer extremely closely, every time he or she stops, or changes pace. And all this must happen without the lead being pulled tight. Out of the corner of its eye the dog must follow the movements of its trainer by adjusting to his or her stride. Above all, make sure that the dog does not get used to following without using its eyes, but by basing

its speed and movement solely on the pull on the lead when there is a change of direction. If this happens the dog will never feel the need to keep its attention focussed on its owner; it will have learnt that any change of direction will be communicated by a pull on the lead. A dog trained in this way will never stay properly to heel: it will be

more like a hauling dog, pulling its owner this way and that. Its attitude will be to the detriment of all forms of discipline, hampering its progress in training, and showing up its poor up-bringing.

Walking on the lead with the command 'Heel!', which makes the dog keep its head behind the trainer's left knee, is rounded off by the command 'Back!', which means that the dog must stay behind the trainer's heels. 'Back!' is a very important command for all hunting, police and military dogs, and, as a general rule, whenver anyone is carrying a firearm.

The technique of the exercise: In order to teach a novice that its attention must be focussed on its trainer, and not stray elsewhere, do the following. Place yourself so that the wall of the training room is on your left-hand side. If you are working in a courtyard, have a wall on your left, and if you are working in an open place, find one where there is a wall, a metal or wooden fence, or something similar. The dog must be positioned on your left, between you and the wall. Like all working dogs, your dog must stay on your left-hand side to give you complete freedom of movement and above all so as not to impede your right arm. The command to be given when you start to move, or when you want the dog on your left, is 'Heel!'.

For the first exercises use a tight collar (not the training collar) and a lead or a piece of cord at least 2 m (2 yd) long.

When you are in the correct position in relation to your dog and the wall, talk to it in a friendly voice. Calm it by patting and stroking it, if it looks nervous or excited, and comfort it with a titbit or two if it seems frightened. When it looks composed, give firmly the command 'Heel!' Then walk slowly beside the wall. It is likely that the dog will happily follow you until, at a certain point, it will try to get out of the narrow space between you and the wall. A dog with a lively temperament will usually tend to walk a head of its owner; a more timid dog will tend to lag behind and pull on the lead; a dog that is easily distracted will try to move to your right-hand side. Whatever the dog does, you, the trainer, must keep moving straight ahead, changing the length of the lead to make the dog stay constantly in the same position, i.e. with its head close to your left knee. If you talk to it kindly, and pat it, the dog will not be anxious, and will even get the feeling that this is just another game.

The three possible mistakes must be put right in the following three ways: (1) Whenever the dog tends to push ahead of you, stop it by nudging its muzzle with your left knee. (2) If the dog lags behind and refuses to move, you must overcome its resistance, but still encourage it all the time with kind words.

Golden rule: During training your tone of voice is all-important. the dog will not pay attention to words but rather to the tone in which they are spoken. (3) If the dog tries to move over to the right, stop it by pulling on the lead.

After a few days, the dog will have learnt what is wanted of it and will walk as it should, close to the wall. Things start to get more complicated when you leave the training room and move outdoors; here there will be no wall-like obstacle on one side, with the trainer on the other.

In the case of strong-willed dogs the lead exercise will have good results if you keep your thin, supple bamboo cane in your right hand and tap the dog's muzzle when it tends to move ahead of you.

A tree-lined road: The following excellent teaching system can be used on a tree-lined street, or in a field with lines of plants. Let the dog go ahead of you and have a good sniff. When you reach the first plant or tree, let the dog go ahead on your left; letting the lead go slack, go to the right of the plant or tree. The lead will quickly form a loop round the tree, with the dog on one side and you on the other. When the lead comes to an end, the dog will find itself suddenly pulled up short. Then, with a firm 'Heel!', pull hard on the lead, dragging the animal backwards, forcing it to move round the tree, back to your side. When the dog is back in the proper position, praise it, regardless of the confusion, and carry on walking, repeating the exercise when you reach the next tree. After ten trees at most the dog will no longer fall into the trap and will pay closer attention to you – just as you wanted it to do.

Get the dog frequently to walk by your side while you twist and turn instead of moving in a straight line: quicken your pace, slow down, turn to the left and right, suddenly turn right round, and sometimes run ahead a few steps.

On the command 'Back!' you want the dog to drop back behind your heels about one pace. You will have to put it in the right position, using the lead, until it understands what is wanted of it. You will soon succeed if you give the command when the dog is tired. Here, too, it is a good ploy to walk close to a wall or along a path between hedges.

Important: During exercises on the lead using the commands 'Heel!' and 'Back!', as soon as the dog behaves correctly, remove the lead and give the release command 'Go!', and let it run off. The 'Go!' command was discussed in the sections on the First and Second Programmes (pp.228-42), and will be dealt with again on page 259.

A word of advice: Never punish the dog with the lead or with your hand. A dog that behaves well on the lead will focus its attention on its owner and establish with him or her that sense of co-operation that is necessary if training is to progress.

Command: 'Sit!'
The First and Second Programmes did not deal with the sit position. With very young puppies it is in fact important to concentrate on the down or lie-down position. Even with young and adult dogs the down position is more important than the command 'Sit!' However, it is given here as the second exercise after lead training, to make the training sequence smoother. When it comes to the command 'Sit!', it is not necessary to wait until the dog has grasped all the rules about being on a lead. For the exercises in this section it is a good idea to use the principle of repeating, in every lesson, everything that the dog has already learnt. So, before starting on the second exercise, go through the first

one again. To achieve a proper response to the command 'Sit!' use the wall technique, with the dog once again on your left in a narrow space. The best place to use is the wall of a training room.

The aim of the exercise: the sit position is the first standard position of the working dog, just as the basic standard position of the military dog is a response to the command 'On guard!'.

The technique of the exercise: Start off as for the lead exercises, but after a few steps, stop, tapping the ground with your heels a little, and bending down to put your left hand on the dog's croup and your right hand on its collar. A lot of dogs are reluctant to adopt the standard position of their own accord. The command alone is not enough; they will decide to obey only if they feel pressure from your hand on their hind-quarters − quite light pressure, of course. You must get them out of this: give the command in your normal voice, but firmly, and only use your hands once the order has been given, so that the dog has a chance to carry it out of its own accord.

Be sure, too, that the dog assumes the correct position; tell it off, with your hand on the scruff of its neck, give the command 'Heel!', walk forwards a few steps, and give the command 'Sit!' once again, until the dog is in the right position. When it is, praise it, stroke it and give it a reward. After a time substitute for the command 'Sit!' a short 'Sss' sound.

When the dog carries out the order as soon as you tap the ground, or as soon as it remembers the sound of the command, move away from the wall. Without this to make it take up the standard position − parallel to its trainer − the dog will have a tendency to sit in the wrong position. The only position in which the dog will not be in your way is the standard one, so you must stop it sitting in any other. To achieve this, when you stop and give the command 'Sit!' stretch your left hand out to the dog's left thigh, so that it cannot move out of the parallel position.

Do not feel that all this patient work is an exaggeration and expect the dog

to obey the 'Sit!' command perfectly the very first time. It is only by precise training that full and satisfactory results will be achieved.

The first exercise should not last more than ten minutes. The second one can be extended to a quarter of an hour, because it embraces both the command 'Sit!' and the lead exercises. The lesson should end on the lead.

Golden rule: Every lesson should end with an exercise that the dog knows how to carry out so that it earns words of praise and a titbit as a reward.

At the end of the daily lesson the dog should be lively, happy and have a sense of achievement. This is the only way of ensuring that the next day's lessons will be carried out with enthusiasm.

Command: 'Come here!'

With this exercise, too, do not wait until the dog is fully acquainted with the two previous ones. After two days devoted solely to working with the lead, you can happily move on to the command 'Sit!' and after two more days to the command 'Come here!' If the dog does not appear tired, extend the lesson to twenty minutes.

The aim of the exercise: To get the dog to stop on the spot, and above all to react perfectly to the call. You will need a helper, someone to run to you as soon as you have given the first call. Remember: a dog that does not respond to its call is of no use. The same

To make your dog stay put while you move away you must give the dog assurance that you will come back.

goes for a dog that is left in a certain spot and does not stay there until its owner returns.

The technique of the exercise: After running through all the previous exercises, when the dog is sitting down, stand in front of it, step slowly backwards, holding out your right hand close to its muzzle, thus stopping it from moving. Count up to twenty to yourself, then give the command 'Come here!' in a friendly tone of voice.

At the same time, walk backwards quickly to encourage the dog to come towards you at a brisk pace. Once it is close to you − always get it to come right up to you − praise it and give it a titbit. Next put the dog on the lead, give it the command 'Sit!' two or three times then stand in front of it again, and step very slowly backwards, so that it hardly notices. Keep the lead in your left hand, and use it to pull the dog lightly if it does not obey the 'Come here!' command straight away.

As the daily lessons progress, make the dog stay where you have left it, without moving, while you take several steps backwards. Make it stay put until you have counted 10, then 30, then 40, up to 100 to yourself. Above all, make the dog come to you at speed, trotting at least, but better still at the gallop. As soon as you notice that on the command 'Come here!' the dog comes towards you looking tired and reluctant, step back again with short steps, but quite quickly, to encourage it to run to you. The main reason for it to do this is the certainty that, once it is close to you, it will be rewarded with something tasty to eat.

Make sure that this lesson does not involve any kind of punishment, not even scolding or a cross tone of voice. The keynote is persuasion – firm persuasion: for the dog, being called by its owner and going to him or her, must always be pleasant, a way of being patted, praised and rewarded.

It is, in fact, better not to punish a dog that comes to you when called, even if it has done something wrong. Some readers may well ask 'How do I punish my dog, when it has done something wrong, if it obeys the command that I have given it precisely to punish it?' In such cases it is advisable not to call the dog; rather, from some way off, give it the command 'Lie down!'. The dog will obey, and you can then go over to it and scold it. Before doing so, ask yourself: 'How shall I get my dog to understand me?' If you find a way of making yourself understood, the rest is easy, but if you treat your dog roughly this will frighten it, and affect its understanding and intelligence. Always remember that it is never necessary to hit a dog in order to make yourself understood.

Some people may object that the dog has first learnt the 'Down!' command from a distance. The answer is that before this point it is a good idea to reduce corrective methods to a minimum. Throughout the first part of training you need, above all, to win your dog's trust and confidence. It has to put up with the lessons, which may often be irksome to it. For the rest of the day it is good tactics not to scold.

To round off the exercise, gradually replace the command 'Down!' with a whistle. First follow your 'Come here!' straightaway with the whistle, then alternate your vocal command with the one given by the whistle. The call whistle, vital over long distances, must be a series of short blasts. A long unbroken note is for the command 'Down!' dealt with below.

Points worth remembering: (1) If, when you call, the dog fails to come, step back with a few brisk short steps, calling it in a friendly voice. (2) In the case of many dogs that do not react naturally to a call, a good ploy is to call and get down on the ground at the same time: the curious and surprised dog will usually run straight over to you. (3) When you give the call, you must feel well disposed towards the dog, because dogs are highly sensitive to mood, and if their trainer is, in fact, in a bad mood, they will soon realize it, whether the command is given in a gentle voice or not. (4) Whenever the dog fails to obey and has to be called firmly, make sure, as soon as it has come to you, that you encourage it with a few 'Good dogs'; this will once more make answering the call a pleasant experience. If the dog hangs back a second time, you can allow yourself a gruff 'Bad dog', quickly changing that to a 'Good dog', as soon as it moves towards you. (5) In the case of dogs that do not react well to their call, you can get help from some-

The 'Down!' position is basic to all training; it is a naturally submissive position, to do with hierarchy. In the pack every dog has its own place; training leads to the acceptance of the owner as dominant.

one who is good with a catapult; when you call, your helper should shower the dog's hindquarters with a slingful of small pebbles, while you call again with a gentle 'Come here! Good dog, Come here!' so that you become a handy refuge. (Instead of a catapult you can use a bunch of keys or a small chain; but this system is only useful if the call is already established and if the dog already knows that nothing unpleasant will happen to it if it goes to its trainer. (6) A trainer who has no assistant but wants to use the chain or bunch-of-keys method for the call exercise should remember that it should only be used for this particular exercise and not for the 'Down!' command, for example; the dog should not notice you throwing the chain or keys, or preparing to do so; do not throw anything if the dog does not come because it is scared: if you do, it will become even more frightened; on the other hand, if it is distracted or playing, you can throw something: the chain or the bunch of keys should land out of the blue, making the dog jump; it will run away from what has disturbed it towards you, and you should then comfort it with 'Good dog' repeated several times and a reward. (7) When the dog is sniffing at a strange dog, it will take its time to respond to the call because it knows that if it moves away, the other dog may follow it and possibly attack it; this is quite natural; it is best to call it when it is some way from the other dog, but if it is already close to the other animal, walk nearer to it, to give it a sense of security.

Commands: 'Down!' 'Go!'

Having reached this point, the daily lessons should be extended to a maximum of 25 minutes. If you have the time, you might even go through two lessons a day. Avoid lessons during the heat of the day in summer. Do not work at night, because the play of light and shadow will stop the dog from concentrating. However, if you have at your disposal a training room with lighting, you can go through the lessons perfectly well after dark.

The down position is a natural one for any dog. When there is a scrap between two members of a pack of street-dogs if one of them reckons it is the weaker it will lie flat on the ground, with its body slightly on one side. The victor will quickly give up any idea of a fight. For the trainee dog the command 'Down!' provides a natural means of breaking off a fight and avoiding punishment. Keep this in mind, and never punish a dog when it has lain down of its own accord.

To get a good response to 'Down!' you will need to work hard every day for at least three or four weeks, the exercises can be combined with others.

The aim of the exercise: The down exercise is rightly regarded by many as the nub of all training. In fact, this command instils in the dog absolute submission; it enables you to control it from close by and far off; it is the keystone of the whole framework of discipline that you are trying to create. But always follow it with a cheerful 'Go!'

The technique of the exercise: Once the dog is in the sit position, stand in front of it, take hold of its two front legs and, repeating softly the command 'Down! Down!' pull it forwards into the standard down position. When its belly is on the ground, put your right hand on its head, forcing it to put its muzzle between its front legs, repeating softly the command 'Down!'

Golden rule: Command words should be repeated several times only when the trainee dog is learning a new word and a new exercise.

As soon as the dog has clearly understood the exercise and the corresponding command word, it should only ever be used once. It is a mistake to shout it, louder and louder. In fact, if the dog does not respond to the first order, give the second one in a quieter voice, and the third one even more softly. Shift from **piano** to **pianissimo**, not from **piano** to **forte** to **fortissimo**. Too many people have the bad habit of talking too loudly to their dogs and repeating their commands until they are screaming them; they do not realize that, by doing this, they are making their poor pets 'hard of hearing'. A dog is described in this way when it waits for its owner to run out of breath before carrying out a command. The fault never lies with the dog, always with the owner or trainer. Talk very gently to your dog, alternating gestures with murmured commands, so that it always keeps its eye on you, waiting, alertly and happily, for your slightest word or movement. An alert and happy dog will always be ready to do what you ask of it.

As soon as the dog shows that it has understood what you want of it, and stays happily in the down position, with you crouched close at hand, get to your knees, keeping your hand on the dog's head. Later on just touch its head with the tip of a forefinger, and finally with a bamboo cane.

The command 'Down!' should always be followed by the release command 'Go!'. The dog should dash off, and you could well run with it for a minute or two to give it a sense of fun and well-being.

Once the dog has understood what is required by the command 'Down!', you must tackle the next step. What you are after is a dog that, at the very first command 'Down!' will drop to the ground as if its legs had suddenly given way. A bamboo cane helps to get quick results.

The use of the cane is very much a question of balance. Incorrect or excessive use of it as a crop will ruin the dog. Careful, clever use of it will make for quick and impressive progress. The pitfall to avoid is a scared dog: there is nothing sadder – and no more glaring sign that you have failed.

Walk with the dog's lead in your left hand. In your right hand, hidden behind your back, have the light, supple bamboo cane. Without warning, give the command 'Down!' in a dry, authoritative tone of voice. At the same moment, and using only the force of your wrist, not of your whole arm, tap the dog's back with the bamboo, slightly below the withers.

Surprised and a bit alarmed, the dog will tend to 'break ranks': stop it from doing so by keeping the lead very short indeed, and then pull the lead downwards to get the dog to lower itself to the ground. Keep repeating the command 'Down!' in the same dry, sharp tone, and accompany the word each time with a tap with the cane.

As soon as the dog starts to carry out the command, stop any form of coercion and give the command 'Go!' along with some warm words of praise, plenty of patting, and a titbit, too. Then suddenly put a stop to all this cajolery with a crisp 'Heel!' Run with the dog for a dozen or so paces, and when it looks in obvious good spirits, repeat the command 'Down!' and at the same time tap it with the cane. Before long the dog will drop to the ground as soon as it hears the command. Continue to follow this up with the release word, 'Go!'

The risk in using the cane is that the dog will become frightened. At the first sign of fear, move on to other exercises which the dog knows well and can carry out without any bother. When you have regained its trust, and it is in good spirits once again, return to an exercise with the command 'Down!' still using the bamboo cane. To avoid the dog taking fright at the mere sight of it, stroke it gently with the cane as soon as it does what it should. Be sure that the taps with the cane are given without any signal movement from you, the trainer: they must appear to come out of the blue. If the dog notices that the taps are regularly preceded by some movement from you, you will have the responsibility for hitting it, in the dog's eyes, and this will have very adverse consequences.

As time passes you can make the actual pronunciation of the command 'Down!' slightly less precise.

It is worth repeating that during this exercise you should be satisfied when the dog merely lies on the ground; do not necessarily expect it to rest its head on the ground. This should happen later, when the dog's response to the command has become instantaneous. The taps from the cane should, of course, represent a threat, not a violent gesture. In other words, they should not be hard enough to make the dog whimper, but brisk and firm, almost as if they were an extension of your voice when it gives the no-nonsense command 'Down!' Lastly, they should be given with the word of command. This is the only way to get positive results.

Once the dog responds immediately the next step is for it to carry out the command when it is not on a lead, on its owner's left-hand side. Training is aimed at the point where the command is effective at any distance. A spoken command or a whistle should be able to stop the dog in its tracks, wherever it is and whatever it is doing.

The command 'Go!' is important as the other half of the exercise, and to make the dog understand what is required; it will also maintain the dog's willingness to carry on working, and will not suppress its initiative. On future occasions it will carry on doing what it was doing before being interrupted by your 'Down!' – a command that must be given for a good reason.

When the dog is at a distance from you, and you want it to lie down, start off by giving it the order standing in front of it and raising your arm at the same time.

To begin with, because of your new position, the dog will be surprised, and will wait a while, or else carry out the order slowly: it will not immediately drop to the ground as before. You can get over this with the help of an assistant who stands behind the dog and taps it with the cane at precisely the same moment that you give the command 'Down!', standing in front of the dog with the lead in your left hand and your right arm raised. Before long you will not need your helper any more, and you will increase the distance between yourself and the dog, and get rid of the lead altogether. (Again, after each 'Down!' release the dog with a 'Go!')

From this point things will be much simpler. Get the dog to sit, leave it where it is, and give the command 'Down!' from a distance – sometimes from in front, sometimes to the side, and sometimes from behind. When your results are good, move on to the next step. With the dog sitting 10 m (11 yd) or so away from you, call it with a 'Come here!' When it is halfway to you give it a firm command 'Down!' It should drop to the ground immediately, in mid-gallop. If this slightly more complicated exercise is not properly understood by the dog, you can call on your helper again. Fix a

10-metre (11 yd) cord to the dog's collar, and get your assistant to hold it, standing behind the dog, which will be sitting down. Position yourself about 10 m (11 yd) from the dog, and call 'Come here!' When it is halfway to you, give the Down command and if the dog does not lie down at once, the assistant should give a firm jerk on the lead; this will make the dog obey the command. This exercise should only be carried out when your call is good and the dog knows the basic exercise; otherwise, when it is expecting the command 'Down!' the dog will come to you at a very sluggish pace. Intersperse the exercise with others that are enjoyable, and do not interrupt them with the command 'Down!'. Never forget to give the command 'Go!' afterwards.

Some experts recommend for this exercise a 'braking' device for impetuous dogs that run off of their own accord as soon as they are set free. This is a roll of material round the collar, and hanging down in front: it hits the dog's legs and because it makes running difficult, the dog will soon become more obedient. As soon as this happens, remove the cloth.

By now you will be able to give the command 'Down!' in circumstances of varying degrees of complexity: close to the dog, from a distance, when the dog is tired, when it is running flat out, when it is coming towards you, when it is running away from you, and so on. It is worth repeating this crucial exercise as often as possible. Aim at reaching a point where the dog can carry out these commands in the order they are given in the following exercises:

(1) 'Sit!' and 'Down!' on the lead. 'Go!'

(2) 'Down!' on the lead, with only the trainer's arm raised. 'Go!'

(3) 'Down!' with the lead on the ground and the trainer standing behind the dog. 'Go!'

(4) Sudden 'Down!' while walking. 'Go!'

(5) Sudden 'Down!' while the dog is running. 'Go!'

(6) 'Down!' from a distance, with a long leash. 'Go!'

(7) 'Down!' close to and from a distance without a leash or long cord, the

command given both verbally and by raising the arm. 'Go!'

(8) 'Down!' from any distance in all circumstances, the command given verbally, by raising the arm or with a whistle. 'Go!'

(9) 'Down!' when firing, for all hunting dogs. For this exercise, and how it is gradually developed, see the First and Second Puppy Programmes. Guard- and watch-dogs should not lie down at the sound of a shot; they should remain indifferent and untroubled.

To accustom your dog to dropping to the ground at the sound of a whistle, blow a long note immediately after your verbal order. Within a few days the dog will obey any one of the three ways of giving the order: verbally, if it is close by; with a whistle, if it is some way off; and with the raised arm.

As soon as it has had the command 'Down!', a dog will tend to move towards its trainer/owner. This can be a drawback later on in hunting, or in general working duties. In fact, the command 'Down!' does not mean that an action stops – an attack, say, in the case of a guard-dog – but rather that it is briefly interrupted. After obeying the command 'Down!' the dog should go on with what it was doing. If, from the start, it makes for you at the command 'Down!', you must quickly teach it to stay where it is before the command is given, without turning its head towards you: when it is in the down position and before you tell it to 'Go!', throw a titbit in front of its nose that it can take as soon as it is released.

Never forget that when you give the command 'Down!' to a distant dog that is running free, there is a risk that it will not obey – quite a large risk, since the dog can persuade itself that obedience is not compulsory, and if it does, all the training it has gone through will be undone. So, go carefully before you give commands to a frolicking dog that is not on a lead, and only give them when it has carried out the exercises perfectly on a long leash. If it does not, do not raise your voice, threaten the dog, or become impatient

An advanced 'Stay!' exercise: by now the dog knows that its owner will not be gone for long.

and undo everything that you have so far achieved. The golden rule is that it is better to call your dog to you gently, pat it for coming, put it on a long lead, take it back to the place where it failed to carry out the exercise in question, leave it there while you walk away, lead in hand, and at a distance repeat the command that it failed to obey. This rule applies to the 'Down' and other obedience exercises.

Command: 'Stay!'
You need a dog that will, on any occasion, stay put while you go off somewhere for ten minutes, half an hour or even longer, confident that it will not move until you get back. If you could simply say to the dog, 'Wait until I get back', the dog would undoubtedly do so without any problem, but, unfortunately, human beings do not know enough about canine language to make themselves understood in it. For the dog, staying in one place, at your command, is a matter of trust. When it watches you walk away, its natural impulse will be to follow. If you

manage to get it to stay where it is for a few seconds, after you have disappeared, it will soon bound off in the direction in which you have gone. It will not stay put because it is afraid that you might forget it and never return for it. So it is a question of giving the dog confidence, of making it understand that it can wait without being worried or anxious, that you will not forget it, and that you will not fail to come back for it. To get your dog to understand all this, carry out the following exercise.

The technique of the exercise: Put the dog in the down position, leaving the lead attached to its collar, and arranging the other end of the lead over the dog's back. The slight weight of the lead will have a mild coercive effect, but one that works quite well. Since the dog must stay where it is for quite a while, do not expect it to keep its head on the ground.

Stand in front of the dog; take a step backwards, giving the command 'Stay!' If the dog stays still, take another couple of steps back, but look

at the dog all the time. Start walking in a semi-circle round the dog, and then walk all round it, and last of all move about 20 m (22 yd) away and hide for a few seconds behind a tree or some other large object. The process of gaining the dog's trust must be worked through gradually, until the dog feels sure that it will not be left alone and forgotten.

Of course, every now and then the dog will make a mistake, get up, and come and find you in your hiding-place. Tell it off by shaking its collar and take it back to where you had left it, making sure that you put it a few metres (yards) further back than it was at first. In other words the dog must quickly absorb a basic point: that getting up after being given the command 'Stay!' is not to its advantage; in fact, it is to its disadvantage because after it has moved it will be put somewhere even further from its owner.

During these exercises dogs that have clearly shown themselves to be undeniably intelligent will get up when their owner is out of sight; they will move forward and then lie down again wherever they happen to be when the owner/trainer reappears. They should be given a scolding – just a mild one. It would be a very serious error to let the dog stay in the new position, because it would take this as proof that its tactics work, and would do the same thing again on the very next occasion. If it is taken a few metres (yards) further back from the original spot it will soon realize that disobedience will not get it anywhere.

When you have managed to get the dog to stay put in a given place for three minutes, it will be quite easy to extend the time gradually to 15, 30 and finally to 60 minutes. Your goal will then have been achieved.

There are, however, certain particularly sensitive dogs that cannot bear to be left, and once their owner is out of sight will get up and follow. These dogs must be treated differently. With the help of special traces for the compulsory down position a couple of lessons will achieve what would otherwise take a week or more. Attach the traces to the collar and the dog will stay put. To begin with keep an eye on

it from close by, repeating the commands in a gentle voice, but with firm insistence, as if there were no traces. If the dog moves, jumps up and rolls over, scold it, put it back in the proper position, and carry on calmly with the exercise. The dog will soon give in and learn that, once it is down on the ground, it must not move until the trainer arrives. The traces can then gradually be slackened and finally undone, but left close to the dog's nose; after a while they can be dispensed with altogether.

The one-month programme
After reading about these obedience exercises, some dog-lovers may won-

der how long it will take for a dog to carry out all the basic ones. If you work with your dog for a little while each day, depending on how much free time you have, your goal will be achieved in a month. In general terms, a good trainer and a bright dog will require 15 hours work per month. A novice trainer, with plenty of determination and a reasonably gifted dog, will need about 30 hours – or an hour a day.

Here is a one-month training programme that has been used with all types of dogs (hunting, working, companion) and has always given excellent results.

Day 1: Lead exercise. 'Sit!' (10 minutes

in the morning and 10 minutes again in the afternoon/evening).

Day 2: Lead exercise. 'Sit!' 'Come here!' (15 minutes morning and afternoon/evening).

Day 3: Lead exercise. 'Sit!' 'Come here!' 'Down!' (20 minutes morning and afternoon/evening).

Day 4: Lead exercise. 'Sit!' 'Come here!' 'Down!' 'Stay!', for a few seconds (20 minutes morning and afternoon/evening).

Days 5, 6, 7, 8, 9, 10: Lead exercise, well away from the wall (if possible in a tree-lined road). 'Sit!': from a distance, well away from any wall, with the dog in the standard position. 'Come here!' Step back up to 9 m (10 yd) and wait up to 90 seconds before calling the dog to you. 'Down!': make the dog assume the 'sphinx' position with its chin on the ground, then give the command from in front of the dog. 'Stay!': walking round the dog and leave it where it is for up to 30 minutes (25 minutes at the morning lesson, 30 minutes in the afternoon/evening).

Day 11: Lead exercise outdoors (if possible somewhere where there are plenty of distractions). Frequent 'Sit!' commands, every 9 to 11 m (10 to 12 yd) during the lead exercise. 'Come here!': step back up to 13 m (14 yd) after a couple of minutes. 'Down!': start to replace the verbal command with the whistle or raised arm. 'Stay!': keep out of sight for a moment (30-minute lesson in both the morning and the afternoon/evening).

Days 12, 13, 14 and 15: Lead exercise: increase and decrease your pace; turn left and right; make a sudden right-about-turn, and dashes forward. 'Sit!': give this command as often as possible during the day, not only during lessons, but also whenever you are simply with the dog. 'Down!': alternate the three types of command. 'Come here!': hide so that you are invisible and, after 10 secods or so, call the dog; during this exercise it must re-

main in the sitting position, and not lie down of its own accord. 'Down!': sudden commands in the midst of a run given at a distance with the dog on a long leash, and always with alternation of the verbal command with the raised arm and the whistle. 'Stay!': keep out of sight for up to 20 seconds (30-minute lessons both morning and afternoon/evening).

Days 16, 17, 18, 19 and 20: Lead exercise, to be done without any mistake. 'Sit!': standard position taken up instantly. 'Come here!': do this exercise as often as possible during the day, even when you are not involved in actual lessons, giving the command verbally and with a whistle. 'Down!': the command given from close by and far off, without a lead and with a long lead, verbally, with raised arm and with the whistle. 'Stay!': use traces if necessary (30-minute lessons both morning and afternoon/evening).

Days 21, 22, 23, 24 and 25: Concentrate on the previous exercises, with the following variations: 'Down!': from a wide range of distances and conditions. 'Stay!': remain out of sight for up to 5 minutes (30-minute lessons morning and afternoon/evening).

Days 26, 27, 28, 29 and 30: Repeat all the exercises already described: in the case of the 'Come here!' command alternate the verbal and the whistle summons (30-minute lessons both morning and afternoon/evening).

This programme can, of course, be

stretched over a longer period of time, without any adverse effects, but should not be shorter than a month: give the dog plenty of time to absorb the various lessons.

The second month's programme is a natural extension of the first, and has no special problems attached to it. Even retrieving or fetching, which is regarded as the main 'stumbling-block', is quite straightforward if you follow one of the various systems described below.

Command: 'Come on! Come on!'
This exercise will start off the second month's programme, which includes: Running, Walking without a lead, Go, Stay, Jump, Bicycle, Refusing a 'bribe', Barking to command, and Fetching or Retrieving. The exercises should be gone through as a well co-ordinated sequence.

Running is an exercise that makes the dog come to you more quickly, along the route that it is already taking. This can be very important in hunting, tracking, retrieving and so on.

The aim of the exercise: To establish a command that will keep the dog on its route, but make it move faster.

The technique of the exercise: On an ordinary walk, suddenly give your dog the command 'Come on! Come on!' and at the same time sprint away from it. At home, when you find yourself right behind the dog as you are climbing the stairs, for example, suddenly

Opposite: Lead exercising should involve walking, trotting and galloping.
Right: The call must be made from a distance leaving the dog on the spot.

give the order 'Come on! Come on!', clapping your hands and running on up the stairs, so that the dog also will have to move faster. Another occasion to use: your dog is some way off and coming towards you; do not move. When it has almost reached you, suddenly give the command 'Come on! Come on!' and move back quickly, so that the dog has to accelerate from a trot to a gallop to catch up with you. There are plenty of other similar opportunities for instilling this command. The important thing is to use them all to create in the dog the habit of reacting by increasing its speed every time it hears your command 'Come on! Come on!'

Without the lead
Command: 'Heel!'

Once a basic obedience has been established with the dog on the lead, you can then, but only then, start working without a lead. However, if you notice signs of uncertainty, put the lead on again at once.

If your lead exercises have been properly conducted, the dog will follow you happily, showing strong trust in your left hand, which it will tend to want to play with.

The aim of the exercise: The dog must follow its trainer when it is without a lead. It must become more and more reliant on its trainer so that it will obey as if it were second nature to do so.

The technique of the exercise: In the training room or usual work place replace the lead with a length of light string. Walk short, straight stretches, leaving the string over the dog's back. Give the command 'Heel' quietly when the dog is about to move away. Make it follow you by slapping your left thigh with your hand. At first make sure there are no distractions. If the dog lags behind, run on ahead and call it quietly. If it goes ahead of you, run back.

If things are going well, make some quarter-turns. Zigzag a little, make some sharp turns, run and then sprint. Repeat the exercise out of doors. Never forget to pat the dog and give it the odd reward every time it does the exercise properly. Do not make the lesson last too long. End each session with an exercise that the dog can do, and stroke it.

Now your dog will follow you, with or without a lead, staying close to your knee and never walking ahead of your left leg. In the place where you usually go through the exercises, let the dog wander off and, after a while, when it is a few metres (yards) away and perhaps lying down or busy doing something, briskly give the command 'Heel!'. The dog should come to you, stay close to your left leg and stay close while you walk along. Repeat this exercise in different places and at unexpected moments. Reward the dog when it behaves correctly, persuade it to obey you if it is reluctant, speaking affectionately to it. If it comes unwillingly when you give the command, slowly and with its head down, back away quickly so that it has to break into a trot to reach you. Walk normally when it is by your side. Make it come quickly as soon as you give the command. Offer it a titbit.

If the dog does not behave correctly several times running, put it on a lead, keep the lead very short, and walk with it like that for about five minutes. At the end of the time, give the dog a titbit, and pat it. Do not allow it to be distracted or hesitate. Be firm, but keep the dog in good spirits. If you are too severe you will achieve nothing. If you become impatient, stop the exercise and start again next day. And always end with an exercise that the dog can do well.

A word of advice: Let the dog miss one of its meals, and have some pieces of meat or biscuits with you during the exercise session. While the dog is distracted, call it ('Heel!'), walk with it off the lead and make it sniff your left hand, in which you are holding the titbit; hand out these treats from time to time. Before long the dog will start to enjoy the exercise, whether it is rewarded each time or not. Always adopt a positive approach to training.

'Go!' and 'Go on!'
Command: 'Go!'
The Puppy Programmes have already mentioned the use of the command 'Go!' after the 'Down!' exercise. It is a very important exercise and command, and must be properly worked through.

The aim of the exercise: To send the dog ahead, releasing it from any stationary positions ('Sit!', 'Down!', 'Stay!', etc.); this will put the dog in good spirits, and enable it to run about. The exercise is also used to make the dog carry on with what it was doing when it was interrupted by the command 'Down!' etc., and to encourage it to check the terrain and, in the case of hunting and tracking dogs, to seek out game.

The technique of the exercise: After finishing exercises with the commands, 'Down!', 'Sit!' or 'Stay!', or a lesson on the lead, give the command 'Go!' and start to run with the dog, looking as if you're enjoying yourself. If it does not run ahead of you give it

Opposite: The 'Stay!' exercise at a distance and without a lead is designed to teach the dog to stop, for instance, in the midst of traffic.

the command 'Come on! Come on!' It will soon realize that 'Go!' means that it has permission to go ahead of you. If the dog is timid, tending to stay close to you, throw a ball, stick or else a titbit, and the dog will soon change its behaviour. Make an appropriate gesture as you give the command 'Go!'

Keep an eye on these things in connection with this exercise: (1) At the beginning of the exercise without the lead, do not give the command 'Go!', or the dog may be inclined to run off without being told to do so. (2) Do not remove the lead and immediately give the command 'Go!', or the two things may overlap in the dog's mind, and as soon as you remove the lead on future occasions it will dash off. (3) After the command 'Go!', do not at first immediately give the counter-command 'Down!', or the pleasure of the 'Go!' will be lost. When it hears 'Go!' the dog must sprint away.

Command: 'Seek!'
This is an excellent exercise, vital for hunting- and herding-dogs, and for those doing rescue work.

The aim of the exercise: To get the dog to seek some way off, in the direction and place indicated by its owner so that it will thoroughly explore the area in which game has fallen to the ground (for hunting-dogs) or where a sheep or cow has gone astray (for herding-dogs) or where there may be an injured person (rescue dogs), and so on. This exercise takes the dog off the beaten track, where its owner will guide it by a kind of remote control, with movements of the arms and whistles. This exercise will take the dog up to 500 metres (550 yards) away from you.

The technique of the exercise: The dog must already be good and practised at retrieving. Now it must seek out and retrieve an object in the direction indicated by a gesture of the trainer's arm. Here are the exercises:
(1) Knot or roll a rag round a titbit (which the dog will easily find and eat) and throw this over a hedge, stream, low wall, etc. Giving the command 'Seek! Seek!', show the dog how to find a way to reach the rag and bring it back to you. Repeat the exercise until

the dog has got the idea and will find its own way to the object to be retrieved.
(2) Throw the rag (again containing a tasty morsel) into a hollow, or down a slope, or hide it in a ditch, or the hollow of a tree, or in some long grass, and with just a gesture or two guide the dog towards it, helping it with the words 'Seek! Seek!', if necessary. If the dog becomes impatient and gives up looking, give the command 'Down!', wait a moment, and then start again, helping the dog this time until it brings back the rag, wagging its tail.

Each time indicate with your arm at full stretch the direction in which the dog must look: it will soon learn to head in the right direction. Repeat the command 'Seek! Seek!' each time.

When you have reached this stage during your walks, every so often point in a particular direction and, if necessary, run in that direction too, encouraging the dog to go ahead of you with the command 'Go! Go on!' Next, call it back, running in the opposite direction with your arm outstretched, repeating the command. The dog will learn quickly, and it should enjoy this exercise – all the more so if there is a titbit at stake.

Now move on to the 'Go on! Go on!' command, which merely increases the working distance:
(1) Get an unseen assistant to place the titbit twice as far away as usual. Guide the dog with the command 'Go!' and 'Seek! Seek!' and make a sweeping circle above your head with one arm, stopping the gesture when you are pointing in the direction in which the dog must look for the titbit. It will soon understand where it must look, and it will also realize that the new gesture means that the object is further away. When it returns with whatever the object may be, give it a reward.

With regard to rewards – words of praise, pats and titbits – it is most important to remember what has already been said about the risk of rewards becoming monotonous, which will make the dog rather unenthusiastic. Vary them. To make the searches more energetic, let the dog miss a meal every now and then, and replace it with some meat and biscuits

Jumping and retrieving combined, showing a high level of discipline.

that the dog will have to find during these exercises. A good appetite will always act as a spur.

(2) After a certain number of exrcises, a longer search will be possible without you having to guide or accompany the dog: your gesture in the right direction will do the trick.

If the dog wants to come back to you before it has found the object, get it to lie down, keep it there for a while, go to it, and repeat the exercise. When it finds the object, and brings it back, reward it.

(3) Step up this exercise with the help of an assistant – a child can help – and everyone – dog, owner and helper – will have an enjoyable time, especially in the country. When the dog has fully understood, it will head straight in the direction indicated by your gesture, then stop and look at you; you should then make another directional gesture, and so on, until the dog finds and retrieves the object.

With a little care and attention the dog will soon find things hundreds of metres (yards) away, which will be a source of satisfaction to dog-lover, hunter and trainer alike.

Command: 'Stop!'
In some ways this is the opposite of the previous exercise. The command 'Go!' or 'Seek!' sends the dog running off rather as if it were an avance guard; the command 'Stop!' is given to halt the dog in its tracks, whatever it is doing at the time.

The aim of the exercise: To enable the owner to stop the dog immediately; rather like the 'Halt!' used in the army, replacing the command 'Down!' in wet or damp places, or on rainy days. The down position is a submissive one, the command 'Stop!' will keep the dog alert and at the ready – when it is looking for game, for example, or attacking a wrongdoer; in city traffic it may well prevent the dog from being run over.

The technique of the exercise: When you are walking with your dog on a

lead – a very short lead – stop without warning and give the command 'Stop!' Put the palm of your right hand over the dog's eyes. Keep the dog still, quietly repeating 'Stop! Stop!' If the dog tends to sit down, or change position, put your left hand under its belly and set it back on all fours. Move slowly in front of it. After it has remained in the one position for a few seconds, praise, stroke and reward it, and afterwards run with it. Repeat the exercise suddenly: the dog will not take long to get the idea. Do not overdo things if you see that the new command is having the desired effect.

Next, stay at a distance from the dog until it carries out the command, first on a long lead, and then without any lead at all. In the end it will stand still on the spot even if it cannot see you. Do not praise the dog too much while it is still, because its pleasure may make it change positions.

By alternating the commands 'Down!', 'Go!', 'Go on! Go on!' and 'Stop!' you will soon have an all-round hunting-dog – or an all-round police dog. Any skilful trainer can turn a dog of any breed into a hunting-dog, and, what is more, a specialist, at pointing, seeking, working in burrows or tracking game.

Commands: 'Up!' 'Back!'
Jumping, when they are told to do so, is very important for all trained dogs. As well as being a good physical exercise – it can easily act as a substitute for long walks – jumping has to do with submission, since the dog is instructed to jump, not for its own pleasure, but simply because it has been given the command.

The aim of the exercise: To enable a trained dog to jump any kind of obstacle: its work should not be interrupted when it encounters a watercourse, ditch, wall or hedge in its path.

The technique of the exercise: A dog that has not been taught jumping exercises is often not aware that it can jump. Dogs kept in an enclosure often realize for the first time, after the exercises, that they could easily have jumped over the fence had they wanted to. The problem in training a dog to jump lies in persuading it that it is capable of carrying out the exercise. Once its fear has been overcome it will jump without any difficulty.

Carry out the first exercise with an obstacle not more than 70 cm (28 in) high for a large dog (such as a Great Dane), not more than 50 cm (20 in) for an average-sized dog (Boxers, Setters, etc.), and not more than 25 cm (10 in) for small dogs (Spaniels, Dachshunds, etc.).

If the dog lives indoors, a good system for teaching it how to jump is to put the obstacle in a doorway between rooms. Leave the dog in one room, call it to you and, just as it is about to jump, give the command 'Up!' Later on you can use natural obstacles outdoors.

If, on the other hand, you have all the equipment necessary (a low gate, and a series of bars for a long jump) you can go ahead as follows. The first exercises must always be carried out with a stake-fence, never with a complete gate, and the fence must be very low, so that both trainer and dog can jump over it easily. In effect, this is an extension of the lead exercises, and

so, naturally, the same rules apply: the exercises must be enjoyable, with plenty of words of praise and rewards when the dog behaves well; and there must never be any use of violence, and even less brutality, unless you do not mind a resounding failure.

When the dog starts carrying out the exercise properly, stop jumping the fence with it; just pretend to jump it, but stay on your side. When the dog on the command 'Up!' has got over to the other side, call it back with the command 'Back!' or 'Come back!', giving, if necessary, a quick tug on the lead (keep the dog on the lead, incidentally, until it is making all its jumps correctly). Increase the height of the fence little by little, and then start using the low gate. In order to get the dog to jump, all you need do is stretch out your right hand, giving the command 'Up!', and then call it back with the command 'Back!', beckoning it at the same time. It is advisable to let the dog have a good run-up to the gate, so that it can jump it without touching it with its feet.

Every time the dog touches the obstacle, lower it a little. Never ask too much of your dog; be happy with small improvements, and do not worry if the dog seems to be slipping back now and then. Keep a close eye on the condition of the dog's feet: sometimes it may be prevented from jumping by a painful graze.

On the other hand, pit the dog fairly and squarely against the obstacle, teaching it to scale the fence, because it must learn to take off for a jump, when necessary, without any run-up. This will develop its hind-quarters, stretch its muscles, and considerably increase its strength and agility. To begin with it is a good idea if you stand, lead in hand, on the other side of the fence and call the dog to you. Later you can simply tell it to jump, and the dog will obey you. If the fence is very high, do not give the command 'Come back!' For average-sized dogs, 10 to 18 months of age, avoid jumps of more than 1.2 m (4 ft). Climbing – and jumping – are excellent ways of developing the back and shoulder muscles, because when the dog has reached the top it must hoist its whole

body with it. The major difficulty in the case of high obstacles – more than 2.4 m (8 ft) for medium-sized dogs – is coming down the other side, because the downward jump can sometimes 'cramp' a dog if it has not yet acquired the proper technique.

Although the dog must learn to cope with the obstacle, it should not be dragged over it by the lead if it refuses to jump: if it is it will let you pull it over every time you ask it to jump. Climbing over an obstacle is more tiring than merely jumping it, so do not demand too much, and make the exercise quite short. The ground must be soft where the dog has to land: if it is not, jumps more than 2 m (6 ft) high may cause injury. Carry out the exercises in the training room with plenty of mats on the far side of the fence. From the outset the dog should approach the centre of the obstacle at right angles to it, otherwise it may show a tendency to run away round the sides. For some time make the dog climb the obstacle on its lead. If a dog when it reaches the top tends to turn back instead of jumping down the other side, give it a slight push or move round to the other side of the obstacle and take it by the lead. Increase the height very gradually and with great care. Let dogs that prefer a short run-up have it. After a jump of more than 1.5 m (5 ft) do not ask the dog to jump back. When it has made a good jump, move on to another form of exercise.

When the dog has mastered the first two jumps, it will easily master the long jump. Gradually increase the distance to be covered, starting at 30 cm (12 in) and ending at about 2 m (6½ ft). With proper use of your equipment, all kinds of jumps can be carried out perfectly well even by Toy dogs.

It is not advisable to give the dog jumping lessons alone. Alternate jumping with the other customary lessons. You can start off the lesson with a few jumps: the dog will be fresh, willing and able. Let it do a couple of climbing jumps half-way through the lesson and end with a long jump. After a time do not go with the dog to the jump: remove its lead and in the end give just a verbal command or gesture with your arm.

262

Refusing bribes

This exercise, though claimed by some experts to be of use, may be considered otherwise to be somewhat barbaric in its techniques. Nevertheless, it is included here as an example of the lengths to which some people are prepared to go, in order to train their dogs. It is quite a tricky exercise, because it is not possible to explain to the dog the reason for and purpose behind refusing something. You are therefore up against a very strong impulse: the desire to have a good meal. In certain specific circumstances it is quite easy to get the dog to refuse — when it is tied up, for example — but it can be much harder in other conditions.

The aim of the exercise: The dog must refuse food or 'bribes' offered to it by a stranger, and it must not eat anything it finds by the wayside, in the home or in the garden. A dog who will not eat poisoned food will be assured of healthy survival — and will not be hoodwinked by a burglar, say, who offers it a titbit.

The technique of the exercise: Stop friends or strangers feeding your puppy with snacks. It is a good idea to get visitors to offer your dog a mouthful or two, and then do the following:

(1) Offer a piece of meat with a pin sticking out of it by about a centimetre (half an inch). As the dog noses forward, the pin will prick it slightly; at the same time you should gently call the dog and offer it some food it likes even more.

(2) The same exercise can be carried out with a fork, which will also prick the dog's outstretched mouth, and prevent it from swallowing the food. Whichever method you decide to use, the important thing is that you should reward the dog immediately afterwards, in this way explaining to the dog that it is not good to take food from strangers, but that it is good to accept from its owner.

The methods described above are definitely preferable to those that entail hitting a greedy dog. It is as well if anyone who helps you with the exercise does not make threatening or hostile gestures: some dogs could be intimidated by them, sometimes on a

long-term basis; whoever offers the titbit should be affectionate and friendly, but despite this, the food they offer must strike the dog as being horrible.

These exercises should be repeated in different places, when you, the owner, are some way off. Repeat them as often as possible, varying the circumstances, places and people. Bear the following in mind: (1) The dog must not pick up bits of food when it is walking on a lead, or when it is off the lead and running about freely. (2) The dog must not accept food offered by anyone either at home or outside, whether on the lead or not.

The hardest exercise is when the dog is off the lead and out of sight, as

is often the case with hunting dogs. When you are following this exercise in open countryside you may find it useful to use small mouse-traps, with tempting bait; let the dog go, and when it tries to take the bait it will receive a nasty shock.

Barking and not barking, to order
Command: 'Bark!', 'No!'
This exercise can be started in the first month of training.

The aim of the exercise: To make the dog bark when told to do so, increase its obedience, prepare it to give vocal signals when it is trained, and stop it barking when bidden.

The technique of the exercise: If you

know someone who has a dog that barks to order, ask him or her to bring it to a training session. When the other owner has got his, or her, dog to bark, give your dog the same command. Your dog's potential jealousy will work wonders, especially if you pat the other dog each time it barks.

If you cannot find a dog that barks when it is told to do so, try another way. Encourage the dog to bark by repeating the command and even making barking noises yourself, when its meal is ready. Hold the plate in your hand, invite the dog to bark and only give it its bowl when it has at least made an effort to obey you. If this does not work well, here is another method. At the time for your dog's daily walk, go to it, stroke it, put on its collar and then go out by yourself, as if you were going to leave it. From outside the door give the command 'Bark! Bark!' The dog will become excited and will start to bark, to call your attention to it. If it does this, reward it, and take it out straight away. If this method does not work, find out when your dog tends to bark of its own accord. When you have pinpointed a particular moment, choose it to give the command 'Bark!' precisely when the dog would have barked in any case. Congratulate it, reward it and quickly repeat the order.

With a little shrewdness and careful observation you will soon achieve your goal – within a few days, in fact. Repeat the exercise whenever you can, in different places. Make the dog bark decisively and loudly. On the other hand, it is a good thing if the dog does not bark to excess, deafening all and sundry whenever the doorbell rings, dashing out into the garden or on to the balcony, and disturbing the neighbours, who may well object – especially if this happens at night.

Small dogs bark more enthusiastically than large ones, which is why the latter are less useful as guard-dogs and

Opposite: A dog on a lead will be more aggressive than when it is free and alone.
Right: A retrieval exercise. Retrieving is the crux of training and the abilities of the trainer are paramount.

watch-dogs in the house or the garden. Large dogs are indispensable for protection duties. To teach both a large or a small dog that it must stop barking on the command 'No!', close its mouth with your hand just when it wants to bark, and repeat the command 'No!', even though the dog may be trying to free its mouth to have

another good bark. After this exercise has been done twenty times or so, an already trained dog will bark and stop barking at your bidding.

Some people suggest tossing a handful of earth on to the muzzle of a dog that barks when it should not, with the command 'No!' This is an effective way to stop a dog barking.

In dire cases, or if you simply cannot impose your training method, muzzle the dog, and this will definitely rid it of any desire to bark. Do not, however, use a muzzle in summer, when dogs need to be able to pant because of the high temperature. If a hot dog is forced to keep its mouth shut, it may die.

Retrieving for fun
Commands: 'Fetch!' 'Drop!'

As we have seen in puppy training, a dog has a natural impulse to chase after animals or moving objects that may look to it like prey. This impulse is useful for retrieving. A police- or hunting-dog that does not retrieve, or retrieves poorly, bites its prey, drops it or gives it to the first person it comes across, is of little use. It is up to the trainer to improve its performance. The following is one of the best methods for teaching a dog – any type of dog, for any type of work – how to retrieve.

The Delfino method of retrieval: Born in 1875, Colonel Delfino lived to the ripe old age of 93. He was a shrewd ethologist and a keen experimenter. He had a famous trianing school at Cuneo, and his retrieval method takes 30 to 40 days to learn:

(1) For the first lessons (in an enclosed place), simply make the dog sit in front of you obediently, preventing it from changing positions or walking away, before you give the command 'Go!' Extend the period gradually.

(2) After teaching it to stay in the sitting position, put a cotton rag between its teeth, about the size of a person's fist, and tied in a knot. The rag is not comfortable to the mucous membranes in the mouth.

(3) The dog will naturally spit out the inedible rag: put it back into its mouth until it keeps it there, if only for a split second. At once say very quietly 'Fetch!', but do not let the dog go. Remove the rag and reward the dog with a titbit and plenty of patting.

(4) If it has the right kind of reward regularly (especially if it has a healthy appetite, and is on a form of 'diet'), the dog will put up with the rag from the start, and soon open its mouth of its own accord, when it has understood that the rag is followed by a titbit. At

this point the hardest part is over. Gradually extend the exercise with the rag in the mouth.

(5) Drop the rag from time to time, as if by accident, when the dog has clearly understood that the titbit depends on the rag. Take your time. After a few attempts, the dog will pick up the rag and hold on to it while it sits down, and, as Delfino would say, 'The miracle is complete, you have a retirever.'

(6) When the dog invariably picks up the rag and sits down in front of you to get its titbit, start throwing the rag a metre (yard) or so, then two or three metres (yards), so that the dog has to leave its place, fetch the rag, come back, take up the sitting position, offer you the rag and then have its titbit. Extend the distances gradually.

(7) Replace the rag, little by little, with other things: cloth balls, sewn together in different shapes and sizes; woollen rags, followed by silk ones; balls made of waste paper, rubber, and leather; straw objects of varying sizes; twigs and sticks, of differing sizes and weights; bags full of shavings or sawdust, sand, gravel, beans and so on, varying gradually in size and weight, depending on the build and strength of the dog; and for dogs that are being trained to retrieve game, stuffed toy rabbits containing sawdust, pebbles, sand, etc. to vary the weight; bags of sawdust and sand, covered with feathers or large bundles of gamebird feathers.

After this the dog will learn to retrieve eggs, toothpicks, plates, bottles, glasses and anything else that comes to hand.

(8) When the dog is retrieving well in the enclosed space, take it out into the country. Hide whatever is to be retireved in some grass and get the dog to look for it. Throw the object into small pits, over hedges, ditches and walls.

(9) Throw it a good way off; the dog will run to fetch it; give the command 'Down!' and stop the dog coming towards you: it must stay where it was when you gave the command. Give the command 'Go! Fetch!' This exercise will make the dog lie down when game is flushed out and also when it falls to the ground after being shot.

With this preparation, the dog will easily learn to retrieve in water. The Delfino method will work for all specialized duties, hunting and otherwise.

Distractions

The dog is now well disciplined. It will behave properly with or without the lead; it will sit and lie down as soon as it is told to do so; it will stay put where you have left it; it will respond well to its call; it will advance 10 metres (11 yards) when told to do so; it will stand still in one spot, and jump and climb over obstacles; it will follow you on your bicycle or scooter; it will behave well in the car, refuse 'bribes' from other people, bark on command, and retrieve.

But there is still a lurking danger. The dog will work extremely well in normal training conditions (places it is used to, calm surroundings, with people it knows round it) and it will behave erratically and even disobediently in new places where there is plenty happening, where there are other dogs, or where there are unusual conditions. This gives rise to the need to cause distractions on purpose, so that the dog will learn that it must carry out its commands in all circumstances.

Everyday rules

If the dog lives close to you, in your home, you must put the exercises that the dog has learned into everyday use. Give it the commands familiar to it, in the usual conditions. It is a good idea to go through obedience and retrieval exercises before the dog eats. In some military kennels the dogs have to take their metal bowls to the cook, who will then fill them. Retrieval thus becomes enjoyable and faultless. The commands 'Sit!', 'Down!' and 'Stay!' can be used whenever an opportunity arises, and dog and trainer/owner alike can derive plenty of enjoyment from each exercise.

One of the everyday rules is to get the dog to walk safely on busy streets. Strays roam the busiest streets quite happily, while trained dogs, used to being on the lead, end up under a car before anyone knows what is happening. In police-dog trials in Germany one test takes place in city traffic.

To make your dog traffic-conscious, you must look for situations that will make it wary of buses, motorbikes, cars, bicycles and trucks. Take it to a street that is not too busy. Get a friend with a car or a motorbike or cycle to drive or ride close to the dog (which is on its lead) and tap it with a stick, or hoot as they pass it. All this will make the dog cautious.

Street hygiene

There is nothing worse than seeing city streets and pavements fouled by dogs. It gives people who do not like dogs all the leverage they need. A trained dog will not foul the street: it can easily be taught to step off the pavement and relieve itself in the gutter, or where there is some grass other than in parks or public places.

From 'don't-do-this' to having fun

With plenty of distractions, and having got rid of mechanical as well as undesirable associations, your dog will now really start to enjoy its life. You will gradually see it carrying out its exercises with pleasure and its work with enjoyment. Remember the rule already referred to: as soon as an exercise has been carried out properly, do not repeat it, even if the dog has been in the sit position for a minute. Do not be sparing of praise for the dog if it does not look as if it is enjoying itself. Be less expansive when it is having fun. Exercises, which earlier seemed to be boring the dog, because they were going against its natural inclinations, if they are repeated in a spirit of co-operation and enjoyment, will eventually become unnecessary.

Second month's programme

Week one: Jumping, lead exercises, without lead, without warning the commands 'Go on!' and 'Stay!' or 'Stop!' Jumps. Retrieving for five minutes; refusing food and barking on command. Climbing. Home following a bicycle. If you prefer, the walk can be separate, at another time of day. A daily lesson of 30 minutes will probably be plenty, whether it is given in the morning or afternoon. If you can, have the lesson in the morning, with another shorter lesson of 15 to 20

minutes in the afternoon.
Week two: As week one, but focusing mainly on the dog's weak points. Concentrate on retrieving. If possible, extend the bicycle walk at the end of the day and if you are in open country, let the dog run off for a while. If this is not possible during the week, make sure that it is at weekends.
Week three: Vary the order of the exercises, and the places where they are done, if possible. 'Go!' and 'Go on! Go on!' Make sure that the first month's exercises are all properly carried out. Increase the distractions all the time. The main problems to do with retrieving are now almost over.
Week four: If possible, change the

Training that is fun leads to mutual trust between man and dog.

place where you and the dog work every day. Extend the lessons to a maximum of 40 minutes. Retrieving should be much improved by now. At the end of this week your dog will acquit itself well. The basis of training, discipline and obedience have now been laid. If you want the dog to go further, choose the speciality for it best suited to your own talents and requirements: different types of hunting, and the various general duties.

At this point your dog is well trained and well disciplined and may be suitable for special further training.

TRAINING WORKING DOGS
The hunting-dog
The sense of smell — more detail

How dogs identify by smell what we humans identify by sight is made clear by the excellent example recommended by the Belgian dog-expert, L. Huyghebaert. Suppose that the person or the game whose track the dog has found does not leave a scent behind him or it, but is equipped with a container that releases a continuous trail of white liquid. The human eye would find it easy enough to detect the white line running over the ground. After a little practice, and depending on the amount of liquid spilt on the ground, we should be able to tell whether the person or the game had walked slowly, or been in a hurry, whether he or it had stopped for a moment, or had rested for quite a long time. But in the long term this white trail would fade and then vanish, as a result of weather conditions or the type of terrain. When this happened we should find the last traces of the trail in those places where the largest amount of liquid had spilled on to the ground, or where not washed away.

With its nose a dog can tell one hare apart from another, just as we can tell two cats apart from one another with our eyes. When we see an emaciated horse we can tell that it is in a bad way by looking at its colouring and its size. Smells give a dog the same impressions and information. The hunting-dog knows whether the track it is following is that of a healthy animal, an injured or sick animal, a lively prey that will put up a fight, or prey that is exhausted and terrified. In order to explain, in the broadest terms, how a dog's mind reacts to smells and scents, the German cynologist, Jagers, refers to the impressions that people receive when they go to a zoo: it does not take a person long to distinguish between the smells of, say, big cats, ruminants and monkeys. The smell of an aviary can never be mistaken for that of a mammal-house. In order to have a good understanding of your dog, whether you are training it at home or in the street, you must never forget that it thinks with its nose.

Age, stress, physical conditions,

temperature, the time of day, the time of year, the atmospheric conditions, the nature of the terrain and a thousand and one other factors will alter the communicative potential of particles, fragrant or otherwise, with regard to the dog's nose.

The wind plays a vital part in a dog's sense of smell, causing currents that waft smells towards the dog when it is walking into the wind, and away from it when it is walking with the wind behind it. Wind can also speed up the rate at which a smell fades, until it finally disappears altogether. What is more, it can have a direct influence on the dog's nose: very cold and dry winds, or excessively hot ones, alter the membranes in the dog's nose, and thus stop its sense of smell from working properly.

A dog's sense of smell can be improved beyond all recognition, if it is backed up by intelligence, good working methods, and perseverance, and the process of improvement can be enjoyable to owner and dog alike. If a dog feels that offering the use of its

sense of smell — for hunting or tracking, for example — is enjoyable and to its advantage, it will become increasingly enthusiastic and eager. But if a dog is mistreated while it is working with its nose, it will end by finding work boring, and lose its keenness.

It is important for a dog to have nasal mucous membranes in perfect condition, as well as healthy nerves to carry sensations of smell to a healthy and sensitive brain; but it is even more important for there to be a sound mind at work behind this whole physical mechanism. The dog's mind must be bright and alert; it must be interested, and keenly so, in the smells about which its nose tells it. It is better to have an enthusiastic dog with a mediocre sense of smell than a champion with a perfect sense of smell and little

Above: The English formula for the gundog is well represented by the Setter.
Opposite: The Continental formula, on the other hand, is well represented by the Wire-haired Pointing Griffon.

interest or efficiency when it comes to interpreting the sensations which its flawless nose communicates to it. Zeal can often be dimmed, or even exting-uished altogether, by incorrect train-ing. Think of all those fat Cocker Spa-niels that have spent years indoors, unaware of such a thing as the hunt, and that eventually become as affec-tionate 'puddings', capable of no more than picking up the scent of the urine left by other dogs on the pavement, the place for their daily walk.

A word to the hunter

All moving game leaves behind it a scent, which is specific to each species of animal: a dog can identify the scent, but it will not always react as you would like. The causes of this are still obscure and cannot all be attributed to the dog. Sometimes the game is so utterly still that it does not spread its scent. Other types of game flatten themselves to the ground, which has 'insulating' properties. The level of humidity affects the scent, which soon disappears in hot, dry terrain. Some

game has only a limited scent (quail, partridge, pheasant, hare), while other animals give off a more marked scent. Tall vegetation is more retentive of a scent than low plants. A gust of wind can release a scent. Variations in weather are important, and so, too, are variations in terrain and game. Much is expected of the hunting-dog, and the hunting-dog will give much in return if you make an effort to under-stand and guide it in its strenuous work, which is at once complex and thrilling. Note that a dog picks up a scent when it inhales, not when it exhales. So when a dog is out of breath and puffing and panting after running or because of the heat, it will find it harder to pick up the scent of game or follow a human scent.

Choosing a Pointer

There are several dozen breeds of Pointers throughout the world, some of which are only found in their native countries. The main ones have already been illustrated. They can be divided into three groups.

(1) **English formula**: All-round Poin-ters, very swift, good at the gallop. Breeds born in the lowlands of Britain, winners of many field trials, often not good at retrieving, but can be trained to become so. According to their sup-porters, English dogs are useful where game is rare, because they have a very wide range, and thus a better chance of finding prey. Their supporters say that the faster the dog, the better its nose, and the greater the distance at which it can point; there is thus less risk of flushing out and disturbing game-fowl and hares.

Their critics maintain that by running so far, these dogs end up missing a lot of game, especially if it is windy weather.

(2) **Italian formula**: Dogs with a res-tricted range, halfway between an ex-tended trot and a half-gallop. Breeds raised in various parts of Lombardy and Piedmont – Spinone (Griffon), Bracco (Pointer) – used by the all-round hunter who prefers to have a one-man dog. According to their sup-porters, the Italian Pointers – and this

formula incidentally includes breeds from other countries, such as the various French Pointers (Braques) — are useful where game is rare, because they will explore every nook and cranny within their range, because they are interested in everything and anything, and because they look for tracks, and work closely with the hunter, thus increasing the chances of coming across game. Their supporters say, too, that the closer to you the dog stays, the more enjoyable is the hunt. But their critics complain that by sniffing at anything and everything the dog ends up by giving the prey time to escape.

(3) **German formula**: Dogs that are midway between the two groups described above, with a sustained gallop and good endurance. Breeds selected in Germany and adapted for all types of hunting: German Pointer, Wiemaraner, Münsterländer, Poodle Pointer (Pudelpointer) and a few dogs from other countries such as the Epagneul Breton (Breton Spaniel) and the Korthals Griffon. These German dogs are also capable of keeping wrongdoers at bay, and guarding the hunter's equipment and game-bag. According to their supporters, dogs in the German group are the only all-rounders; they are more useful today than they have ever been: they can follow the trail of blood of a wounded animal, nose to the ground, retrieving light game, and indicating in various ways where larger game is lying. Their critics maintain that only a dog that is an all-rounder can be a thoroughly contented dog. They take the view that because these dogs are trained in all the various skills, they tend to lose their initiative.

So, which kind of Pointer should you choose? The choice depends not so much on the breed but on the individual and, above all, on the hunter — his personal tastes, the type of terrain available, his favourite game, and his method of hunting. A dog that weighs more than 25 kg (55 lb) as an

The most recent training techniques in German and American dog circles are quite innovative, even using cages holding chickens or rabbits set in the ground to train dogs to game.

adult will soon tire. A short-haired dog will not be able to hunt for long periods in cold weather.

Nevertheless, the Pointer is only really useful if it has been properly trained, if it is 'in control' — meaning that it will come back to you at a whistle from a distance of 500 m (550 yd); a dog that is not 'in control' will not obey orders even at 50 m (55 yd).

The Granderath method for Pointers

Franz Granderath is a well-known German cynologist who has described various surprising methods for training the Pointer. His results are excellent, even though they might, at first glance, appear to be revolutionary.

After taking your dog once or twice into a field, and seeing how it reacts to the scent put up by game, you can proceed with training it to point; do not use haphazard methods; abide by a pre-established plan so that, from the outset, you can ward off any unpleasant surprises that might crop up on the hunt itself.

The first such 'surprise' to be avoided is the pursuit of, for instance, game-fowl that has just taken flight. Use the following method: in flattish terrain, place small wooden cages, surrounded by barbed wire at a distance of 30 m (33 yd) alternatively to left and right of a central line and 300-400 m (330-440 yd) apart from each other. Put a pigeon or a hen in each cage, or a duck or a rabbit. Sink the cages in the ground, with just about 10 cm (4 in) or so showing.

An hour after positioning the cages, take the dog to the place where they are. Position it so that the wind is blowing from the cages, towards it and keep it on a 30 m (33 yd) lead.

In many cases the dog will actually point on the very first occasion; if it does not, it very soon will. When it shows that it has picked up the scent of the caged creature, give the command 'Down!' and back it up with a firm tug on the lead.

Leave the dog in position for a few minutes, and walk round it, calming it with kindly words.

Move back 20 m (22 yd) or so and

call the dog, greeting it when it comes with pats and titbits.

Because you know exactly where the caged birds or animals are, you can help the dog much more effectively than when you are actually hunting, when unforeseen things will crop up, and when you may tend to be over-keen to shoot, to the detriment of paying enough attention to the dog. This method has the added advantage of being applicable at all times of year, in any kind of terrain.

All dogs trained by this method have subsequently behaved perfectly in the presence of wild game. The change from the habit of pointing with the scent of caged domestic animals to the use of wild game has always been automatic and natural. When the dog comes across an animal smell or scent, it does not stop to think; it has no idea about the meaning or purpose of pointing. Once it has picked up the scent, its body assumes the rigid pointing posture quite naturally.

Later the dog will become aware of two things: (1) that pointing and staying in the pointing position for a period of time will earn it praise, stroking and a titbit from its trainer; (2) that breaking out of the pointing position, in the hope of getting hold of the game, will involve being told off by the hunter/trainer, a painful jerk on the lead attached to its collar – possibly a training or choke-collar for very impetuous dogs – and still no chance to get hold of the game.

These two experiences will be quickly understood by the dog and will make pointing a basic and automatic posture, which it will hold until its master gives the commands 'Down!' and then 'Fetch!' when he has fired. Obedience in the presence of wild game and extended pointing will soon become second nature. During the preparatory exercise, it is a good idea to encourage the dog every so often by allowing it to retrieve.

At the end of a day when the dog has worked perfectly with the cages, fire a blank at the closest cage. Walk 50 m (55 yd) or so away from it with the dog, while a helper replaces the cage with something appropriate, a dead rabbit, hen or pigeon, depending on what was originally in the cage in question. Then tell the dog to fetch it, and when it does, show it a great deal of attention; this will heighten its enjoyment of its work.

Using this system – whether you have some land with plenty of game on it or not – you can train a dog to point correctly, abiding by all the rules, and with a guarantee of success.

There are essentially two objections to this method: (1) a dog trained with domestic animals should not be interested in poultry, pigeons, rabbits and so on; and it should certainly not start pointing with them; (2) domestic pointing exercises may harm the dog's skill by encouraging it to point at every bird it encounters in the street or the countryside.

These points are not valid. In fact, this method only needs to be put into practice once for the dog to adopt it.

The weak scent of a hen, pigeon or rabbit, which the dog suddenly picks up on the ground, will produce the same effect as the scent of wild game: in both cases the dog will start to point to the same degree. But in villages, or country homes or in streets where the air is charged with the scent of domestic animals, this stimulus will be missing.

In addition, for the dog, the discouraging sight of these animals among houses and streets has nothing to do with the detection of wild game hidden away in the secrecy of its own hide-out.

Using the Granderath method it is also possible to train precocious dogs to point – those dogs that have been put through the two Puppy Programmes and are looking promising by the age of five to six months.

When the Granderath method is well under way, quail are put in the cage (see pp.269-70 on caged animals), and then the dog is put on to wild game proper; the trainee dog must stay stock still when the game flies up into the air, or breaks cover, and when you fire.

When you are hunting with an obedient dog trained by the Granderath method (or the Jackson method – see below), you must be patient and tolerant; do not give commands ('Down!', 'Stay', etc.) unless they are relevant. If you treat a dog with military precision, it will end up by losing its initiative and zeal. Remember: empathy, and remember that French hunter's saying, 'Nous deux, mon chien.'

The Jackson method for Pointers

The American cynologist M.R. Jackson has developed a popular method for pointing. The aim is still the same: to teach the dog that, when the game breaks cover, it must lie down at once. The Jackson trap makes it possible to move dog and game about as required, and this shortens the training period. The method is clearly explained in the diagrams overleaf:

(1) **The closed Jackson trap:** The trap is placed in a hole in the ground, as with the Granderath method. The trap is in two sections: a box with a lid, containing a pigeon, and a cage containing two quail, or a woodcock, or pheasant or whichever game fowl the hunter chooses. (It is said that throughout its working life a dog will have a preference for the game to which it was introduced in its early life.)

(2) **The open trap:** The trainer opens the lid of the box, and the pigeon can fly away. At the same time, the trainer makes the cage holding the quail drop into a hole in the ground, and so the birds disappear from view.

(3) **Pointing:** Picking up the scent of the quail, the dog will start pointing.

(4) **Spike:** The trainer now drives a metal spike into the ground, inside the ring through which the long cord is passed.

(5) **Breaking cover:** With a wire (or light cord) the trainer effects a double action in the trap: the pigeon breaks cover, the quail disappear, and the dog runs after the birds.

(6) **Stopping the dog:** The dog is pulled up short by the long lead; the trainer gives a firm command 'Down!', and the scent of the game has vanished.

Jackson traps can be bought in the United States, but they are not hard to make. Thousands of Pointers have been trained with this method.

Caged animals

At this point the trainee Pointer is

ready to join fully in the hunt – with considerable enjoyment. All it needs now is practice.

Quail are sometimes used at this stage in training: they stay put for a long time, they have a short flight pattern, they are quick to excite the novice dog, and they are easy for you to hit. Caged birds are positioned in a spot where there are scattered clumps of tall, dense grass.

Do not get the novice dog to retrieve the quail: it is a delicate bird, and the dog might be tempted to bite on it. Never get your dog to retrieve game that has fallen in view, if you want to avoid undesirable associations: the apprentice dog will soon associate breaking cover, the gun-shot and the game falling to the ground with retrieving, and this may give rise to a tendency for it to interrupt the pointing exercise, not even waiting for the gun-shot before going off in pursuit of the game – something that is quite out of order. If a bird falls to the ground in view, always go and pick it up yourself and leave the dog in the down position. The sight of its master picking up the game will not make it feel inferior: in the pack, all the members take part in the hunt, but only the head dog actually picks up the prey that has been caught. However, it will be up to your dog to seek out and retrieve game that has been hit or wounded, or that cannot be found. Retrieval is as important as seeking.

If you want your dog to become an all-rounder, capable of helping in any type of hunting, change the game being hunted as often as possible. This will extend the dog's range of experience, improve its skills, and provide the trainer with plenty of satisfaction. But if you are more inclined towards big game and field trials, do not present your Pointer or Setter with woodcock and partridge: these fowl are best for all-round hunting-dogs, or for specialists – not for English breeds of hunting-dog.

Left: The various steps described above in the Jackson method for training pointers.
Opposite: The Jackson method for training seeker dogs.

Seeker dogs

The Pointer is not suitable for certain hunting grounds and for certain types of game. It is not at home, for example, in thick undergrowth and low, dense vegetation; nor is it equipped for dense forests. The best place for it to work is in open woodland. Where there are thorns its long tail will become snagged and scratched, and may bleed. If its noiseless technique takes it into scrub, it is very hard to find as it lies in wait, stock still; this means that the hunter must go in search of his dog rather than game. In densely covered terrain the Pointer's large nose is not much use; this type of country requires initiative, determination, cun-

ning and, above all, a small dog that can move easily through the undergrowth. For woodcock, bear in mind the following: a dog that points at 15 m (16 yd) and so allows the 'queen of the woods' to fly away into inaccessible areas is useless; there is nothing to be gained by trying to direct the dog, which will be hampered mainly by natural obstacles; you need a dog that is in control, one that will force the bird to take to the air under fire. In marshland and bogs, too, you need a tireless, innate retriever. In a word, what you need is a seeker dog.

The Jackson method of seeking

M.R. Jackson has found an excellent way of teaching seeker dogs to go in pursuit of game-fowl, instead of lying down and waiting for the hunter. This soon gives rise to a strong sense of collaboration.

(1) and (2) **The closed Jackson trap** and **The open trap**: See above, and the drawings on this page.

(3) **Seek**: Having picked up the scent of the quail, the dog starts to seek them out.

(4) **Breaking cover**: When the dog comes up against the cord surrounding the trap, it causes the door to open and the pigeon quickly flies off (starlings also are used in the United States). At the same time the cage holding the brace of quail drops into the ground and the scent vanishes. The dog can no longer see the cage. As the pigeon breaks cover, give the firm order 'Down!'

A cord runs freely through the eyes of the spikes, forming an enclosure. The end of the cord is attached to the release system for the trap. Any pressure on the cord sets the trap in motion. The Jackson method achieves quick results, even with very active and impetuous dogs.

The Granderath seeking method

The German cynologist has worked out his own method for hunting in woodland, described here briefly in its application specifically to the training of seeker dogs.

A couple of rabbits are released in uneven, preferably enclosed, terrain, measuring not more than 200 sq m (236 sq yd), dense with scrub, bushes, brambles, etc. The rabbits will quickly hide away in the brush. On the command 'Go!' the dog must head into the undergrowth and brambles, testing out its skills as a seeker, not giving chase when the prey breaks cover, lying down, waiting for the gun-shot, and then retrieving the prey as taught. You can also use other farmyard animals, as indicated in the earlier Granderath exercise. It is a question of teaching the dog how to behave 'on the job', in artifical conditions, which, precisely because they are contrived, enable you to make the dog understand what it is that you expect of the animal.

The Hegendorf method for working in water

The 'great' Hegendorf, as he is known in his native Austria, is the author of the famous **Der Gebrauchshund** (The Working Dog). He has suggested an ingenious and effective method for both hunting and working dogs.

The system involves two apparent contradictions: (1) forcing the dog into water; (2) increasing the dog's trust in its trainer and its self-confidence.

The right place: A watercourse 5-6 m (6-7 yd) wide, with easy access, and not busy. Before the water exercises, take the dog fairly often to the place you have in mind, so that it becomes familiar with it. This familiarity is vital, if you want the Hegendorf method to achieve good results.

Equipment required: (1) A long, light cord 15-20 m (50-66 ft), with a spring-clip at either end: it must be able to reach the far bank and back. (2) A wooden post about 90 cm (3 ft) long; it should be driven into the ground up to 75 cm (30 in) and have a strong metal ring at the top, firmly attached. (If there is a telegraph pole or strong tree close to the bank, the post will not be necessary.) (3) Put the usual metal training or choke-collar on the dog.

Phase one

With the dog lying down, put the cord through the ring on the post or round the telegraph pole or tree. Take the two ends of the cord and throw them across to the other side of the stream/ watercourse. Take the dog to the opposite bank, where the two ends have come to land. This is when the exercise proper begins. Take the spring-clip at one end of the long cord and attach it to the ring on the dog's collar (but not in the choke position). Attach the other spring-clip either to the same ring, or to another ring in the chain, again avoiding the choke position. Now the cord is a continuous circle.

Approach the water with your dog and give the command 'Go!' At the same time pull on the cord so that the dog has no option but to enter the water, no matter how reluctant it may feel. Before it fully realizes what is happening, it will find itself having to swim, or at least having to try to swim.

Good swimmers will start swimming properly from the start; a dog that is not cut out for swimming will tend to splash a lot with its front legs, and its inclination will be to get to the other bank as fast as possible.

You must not let it do this. During the first exercise, when the dog has got halfway across the water, call it back with the command 'Back!' or 'Come back!' Without waiting to see whether the dog will obey of its own accord, pull on the cord, making it swim back to you. You will only need to pull on the continuous cord to do this. As the dog reaches the bank, be close by to stop it shaking itself dry as soon as it has arrived; make it sit, praise it warmly and then allow it to have a good shake. From the start you must not let the dog develop the habit of shaking itself as soon as it gets out of the water. If it does develop this bad habit, when it has been in water to fetch an object or an animal, it will drop it as soon as it is on dry land again, to shake its coat free of water. It must learn that it may only shake itself dry when it has delivered properly what it has retrieved.

Phase two

The exercise described above will make it clear to the dog that you are in charge, even when it comes to water. The most common stumbling-block encountered when making a dog work in water is precisely the fact that the dog will soon realize that, once in the water, it can become its own master, and that its real human master is out of range. Lack of discipline in water can soon become firmly rooted and can even spread to working duties on land, resulting in a disobedient dog.

This cannot happen with the Hegendorf system. Before embarking on this exercise, the dog will already have gone through all the submission and retrieval exercises, and will therefore be highly disciplined. The new water exercises will make it even more submissive.

Repeat the exercise until the dog takes to the water on its own, on the simple command 'Go!' Five exercises will usually be ample (remember: just one exercise a day) to achieve good results. Sometimes you may need

eight days. One – exceptional – case needed eleven days. A dog will rarely be afraid after the fifth exercise. By the second its fear will be much less marked, and by the third and fourth lessons a slight tug will be enough to get it into the water. Even a very frightened dog will quickly overcome its initial fear, because it will have been taught to trust you, its trainer and owner, just as a person trusts a swimming-instructor. The call into the water leaves a particularly marked impression, and the dog must obey you at once when you give it the command 'Come back': pull on the cord to help it if necessary, at first.

Phase three

Once the dog will enter the water of its own accord at the command 'Go!', let it reach the other bank for the first time. When it gets there, the dog will hope to be let loose, so that it can roll in the grass, shake itself and run about. This is when you must give the command 'Come back!' or 'Back!', simultaneously tugging on the cord, and make it get back into the water and swim back to you. You can reckon that the lesson has been well learnt when the dog goes to the water at the very first command, responds to your call halfway across, then, when you say 'Go!' again, swims towards the other bank and, once there, plunges back into the water as soon as you give the command 'Back!' It goes without saying that in every phase of these water exercises on the long cord, the best pupil will be one that is generously praised and stroked. As far as titbits are concerned, a dog will not normally feel like one as soon as it comes out of the water. There is no need for constraints either, given that the cord itself already represents an effective one that is in no way brutal.

Phase four

These exercises must now be done without the cord. As an intermediate phase, you can cunningly pretend to attach the ends of the cord to the collar, without in fact, attaching the spring-clips, so that, while the dog is in the water, you can slip them loose and give all the commands: 'Go!', 'Back!', 'Go!' etc. Then get rid of the cord altogether. If the dog shows the slight-

est sign of disobedience, resort to the cord again at once.

A word of advice: The novice dog should work in water only in fine, warm weather; the exercises must not last more than half an hour, and when they are over, let the dog run about as the spirit takes it. If this is not possible for some reason, rub it and warm it, and put it in a sack full of dry straw with just its head showing.

The tracker dog

The Hound's job is to seek out, flush out and pursue wild game, large and small. All dogs are natural chasers.

The use of tracker dogs has traditionally involved hunting on horseback and on foot, either with a single dog, or with a whole pack, by day or by night, for dangerous carnivores such as bears and pumas, or for harmless herbivores such as deer and gazelle. The game being hunted has invariably been a mammal, except in South America where people have hunted the nandu, a large flightless ostrich-like bird.

There are many different breeds of tracker dogs, all with their various uses. The Indian Sharil has been used to flush out a tiger, the Rhodesian Ridgeback for hunting lions, the Deerhound for chasing fallow deer, the Wolfhound wolves, and so on. There are breeds, too, that have been used

The Sicilian Hound (Cirneco) is an uncommon breed used for hunting wild rabbits on the slopes of Mt Etna in Sicily.

for pursuing seals, leopards and caribou as well as the more conventional game animals, such as rabbits, hares, foxes and stags.

Hunters rarely train dogs that work in a pack. They will at most prepare them for working collectively, and then follow them rather than direct them.

The underground hunting dog

The task of the underground hunting dog (broadly speaking, the 'Terrier' type) is to seek and then flush out wild game that lives in dens and burrows in the ground, in hollows at the foot of trees, in cracks in rocks and in other places where ordinary tracker dogs cannot go.

The breeds best suited to this work are the English Terriers, the German Dachshunds, and the German Jagdterrier. The game they have been used for includes, as well as vermin in general, the badger, the fox, the otter and the wild cat. The Jagdterrier is a recently selected breed, subject to very high standards: breeding dogs must prove themselves in field tests, above and underground, and in water, for retrieving, barking in pursuit of hares and so on. They are badger specialists, so much so that if one was to be used for fox-hunting, it must not be introduced to badgers beforehand.

The English Fox Terrier is a fox expert when it is selected for hunting and not for showing or as a companion dog. It is said that the Wire-haired Fox Terrier has a greater tendency to bite that its short-haired relative. German Dachshunds have been used successfully for all types of underground game; they hav e also been used for seeking, retrieving and following trails of blood left by large game. The Norwegian Lundehund is very skilled at flushing out birds from cliffs towering above the sea. French Dachshunds were once renowned for their skill at **déterrage** (flushing out), as were the Pinscher and the Bull Terrier among other small breeds.

The Granderath method for Terriers and other small hunting dogs

As a breeder of Dachshunds, Granderath recommends making frequent offerings to the litter of badger-, fox- and wild-cat-hides. Doing so will cause fierce fights among the siblings, and this in turn will make dogs prepared in this way extremely keen to get at the vermin itself. It is also a good idea (even in your own garden) to build a tunnel at ground level with bricks or clay: it should be up to 3 m (10 ft) long.

Five-week-old pups will get used to playing and fighting in the tunnel. It will be quite dark inside, which might scare older Terriers, etc., which are not accustomed to tunnels.

Next, make two tunnels, each one 3 m (10 ft) long, at right angles, ending in a circular hollow, built in such a way that it can be exposed. Young Terriers will soon use these tunnels for energetic games and mock battles. Last of all, use a tunnel 1.5 m (5 ft) long and 20 cm (8 in) in both width and height, made of planks. The tunnel must be open at one end and closed at the other, except for a quite small aperture. Through this hole push a broomhandle with a dead fox's head nailed to it – or the head of some other animal. Let the young dogs loose and from outside the tunnel move the handle carrying the head. The keenest Terriers will venture into the tunnel, barking; the most hot-blooded will bite the 'enemy', and not let go.

Through this sort of training the young dog will now know how to behave when, a few months later, you take it into the field to start the real training programme.

The truffle dog

Truffle-hunting is an enjoyable and, in some areas of Europe, a highly profitable pastime. The seeking and unearthing technique described here originated in Piedmont in Italy. The most suitable breed is the Poodle.

(1) Present the dog with a fresh truffle (not a preserved variety): if it tucks into it, the first test has been successful. A dog will only hunt out truffles if it enjoys eating them.

(2) Truffles grow best of all in the roots of certain oak trees, but they can also be found in woods of holm oak, poplar, willow, hazel, and even hornbeam and ash. Leave the dog at home and take a trip to the woods. In clearly marked spots bury small pieces of fresh truffle, at increasing depths and in gradually less and less obvious places.

(3) Take the dog, unfed, to the wood, and set it looking; make it dig from

The Smooth-haired Fox Terrier is one of the breeds selected and bred to flush out foxes that have gone to ground.

... time, then pick up the truffle
... d offer it to the dog, letting it
... your hand.
... the dog has learnt what to
... an start the real truffle-hunt,
... th you a bag holding pieces of
... meat and biscuits to offer the
... rewards. A vital tool is a pick
with a handle 12 cm (1 ft) long for
removing the truffles once they have
been located.

(5) The dog must be allowed to act as
a free agent: he must guide you; only
the dog, with its keen sense of smell,
can tell you where to dig. Have it on a
2 m (6 ft) lead. Do not use a choke-
collar – in fact the best arrangement is
to use a harness. Let the dog pull you
along.

(6) If the dog starts taking an interest in
mice or rats in the wood, take no
notice, and do not reprove it. The
truffle dog must be allowed complete
independence; you are just an assistant – the tables are turned! No obedience training here, and no coercion.
The dog is looking for truffles because
it is hungry and because it enjoys this
game, and in the end you will benefit
from it.

(7) When the dog finds a truffle, let it
have a good smell, still keeping it on a
short lead, and at the same time reward it with a few chunks of meat. In
its mind it must associate finding truffles with having its own appetite satisfied.

(8) When the dog has discovered
some truffles, and if it wants to have a
rest, let it do so until it wants to start
working again. Make sure that it does
not damage its toes when it digs.
Digging should, in fact, only be an
indication that it has found something;
you should quickly take over with your
pick, while the dog watches you. Always remember to reward the dog as
soon as it discovers a truffle, no matter
how small.

The guard-dog
Choosing a guard- or police-dog
A great many breeds are suitable for
these and similar duties. They include
the German Shepherd Dog, the Belgian Malinois, the Boxer, the Schnauzer and the Neapolitan Mastiff, but the
list might go on ad infinitum.

Biting
Although it may appear strange, as a
rule dogs do not bite as effectively as
their teeth might actually permit. In
fact, they tend to gnaw and (except
when involved in a fierce fight with
another dog) will not seize hold of prey
with their mouth at full stretch.

The aim of the exercise: To teach the
dog to bite as required.

The technique of the exercise: Put the
dog on a lead, wherever you have
decided to work, and attach the lead to
a wall, post or tree. You will need an
assistant who is a total stranger to the
dog. Take with you an empty sack,
rolled up like a large sausage, with
string wound round it. Stand beside

The Groenendael, like other dogs
used for guarding, must learn to bite
using the proper technique.

the dog while your assistant walks
towards you, armed with the sack.
About a metre (yard) outside the maximum range permitted the dog by the
lead, the assistant must start annoying
the dog, tapping it on the head with
the sack. At the same time you should
begin to excite the dog, inviting it to
react, and encouraging it to bite the
sack. It will soon do so. The assistant
must then start pulling on the free end
of the sack, while the dog grips the
other end in its mouth.

Repeat this exercise several times; the dog will soon learn to take a firm hold on its 'prey'. After a few sessions, remove the lead so that the dog feels free. Consider it a satisfactory day when the dog clings on to the sack while the assistant holds it in both hands, then spins round and tosses it and the dog into the air together, without the dog releasing its hold.

Guarding an object
Command: 'Watch!'
You have to get the dog to understand that it must guard and watch over whatever is left in its charge, until you, the owner, have returned. Before this, the dog will have been taught to stay put for up to four minutes, on its own, in familiar and unfamiliar places, in the down position.

The aim of the exercise: Choose a place where you can approach the dog without it seeing or hearing you. Get it to lie down in a comfortable position, head raised, so that it can see all round it. Lay your jacket in front of it, or a pair of your gloves or your handkerchief, and give the command 'Watch!' Move back a few steps: if the dog wants to follow you, threaten it by shaking your finger, repeating the command 'Watch!' Walk round the dog, repeating the order. Move further and further away and then duck out of sight, hiding in a place where the dog cannot see you. If it stays put for a full ten minutes, return to it, walking round it for a few minutes, before allowing it to get up and praising it warmly. Repeat this exercise somewhere else. From your hiding-place, throw a bunch of keys at the dog (or a chain, or a handful of gravel) if it tries to move before the time is up. You will manage to get the dog to stay on the spot for at least half an hour. See also the earlier section describing the exercise to the command 'Stay!'.

Further stages
The technique of the exercise
(1) Go back to where the previous exercise took place, with an assistant. Set the dog down in front of your gloves or something else belonging to you. Attach it by its lead to a tree or post and move 10 m (11 yd) away,

with your assistant, who should be provided with a long thin stick. The assistant returns in a semi-circle to within 3 m (10 ft) of the dog, calling it, but going no closer, and not touching it in any way whatsoever. You, in the meantime, have hidden. If the dog does not respond to the assistant's first call, he or she should not press it too hard on this first occasion, but, rather, more away while you return to the dog. On the other hand, if the dog, which is on a slack lead, gets up to answer the call, come out from your hiding-place, tell the dog off and repeat 'No! No!', Watch! Watch!' If necessary get the dog to bark. Before long it will no longer respond to the assistant. As soon as this has been achieved, the assistant, in your presence, should walk forward with the same sack used to get the dog to bite and hit the dog lightly until it becomes excited and bites the sack. After that leave the sack at the dog's feet, close to the gloves, and give the command 'Watch!' The assistant must now come to remove the sack, threatening the dog with the stick, and making other intimidating gestures, before reaching out towards the sack. The dog will be quick to react. Whenever it makes the slightest aggressive move, the assistant must step back at once, as if very scared, then go on to the attack again, then step back again, repeating these actions several times.

(2) This exercise must now be taken still further: the dog must start to bark as soon as the assistant is about 3 m (10 ft) from it. This is a very important detail and it must be achieved to perfection, first of all because the dog must learn to issue a warning by barking as soon as whatever has been left in its charge is under threat. Secondly, if the dog is in a public place, guarding a child, a bicycle, or a suitcase, for example, it is necessary to avoid an absent-minded passer-by being bitten by the dog because he or she has strayed too close to it, without warning. If the dog barks at the right moment, anyone passing it will make a detour, to keep well out of its range.

To get the dog to bark, work in the following way. Armed with the stick, 1.8 m (6 ft) long or more, the assistant

will advance on the dog, while you stay back. When 3 m (10 ft) away from the dog, the assistant will raise the stick, and you will give the command: 'Bark! Bark!' If the dog does not obey, it should be tapped lightly with the stick; if it does obey, the assistant must back away, as if frightened. The dog will soon learn when to bark.

Repeat the lesson, with the assistant circling the dog for a time, getting closer and closer, until when he (or she) is 3 m (10 ft) away, he raises the stick and you give the command 'Bark!' If the dog barks prematurely give the command 'No!' Afterwards carry out the exercise while you are hidden.

(3) Next, despite the dog's barks, the assistant approaches with hand outstretched to take the sack, jumping back as soon as the dog makes to bite him. Later, replace the sack with other objects. Later still, repeat these exercises with the dog off the lead and no longer attached to a tree or post. Make sure that when the dog goes to pursue the 'attacker' or 'intruder', it does not move more than a metre (yard) or so from the object in its charge. Repeat the same exercise with a bicycle, lying on the ground, so that it will not fall on top of the dog, and frighten it. Attach the dog to the bicycle by a long lead, so that a possible thief intent on stealing the machine would have to take the watch-dog as well. Repeat the exercise, using other objects that you

Opposite: At the order, the guard-dog must assume an aggressive posture, growling or snarling.
Above and below: Two stages in the training to attack.

might want the dog to watch over, or with the help of a child. Change assistants as often as possible so that the dog does not get the idea that it must protect things from the one person only, and not from others.

Small dogs, no matter how small, are always very quick to learn these exercises. It is worth mentioning that a dog will be all the more vigilant and prepared to bite if it is attached to something by its lead. Firstly, this will prevent it from running off — perhaps to fetch a stone that has been thrown — and secondly it will make the dog that much keener to defend the object in its charge, even if it is a fairly docile creature normally. The same principle applies as when a dog held on a chain barks and growls like an animal possessed, whereas in many cases, if it is not on a chain, it will behave gently

and good-naturedly. Thirdly, a fixed lead will stop accidents happening, if a passer-by comes too close to the dog, for example.

Guarding a car
The technique of the exercise: First of all, you must accustom the dog to

staying in a car for long periods of time. Then proceed as with the exercise for watching over objects. (See also **Barking to order**, p.262).

Above all, it is important to teach the dog to bark distinctly and loudly, and for a long time, when it senses that the car is under threat. By doing this it will be able to give the alarm in good time. No matter how daring a thief may be it would be hard for him to take possession of a car in which there is an excited dog, barking loudly and attracting attention, and ready to bite anyone who dares to venture inside the car.

A dog will willingly stay in a car for hours on end, or even throughout an entire night, but be sure to leave the windows – or at least the side-windows – open a little. Lack of oxygen can easily cause a dog to die, especially if the car is parked in the sun, but sometimes even if it is in shade.

Attacking people
Commands 'On guard!' 'Attack!' 'Let go!'

By now the pupil-dog can assume an aggressive posture towards anyone threatening children, adults, bicycles, cars and so on, put in its charge. It can also bite hard, thanks to the exercises with the sack.

From the very start of the exercises for teaching the dog how to attack a person, it is important that it should not sense the slightest element of play-acting or 'having fun' among friends. As soon as the command to attack is given the dog must be convinced that both it and its master are in danger.

During the attack exercises the assistant must have special protective clothing. There is a wide range of this. You can use an old coat, if it is well padded, or a leather jerkin with extra patches sewn on to it. Wear it under your top clothes so that it cannot be seen. The important thing is that the protective clothing should be as nondescript as possible, so that the dog's reactions are not triggered off just when it sees that type of clothing.

Protective items are quite costly. If you cannot afford the right ones, get in touch with a training school that might allow you to use its equipment. If you cannot put your hands on proper protective clothing, you can make do with a simple sleeve, which should be worn on your right arm. It can be bought, but it is quite easy to make, from tough sacking, filled with plenty of wadding. The sleeve must be longer than your arm, and reach as high as

After the attack exercises, the dog should be put into the 'Down!'.

your shoulder. Use a strong canvas strap to attach it to your ribcage, and tie it tightly on the left-hand side of the body. As well as the sleeve, your assistant should wear a pair of boots.

It is, in fact, advisable not to train your dog exclusively with the help of people wearing protective clothing. At times put a strong muzzle on the dog, and get it to attack people in ordinary clothes. On other occasions, set the dog against someone with a stout stick or a sack, which he will let the dog bite, while you give a firm 'Down!' command and call the dog.

You should also change the place of training frequently, so that the dog realizes that it may be called on to attack in all sorts of places. For any dog being put through these exercises, the important factor is not so much its degree of aggressiveness (which can always be brought out and heightened), but the effect of your call. This must be perfectly understood: no mat-

ter how excited it is, as soon as the dog hears your call, it must return at once to you.

The aim of the exercise: To get the dog to confront anyone who is threatening its master or mistress.

The technique of the exercise:
(1) Take the dog to the place where it has often watched over things. Give it your jacket to guard. Keep it on a lead about 2 m (6 ft) long. The assistant should come towards it slowly, wielding a stout stick, and wearing protective clothing. You give the command 'On guard!' From now on you should use this command to put the dog on the alert. In future, when there is danger about, you will have at your disposal a command that will at once prepare your dog to attack.

When the assistant is within 3 m (10 ft) the dog will bark. Instead of reaching for the object entrusted to the dog's care, the assistant brandishes the stick at you, the trainer, and starts to hit you. Give the command 'Attack!' and see how your dog reacts. Many dogs will attack straight away. If this happens, the assistant should quickly offer the dog the sleeve to bite. This is most important: the dog must get used to always attacking the right arm. The assistant should act frightened and move back, while you spur the dog on. Then give the firm command: 'Let go!' or 'Drop!'. Once you have done this, the assistant should keep still. If the dog has mastered the retrieving lessons, it will automatically open its mouth, although it will keep its hostile attitudes towards the assistant. Give the command 'Heel' and, if the dog is slow to obey, pull it towards you with the lead.
(2) If the dog does not attack after you have been hit, your assistant should use the stick on the dog, tapping it lightly to excite it. If earlier guard-dog exercises have been successful the dog will be quick to react. Some dogs, however, may be timid of fearful by nature and if a dog's timidity is inherited, it may present a problem. The best way to avoid difficulty is to buy puppies born to trained parents. In their case a timid or fearful attitude can only be put down to poor training, which can be overcome as follows.

Take the dog home and let it rest for a couple of days. On the third day ask your assistant to come to your home and hide behind a gate, a door, or a screen made of boards. Take the dog towards the spot on its lead (a dog on a lead is always braver).

Staying out of sight, the assistant starts making strange noises, and hitting things with the stick. Give the order 'On guard!' and make the dog excited. When the dog barks fiercely, the assistant must let it see the stick and wave it about, until the dog seizes and bites it. Then the assistant must hold out his arm, protected by the sleeve. Highly excited by now, the dog will bite when you give the command 'Attack!' After a successful exercise, all you will have to do is modify it a little to achieve complete success. To start with, repeat it at home, with the assistant first only half-hidden and then completely visible. Finally, go back over the first part of the exercise described here.

(3) To round off the exercise, during the attack, the assistant must hit the dog with the stick, holding it in his left hand. The blows should be light at first and then gradually somewhat harder so that the dog will not become scared during a real encounter. When you give the command 'Let go!' make sure that the dog slackens its hold, and returns to you when you say 'Heel!', no matter how agitated it may be. When you give the order 'Let go!', the assistant must keep absolutely still. Go on urging the dog to attack him. The dog's tendency will be not to attack an enemy who is not moving. Encourage this, getting the dog to bark fiercely at the assistant without attacking him, but being ready to attack as soon as he makes a move or tries to run away. If this tendency is not evident (which is rare), instil it in the dog: stop it from biting the assistant when he is motionless, even if it is only in the sleeve. At each attack, the assistant should at once offer his right arm, to accustom the dog to doing battle with this part of the body on every occasion.

(4) Repeat the exercise, with or without a lead, in tree-lined roads, by night, and in other circumstances. Sometimes the attack should be made with a pistol or knife, to teach the dog to go straight for the arm wielding the weapon. Make sure it always gets a firm hold, in spite of shots or blows. It would be wrong to think that these defensive exercises are difficult: in fact, they are easier and more enjoyable than obedience exercises.

Dealing with runaways
The aim of the exercise: When ordered, the dog must pursue a fleeing enemy, leap on his back, bring him down and keep him immobilized until its master arrives.

The technique of the exercise: The assistant moves towards you with the dog sitting at your side. The assistant becomes excited, raises his voice, pretends to pick a fight, and punch you, or produces a weapon. Set the dog on him, making sure that it only moves when told to do so. The assistant runs off. Follow him with the dog on the lead and when you are close behind the 'fugitive' give the command 'Up! Up!' – the same command as for ordinary jumping. Encourage the dog to leap on the asisstant's back. As soon as the dog has jumped up – no matter how badly – the assistant drops to the ground, face downwards, not moving. Pat the dog, give it the commands 'Down!' and 'On guard!', setting it down a couple of yards from the assistant, at right angles to him. Lay down the lead in such a way that the dog will move towards the man. Move away, then come back again, with the command 'Attack!' As soon as the dog seizes him, your assistant must stay motionless. Give the command 'Let go!' Move away, giving the command 'Heel!' As soon as the dog is by your side, take it back to the assistant, who is still on the ground.

Next, try to improve the way the dog jumps on to the 'wrongdoer's' back: it must push against it hard enough for the assistant to lose his balance. When he is on the ground, the dog must stay close beside him, in the down position, and attack at the slightest sign of a threatening gesture or any attempt to escape. The dog has to be taught beyond any doubt that it must not attack anyone who is not moving. If there is too great a readi-ness to bite, go through the whole exercise with the dog muzzled. For large dogs, weighing more than 50 kg (110 lb), knocking the 'criminal' to the ground is an ample substitute for biting, which might become too dangerous. They can be taught to knock down attackers as well as fugitives soon learning to hurl themselves at an adversary, whether the attack is head-on, from the side, or from behind. (A Neapolitan Mastiff will attack someone quite naturally with powerful butts of the head, not with bites.)

In the case of dogs that are reluctant to jump at a person, put the 'enemy' against the practice jump, and tell the dog to jump. It will have to jump at the man, who must then pretend to fall down.

The police-dog
For the policeman, the security guard and the night-watchman the dog can be an extraordinarily useful 'right hand'. In fact, in many countries police-dogs are considered vital. But they must have very special qualities. First and foremost they must be made to regard all strangers as friends, at least in principle. There is no place for a dog that bites too readily. A police-dog must only become aggressive when ordered to do so. Dogs used by the police force, and the army, often for peace-keeping duties, are required not so much to bite, as to bark and to detain a suspect. This needs special training and, more importantly, dogs with special skills; they must not bite at will; they must have a strong protective impulse; and not a strong impulse to attack people.

The private individual is generally unarmed and therefore needs a dog with a powerful set of teeth. As far as the policeman is concerned it is not desirable for his dog to attack all and sundry, regardless of how much it is hit, because it would certainly be too easy a target for many criminals. The police-dog must be cautious and have foresight; it must avoid being hit, and not put up senseless and stubborn resistance. It must also be a good seeker, able to track down a thief on the run, and find people who have gone into hiding. If this kind of dog

bites at random, it will inevitably end up hurting some harmless passer-by. This will not happen if the dog is capable of stopping a stranger and barking to attract its handler's attention, without biting anybody.

The police-dog must always be trained so that it will only resort to using its teeth in two instances: (1) when the offender or suspect runs away; (2) when the suspect attacks it or its handler. When the suspect stops running or attacking, the dog must instantly stop biting him.

The down position, when the fight is over

The aim of the exercise: To instil understanding of a command whose meaning, for the dog, is that it need no longer keep up its aggressive attitude.

The technique of the exercise: During a police raid, for example, it can happen that people with nothing to do with the crime in question may be arrested or stopped. When the command 'Down!' is given, the dog must disregard these people at once. To achieve this, every so often give the dog a 'Down!' command while it is dealing with your assistant, and then let the latter walk quietly away, while you take the dog elsewhere, to play for a little while. With a methodical approach the dog will soon learn that the command 'Down!' is followed by an end to all 'hostilities'. If the dog stops a peaceful passer-by, the simple command 'Down!' will be enough to disengage it. When the command 'Down!' is given the dog must naturally stop barking.

Tracker-dogs

Here we are venturing into the broadest, most mysterious and most intriguing area of dog-training – a world of smells of which we humans know nothing. On human trails the handler must establish with his dog an almost exclusively intuitive relationship, because what the dog 'sees' on the ground is – for human beings – just grass, or a path, or a pile of dead leaves. Training a tracker-dog requires plenty of common sense, energy, calmness and keen understanding.

The potential of the tracker-dog

It is not possible for ordinary dogs belonging to common working breeds (German Shepherd Dogs, Belgian Shepherd Dogs, Airedales, Dobermanns, Boxers, Rottweilers, mountain dogs) to follow human trails over dry, stony ground, or over asphalt, but over this kind of terrain they can follow short, damp trails. They cannot work on bare, sandy terrain when it is dry, but if the ground is wet, and there are favourable weather conditions, it is possible for them to follow trails and tracks up to twelve hours after they were made. 'Favourable weather conditions' means moist air, moderate winds and no sunshine. In such conditions twenty-four hour old tracks can be followed over grassy and wooded terrain. On terrain where there is no shade, the track fades in three hours if the air is dry, the wind brisk, and the sun strong. In the same weather conditions, a track can be traced for up to twelve hours if the terrain is partly sheltered from the wind and in shade. A track left at sundown will usually be good the following morning. Given that criminal activities usually occur at night, this is a plus-point for finding the tracks of thieves, murderers, spies and so on. Tracks in snow are better preserved than tracks on terrain that is not snow-covered, even if a new fall of snow covers them to a depth of 5 cm (2 in). If the new fall is deeper than this, the track will not be found. Stormy weather and heavy rain make tracking very tricky, whereas a short shower makes things easier. Cold weather – even extremely cold weather – does not affect the possibility of detecting tracks.

Opposite: The trained Bloodhound, which will even track through water. Right: Training a German Shepherd to track.

The tracker-dog must work with its nose, and ignore any information from its other senses (sight, hearing). In order to achieve this exclusive use of the sense of smell in the exercises to come, there are some cardinal rules to be observed. They are as follows:

(1) Make sure that the dog cannot find the person it is tracking by using its eyes or ears. The person being tracked must be very quiet, and keep well out of sight. Special 'blinkers' can come in useful.

(2) Do not let the dog use its memory of earlier tracks as a basis: change both the place and the other circumstances as often as possible. Do not, for example, let the person being sought always hide behind a tree, or a wall, or a bush. Use a tree for one exercise, a bush for another, and a wall for a third. In this way, the dog will learn to rely solely on its own sense of smell, and not on its other senses or memory.

(3) Let there be no distractions during the first exercises.

(4) Set about tracking with the dog on a lead, and wearing its tracking harness. If it is let loose, especially in the initial stages, it will stray to no real purpose.

(5) The first exercise must be carried out in particularly suitable and favourable places: woodland, meadows and fields.

(6) To start with, you must be acquainted with the route of the track, down to its smallest detail. Above all, pick out a good spot from which to start, marking it with something clearly visible. It can often happen that the trainer is unable to find the start again, and this can affect the success of the exercise.

(7) Start off with fresh tracks (never made more than half an hour earlier), no more than about 30 m (33 yd) long, and laid over a straight line. A novice dog should never begin work on a curving track, or on one with corners in it.

(8) Always bear in mind that the track on which the dog is set must not be near other fresh tracks or ones that are in some way more marked. This is a very important point.

(9) At the end of the track the dog must always find what it was looking for, or else it will lose heart.

(10) During the exercises using objects left on the track, make sure that they are right on the track, and not to the right or left of it. If the track is a tricky one with corners in it, do not put any of the objects on a corner, but where the track is straight. They should not have conspicuous shapes or be brightly coloured, but merge with the terrain and always have a human scent. If, for some special reason, you do not want the dog to find things that have a canine scent also, never repeat an exercise with things that your dog, or other dogs, have already retrieved.

The Whitney method

A number of famous American trainers have experimented for years with the best training methods for Bloodhounds. Captain V.G. Mullikin achieved countless successes and reached a point that can only be called perfection. Leon F. Whitney's excellent work, **Bloodhounds and How to Train Them** (New York, 1947) is certainly thought-provoking.

The American criminal court recognizes the identification of a suspect or accused if it is made by a Bloodhound (but no other breed of dog), as long as the Bloodhound is a thoroughbred. This is demonstrated by its pedigree, which must be authenticated by the American Kennel Club.

Modern means of transport do not present a problem for the Bloodhound. In fact a vehicle that has been abandoned by criminals on the run is a perfect start for any tracker-dog. A pair owned by Whitney once tracked twelve patients who had escaped from mental homes, after sniffing the sheets in which the escapees had slept. The two dogs followed the track together, until they came to a river, where a small boat had been stolen. One of the dogs instantly leapt into the water and concentrated on following the track as it swam, while the other worked on the bank. The dog in the river headed at a certain point towards the opposite bank, where six of the escaped patients were found. The other dog carried on to a house where the other six patients were all fast asleep.

The first thing many burglars do after a theft is to hide whatever they have stolen. By following the track, a Bloodhound starts off by recovering the 'loot'. In the summer of 1937, in just one week, Whitney's dogs tracked down fourteen people: four escapees, two murderers, four mental patients, two lost children, a woman who had become unconscious, and a dead angler. The presence of a Bloodhound in an area may discourage criminal activity. At the time of the notorious Jack the Ripper, crime virtually ceased altogether when Bloodhounds were used by the police, and only started again when they were called off the hunt.

Preliminaries

The best age for training a potential tracker-dog, and Bloodhounds in particular, is 18 months. A dog trained at 10 months and another trained at 18 months will be at precisely the same stage at the age of 20 months. Training will take six months. It must be carried out always and only on a long leather leash attached to a harness. Bloodhounds, obviously enough, make no noise at work. They can be used in pairs, or singly, three dogs can be used at the same time, but not more. Comparisons made in the United States between Bloodhounds on the one hand and Dobermanns and German Shepherd Dogs on the other have all come down fairly and squarely in favour of the former.

Your dogs must be kept fit by being regularly exercised, both during and after training, at least twice a week. The ideal place for training all tracker-dogs is the countryside, but Bloodhounds will also achieve good training results in town.

Your working equipment is as follows: a leather lead, a leather harness and a wide collar. (It is customary for the harness to be decorated with copper plaques.) The most widely used lead is 2.4 m (8 ft) long – usually a horse's old rein. At the end of the lead, before the spring-clip fixed to the harness, attach a length of chain. This can be used as a corrective device, when you want to pull the dog to keep its attention focused on the job in hand, and stop it sniffing at bushes where other dogs have left their mark. As a rule, the dog will have its lead attached to its collar. Change to the harness when the tracking proper starts. When the day's work is over, put the lead back on the collar.

The trainer must have a good knowledge of the track to be followed. Here are good American systems:
(1) The person being pursued carries with him several strips of cloth (not unlike bandages in shape and size) and every so often stops and ties them to bushes, hedges, posts, etc. In this way, even from a distance, the trainer will always know which track the dog must follow.
(2) The person being tracked carries six or seven newspapers and as he moves along tears them first into strips the width of his hand, and then into squares that will be clearly visible.
(3) Armed with a good knife, the person being pursued makes frequent nicks in branches, and cuts off small ones to lay on the ground, pointing in the direction of the track. A freshly cut branch makes an easy signal for the trainer.

The American method

The first difficulty in training a Bloodhound (and this goes for all other breeds, incidentally) is to make it understand that it must always follow the original track and not change, during the pursuit, to other fresher or different tracks. Because we cannot pick up the scent of the track, we do not know when a dog is changing tracks and this can give rise to confusion, problems and setbacks. The second problem is to get the dog to track keenly, with total commitment, and so that it can use all the qualities of its sense of smell. American trainers use the following method.

The person being tracked or pursued carries a jacket or some other piece of clothing which is pale in colour, and a container filled with boiled liver, which most dogs like. (If your dog does not enjoy it, choose a titbit that it does like.) The dog should miss a meal, so that its appetite can be used to advantage. The trainer keeps the dog on a short lead in front of the person being tracked, who offers the dog a morsel, then a smaller one, then a sliver and then an even tinier scrap, until the dog is more or less beside itself with anxiety to get its teeth into the meat. At this point, the person being tracked gradually drops back, and when the dog starts to stare at him, suddenly runs off, calling the dog and waving the jacket in the air. About 10 m (11 yd) away, the 'fugitive' hides behind a wall or a hedge, but before doing so, drops the jacket; then he runs for about 50 m (55 yd), and lies flat on the ground or hides behind a tree. (The place must, of course, be carefully inspected before these exercises begin.)

A few minutes after the 'fugitive' has disappeared, the trainer invites the dog to look for him with the command 'Seek!' As far as American authors are concerned the important thing is that the dog is made to run during the first exercise. Stop at the jacket and let the dog have a good sniff at it. The following procedure is even better: 2 m (6½ ft) away from where the jacket is, grab the dog by the collar and pull its head up; when you are almost on top of the jacket, let the dog go, so that its nose drops straight on to it. In time, the dog will learn that the jacket is the thing that will provide the scent that it will then have to follow.

It will not be hard to go from the jacket to the 'fugitive', who should be the one to reward the dog. Be sure not to give the dog the whole of its reward at once, because the fierce appetite of the dog will stop it tasting the food, and may even make it swallow all of it on one gulp, without getting any enjoyment from it. The 'fugitive' should hand out the prize bit by bit, so that the dog tastes it properly.

Make sure that you avoid the serious mistake of changing 'fugitives' on the same day, because it would encourage the dog to change from track to track on future occasions. You should change 'fugitives', certainly, but only at the right moment, and never during a working day.

The exercises should be continued with the help of two assistants. The dog will see them both running away, but only one will have the pale-coloured jacket, which will be dropped 10 m (11 yd) or so from the dog. Take the dog to the jacket, holding on to its collar, to keep its head held high.

When you get to the jacket, let the dog drop down beside it and attach the lead to the harness, at the same time giving the order 'Seek!'. In the meantime the two 'fugitives' will have vanished, either lying flat on the ground or hiding behind a tree, some 20 m (22 yd) away. The two tracks will be close together, but not overlapping. If the dog now follows the good track, praise it; if it makes for the wrong one, pull it up short on the lead and admonish it until it returns to the right track and seriously sets to work. It is a good thing if the dog makes the odd mistake. It gives you – the trainer – the opportunity to make it understand that it must not follow tracks other than the one on which you have set it. Having reached this stage, use four 'fugitives', of whom only one has a jacket to leave on the ground. The four will move away in the dog's view, one after the other, covering some 50 m (55 yd) once they are out of sight. Their tracks will intersect, only separating towards the end of their run. Let all four of them vanish from sight and then take the dog to the jacket, still keeping its head high; let it have a good sniff, and keep up with it as it tracks.

L.F. Whitney likes to end his Bloodhounds' training programmes on a golf course. At 4 pm he gets an assistant to make a track or trail, about 5 km (3 miles) long, all round the course. In the evening, when other golfers have left plenty of traces, he sets his dog to work on the course, carrying the jacket of the 'fugitive' along the track and letting the dog sniff at it when it is clearly having trouble in following the scent. If the exercise is successful, the helper makes a trail the following morning, and the dog seeks it out in the evening. When it can do this, a Bloodhound can be regarded as well trained.

The guard-dog

There are two types of guard-dog; the dog that raises the alarm as a warning, and the 'armed' guard-dog, whose function is to attack any intruder (man or animal) into its territory. An extremely alert and vigilant dog must be selected from among dogs that are markedly suspicious and thus, to a certain extent, timid and fearful. A very courageous dog, although it will be a fearsome attacker, will also be less alert.

The function of the first type – the dog that warns – is very important. It is hard to enter a property where there is a barking dog with a pair of fiery eyes (no matter how small it may be) standing by the entrance, threatening you with its bared teeth. That is why some criminals deal first of all with any guard-dog there may be by giving it poisoned food.

The first thing, therefore, the guard-dog must learn is not to pick up any food from the ground, or accept food from strangers. With a little patience and using the severe techniques already described you can train a guard-dog to be unbribable, no matter how tempting the bribe. See **Refusing bribes** (p.262).

On the chain

Keeping a dog on a chain has its advantages and its drawbacks. The advantage is the same as that of having it on a lead: in other words the dog will be bolder and more threatening towards strangers than when it is loose. There are, however, chains and chains. Some chains are nothing more than a form of punishment: the unfortunate dog cannot even follow its natural instinct to move away from its kennel or basket to obey its bodily needs. Another type of chain, from Germany, enables the guard-dog to walk round the building in its care. A third type, which is American, gives the guard-dog the chance to move about within a given radius, depending on the length of the chain itself. A fourth type, which is English, is based on the well-known system of the overhead wire, but improves on it with the use of a special runner (see drawing) which enables the guard-dog to keep a large area under its watchful eye, and move about. All animals need to do this, but many guard-dogs are prohibited from doing it, and this makes them unhappy.

Another advantage of the chained-up dog is that although it may bark at strangers, thus warning of their presence and making them afraid, it cannot directly attack them. This is regarded as important by those owners who are not able to train their dogs, and who want to avoid any bother.

The main drawback of the chained dog lies in the fact that it cannot go beyond the limit of the chain itself, so a potential wrongdoer who stays just a centimetre or two (an inch) beyond this limit runs absolutely no risk of being stopped by the dog. In addition, an armed criminal can easily shoot or hit a chained dog, without any risk to himself, whereas a dog at large presents a real danger.

In general, guard-dogs are chained up during the day, and let loose at night. But this system lays a dog open to being poisoned and probably killed. In addition, a dog kept chained up all day will at night be dangerous to all and sundry, including its master. In fact, it does not consider its master as its 'superior': it has been made savage by the chain forcing it to bark its head off, and possibly preventing it from urinating and defecating away from

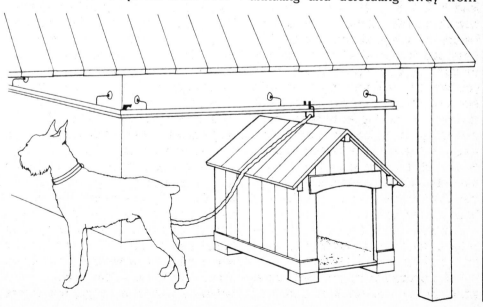

the restricted area in which it has to live. Chained-up dogs may sometimes even bite their own masters.

The ideal watch-dog
A good guard-dog, with the specific task of acting as a warning, must be taught to be broadly submissive, obeying the commands 'Sit!', 'Down!' 'Bark!' and 'Stay!' The command 'Down!' is particularly important if (as is advisable) you use the overhead wire system to chain the animal. In fact, when you want to let someone cross the area under guard, all you will have to do is give the command 'Down!', and the obedient dog will lie down and let the person pass.

During the day, your watch-dog will keep an eye on the entrance to your property. Let it loose at night, in the garden. It must learn not to stray beyond the garden, because, if it did, it would soon become a night wanderer. (If your guard-dog is a bitch, there will be less risk of this happening than there would be with a male. In any case, if there are places in a fence or hedge that the dog can easily jump over or get through, use an electrified wire for a few nights to discourage it.

Of course, any guard-dog must instantly refuse 'bribes', and to reinforce its aversion to things it finds on the ground or things offered it by strangers, put it to the test yourself about once a month. This will produce an ideal watch-dog: lively, strong and suspicous of strangers.

The 'armed' guard-dog
For this type of duty you need an energetic dog that has been through all the main obedience and attacking exercises.

Dogs that are to work as watch-dogs mainly at night are usually fed twice a day: in the morning, at about 8 am, and again at about 1 pm. It is not a good idea to feed these dogs in the evening; because they may tend to doze off instead of staying on guard. This is serious in the case of the 'armed' guard-dog that must be self-confident and aware of its own

Rescue work in the mountains with a well-trained German Shepherd.

strength. It is less so in the case of dogs used to warn, in which a little timidity can act as a stimulus. Excellent results can be achieved by giving the large guard-dog (Neapolitan Mastiff, English Mastiff, Great Dane, St Bernard, Leonberger and so on) a dog from a miniature breed as a companion (Pomeranian, small Greyhound, etc.). The smaller dog, well aware of its own relative weakness, will always sleep with one eye open, and in the event of danger, even some distance away, will wake up its larger companion by barking, and directing it towards the threat.

As a rule, the 'armed' guard-dog prevents any person or animal from entering its territory. It will chase away cats, rats and other dogs. Just as the Bloodhound is a pastmaster at tracking, so the Neapolitan Mastiff – if well trained – is pastmaster as a guard. A rather sedentary animal by nature, this magnificent dog does not need a great deal of exercise, and so is an ideal watch-dog. It has an innate sense of ownership and combines great alertness and vigilance with a proverbial ability to suffer pain. It is impressively powerful, too, and surprisingly intelligent. In addition, its obedience to its master is total, it has a natural respect for other domestic animals (cats, poultry, other dogs, large quadrupeds, etc.), and its appearance is daunting to strangers, and to wrongdoers in particular.

Rescue dogs
With the ever-increasing popularity of winter-sports, mountain rescue dogs, trained to work in snow, are very much to the fore. Every year, hundreds of skiers are caught in avalanches, and some are killed – not on the whole, by the impact of the great wall of snow, but rather by suffocation and exposure, deep beneath the surface. If they could be discovered quickly and dug out, their lives would be saved.

Some time ago, Swiss cynologists began a series of successfull experiments with dogs belonging to the following breeds: Appenzeller Sennenhund, Boxer, German Shepherd Dog, Airedale, Rottweiler and Dobermann. (The St Bernard, which is too slow and heavy, is not suitable for rescue work.) It is worth mentioning here the fame of the Dachshund Moritz in Murren in Switzerland, an expert at avalanche work, that saved the life of the Andermatt mountain guide, Joseph Bonetti.

Training
It is important to choose dogs with plenty of character and endurance, that will stand up to arduous duties and very harsh temperatures. The ideal dog should show a marked tendency to enjoy running about in snow – something quite common. If it appears a little awkward the first two or three times it encounters snow, do not pay overmuch attention to this.

Training involves submission and obedience; the dog must respond extremely well to its call, and lie down when ordered at any distance. You must also teach it to dig in the snow, but not for too long, or too deeply: it need dig for only half a minute at most – rather like the truffle dog.

Command: 'Dig!'

The technique of the exercise: At feeding-time, take a piece of meat from the bowl and while the dog is watching you, hide it under a light covering of snow. Do not give the dog its bowl until it has fetched and eaten the buried titbit. Be methodical: increase the depth of snow covering the food to a few centimetres (inches). As the dog starts to dig, give the command 'Dig!', in a lively tone of voice. When the dog has grasped the meaning of the word, hide several tasty morsels in the snow, allowing the dog to watch you as you do it. Give the command and let the dog eat its fill. Next, hide some titbits out of sight of the dog. As soon as you give the command, it will start to dig. Do not bury the titbits too deep. The dog must not become tired out. Use titbits which the dog particularly likes. Using the same technique you can teach a dog to dig in earth, sand or rubble.

Bear two things in mind: (1) A 'victim' must first lie down in the snow; then be half-buried; and finally completely buried in a hole dug specially for the exercise. Gradually deepen the hole. (2) At the outset of the exercises bury a rich haul of titbits quite close to the 'victim', who should invite the dog to dig. When the 'victim' is completely buried, place the titbits in the same spot, so that he can give the dog the titbits, once he has been removed from the hole. Last of all, put the assistant in small caves, which are quite common where there is snow on the ground, and start a smallish snow-slide, so that the snow in which the dog must work carries no scent of anyone apart from the 'victim'.

Rescue work in rubble and ruins

In Berlin and other German cities during the Second World War groups of dogs were taught to point out where people were buried in ruins and rubble after bombing raids; they were extremely useful, in helping to save a great many lives. In the postwar period squads of dogs have been formed to find earthquake victims. With various modifications, the form of training is similar to that for snow rescue. The 'Dig!' command must be thoroughly established. It is best to work with 'dummy victims' in rubble.

It would be a good idea if all cities, even in peacetime, had squads of dogs ready to go to work in the event of explosions, collapsed buildings, earthquakes and other disasters.

Swiss rescue dogs have saved literally hundreds of people after being taken by air to the sites of earthquakes, for example, in Friuli (1976), in Bucharest (1977) and in Irpinia (1980). They are trained to detect in fumes and the various smells of rubble, the presence of people who have been buried alive. These dogs can be mobilized with their handlers on an emergency basis and taken to the scene of a disaster within minutes, by helicopter and other aircraft.

The show-dog

At dog-shows, the judge examines the dog for a few minutes. If, during this brief inspection, the dog is in tip-top condition, and shows off its qualities to the full, it will certainly be more successful than if it cowers in a corner, and does not let the judge have a good look at it. Hence, the need to train the show-dog to present itself in the best possible way. We all know that at certain moments our dog tends to look its best (when it has scented a cat, for example, or heard a noise at the door), and at others it looks the very opposite (when it is drowsy, or over-excited, or lack-lustre). You must be able to put your dog in its most favourable mood, and keep it in that mood for as long as may be required. First and foremost, the show-dog must be accustomed to the presence of other dogs, so that it does not run wild in the ring, biting other dogs, and getting so worked up that it ends up frothing at the mouth and finally collapsing in a dead faint. Start by getting your dog used to being in the presence of other dogs, and to looking at them with a kindly eye, or at least with indifference. Next establish the need for obedience if your dog is to be considered for a prize at the show.

It is inconceivable that a dog that often travels and stays in hotels with its owner should not be obedient – and totally so. So it is vital that before embarking on training for shows the dog has been through the first stages of submission training: exercises on the lead, and with the commands 'Sit!' and 'Down!'

Training

You can start training with a dog just three months old, by putting it on a table, or a young dog, or an adult.

(1) Start as for the usual exercise on the lead, the dog on your left, and the lead slack.

(2) Suddenly stop. With your left hand pull lightly on the lead (kept quite short), while your right hand moves to below the dog's neck, thus stopping it from moving forward. In the meantime, in a quiet voice, give the command 'Stay!' and repeat it softly from time to time. Do not let the dog sit down, which it will tend to do, as a result of the previous submission and obedience exercises. If necessary, put a hand beneath its stomach, and lift it up if it has already sat down. Ask it not to do so again with the commands 'No! Stay!' spoken quietly, in a friendly tone of voice.

(3) As soon as the dog has understood that it must stay still, kneel or squat beside it, taking great care that your right hand stays under the dog's throat, stroking it gently and the left beneath the base of its tail. Keep still in this position for ten seconds or so, repeating the command 'Stay!' in a quiet voice. If the dog more or less obeys, praise it warmly, stroke it and reward it with a titbit, then get up and carry on with your walk. After 20 m (22 yd), start the whole process again.

(4) Do not worry about the dog's fore-quarters – the feet may be too close together – or its hind-quarters, which will probably be too far apart. During this initial training, the dog will assume unnatural positions, which should certainly not be the ones it takes up after being trained.

Above: Shows are very important for guiding the selection made by breeders. The future of dog breeds depends on dedicated breeders.

(5) After a time, when the dog has learnt to stay still, with you touching it with less and less pressure under the throat and tail, you can start to work on its position. To improve the fore-quarters, take the dog between the chest and the neck, lifting it up a little, and letting it drop down again of its own accord: the legs will then assume the correct stance.

(6) To improve the hind-quarters, push the dog backwards a little: the legs will bend slightly, and this will give the whole of the dog's back a better line. If you regularly correct the dog's position, little by little, it will understand what you want of it and before long, as soon as you stop it, give the command 'Stay!' and put your hands in the positions mentioned above, it will assume the correct position.

Towards the end of training, when you are concentrating on the dog's presentation, first remove the hand beneath the tail, but keep the other one at the neck; later remove both hands, keeping the lead quite taut, at right angles to the dog. Absorbing all these signals, the dog will quickly position itself, and stay in position for an increasingly long time, making it possible for an impressed judge to have a quiet look at the whole animal.

Some breeds – German Shepherd Dogs, for example – are not judged when they are still but while they are trotting and the test can last for several hours in some countries. It is advisable, therefore, to practice trotting with your dog for long periods, making sure that it never breaks into a gallop, but uses its longest and most flowing stride. It is very important for the dog to cover a lot of ground, and to show good endurance. For some breeds there is also a 'character' test, which involves the dog barking when told to do so, assuming an aggressive position on command, and remaining unruffled by a gun-shot. Such tests will not be a problem for dogs that have been trained to protect people and property.

Remember, too, that the judge will want to have a look at the dog's teeth, so accustom it to strangers touching its mouth.

The companion-dog

All dogs are companion-dogs. All dog-lovers know well how much companionship there is to be gained from an eager Pointer, an alert Dobermann, a good-natured Boxer, a noble Great Dane, a protective Mastiff, a placid Bulldog, a sensitive Sheepdog, a bright-eyed Poodle, a proud and comical Pekingese, an eccentric little Schnauzer, or a dignified little Dachshund. People who have no dog at home miss a great deal.

Choosing and training a companion-dog

Not every dog will necessarily adapt to the person with whom it is to live. This is where the breed has to be taken into account. The German Shepherd Dog will attach itself to just one person, while a Boxer will befriend a whole family, and children in particular; the Fox Terrier and the Pomeranian tend to bark quite a lot, and are not suitable for nervous or highly-strung owners; Cocker Spaniels and Dachshunds are quiet, obedient and gentle, but if they do not get much exercise they will soon become fat; an athletic person will be best with an energetic Dobermann; those who like strength should choose a powerful Mastiff, those who like sheer size a Great Dane, those who like small dogs might choose a Corgi, and so on. Choose not only the dog that suits your personal taste, but one that also suits your lifestyle. For example, a Poodle-lover should remember that there are three sizes – toy, medium and large – and choose the most suitable.

Training is vital for any companion-dog. Just as children should be well brought up, so should a dog that lives in the home, whatever its size; toy dogs can be trained just as successfully as large breeds.

The small companion-dog, living most of the time in the home – i.e. in very close contact with people – must learn to behave rather as if it were a small well-brought-up person. Firstly, it must be in no doubt whatsoever about the meaning of the command 'No!', which must be given firmly, but not with a raised voice, every time it does something it should not do, such as jumping up at people, or damaging furniture (it must never be allowed on furniture, incidentally). To increase the effect of your 'No!', you can throw a light chain or a bunch of keys at the dog from a distance; when they hit the ground the noise will scare it and make it stop. The two basic positions, sit and down, are crucial. Before starting on these two, go through the lead exercises since an indoor dog must not be allowed to roam about the streets where, because of its small size, it would go unnoticed by motorists, and would probably be run over. The sit and down exercises should be followed up by the stay exercise.

Small companion-dogs are often required to act a little like circus dogs, to show off their intelligence, increase their self-respect, and give amusement. Start by teaching your dog to stand on its front legs. To achieve this, support its back against a wall and help it to keep its balance with your hand. It will soon learn to stay still in this position, without your helping hand, and little by little without the support of the wall either.

Jumping to order comes in useful for companion-dogs, as well as guard- and hunting-dogs. It is possibly even more important for indoor dogs, because a short bout of jumping will be good exercise. The dog will quickly learn to jump.

By now your dog will be trained, and a full and popular member of the household. However, when you invite it to go for a walk, it may become so excited that it dashes for the door, and straight into the street. Many dogs are run over by cars through behaving like this, so teach your dog to stop on the threshold, make it lie down, and when it has calmed down call it to you, make it sit, attach the lead, and then start your walk.

Retrieving is also important. The dog must be able to hold and carry an object such as a newspaper or a basket, and deliver it to you properly from the sitting position.

When the dog has mastered the art of retrieving (i.e., fetching and carrying) make it look for things inside and outside the home, on the command 'Seek!' To start, leave the object only half-hidden, then hide it in a more complicated way.

To round off the training, teach your dog to refuse food or 'bribes' offered by strangers, so that there will be no risk of it picking up anything poisoned.

Rules for breeders
The responsibilities of the breeder

Thanks to the persistent endeavours of breeders over several generations, breeds have been both consolidated and improved – some have even been created. Because of errors made by some breeders, one or two breeds have become deformed, or even died out altogether. Incompetent, unscrupulous, or profit-hungry breeders out to make easy money or breeders with no clear aim in mind have often brought highly-prized breeds of dogs to the verge of ruin.

Kennels rarely provide financial profits to balance the sacrifices involved and the inevitable disappointments encountered. The breeder's efforts are nurtured by a passion for his work that is sometimes hard for the layman to understand. The future depends on these efforts.

In too many cases, breeders are so keen on dog-shows and competitions, and so set on winning prizes, that all they look for is anatomical and physical perfection; they tend to forget that a dog has mental qualities that are more important than any physical excellence. As a result, many buyers who are keen to have a dog for a specific purpose, such as hunting or guarding, find themselves with the most handsome of, say, Setters without a clue how to point or set, or a splendid Sheepdog that is timid and a coward, or the prettiest of Poodles that bites all and sundry.

The choice of breeding dogs and bitches must not be based on physical qualities only, but must emphasize the dog's mental characteristic. To this effect here are a few hints.

Basic rules

In the section dealing with puppy training, under the sub-heading **Character and personality**, (p.241) dog psychology was discussed. What follows is a method, used on many occasions to good effect, for selecting breeds with a stress on the mental make-up of the

The King Charles Spaniel is one of the many attractive breeds of companion-dogs. The pups, as those in this litter, are particularly endearing.

parents and the improvement of the qualities of the dogs in question. The following features are taken into account:

Courage (C): Disregard of the dog for its own interests in defence of those of the group – such as its master, the family, or an even larger collective group.

Defensive Impulse (DI): Readiness to intervene and take action, in the event of a threat, and in defence of a companion or companions, whether human or animal.

Fighting Impulse (FI): Taking pleasure in a good 'brawl', a combative tendency.

Readiness of bite (RB): A hostile reaction to unpleasant stimuli.

Constitution of Character (CC): Tolerance of unpleasant actions.

Vigilance (V): Direct reaction by barking, growling, etc., to an unusual stimulus.

Temperament (T): Speed of reaction to external stimuli, energy.

Docility (D): Easily accepts human society, so allowing a person to be in charge.

Endurance (E): Capacity to summon new strength from within to confront a situation and, above all, to carry on with the job to be done.

Classification according to these mental qualities is as follows:
Courage + 1 means that this feature is necessary to a breed, though not to any marked degree. Courage + 2, however, means that this feature must be conspicuous, so that the breeding dog or bitch, when well mated or paired, will improve its offspring, which may be destined to become rescue-dogs, or to be used for hunting underground game, or for night-watching duties. Courage + 3 means that this must be the salient quality in the parent, to produce offspring that will become guard-dogs, police-dogs, or even dogs used for hunting certain game. Courage − 1 means that this quality is not a requisite for the function(s) envisaged for the future offspring (as companion-dogs, for example); timidity or fearfulness is indicated by C − 2, and timidity bordering on cowardice by C − 3.

Using these formulae, it is possible to work out not only whether a male dog will be a good breeder if it is mated with a suitable bitch, but also whether the young dog in question will be suitable for a specific type of training: guarding, pointing, tracking, attacking, working in water, working underground, herding (sheep or cattle), hauling, pack-work, companionship, or for showing.

The tests

In Europe the first people to embark on methodical studies of the selection of the mental characteristics of dogs were the Menzels, a husband and wife, who lived first in Linz and later in Israel. They referred to their studies at the International Cynological Congress held in 1935 at Frankfurt-am-Main. Their research was spread over a period of sixteen years, using almost 800 Boxers, all belonging to a single family over ten successive generations. (If the same psychological tests were to be carried out on human beings over ten generations, they would take three centuries.) The Men-

zels' methods have since been developed and completed by later students.

The author's own experiments in this field, involved about 1000 dogs, with specimens from some thirty breeds of working- hunting- and companion-dogs and took place from 1947 to 1960, at Rome Zoo.

The research and studies were focused both on the hereditary nature of mental characteristics, and on the innermost qualities in the young dog that was to undergo specific training. The tests that follow can therefore be used in the two ways.

The best age for putting a dog through the tests is between 6 and 10 months. Earlier than this, the dog's immaturity does not permit you to make accurate assessments, and later, the influences of training and upbringing can alter the authenticity of the results.

The preferable age is also good for establishing the mental qualities of dogs that will later become breeding animals, and of dogs that, although

not earmarked for breeding, will nevertheless have to show the right qualities in order to be trained in specific tasks.

Character test

This takes place out of doors, where there is no traffic, and not too many distractions, preferably with a few other dogs present. It is worth having an expert examiner with you. If this is not possible, you, the owner, or a friend, can act as examiner, working according to the following suggestions.

Walk with the dog on the lead, in a natural and ordinary way. Suddenly, and apparently without any specific purpose, cut across the dog's tracks, gently treading on its feet. The dog's reaction will show its 'character', the resistance it puts up against unpleasant actions. A dog with plenty of 'character' will tend to make at least a gesture of snapping at the shoe that has hurt it (CC + 3). A young dog with a good character will not react by biting, and will continue walking as if nothing had happened (CC + 2). A dog with an average character will show signs of being hurt (an instant yelp, a moment of limping, etc.), and then suddenly carry on its way (CC + 1). A dog with a weak character will prolong the signs of being hurt, all the more so if it is really lacking in character (CC − 1, 2 or 3).

If there is any doubt, move on to other tests, but always with the aim of clearly establishing − not just after a single exercise − the degree of resistance or tolerance being shown by the 'examinee' to an unpleasant action.

Temperament test

The character test has already given the first indications of the dog's temperament. The young dog (or bitch) with plenty of temperament will walk in a lively way, react straight away to being lightly kicked, and turn its head in a flash towards anything that attracts its attention (e.g., other dogs round about).

Go to a rather secluded and quiet spot, and start to play with the dog. See if it immediately accepts the idea of playing, or whether it holds back and needs considerable encourage-

ment. In the first instance, it has a positive temperament (T + 1, 2 or 3); in the second, its temperament is fairly negative (T − 1, 2 or 3).

Next, tap the dog's head playfully, as well as its tail and legs and feet: if the dog has a good temperament, its reactions will be very quick; it will fend off the hand before it has even been touched, and will even bite it quite hard.

This will give you a clear sign of the dog's temperament: if it is extremely positive, it will bare its teeth. Another excellent indication of a strong temperament is the dog's biting itself while at play. To assess this, give the dog at play its own tail or paw to nip.

Above, top: Training a Golden Retriever. This gundog breed is nowadays frequently trained to sniff out drugs.
Above: A pair of Bearded Collies, a breed originally used for herding sheep, undergoing police-dog trials.
Opposite: Two German gundogs being trained.

Any dog that has the look of an 'oppressed' partner, instead of playing enthusiastically with you, has a weak temperament. But if an owner has adopted the bad, and sad, habit of hitting his or her dog, those mistakes will hamper the dog's genuine reaction.

Just as a dog's character can be strong or weak, so its temperament can be resolute or soft, but these terms imply neither praise nor criticism. A soft dog can be perfect for some tasks. If, for example, you want your dog to be a playmate for your children, you will be better off with a dog that does not have a resolute temperament. Guide-dogs for the blind must also be quite pliable, as must Retrievers and companion-dogs. As a general rule, a dog with a pliable temperament will not play a great deal, soon losing interest, whereas dogs with plenty of positive temperament become increasingly more playful and enthusiastic in their behaviour.

Another temperament test consists of putting the young dog between your legs and trying to part its lips to have a look at its teeth, without opening its jaws. A dog with a very marked, strong temperament will try to free itself, and prevent the examination, sometimes even resorting to a menacing growl: it will, in short, try to get the upper hand. A form of counter-test is to put the dog on its back, again playfully, and see how it reacts. You will now be able to score the dog.

Vigilance test

It is best if this takes place somewhere familiar to the dog: a garden, courtyard or terrace, for example. Lie back in a deck-chair or something similar and pretend to be dozing. Arrange for a stranger to approach after about ten minutes, looking obviously furtive: it is best if the dog spots him when he is some way off. If the dog (on a 1.5 m (5 ft) lead) growls, barks, and threatens the stranger, it has a high degree of vigilance.

Repeat this test in a place that the dog does not know; pretend to doze for about ten minutes, without moving.

Docility (obedience) test

In the same place where you carried out the character and temperament tests, remove the dog's collar and lead and let it loose.

If the dog 'has temperament' (and courage), it will run away from its owner at once, sniffing this and that,

going up to other dogs, and attending to its bodily needs. If it is low on temperament (and fearful), it will not leave its owner, straying off at most just a few metres (yards).

Remember that even a dog with plenty of temperament and courage will do this if it has always lived in a small space, without going out and seeing other people and dogs.

Do not confuse docility with timidity or fearfulness. A docile, timid dog will stay close to its owner, tail between its legs (fear), looking intently at its owner's face (docility) to find out what it should be doing. A docile and courageous dog will move away, but turn round every now and then to have a quick look at its owner, as if it were asking permission to leave his side. When called back, it will come readily, at a brisk trot.

The call is very important in establishing an attitude of docility or obedience: many owners mistreat a young dog when it comes back to them, and this damages the effectiveness of the call.

To establish the strength of a dog's attachment to you, move away without fuss when the dog's attention is distracted, and hide out of sight. See how much time elapses before the dog becomes aware of your absence, and when it has realized that you are somewhere else, check its attitude. This will give you only an indication, however, because there are several factors at work here: (1) courage, (2) the desire to play, (3) the desire to move, and (4) suspicion.

A dog that shows great courage, and a keen desire to play and move, but that also hurries to look for its owner as soon as it realizes he is not present, is healthily attached to him, and has great potential docility.

The degree of docility becomes apparent during the temperament test as well, when you play with your dog: how does it react if, in the middle of a good romp, you give it the command to stop playing? How often do you have to repeat this order?

In this assessment it is important to remember that the dog with a weak character is more sensitive to command than the dog with a strong character, which does not mean that it is more docile, but simply that even a minor command tends to impress it, and its weak character is thus more malleable as a result. Do not forget that docility is a deep-seated and voluntary attitude — a talent, in fact — whereas malleability if due to a weak character, and caused by fear.

Endurance test

Temperament and endurance are closely connected to one another, and there is also a link between endurance and character.

During the character test it is possible to observe the dog's endurance in the face of unpleasant situations; and the temperament test may reveal that endurance in action. Lengthy periods of barking during the vigilance test also give another pointer.

The usual behaviour of the dog when not undergoing tests starts to come to light at this stage. Does it tire easily? Will it walk willingly and for a long time? Even if tired, will it get its second wind, if asked to play or run?

Above: In some countries there are trials for water-rescue dogs. The illustration shows a Newfoundland in training in Great Britain. The New Foundland is the classic breed for this kind of work, its great strength being one of its assets.
Opposite: An American Cocker Spaniel being exercised with a ball.

Remember that you are with a young animal that will tire faster than an adult. Above all, do not look for signs of physical endurance but of mental endurance. A young dog that plays a lot and never 'gives up' usually has good qualities of endurance.

Other tests

Separation from the owner: A stranger approaches the dog, which is near its owner, and starts playing with it. As soon as the young dog agrees to play, the stranger takes the lead and quietly draws it away from its owner (who meanwhile hides), playing all the time, perhaps with a ball.

This will give an interesting indica- tion of the dog's attitude when it notices that its owner has vanished. Will it try to head back to the place where the two parted company? Will it stop playing altogether, or go on, but half-heartedly? Will it forget about its owner if the stranger inveigles it into playing harder?

A dog with considerable courage, and a keen desire to play, move and chase, will not mind being parted from its owner, whereas a fearful young dog, with poor means of defence at its disposal, will not want to be parted, or go with a stranger, at any price, not so much because of its attachment to its owner, as because it is afraid of those it does not know.

Negotiating obstacles: For this exer- cise use a fence or a wall with a gate in it, and about 12 m (13 yd) away, a large opening through which the dog can easily pass. The fence should be reasonably high, so that the dog can- not get over it except by making a good leap of 2 m (6½ ft) or so.

Place yourself with the dog 10 m (11 yd) from the fence. Hand the dog over to a stranger, who must hold it firmly by the lead. In full view of the dog, walk up to the fence, open the gate, walk through it, close it, and walk about another 10 m (11 yd), when you will obviously be invisible to the dog.

The dog should now be let off its lead. How will it act? Will it stop by the gate, looking desperate? Will it look about to find a way of getting to its vanished owner? Will it skim over the fence, not having noticed the opening on its panic? Will it find the opening straight away? Will it try to get over the fence? Will it succeed, or will it need several attempts?

All this will provide you with clear indications about its intelligence, tem- perament, character and endurance.

Sensitivity tests

Arrange for various people to hide along a road that is unfamiliar to the dog. When you appear with the dog they behave in ways that produce the following sequence of stimuli, each one on a different walk:

(1) As the dog passes one person steps forward and opens an umbrella close to it; when the umbrella is closed, another person throws some rags into the air, which fall to the ground close to the dog.

(2) One of the people in hiding will suddenly set light to something that burns easily (straw, rags soaked in paraffin, etc.).

(3) Next, someone will make strange and unexpected noises: using a horn, a pan beaten with a stick, a rattle, a bell, or something similar.

(4) Next, someone fires a blank pistol about 10 m (11 yd) away from the dog.

Between these different walks and experiences, you should stroke the dog, and reassure it if it looks scared. It is important to have a lead at least 2 m (6½ ft) in length so that the dog is not held back: it must be able to walk ahead freely, go back, and dart off to left and right without being restrained by the lead; if it is, a slight feeling of fear will turn into fully fledged fright.

Some dogs are indifferent to aural stimuli and extremely sensitive to visual stimuli (fire, the umbrella being opened, etc.). Having once established the dog's weak spots, you can set about attending to them during training, until they no longer exist. It is vital to detect them at an early stage. From the dog's different reactions, which emerge from the tests, the examiner can deduce various things which go to make up his general assessment. The results can be summed up as follows:

(a) Faced with one, several or all four stimuli, the dog assumes a hostile attitude (barking, raising its tail, opening its mouth to bite, hackles standing on end) with no sign of being afraid. This attitude implies courage and a readiness to bite.

(b) Faced with one, two, or all four stimuli, the dog appears reluctant to fight, but does not look frightened. It reacts to the stimuli with curiosity or indifference. It may try to head for the place from which the unusual phenomenon is coming, wagging its tail cheerfully, and then lose interest and go on its way beside its owner. This attitude implies courage, but no readiness to bite.

(c) Faced with one or more or all four stimuli, the dog looks worried, ready to defend itself, with its hackles standing on end out of fear, growling or barking and its tail usually carried low (although not always; some breeds carry their tail high in such situations). It will try to move away from the place from which the presumed danger is coming, pulling on its lead, no matter how long it is. This is an attitude of frightened hostility, which embraces a readiness to bite.

(d) Faced with one, two or all four stimuli, the dog looks anxious, ready to take to its heels, with no intention of defending itself, and with not the slightest hint of hostility. Its tail will be between its legs and stiff. In extreme examples of this attitude, the dog will yelp from fear, or urinate. This attitude is fearful, with no readiness to bite.

In cases (a) and (b) the dominant impulse is to fight, giving rise to the show of courage and an aggressive readiness to bite. In cases (c) and (d)

The Labrador Retriever is a great expert when it comes to fetching and carrying.

the defensive impulse is the dominant one, giving rise to a desire to run away, combined with an apparent readiness to bite, i.e., a defensive readiness to bite. Do not forget that all dogs have all the different impulses, and their derivatives. Even a fearful dog, if well trained and used to carrying out the tasks allotted to it, will lose all or some of its fearfulness. These tests are also helpful indicators of the dog's vigilance.

Water tests

Whatever its speciality (pointing, seeking, retrieving, tracking, recovering wounded game), the hunting-dog must be able to work in water: and the same goes for other dogs (guard-dogs, herding- and rescue-dogs, etc.). Some dogs are specialists, trained to help fishermen. What is more, the dog's reaction to water is an important test that establishes many of its mental traits. Some dogs hate getting even their feet wet; others will splash about in water all day long.

Get a friend, who is a hunter, to help you, and lend you his own hunting-dog, which should be good at retrieving duck and other waterfowl. Confidence in water can be detected very early. If possible, choose a fine spring day, when the water has started to warm up a little. Take the older and more experienced dog with you, and make sure that it and your dog see eye to eye. When you are near a watercourse, see how your dog behaves when the older dog leaps in with obvious delight. If it is confident about water, it will follow the other animal without hesitation, and will show obvious pleasure as it runs into the water. If this happens, you have no worries; you can be sure that on future occasions the dog will not let you down when you command it to swim over a long distance, or for a long time. However, it is possible that the young dog will enter the water cautiously, not spurred on by the older dog's example, or, worse still, that it will stay firmly rooted to the bank, looking apprehensive, and making sure that it does not get even its toes wet. Do not

lose heart even if this happens. Repeat the test on other days, if possible when it is sunny and warm.

When the young dog enters the water of its own accord, watch closely how it behaves when it comes back on to land again. Dogs with little inclination for working in water will want to do only one thing when they come out of it: shake themselves dry of that horrid wet stuff! This type of young dog will turn into an adult that will drop whatever it is carrying out of the water as soon as it is on terra firma, so that it can shake itself. Dogs that shake themselves immediately and thoroughly, and young dogs that tremble and shiver once on dry land, and busily lick their legs and paws, will be dogs that will only ever give a mediocre performance when asked to work in water. Of course, any lack of natural liking for water can be improved by training, which can get a dog to run into a lake despite its suspicion of water. If you get your dog to work in water during the summer and early autumn, you may have better results. However, if you want a dog that will work in water at all times of year, and in difficult and sometimes severe conditions, you must choose a young dog that shows a natural love of water. Such animals are far from uncommon and their pleasure is self-evident.

If your dog is reluctant to come to terms with water, you can try a further test. On a fine warm day, go to a fairly shallow expanse of water, where there are some wild duck. If there are no wild duck, take a domestic bird with you. Tell the older dog to go and fetch it. Faced with this threat, the bird will head off to deeper water and then hide. If this exciting sight does not get your young dog into the water, and it simply stays happily on dry land, you will know for sure that it is not cut out for working in water, and that when it breeds, its offspring will have the same attitude.

The attitudes of your dog during these water tests also help to establish its character, temperament and endurance. A dog's qualities in water are marked as follows: W + 1, 2 or 3, W − 1, 2 or 3.

Testing the sense of smell

These tests must also be carried out in an open space, where there is no traffic, but where there are a few other dogs, acting as a distraction. The test should not be done on a rainy day when the ground is too sodden, when it is very hot, or when there is snow on the ground. The best conditions are to be found on a mild morning, in a field or meadow.

During the 'exam', bear in mind what has already been said about the mechanism of the dog's sense of smell, even though this test can be useful not only for young hunting-dogs, but also for specialized working-dogs which must have a keen sense of smell. The test has a dual function: to establish the young dog's natural qualities for future training, and those natural skills that the dog will probably hand down to its offspring, once it is an adult.

Owners of Pointers (often almost obsessed by their work) should not worry if, on some occasions, this test might make the dog point with its head held quite low (Pointers point with nose carried high as a rule).

Play with your dog first, using an object that the dog likes: a sock, an old sack or glove, etc. When the dog is thoroughly enjoying the game, get an assistant to hold it on its lead at the edge of the field, while you move away from the area immediately in front of the dog, showing it the object all the time and inviting it to come and play. As you walk, drag your feet in the grass a little, or perhaps show the dog the play-object and then drag that along in the grass, for about 50 paces. At the end of this short trail, drop the object, without letting the dog see exactly where it has fallen. Retrace your steps, following the trail exactly, and invite the dog to seek. Do not waste time, or the dog may start to lose interest, and to forget what the exercise is all about. It is important that the dog works on its own initiative, and is not taken to the start of the trail. If you feel that the lead is getting in the way, let the dog run free. Having reached the spot where the object is, if the dog takes it, or even just points to it, showing that it has recognized it, give it

much praise. If it looks uninterested, get its attention back by playing with it again, for this purpose using the same object.

If the exercise works on the very first occasion, repeat it, over a distance of 60 paces, with a sharp bend halfway along the trail. The way the dog reacts to this corner is very important and indicative. There are three usual forms of reaction: (1) the dog starts to walk round the spot where the trial makes the turn, and has a long sniff; (2) the dog follows the bend exactly, as if it presented no difficulty at all, acting as if it is more or less on rails − an indication of a dog with a good nose; (3) the dog looks bewildered when the trail, which it had been following with interest, no longer goes straight ahead. This indicates a dog still very much lacking in experience.

Looking for the owner: There are some dogs that, to begin with, show no interest in following tracks. When the owner comes back after having walked away across the field − something which had worried the dog − it is preoccupied with sticking close to the owner, and pays no attention whatsoever to invitations to get its nose to the ground and start to seek. Do not be too quick to conclude that the dog has a poor nose. It is merely an animal that has not yet understood what is wanted of it; as soon as it has understood this, it may well reveal some useful skills. In such cases conduct, the 'looking for the owner' exercises as follows.

Stand a few metres (yards) away from the dog and let it see you kick the starting-point in the field, with the same foot movement that you make when cleaning your shoes on the doormat before going inside. As soon as you move away, your assistants must position themselves in front of the dog, blocking its view. When you have hidden in the field, about 50 paces away, an assistant should take the dog to the starting-point. Watch the dog's behaviour closely. Do not forget that the trainee dog is often so upset by the disappearance of its owner that it will naturally start to seek him out with all its senses, not just with its sense of smell, and you may see it changing from a tracker to a burrower,

Sheepdog trials, governed by strict rules, are a feature of rural life in countries such as Scotland and New Zealand.

with its nose close to the ground, its ears quite erect, and its eyes glancing hither and thither as it runs to and fro. Sometimes, as it runs all over the place, it may find the track, and trust to its nose, running along nose to the ground until it finds its owner. Remember that you must make a curving trail; if you made a straight one it would be hard to establish if the dog was really following it with its nose.

In most cases, this exercise produces good results but they are only really indicative at the third or fourth attempt, when the dog has by now understood that its owner has not disappeared, but is playing a game of hide-and-seek. Of course, every time you embark on this test, the trail must be different, and it should not overlap with the previous one. You should change your hiding-place each time, too.

Disappearance of the owner: If there is some doubt about whether the dog is following with its nose, carry out the following experiment. On a walk in an open and isolated place, when your young dog has strayed away from you and is running about with not a care in the world, hide somewhere carefully, preferably flat on the ground, behind a bush or tall plants, in a ditch, etc. but somewhere from which you can watch how the dog acts. You should be completely invisible and absolutely quiet.

The dog turns its head towards the spot where it last saw you, and where there is now no one. Until now it had always easily found you, just by looking round. But now you are nowhere to be seen, as if the earth had swallowed you up. If there is a passer-by some way off, the young dog will run up to him, mistaking him for you. But when it is closer, it will realize its mistake and be sorely disappointed. Its fear now increases and is expressed by a frantic dashing about all over the place. A dog with a poor nose will

sit down after looking for you for half an hour or so, and start whining and whimpering.

A better equipped young dog, with better endurance (something that is valuable on the hunt), will keep on looking until, by sheer fluke, it stumbles upon you, or else drops to the ground, exhausted.

A well-equipped dog will behave quite differently. It will undoubtedly look worried, glancing to left and right, and it will also run up to the first person it spots in the distance. But before long it will remember having seen you for the last time in a specific place, and because of its excellent sense of direction (of prime importance to any hunter), it will quickly get back to the spot. It will, of course, not find you there, but it will realize that a track starts from the place, and it will start to follow it with its nose in the air, or on the ground, until it discovers your hiding-place.

If your dog acts like this from the start, you are lucky: it will become a fine hunting-dog. If it fails the test the first time, be patient and repeat the exercise the following day, and after that whenever it seems a good moment to do so. Remember to give the dog a warm welcome when it has found you, and a titbit as well. A dog's ability to seek with its sense of smell is scored with S + 1, 2 or 3, or S − 1, 2 or 3.

Retrieval test

To find out whether your dog is a natural retriever (and whether these skills can be handed on, by mating it with equally gifted dogs), see how it behaves with objects you throw ahead of it, not too far.

Does it show lack of interest? Does it chase and sniff them, but never pick them up in its mouth? Does it pick them up and bring them back to you, but leave them some way away? Does it bring them directly to you? Does it drop them right at your feet?

If, at the beginning of the test, the dog appears to be uninterested, get its attention, making it gnaw on the object (an old sock, a piece of sack, or a glove, for example) and then throw it a short distance. Try this, too, with the dog on the lead and off it. If things are going well, repeat the exercise two or three times, to get a good idea of the dog's endurance.

If the dog runs some way off with the object, try again with the lead. If that makes the dog feel intimidated by a stern owner, it will not play readily, and will be happier with a stranger who appears friendly, or with a boy or girl who is used to dogs. Remember that wary dogs like playing with children.

After several tests you will have a clear idea about the natural qualities of your dog, and you can mark it as follows: R + 1, 2 or 3, or R − 1, 2 or 3.

Visual curiosity test

This is not so much a test as an overall examination: it is the outcome of observations made during all the other tests.

In any dog, visual curiosity is a keenness to see, to know and learn, by looking, about what is going on around it, and particularly about its relationship with its owner.

Sight is undoubtedly the sense that can most easily play tricks on a dog. However, the very alert expression of a dog (often referred to its 'intelligent look') indicates good physical qualities as far as all forms of training are concerned: the alertness of the expression is the product of the completeness of the other senses, which provide the eye with its proper sense of direction. This feature can therefore be marked as follows: VC + 1, 2 or 3, or VC − 1, 2 or 3.

The minus marking has to do with dogs that never look you straight in the eye, but turn their head away, almost as if they are avoiding any contact with people. This arises, as has already been mentioned more than once, almost invariably from mistakes made by human beings.

Score-card

The examiner should summarize the outcome of the various tests on a card, something like this:
Name of dog:
Breed and sex:
Height at withers, and weight:
Age, and teeth (complete or incomplete):
Father and mother:
Breeder and owner:
Handler (instructor): Is the handler during the tests the owner or someone else? Is the dog attached to him?
Visual curiosity: marks.
Character: Does the dog try to bite? Does it yelp? limp? show its teeth when playing? bite itself at play? Marks.
Temperament: Does the dog show plenty of energy? Does it play readily? Is it submissive? Will it allow its teeth to be examined? Can you roll it over on its back? Does it stray away when let off the lead? Does it stay between its owner's legs? Is this the first time it has been away from its familiar environment? Marks.
Vigilance: At home, does it bark to warn of an approaching stranger? Will it attack if the stranger actually enters? Does it run round the stranger barking fiercely? Does it stop acting hostilely after having a good sniff at him? Is it usually suspicious or trusting towards strangers? Does it let strangers stroke

it? How does it behave when its owner pretends to be asleep? Marks.
Docility: Does it wag its tail when it has understood what its owner wants, and obey? If it runs off, does it often turn round to see where its owner is? How does it respond to its call? If it is playing with its owner and is suddenly told 'Enough! Stop!', does it quickly obey? Marks.
Endurance: Does it soon refuse to run or jump? Does it play only for short periods? Does it bark for a long time, or stop quickly? Does it enjoy long walks? Marks.
Courage: Is it courageous and ready to bite? Courageous and not inclined to bite? Timid and inclined to bite? Does it have phobias to do with its sight or hearing? Does it have a fighting impulse? Does it put up with being hit with a stick? Marks.
Water test: Marks.
Seeking by smell: Marks.

The ideal formulae

Guard-dog: For dogs used only to warn, the best formula is the following: V + 3, RB + 2, C − 1, DI + 2, FI − 1, T + 2, CC + 2, E + 2, D + 1.
'Armed' guard-dog: V + 3, RB + 2, C + 3, DI + 3, FI + 3, T + 2, D + 2, CC + 2, E + 2.
For these two types of duties, there is no point in going through the disappearance tests, the obstacle test, the test to assess sensitivity to stimuli, the water test, tracking by smell and retrieval. In fact a guard-dog needs only to give fairly limited performances.
Attacking dog: The formula takes into account that this duty requires a dog that enjoys fighting, is quite brave, capable of enduring pain, but docile enough to stop fighting as soon as it is told to: C + 3, FI + 3, DI + 2, RB + 3, T + 3, D + 1, CC + 3, E + 3, V − 1.
Dog for underground work: This duty involves both general working-dogs (looking for missing persons, injured people, people buried in ruined buildings, etc.) and hunting-dogs (pursuing large game that is injured, retrieving fowl lost in cane-brakes). For this special duty the dog must be able to use all its senses: RB − 1, FI − 1, DI − 1, C + 2, T + 3, D + 3, CC − 1, E + 3, V + 2.

294

Guide-dog for the blind: Attachment to its master is extremely important: C + 2, DI + 2, FI − 1, RB − 1, T + 1, D + 3, CC + 1, V + 3, E + 2.

Herding-dog (sheep): It is necessary to have an additional test to check the dog's impulse to herd, i.e. not to allow the flock under watch to scatter: C + 2, DI + 1, FI − 1, RB + 1, T + 2, D + 3, CC + 1, V + 3, E + 3.

Herding-dog (cattle): Look at the reaction to the herd (cattle or horses), and remedy it if necessary: C + 3, DI + 3, FI + 2, RB + 1, T + 2, D + 3, CC + 3, V + 1, E + 1.

Message or errand dog: A specific and indicative test to be added to the rest is the following. Look at the attitude of the dog when it is held by a stranger while its owner goes away and hides among a group of people. Will the dog find him at once? C + 2, DI + 2, FI − 1, RB − 1, T + 1, D + 2, CC + 2, V − 1, E + 3.

Hauling- and pack-dog: Common in Switzerland (Mountain Dogs are used), Belgium (the Belgian Mastiff), Holland and northern France. There may be two or four dogs in a hauling team. Milkmen, bakers, butchers and travelling salesmen use them. The harness is a very important feature. Pack-dogs are used in North America: if they are at least 60 cm (24 in) at the withers they can carry loads of 15-20 kg (33-44 lb). E + 3, C + 1, DI + 1, FI + 1, RB − 1, T + 1, CC + 2, V + 1.

Companion-dog: It is not possible here to give even a suggested formula, because of the huge range: the companion-dog of a young, athletic person will be energetic and impetuous, of an elderly lady gentle and affectionate, of a bachelor a good walking companion, of children a patient animal. Each owner can carry out his own tests.

Hunting-dog: Here, too, the special types are many and varied: pointing, seeking, tracking, retrieving, recovering, working in water, working in pairs, in packs and so on. What is more, the demands of each hunter will vary; each will have his favourite form of hunting, and so will need a specific type of dog. The tests must be appropriate, especially with regard to seeking by smell.

For breeders

In order to keep dogs in their role as man's principal helper, and as the chief of all working animals, breeders must intensify their selection of mental characteristics. When their dogs are still young (five to ten months) future breeding animals must be subjected to tests and marked on the basis of their actual features. These will be clear at this age: later on, with training, they may become completely blurred.

A male dog, timid or fearful when young, will appear courageous with good training. If mated with an innately fearful bitch, whose fear is also concealed by training, the offspring will be even more timid or fearful. If these features are detected in good time, any such pairing should be avoided. This goes for all the other mental characteristics.

Example of an ordinary pairing: An example of a pairing of two good guard-dogs, which nevertheless gives offspring that are ill-suited to the same task, or that are, at least, not as good as their parents. This is a common example, but it could be worse. There are also apparently good matches that produce disastrous results.

Mental characteristics of the DOG (test at the age of 7 months)	Mental characteristics of the BITCH (test at the age of 7 months)
C−1/DI+3 FI+1/T+3 Good guard-dog as an adult	C−1/DI+2 FI+2/T+1 Good guard-dog as an adult

Mental characteristics of three PUPPIES (test at the age of 7 months)

C−3/DI+2 FI+1/T+1	C−3/DI+3 FI+2/T+2	C−1/DI+2 FI+1/T+1
Not suitable as a guard-dog	Poorly suited as a guard-dog	Less suited than the parents

Example of good pairing

The example given below is of a successful mating for the improvement of guard-dog stock. On a similar basis there can be improvement of hunting-dogs or dogs suitable for any other kind of duty.

It is worth noting that the two parents in this example are inferior to the parents in the previous example, but none of the offspring is inferior to the parents; in fact, many of the children are clearly superior.

Mental characteristics of the DOG (test at the age of 6 months)	Mental characteristics of the BITCH (test at the age of 6 months)
C+3 DI+1 FI+3 T+1 Good guard-dog as an adult	C−1 DI+3 FI−1 T+3 Good guard-dog as an adult

Mental characteristics of the PUPPIES (test at the age of 7 months)
3 pups noticeably influenced by the father

C+3/DI+3 FI+3/T+3	C+3/DI+3 FI+3/T+1	C+3/DI+1 FI+3/T+1
Better than parents	Better than parents	Same as father

The three pups noticeably influenced by their mother

C+2/DI+3 FI+2/T+3	C+1/DI+3 FI+1/T+3	C−1/DI+3 FI−1/T+3
Better than parents	Better than the mother	Same as mother

Of a total of six puppies, three are excellent guard-dogs, better than their parents; two are very good guard-dogs, as good as the less efficient of the parents (i.e., the dog); only one is the same as the mother, but this pup has within it an improving genetic inheritance, which will have good results for its offspring.

FURTHER READING

A to Z of Dog Care, Collins/Fontana, London, 1979

All About Dog Shows, TFH Publications, USA, 1982

Atkinson, W. Ian (ed.), **Emergency First Aid for Dogs**, Muller, London, 1982

Bennett, James Gordon, **Command Train Your Dog**, Prentice-Hall, USA, 1979

Bruette, W.A. and Donnelly K.V., **Complete Dog Buyers' Guide**, TFH Publications, USA, 1983

Burke, Lew, **Dog Training**, TFH Publications, USA, 1976

Canadian Kennel Club Book of Dogs, General Publishing Co., Canada, 1983

Care for Your Dog, in RSPCA Pet Guides Series, Collins, London, 1980

Cavill, David, **All About Mating, Whelping and Weaning**, Pelham Books, London, 1981

Cavill, David, **All About Showing Dogs**, Pelham Books, London, 1984

Cavill, David, **All About the Spitz Breeds**, Pelham Books, London, 1978 (In the "All About" Series published by Pelham Books there are books on many individual breeds.)

Chandler, J. **Best Loved Dogs of the World**, Ward Lock, London, 1979

Complete Dog Training Manual, TAB Books, USA, 1978

Cree, J. **Nosework for Dogs**, Pelham Books, London, 1980

Craft Dog Book, Foulsham, London, 1983

Dangerfield, S., **Dog in the Family**, Popular Dogs (Hutchinson), London, 1973

The Dog, Orbis, London, 1980

Dog and Hound in Antiquity: 'De Canibus', J.A. Allen, London, 1971

Dog Care Question and Answer Book, Orbis, London, 1983

Dog for You, Houghton Mifflin, USA, 1984

Dog Grooming Guide, Gifford, London, 1977

Dog Owner's Home Veterinary Handbook, Howell, USA, 1980

Dogs: A Practical Guide to Breeding and Showing, Batsford, London, 1983

Dog's Medical Dictionary, Routledge, London, 1976

Dog Training Weekly Club Directory, **Dog Training Weekly**, UK, 1981

Encyclopaedia of the Dog, Octopus Books, London, 1981

Encyclopaedia of Dogs, Hart-Davis, London, 1973

Erlandson, Keith, **Gundog Training**, Barrie & Jenkins, London, 1976

Field Guide in Colour to Dogs, Octopus Books, London, 1977

First Aid and Nursing for Your Dog, Popular Dogs (Hutchinson), London, 1982

Flynn, **Dogs for Protection**, TFH Publications, USA, 1983

Frankling, E. **Practical Dog Breeding and Genetics**, Popular Dogs (Hutchinson), London, 1981

Glover, Harry, **Standard Guide to Pure-bred Dogs**, Macmillan, London, hardback 1977, paperback 1982; McGraw-Hill, New York, 1978

Good Dog: Basic Training Book for All Breeds, Farming Press, UK, 1977

Gordon, J.F., **Rare and Unusual Dog Breeds**, Bartholomew, Edinburgh, 1975

Halsall, Eric, **Sheepdogs**, Patrick Stephens, London, 1980

Halsall, Eric, **Sheepdog Trials**, Patrick Stephens, London, 1982

Hancock, R.C.G., **Old Working Dogs**, Shire Publications, Princes Risborough, Bucks, 1984

Hancock, R.C.G., **Right Way to Keep Dogs**, Elliott Right Ways Books, Tadworth, Surrey, 1983

Harman, Hilary, **Dogs and How to Breed Them**, Gifford, London, 1974

Harman, Hilary, **Dogs and How to Groom Them**, Gifford, London, 1974

Harman, Hilary, **Showing and Judging Dogs**, Gifford, London, 1977

Hart, A., **Dog Owner's Encyclopaedia of Veterinary Medicine**, TFH Publications, USA, 1970

Holmes, John, **Obedient Dog**, Popular Dogs (Hutchinson), London, 1977

How to Care for Your Older Dog, New English Library, London, 1980

Lorenz, Konrad, **Man Meets Dog**, Methuen, London, 1979

Macdonald Encyclopaedia of Dogs, Macdonald, London, 1983

Maller, D. and Feinman, J., **Twenty-one Days to a Trained Dog**, Pan Books, London, 1978

Marvin, John T., **Book of All Terriers**, Howell, USA, 1964

Messent, Peter, **Understanding Your Dog**, Macdonald, London, 1984

Miller, Malcolm E., **Anatomy of the Dog**, Saunders, Eastbourne, East Sussex, 1979

Natural Health for Dogs and Cats, Rodale Press, USA, 1983

Nelson, Michael, **Pocket Book on Dog Care and Training**, Octopus Books, London, 1982

Observer's Book of Dogs, Frederick Warne, London, 1983

Osborne, Margaret, **The Collie**, Popular Dogs (Hutchinson), London, 1978

Palmer, Joan, **Working Dogs**, Patrick Stephens, London, 1983

Penguin Book of Dogs, Penguin Books, Harmondsworth, Middlesex, 1983

Pickup, Madeleine, **All About the German Shepherd**, Pelham Books, London, 1980

Pemmner, David, **Working Terrier**, Boydell, UK, 1978

Pocket Encyclopaedia of Dogs, Blandford Press, Poole, Dorset, 1981

Portman, Graham R., **Mating and Whelping of Dogs**, Popular Dogs (Hutchinson), London, 1983

Radcliffe, Talbot, **Spaniels for Sport**, Faber, London, 1969

Saunders, Blanche, **Complete Book of Dog Obedience** Howell, USA, 1979

Saunders, Blanche, **Dog Care for Boys and Girls**, Howell, USA, 1964

Scott, J.P. and Fuller, J.L., **Dog Behaviour: The Genetic Basis**, University of Chicago Press, USA, 1974

Scott, Tom, **Obedience and Security Training for Dogs**, Popular Dogs, (Hutchinson), London, 1974

Shedrup, I. (ed.), **Dogs of the World**, David & Charles, Newton Abbot, Devon, 1983

Sheldon, Margaret, **All About Poodles**, Pelham Books, London, 1983

Sheldon, Margaret R., **All About Cross-Breeds and Mongrels**, Pelham Books, London, n.d.

Smith, Guy N., **Sporting and Working Dogs**, Spur Publications, UK, 1979

Strickland, W.G., **Expert Obedience Training for Dogs**, Barrie & Jenkins, London, 1978

Training and Care of the Family Dog in Pet Care Guides, Bartholomew, Edinburgh, 1980

Training and Caring for Your Dog, Ward Lock, London, 1980

Turner, Trevor, **How to Feed Your Dog**, Popular Dogs (Hutchinson), London, 1980

Walker, Alan, **Practical Guide to Feeding Dogs: 'Fit for a Dog'**, Davis-Poynter, London, 1980

West, Geoffrey P., **About Dogs: Veterinary Guide to Health**, Gilbertson & Page, 1966

White, R.C., **Dog's Medical Dictionary**, Routledge, London, 1976

Whitney, L.F., **Natural Method of Dog Training**, TFH Publications, USA, 1983

Wood, Carl P., **Sporting Dogs**, DBU Books, USA, 1984

INDEX

Numbers in bold type refer to illustration captions which do not appear on same page as textual reference